CONCILIUM SERIES

The Power of Naming

*A Concilium Reader in
Feminist Liberation Theology*

**Edited by
ELISABETH SCHÜSSLER FIORENZA**

ORBIS BOOKS
Maryknoll, New York 10545

SCM PRESS

The Catholic Foreign Mission Society of America (Maryknoll) recruits and trains people for overseas missionary service. Through Orbis Books, Maryknoll aims to foster the international dialogue that is essential to mission. The books published, however, reflect the opinions of their authors and are not meant to represent the official position of the society.

Copyright © 1996 by the Concilium Foundation, Nijmegen, The Netherlands

Introduction © 1996 by Elisabeth Schüssler Fiorenza

Published by Orbis Books, Maryknoll, NY 10545-0308 and SCM Press, London, England

All rights reserved. No part of this publication may be reproduced or transmitted in any form or by any means, electronic or mechanical, including photocopying, recording, or any information storage or retrieval system, without prior permission in writing from the publishers.

Queries regarding rights and permissions should be addressed to: Stichting Concilium, Prins Bernhardstratt 23, 6521 AB Nijmegen, The Netherlands.

Manufactured in the United States of America

ORBIS/ISBN 1-57075-094-7   SCM/ISBN 0-334-02660-1

The Power of Naming

Concilium is an international theological journal begun in 1965. Inspired by the Second Vatican Council and the spirit of reform and dialogue which the Council inaugurated, *Concilium* has featured many of the world's foremost theologians. The *Concilium Series*, published by Orbis Books and SCM Press, highlights the contributions of these distinguished authors as well as selected themes that reflect the journal's concern for the mystical-political meaning of the Gospel for our age.

Already published

David Tracy, *On Naming the Present*

Edward Schillebeeckx, *The Language of Faith*

Johann-Baptist Metz and Jürgen Moltmann, *Faith and the Future*

To my feminist Concilium co-editors
Mary Collins, Anne Carr,
M. Shawn Copeland, Mary John Mananzan,
Theologians of Wisdom

Sophia/Wisdom grows bright,
and does not grow dim.
By those who love Her, she is readily seen,
and found by those who look for Her...
She Herself walks about looking for those
who are worthy of Her
and graciously shows Herself to them as they go
in every thought of theirs coming to meet them.

– Wisdom 6:12, 16

Contents

PART II
Naming the Structures of Women's Oppression

PART III
The Theological Construction of Women's Silence

PART IV
Changing Theological Discourses

Introduction

Feminist Liberation Theology as Critical Sophialogy

ELISABETH SCHÜSSLER FIORENZA

More than a hundred years ago, the educator Anna Julia Cooper, a womanist foresister, eloquently expressed the need and rationale for wo/men's[1] public speaking. She insisted that those of us who are wo/men and until now have been excluded from institutions of knowledge and power must be allowed to participate in articulating the full circle of human perception and imagination.

It is not the intelligent woman vs. the ignorant woman; nor the white woman vs. the black, the brown, and the red — it is not even the cause of woman vs. man. Nay, it is woman's strongest vindication for speaking that *the world needs to hear her voice*. It would be subversive of every human interest that the cry of one half of the human family be stifled. Woman . . . daring to think and move and speak — to undertake to help shape, mold and direct the thought of her age, is merely completing the circle of the world's vision. Hers is every interest that has lacked an interpreter and a defender. Her cause is linked with that of every agony that has been dumb — every wrong that needs a voice. . . . The world has had to limp along with the wobbling gait and one-sided hesitancy of a man with one eye. Suddenly the bandage is removed from the other eye and the whole body is filled with light. It sees a circle where before it saw a segment. The darkened eye restored, every member rejoices with it.[2]

Feminist theology, I submit, seeks to articulate such a different theo-ethical religious vision and to reform malestream[3] knowledge about the world and G*d[4] in order to correct and complete the world's and the church's one-sided vision. It seeks to rectify our gendered knowledge and

spiritual perception of the world which is still one-eyed to the extent that
it continues to be articulated in the interest of elite white western men.
How then does feminist theology seek to restore the world's full spiritual
vision? How can it correct the fragmentary circle of Christian vision and
change its narrow and biased perception of the world and of G*d?

Introduction

The present *Concilium* Reader speaks to this question from a very
particular subject location within Roman Catholic theological struggles. It could be easily misread, therefore, as simply addressing Roman
Catholic theological problems. However, such a misconception would
discount that particular theological discourses which are conscious of
their unique perspective can be of universal significance. The individual articles in this volume approach their topics from very different
social-ecclesial locations. They not only seek to introduce the feminist
theological thought engendered by the international Catholic journal
Concilium to the attention of a wider audience. This collection of essays which span a time of almost twenty years also seeks to introduce
college and theology students to a particular form of feminist theology. By presenting a variety of feminist theological voices, it documents
the international and inter-faith work of Christian feminist liberation
theologians.[5] Hence, these essays gathered in this volume indicate both
the structural and ideological limits of feminist discourses in biblical
religions and an array of common goals and visions.

Since *Concilium* has been founded to keep alive and further the reform
initiatives of the Second Vatican *Council,* the specific socio-religious location of Feminist Theology in *Concilium* is both limited and enhanced by
its institutional location. The theological renewal movements in World-
Catholicism, especially the women's movement, have sought to open
the "windows and doors" of the Roman Catholic church and generate
new and exciting theological insights and ekklesial practices. In the past
thirty years they have attempted to turn the monarchic, exclusivist, and
fundamentalist pre-Vatican II church into a church that would respect
religious liberty, privilege the "option for the poor," and strive to reform
Catholicism in light of the radical democratic vision of the people of G*d.
Although the Second Vatican Council did not specifically wrestle with the
problem of women, the ekklesial status of women is the linchpin for any
such social and ekklesial reform program.

The first issue of *Concilium* that explicitly explored the problem of
"Women in the Church" was edited by Gregory Baum and appeared in
1975, more than twenty years ago. More than ten years ago, a spe-

cial section for feminist theology was established in *Concilium*.[6] At that time not only the creation of such a section but also the name of this new section were hotly debated. Some argued for an issue on *Women in the Church*, others for *Women's Theology*, others for *Theology of Woman*. Since by then Feminist Studies in Religion had emerged as an independent discipline, the title *feminist theology* was finally accepted, with the clear understanding that the approaches of this *Concilium* section would be interdisciplinary, ecumenical, and interreligious and would adopt a critical feminist liberationist perspective.[7] Its specific socio-religious location in Catholic ekklesial struggles has shaped the articulations of feminist theology in *Concilium* to be experiential, contextual, particular, systemic-critical, and liberative.[8]

Today, *Concilium* continues to keep the reform program of Vatican II alive in the midst of the forces of restoration and backlash against the vision of church as the people of G*d. As the contributions selected for this volume indicate, feminist theology has been crucial for keeping this dream and struggle vital in the work of *Concilium*. However, this does not mean that feminist theology has restricted itself to exploring the situation of wo/men in the Roman Catholic Church and adopted a confessional, parochial perspective. Rather we have sought to investigate the particular Roman Catholic location of wo/men in conjunction with the ecumenical and global struggles of wo/men against kyriarchal[9] structures of oppression in society and biblical religions.

Consequently, the articles reflect a variety of religious-theological and feminist perspectives. They document that feminist theology is an assembly, i.e., an *ekklēsia* of ecumenical, interreligious, multicultural, and global voices. They also record that feminist theology desires to transform traditional theological discourses not only by interfacing them with a socio-political systemic analysis and socio-political framework but also by interfacing the particular struggles of wo/men in Roman Catholicism with those in other Christian denominations and biblical religions. Just as other religious feminists want to transform their own kyriarchal religious home-base, so Catholic feminists attempt to do so by introducing wo/men as new thinking and speaking subjects into theology. By critically reflecting on their own location within institutionalized biblical religions, feminist theologians are able to claim their own religious voice, heritage, and community. Just as Jewish, Muslim, or Unitarian, so also Catholic feminist "theologies" speak in their own particular theological voices to their own communities and traditions in order to change them. Their critical insights and constructive visions strengthen each other in the global feminist struggles for liberation.

Feminist debates on difference and commonality show that particular feminist discourses are not only shaped by their cultural-religious location but also defined through their interface and interaction with feminist movements and theoretical articulations. Hence the volume first opens with a discussion of women's studies in order to situate the feminist theological discourse of *Concilium* within a wider critical feminist theoretical perspective and practical context.[10] Second, feminist liberation theology begins with a systemic exploration of women's oppression and its ideological legitimization. The articulation of feminist theology as a spirituality of struggle and liberation insists that feminist strategies for change must be rooted in a common systemic analysis. Such a theology of struggle requires the recognition and elaboration of kyriarchal sexism and violence against wo/men as a structural sin. A third section explores the theological-ecclesiastical silencing of wo/men and the function of church and theology for internalizing and perpetuating the structural evil of kyriarchal oppressions and dehumanization. Finally, a fourth section seeks to delineate the very notion of theology from a feminist perspective of struggle. It argues that theology is best understood as sophialogy which places our "speaking of the Divine" within the force field of Sophia/Wisdom. Since feminist discourses not only seek to overcome the theological silencing and marginalization of women but also to re-articulate theology in a feminist key, I argue that a critical feminist theology of liberation must attend to its very task of "naming the Divine." It must explore what it means to "theologize" in a liberationist feminist key. If it wants to change malestream theology, it cannot understand itself simply as "complementary" or "oppositional" but must articulate a Christian sophialogical vision of equality and well-being for everywoman and everyone, a theological vision that can inspire the diverse movements of liberation in and outside the churches.

Feminist Theoretical Contextualization[11]

Since, for many, feminism and feminist theology still (or again) are "dirty words" associated with ideological bias and heresy, it is necessary first to explain how I use the f-word and explicate the notion of "feminism" in order to address the emotional constraints which this term imposes on the intellectual understanding of academic and popular audiences. U.S. polls have shown that about 70 percent of wo/men refuse to identify as feminists because to their mind this label characterizes a person as fanatic, biased, man-hating, and crazy. No wonder women do not want to be brushed with the label "feminist." In a time when affirmative action is maligned, presidential candidates lace their campaign speeches with anti-feminist sentiments, and even some in the academy find it acceptable to speak of femi-nazis, the struggle over feminist discourse intensifies.[12] It has again become a liability for a theologian to be called a feminist or to identify herself as one, since in the academy the term continues to be contested and shunned as either too political or too ideological by those scholars who profess value-neutrality and a positivist ethos of inquiry.

My preferred definition of feminism is expressed by a well-known bumper sticker which, with tongue in cheek, asserts "feminism is the radical notion that women are people." This definition accentuates that feminism is a radical concept and at the same time ironically under-scores that in the twentieth century, feminism is a common sense notion. Wo/men are not ladies, wives, handmaids, seductresses, or beasts of burden but full citizens. This definition alludes to the democratic motto "We, the people" and positions feminism within radical democratic discourses that argue for the rights of all the people. It evokes memories of radical democratic struggles for equal citizenship and decision-making powers in society and religion. Theologically it understands the death-dealing powers of oppression as structural sin and life-destroying evil. It focuses on the rights and dignity of wo/men living on the bottom of the kyriarchal pyramid of exploitation and understands their courage and survival with integrity as the visible presence of G*d at work in our midst.

Although there are many divergent forms and even contradictory articulations of feminism today, so that it is appropriate to speak of feminisms in the plural, most feminists agree nevertheless that contemporary feminism is not only a political movement akin to other emancipatory movements. It also is an intellectual process for theorizing the situation of wo/men in kyriarchal societies and religions. The diverse theoretical articulations of feminism come together in their critique of elite male supremacy and hold that gender is socially constructed rather than innate or ordained by God.

Feminist conscientization makes one realize that cultural common sense, dominant perspectives, scientific theories, and historical knowledge are not only androcentric but that they are kyriocentric, that is, elite male or master-centered. Malestream language and science do not give an objective, value-neutral account of reality. Rather, by making marginalization and stereotypes appear as "natural" or "common sense," they interpret, construct, and legitimize reality from the perspective of elite western men and in the interest of relations of exclusion and domination.

In the past, as in the present, feminist movements have emerged from participation of wo/men in emancipatory struggles: the struggles for full democratic citizenship, religious freedom, abolition of slavery, civil rights, national and cultural independence, as well as those of the ecological, labor, peace or gay movements. In these struggles for religious, civil, and human rights, feminists have learned that words such as "human" or "worker" or "civil society" are gender typed and often do not mean and include the rights and interests of wo/men. Therefore it becomes necessary to focus specifically on the struggle for *wo/men's* rights and self-determination. Hence, feminist movements are engendered and renewed by wo/men's participation in emancipatory democratic struggles, a participation which leads to a different self-understanding and systemic analysis of "common sense" perceptions and visions of the world. Such a different understanding in turn leads to the articulation of a feminist politics and spirituality that can empower women to bring about further change of society and religion.

As far as I can see, the field of feminist studies is presently construed in different theoretical ways which have great impact on how feminist theology is conceptualized. The academic women's movement has defined itself as a women's studies movement. *Woman or women's studies,* however, have been developed in different ways, because they have placed in the center of their attention wo/men simultaneously as objects and subjects of scholarship and research. They have focused on the "woman question" as a generative topos of research and have tended to see wo/men as defined by the sex/gender system rather than as critical agents of change in academic and other institutions.

First, women's studies has tended to re-valorize "woman" and define her in essentialist female/feminine terms. Since scholars have sought to re-value the negative feminine pole of gender dualism, they have understood such a "female" essence in terms of the romantic "theology of womanhood." This approach claims that all wo/men have a special, essential nature in common which defines them all in the same way in their otherness to men.

Second, women's studies has come to mean the study *about* wo/men. According to this understanding, wo/men are the objects of research which seeks to complement malestream academic accounts that do not focus on wo/men and other marginalized peoples. This focus on wo/men as objects of research has generated much new scholarship in all areas of the humanities. It has been especially fruitful in biblical and historical studies.

Third, the emphasis on wo/men as objects of study has been taken up and further theorized by *gender studies* which argue that woman and man are not two independent cultural categories but are correlated and interdependent. Gender categories are not a "natural fact" or "revealed by G*d," but they are socially constructed and hence can become objects of research. In the last decade, *gender studies in religion* have emerged as an alternative approach to women's studies.

Gender studies do not position themselves explicitly in the women's movements for change. Insofar as the conceptualization of gender studies isolates gender oppression from other structures of wo/men's oppression such as racism, class exploitation, and colonialism, it is a step backward, because it reverts to a dualistic theoretical frame of reference which has been challenged by wo/men of all colors as theoretically unsatisfactory and as practically regressive.

Fourth, whereas the disciplinary approach of gender studies stresses the social construction of gender, *feminist liberationist studies* have developed the aspect of women's studies which emphasizes that wo/men are intellectual subjects and socio-political agents of change. This approach seeks to correct the academic-objectivist frame of gender studies by developing feminist theory and theology as a critical tool of inquiry into wo/men's oppression and liberation. Since feminist critical theory seeks not only to understand but also to change our knowledge of the world, it challenges the kyriarchal institutions which produce oppressive knowledges and which in turn are legitimated by it.

This theoretical framework of feminist liberation theology has been developed in interaction with liberation movements and thought. It has also been shaped in interaction with feminist theorists of the so-called two-thirds world. Whether these critical liberationist voices will be successful in destabilizing the objectifying, universalizing, and essentializing Euro-American voice of women's and gender studies remains to be seen. These feminist voices argue that women's and gender studies should stop to construct the identity of wo/men in unitary and universal terms. They must cease to re-inscribe wo/men's identity in objectivist and essentialist terms. For unraveling the unitary Otherness of Woman from Man in western philosophical-political and religious discourses, feminist liberationist voices argue one must focus on the specific historical cultural contexts and on the historically defined subjectivity, as well as on the plurality of wo/men.[13]

By deconstructing the ideological construct Woman and the Feminine, such critical feminist discourses elucidate how the identity of wo/men who belong to subordinated races, classes, cultures, or religions is constructed as the "other" of the "other," as negative foil for the feminine identity of the White Lady. These feminist liberationist discourses, which articulate the interaction between race, gender, class, and culture in kyriarchal structures, compel middle-class women's studies in the so-called first world not to reduplicate the malestream discourse of gender dualism. At the same time they caution middle-class women's studies in the two-thirds world not to reproduce the neo-colonialist discourse on "woman" and "femininity."

Finally, just as the category "woma[e]n" and the "feminine," so also the term "feminist" has become problematic[14] since it is also often construed in essentialist white feminine terms rather than understood historically.

Hence, some two-thirds world theologians have suggested that the qual-
ifier "feminist" should be displaced and replaced with a proliferation of
names and self-designations, such as "womanist," "mujerista,"[15] Latina
and Africana feminist, or that theology should be qualified as done from
Asian, lesbian, differently abled, elder, Protestant, Muslim, Catholic,
Jewish, or indigenous women's perspectives.

While some of the proposed neologisms and self-definitions explicitly
claim to be feminist (cf. Alice Walker's definition of womanist as a black
feminist),[16] others reject the label "feminist" as too radical. Others argue
that abandoning the term "feminism" would be a "mixed blessing" for
wo/men of the two-thirds world. Such a practice not only would credit
the historical achievements of feminism as a worldwide political and intellectual movement to white European-American wo/men. It also would
relinquish the work of feminists around the world who point out that
they have shaped and continue to define the meaning and practice of
feminism in a different key.[17]

Feminists of all colors argue that one needs to rhetorically destabilize
and problematize the meanings of the term, rather than reify "feminist/
feminism" as a white supremacist definition by theorizing it in terms of
the Euro-American sex/gender system. While it is important that diverse
feminist communities articulate their own positive self-designations, a
proliferation of such self-designations along the fault-lines of kyriarchal oppressions easily could lead to the fragmentation and division of
feminist theology and movement. Such a "balkanization" of the feminist
movement[18] is in danger of, in the interest of established powers, turning
differently articulated feminist movements into "special interest groups."

In order to avoid the debilitating impact of academic and religious
fragmentation as well as the forensic academic and doctrinal styles
of malestream discourse, feminist theorists and theologians, I suggest,
would better conceptualize their debates over self-naming as open political discourses that are to be again and again problematized, destabilized,
and defined differently. Only if the term "feminist/feminism" is not reified as a fixed essentialist Euro-American category but understood in
rhetorical-political terms can it foster an "open ended" process of naming which is to be questioned, destabilized, and redefined in ever shifting
historical-political situations of domination.

Systemic Analysis of the Structures of Oppression

A critical feminist theory and theology of liberation understands
wo/men's oppression not just in terms of gender as patriarchy,[19] i.e.,
the domination of women by men but in terms of the multiplicative

inter-structuring of racism, class-exploitation, sexism, and colonialist militarism.[20] Because feminist discourses generally define patriarchy in the sense of sexism and gender dualism or use it as an undefined label, I have renamed patriarchy as kyriarchy, that is, "the rule of the father/ lord/master/husband." *Kyriarchy* (i.e., elite male-defined relationships of ruling) is a socio-cultural, religious, and political system of elite male power, which does not just perpetrate the dehumanization of sexism, heterosexism, and gender stereotypes but also engenders other structures of women's oppression, such as racism, poverty, colonialism, and religious exclusivism. In insisting on such a systemic analysis, I differ with postmodern feminists who reject such an overarching normative analytic as master-narrative.[21]

A critical socio-political analysis of the western patri-kyriarchal system and the function of Christianity in consolidating or challenging this overarching system can provide the normative frame of reference for feminist liberation theologies and movements. With kyriarchal structures, gender oppression is multiplied by racist dehumanization, multiplied by economic exploitation, multiplied by cultural colonization, multiplied by heterosexist prejudice, multiplied by ageist stereotypes, multiplied by religious demonization. Such multiplicative structures of women's oppression are ideologically legitimized, not simply by androcentrism which privileges the experiences, knowledges, and belief-systems of men, but much more so by kyriocentrism that interprets the world and human life from the perspective and in the interest of kyriarchal domination, exploitation, and dehumanization. Kyriarchy/kyriocentrism is a heuristic tool that allows one to investigate the complex interstructuring of systemic oppression which continues to engender western dualistic ideologies of othering and in turn is sustained by its politics of dehumanization.

One of the first explicit theoretical legitimizations of kyriarchy as a socio-political and cultural-religious overarching system is found in classical Aristotelian philosophy. Aristotle not only argues that the order of the kyriarchal household is the heart and foundation of the kyriarchal state. He also makes a case for why certain people are excluded from the full decision-making powers of citizenship in the democratic city-state. In light of the democratic ideal, Aristotle had to argue why certain people — freeborn wo/men, Athenian-born slaves, or young and un-educated wo/men — were excluded from democratic self-determination. Although kyriarchy has changed throughout history, its Aristotelian articulation as democratic kyriarchy or kyriarchal democracy has been and is still powerful in western cultures today.

With the emergence of democracy as an alternate social order, classical and modern philosophy was compelled to develop theoretical arguments why, because of their "different" and "deficient" natures, certain people were to be excluded from decision-making governance. Modern philosophy has also developed the argument that wo/men and socially powerless people have inferior or different natures, in order to exclude them from democratic political power. This is why, in western societies, gendered values and roles such as service, obedience, caring, subordination, emotionality, bodilessness, or licentiousness are not just "feminine" values and roles associated with wo/men but also ascribed to slaves and other subjugated and colonized peoples, both wo/men and men.

The antidemocratic pattern of submission and exclusion has found its way into Christian Scriptures in form of the household-code tradition. Its argument for the inferior or different natures of freeborn wo/men, slave wo/men and men, and colonialized peoples has decisively influenced Christian theologies and western Christian societies. Western kyriarchal structures of domination and their stereotyping theories of dehumanization have not been invented by Judaism and Christianity. However, they have been incorporated into Christianity and mediated through it in western cultures.

Hence, a critical feminist theology of liberation cannot limit itself to trying to understand kyriarchal domination and its theological legitimizations. Rather it strives to change and transform such oppressive articulations. With other liberation theologies, it insists that the central question for theology today is not the modern problem of secularization but the problem of wo/men's dehumanization and exploitation caused by multiplicative oppressions. A critical feminist theology of liberation, therefore, does not begin its work with kyriocentric Scriptures, malestream theological traditions, and ecclesiastical doctrines. Rather it begins with the feminist experience of wo/men struggling against kyriarchal oppressions as well as for liberation and human dignity. It begins with a critical theological exploration not just of wo/men's experience but of feminist experience. I understand feminist experience as an experience that is in the "process of becoming conscious" of its psychological-religious socialization, its cultural-religious formation, and its kyriarchal location within socio-political structures of domination and exploitation. Such a feminist liberationist theology names the death-dealing oppressive systems and powers of kyriarchy as structural sin and evil.

Yet, despite the claim to the contrary, feminist theological discourses have not always avoided the idealist and individualist trap of malestream theology, insofar as they often begin with traditional inner-theological "topoi and loci" of Scripture, tradition, dogmatic and systematic theology or ecclesiastical pronouncements. Some have tended not to take a systemic analysis of wo/men's experience and situation of exploitation as their primary lens for interpreting Scripture and tradition. They have often done so in order to avoid the accusation of presenting a theology that is "unchristian" or just a form of popular sociology.

Such a clean-cut division between theological and sociological approaches cannot be accepted, however, by a feminist theology that seeks to articulate itself as a critical theology of liberation. Its methods and strategies are critical analysis, constructive exploration, and conceptual transformation. As a critical theology, it has to identify not only the kyriocentric dynamics and misogynist elements of Christian Scriptures, traditions, and theologies but also those structures of the church that perpetrate kyriarchal sexism as well as racism, classism, and colonialism. Such a theology has to open up the actual struggles and social situations of wo/men as the primary focus of theological reflection if it should not continue to re-inscribe the kyriocentric dualistic split between masculine and feminine, soul and body, public and private, religious and secular, which comes to the fore in the antagonistic conceptualization of the relationship between theology and sociology or between theology and any other human science.

To that end, feminist theology must investigate how malestream economic, institutional, and ideological structures of kyriarchal exploitation determine its institutional structures. It has to examine how cultural gender assumptions and "feminine" ideals affect theological language and Christian values that internalize and sustain wo/men's exploitation. It must inquire into the structural interconnections between the gendered economic system of kyriarchal capitalism, its racist underpinnings, and wo/men's global poverty.

According to the gendered economic system of kyriarchal capitalism, wo/men's work in the home is not paid as work at all, although reproduction and child rearing are important for the survival of society and church. Because of the mistaken assumption that men are the breadwinners, wo/men's work outside the home is paid only minimally. Since it is believed that wo/men work for pin money until they get married and for pocket money in order to complement the salaries of their husbands, wo/men are generally paid about half as much as men. Such a discriminatory pay scale is already advocated in the Christian Testament,[22] where the Pastoral Epistles stipulate that the widow/elder should receive only half the payment or honor due to the male presiding elder. Whereas male elders and officers of the community should be remunerated independently of their family status and income, widows/elders should only receive financial support from the community when they are absolutely without family support (1 Tim. 5:3–16).

This global exploitation of wo/men is maintained through violence against wo/men in and outside the home as well as through systemic socialization and education of wo/men into freely accepting feminine roles and behavior. Such "feminine" socialization is reinforced through the official "theology of woman" which insists that woman's nature is essentially different from and complementary to that of man. Hence it defines woman's vocation to be that of loving wife and self-sacrificing mother. Whereas in the beginning of the century official ecclesiastical pronouncements insisted that because of their subordinate position wo/men should not work outside the home, more recent papal statements emphasize the equal dignity and responsible equality of wo/men. Nevertheless, they still argue that wo/men's "feminine" calling must be realized first of all in wo/men's self-giving devotion to their husbands and loving service to their children. Wo/men can engage in a profession or take over public-social responsibilities as long as familial duties come first, since they express the true nature and vocation of woman.

The "theology of woman" has been consistently criticized by feminist theologians. However, it must not be overlooked that this theology legitimates an upper-middle-class lifestyle which has been possible only for a small group of wo/men. Only middle- and upper-class wo/men, the ladies of the house, have had the "luxury" of staying at home and taking care of household and family. Their and their husband's prestige required, moreover, that a "maid," a lower-class or "colored" wo/man, should do the heavy work under the supervision of the lady of the house. Economic developments in the past two decades or so have necessitated more and more white middle-class wo/men working outside the home in order to sustain a middle-class lifestyle and pay for the education of their children.

Poor, working-class, and two-thirds world wo/men, however, have never had the possibility and privilege "not to work" and to "stay home." Whereas European wo/men workers and farm wo/men have had to rely on relatives or the older girls of the family for help in household and child care, the white wo/men workers in the USA or in the colonies who could not take care of their own house and children still could hire a Black or immigrant woman to do so. Two-thirds world wo/men workers in turn have had to rely on their oldest girl children for taking care of their siblings as well as for caring for white wo/men's households and children.

Since, as service work, wo/men's work outside and inside the home is minimally paid, a feminist theological reflection must begin with an analysis of the social structures of domesticity and motherhood that foster wo/men's economic exploitation. It does not suffice to struggle for equal rights in the workplace or advocate salaries for housework as long as only wo/men are believed to be destined by nature and by G*d to do such housework as service. Moreover, feminist theology also must critically analyze men's traditional gender role as "heads of household" and on boys' socialization as "breadwinners" and wo/men's superiors. Not only women's role and socialization, but even more so that of men, must be changed if women's "double workload" outside and inside the home is not to be perpetuated.

To give an example: The political, intellectual, and professional work of middle-class men is sustained by the invisible, "shadow" work[23] of wo/men who not only take care of the material as well as emotional needs of the "great men" in society and church, but also do the "leg-work" for their political success or academic research. The situation of church-men and theologians is no different. Feminist theologians therefore not only refuse to remain the "invisible support-staff" of the "great men" in church and theology, but also reject the religious ideal of unpaid service in order to claim creative ecclesial and challenging theological work as their own birthright. Such a refusal is, however, only possible if wo/men scholars learn to understand and articulate their struggle for the financial and professional recognition of their own theological or ministerial work as an integral part of all wo/men workers' struggles for just labor conditions as well as against increasing poverty and violence in and outside the home.

Finally, one must question all attempts to characterize unpaid work as self-fulfilling in opposition to paid work, which in turn is understood as alienating work.[24] A case in point is wo/men's ministry. Because of their religious socialization to self-giving love in the service of G*d, wo/men in the churches still see their ministry as vocation to self-negating service. Yet, as long as wo/men do not understand their ministry in the churches as work but speak of it as service, they cannot see themselves as workers deserving due process and just remuneration.

Several years ago, a demographic study sponsored by the Leadership Conference of Women Religious (LCWR) and the Gallup Institute sought to highlight the number and contributions of wo/men in full-time ecclesial ministry in the U.S.[25] The most damaging result of the study, however, was the observation that wo/men on welfare and poor wo/men cannot "afford" ministry. Whereas men are ministers by virtue of ordination, wo/men are ministers in virtue of unpaid service. As long as wo/men in ministry do not understand themselves as workers, we will not join the global struggle of wo/men for more just labor conditions in and outside the home. Only if wo/men's exploitation and worldwide poverty remain the pivotal systemic socio-political and theo-ethical problem that grounds feminist theology and ministry, will critical feminist theological discourses avoid co-optation into kyriarchal hierarchical status and power and avoid the idealistic pitfall of malestream theology and spirituality.

The Theological Construction of Women's Silence[26]

Feminism is not and never has been just a political movement. It always has articulated itself as a spiritual religious movement, insofar as it
has sought to bring about a coming into a different consciousness, which
in traditional theological terms is equivalent to conversion. This call to
metanoia, to a turning around for engaging in a different way of life, is
heard and becomes realized again and again in the struggle for changing kyriarchal relations of inequity and oppression. Throughout the
centuries, kyriocentric theology and kyriarchal hierarchy have silenced
women, kept us out of religious institutions of authority, and excluded
us from ordained ministry and academic theology. Feminist theology has
as its specific task to empower women for becoming theological subjects,
for participating in the critical construction of religious-theological meanings, and for claiming our authority to do so. Whenever feminist theology
succeeds in such a process of intellectual conscientization, and in the
production of radical democratic emancipatory knowledges, it is apt to
rewrite religious scholarship and Christian theology in such a way that it
changes kyriarchal-theological disciplines and church structures rather
than to become disciplined by them.

Only in the context of the women's movement in the last century,
and especially in the past twenty years or so, have feminists in religion begun to explore the implications and possibilities of articulating
a theology that takes the institutional ecclesiastical silencing of wo/men
into account. As a movement and strategy for change, Christian feminism engages in the struggle to transform the kyriarchal church into the
ekklēsia envisioned as a discipleship community of equals or community
of friends.[27] Therefore it seeks to expose and redress wo/men's subordination, exploitation, and oppression in society and church. Feminists
in biblical religions seek to break the structures of silencing and exclusion that have prohibited wo/men's ecclesial self-determination and
leadership and have prevented them from asking their own theological
questions and from articulating theology in light of their own experiences
of struggle.

Although wo/men always have been the mainstay of the church and
still are the majority of active Christians, the church is represented by
men and becomes publicly visible as a male institution representing
a long succession of clerical men. Kyriocentric religious and liturgical
language excludes wo/men from representing the Divine and makes
us invisible even to our own selves. Feminist theology must articulate
this self-alienating religious experience of wo/men. However, it should
not conceptualize the feminist issue as a problem of wo/men in the
church or as a question of the solidarity of the churches with wo/men,

as though wo/men and not the institutionalized male church were the problem or as if wo/men did not belong to the churches in solidarity with wo/men. Rather, feminist theology must shift the linguistic and theoretical framework of the discussion and analyze the century-old ecclesiastical silencing and ministerial exclusion of wo/men from religious authority and sacred power as a foundational theological problem.

Such a theological exploration points to the kyriarchal roots and deformations of church and theology in order to call the whole church to conversion. It begins its work by exploring wo/men's experiences of being silenced, excluded from ordination, trivialized, and marginalized in theology and church because they are women. It calls the male hierarchy to repent from its collusion with kyriarchal religious structures that continue to marginalize and silence wo/men today, as they have done throughout the centuries. The structural sin of kyriarchal hierarchy has denied, and still does so today, wo/men's baptismal birthright of fully being church. Since wo/men *as wo/men* have been excluded *on the basis of gender* not only by custom but also by church law from articulating theology and ethics, from defining church traditions and from creating the liturgies and symbols of faith, feminist theology seeks to overcome this ecclesiastical silencing and official marginalization of wo/men by claiming the authority of wo/men, especially of those suffering from multiple oppressions, who are the new *speaking subjects* in theology and church.

Consequently, feminist theology not only investigates how centuries of wo/men's exclusion from the academy and theological education was legitimated but also how it can be undone. In the last century, women first gained access to intellectual work and academic studies through special courses or schools for women. In this century wo/men have been admitted to full theological studies and teaching, as long as they could prove they were better than their male colleagues. Despite outstanding qualifications and academic excellence, only a very few wo/men scholars have achieved senior faculty status and scholarly influence. But while at first wo/men just fought for academic access and excelled in malestream scholarship, in the past decades wo/men scholars have developed feminist studies and theology as an alternative to malestream knowledge.

Feminist scholars have realized that it does not suffice to argue for a special sphere or domain for wo/men or to seek for integration into a male-dominated academy and church. Nothing less than the transformation of all academic disciplines is necessary.[28] Theology and ministry will be changed into social institutions that cease to produce one-sided malestream knowledge only if they allow for the full intellectual participation and decision-making citizenship of wo/men.

Almost sixty years ago, Virginia Woolf insisted that wo/men have to set the conditions under which they are willing to join the "procession of educated men." Wo/men also have to ask where this procession will lead them if they join its ranks. In light of the overall systemic exploitation and marginalization of women, feminist liberation theologians have carefully pondered this question as to whether to "join the procession of ordained men." In the past two decades, feminist theologians therefore have explored the theological conditions under which feminists are able to join the hierarchical ranks of church and academy. Catholic feminists no longer simply ask whether wo/men's ordination is possible, since Christian wo/men have been for quite some time ordained ministers, priests, and bishops.[29] Rather they ask, what will ordination do to wo/men and for them in their struggles for liberation? Is ordination into kyriarchal structures good for wo/men if it incorporates them into violent and abusive hierarchical situations of domination?

Feminist theologians have come to understand Woolf's conclusion that simply joining the "procession of educated men" will lead wo/men to war, exploitation, elitism, the greed for power, the degradation of the human race, and the pollution of our natural environment. If one contemplates wo/men's ministry in the context of women's economic exploitation and worldwide poverty, the question seems no longer wo/men's admission to the kyriarchal hierarchy in and through ordination, but how to prevent wo/men's further exploitation. It is the problem as to whether it is possible to change the kyriarchal church and to articulate theology in such a way that it does not continue to foster wo/men's exploitation and self-abnegation. It is no longer "the woman's question" that moves feminist theology. Rather it is the question whether religious institutions and theological disciplines can be changed, redefined, and transformed so they invite rather than prohibit wo/men from speaking as theological and ministerial subjects rather than remain objects of ecclesiastical control and academic research.

Only if feminist theology continues to explore critically wo/men's dehumanization in and through theological traditions and kyriocentric sacred language and the theological politics of wo/men's exclusion from church leadership, will it be able to transform wo/men's lives on the grassroots level in and through the practice of feminist ministry. More and more wo/men become schooled in feminist liberationist theological perspectives and committed to ministry in the discipleship of equals. Such feminist ministers continue to nurture individuals and empower communities for realizing justice and love as the heartbeat of any religious belief system. In liturgy and ritual, in bible study and shelters for the homeless, in preaching and pastoral counseling, in day-care centers and town meetings, feminist ministers proclaim and enact the "good news" that wo/men, the weak, and the marginal are "beloved" in the eyes of G*d and therefore must reclaim their dignity, rights, and power in society and church.

Similarly, feminist theologians and scholars in religion demand not just the admittance of wo/men to academic studies and professorships but ask for the recognition of wo/men's theological contributions in the past and present. They seek to reconceptualize and revise malestream theoretical frameworks, social-ecclesiastical structures, doctrinal ethical teachings, and communicative-educational practices that are based entirely on the experiences and work of "educated western Christian clergy-men."

A feminist theology that understands itself as a critical theology of liberation refuses to be incorporated into malestream theological discourse as one more particular expression of the same. It does not seek to prove its legitimacy in terms of kyriarchal theology and church teaching. Rather, feminist liberationist discourses critically analyze and problematize conceptualizations of theological discourse that do not allow for change because they claim G*d as their author. They insist that only if and when wo/men share fully in socio-ekklesial leadership and the sacred powers of ordination will it no longer be necessary to generate misogynist theories and theologies that serve to legitimate wo/men's silencing and exclusion.

Redefining Christian Theology[30]

Feminist studies in general have elaborated that wo/men's exclusion from the university because of their gender, race, class, or ethnicity has produced knowledge and science that is one-sided, gendered, and biased because it has been articulated from the perspective of elite, educated, mostly western men. Consequently, they seek to correct and transform such kyriocentric Euro-American scholarship by introducing a theoretical perspective and educational practice that systemically reflects on the rich diversity of human experiences.

Feminist theological studies in particular underscore both that wo/men must be recognized as theological subjects[31] and that the practices and institutions of theology must be changed. They want to engender a paradigm shift, to use the expression of Thomas Kuhn, from malestream scholarship produced by kyriarchal academic institutions, to a feminist comprehension of the world, human life, and Christian faith. Such a paradigm shift would not only produce different emancipatory knowledges but also a different kind of theology.

In contrast to fundamentalist, traditional, and liberal modern theologies, feminist liberation theologies of all colors do not see the greatest problem for faith today in the threat of secularization. With other liberation theologians, they see it in the fact that human life is threatened by dehumanization, exploitation, and extinction. Hence, they shift the question from "how can we believe in G*d" to "in what kind of G*d do Christians believe"[32] and ask if religion makes a difference in the struggle for the well-being of all in the "global village." How are Scriptures and religious traditions used in this struggle for liberation and transformation? Which religious teachings legitimate the status quo and which promote G*d's intention for the well-being of all? In short, liberation theologies insist that salvation is not possible outside the world. G*d's vision of a renewed creation entails not just a "new" heaven but also a "new" qualitatively different earth. A feminist spirituality of struggle must explicate that such a world will be free from all forms of kyriarchal domination and dehumanization.

For that reason, feminist liberation theologies of all colors do not derive their lenses of theological interpretation from the modern individualistic understanding of religion. Rather they shift attention to the politics of theological articulation and its socio-political contexts. The social location and religious perspective from which feminist theology is "done" is that of poor and marginalized wo/men. The purpose of such a "doing of theology" is not primarily to defend against secularization, but to interpret daily life in the global village with the help of the biblical G*d of justice and salvation and inspire Christians for transformation with the biblical vision of a world freed from the structural sin of kyriarchal domination.

Feminist theologians and scholars in religion first of all engage a critical strategy that theoretically can explore the ways the structures and ideological systems of kyriarchy have shaped and still shape biblical self-identity, memory, theology, and communal practice. Since feminist critical theological reflection is motivated by the hunger and thirst for justice, it also seeks to reclaim positively those religious visions, memories, and unrealized possibilities that can sustain resistance to oppressive structures and inspire self-affirmation, energy, and hope for their transformation. Reclaiming the authority of wo/men for shaping and determining biblical religions, feminist theology asks new questions and seeks new visions in the global praxis for liberation. In so doing, a critical feminist theology of liberation privileges the experience and voice of those women who struggle at the bottom of the kyriarchal pyramid because their courage and survival against all odds reveal the life-sustaining power of Divine Presence and Wisdom in our midst.

A theologizing from the systemic positionality of oppressed wo/men is by definition ecumenical and interreligious. It seeks to enable and defend life that is threatened or destroyed by hunger, destitution, sexual violence, torture, and dehumanization. Such a doing of theology seeks to give dignity and value to the life of the nonperson — to use an expression of Gustavo Gutiérrez — as the presence and image of G*d in our midst. Therefore it does not restrict salvation to the soul but seeks to promote the well-being of the whole person and insists on radical equality for all. To that end it seeks to inspire Christians to engage in the struggle for transforming kyriarchal structures of domination.

In short, a critical feminist theology of liberation is best understood as sophialogy, as a critical reflection and exploration of G*d at work in the midst of structural sin and the death-dealing powers of oppression and dehumanization. If the Christian G*d is a G*d of liberation and salvation for *all* rather than a G*d of dehumanization and destruction, then Christian theology has no choice but to become more and more a feminist theology of liberation that critically explores the faith experiences and articulations of the people of G*d who are wo/men.

However, this does not mean that feminist theology should be conceptualized as completely different, complementary, or opposite to traditional "orthodox" theology, as is the case in a new college textbook on *Christian Feminist Theology*. Whereas post-Christian feminists see their theology as totally different from Christian theology, Denise L. Carmody seeks to show how the adjectives "feminist" and "Christian" are in harmony and complement each other in a feminist Christian theology. She states from the outset that she has a dual allegiance. Her first allegiance belongs to traditional theology, "the faith handed down through the Christian centuries. . . . Traditional is a badge of honor" for her.[33] She understands theology in the common sense "developed by Western Christianity as 'faith seeking understanding' (Fides quaerens intellectum)."[34] Her theological method is constructive, which allows her to present the "traditional major topics of Christian theology . . . in an orderly, connected fashion, so as to make them emerge as a coherent world view . . . " and as "a consistent harmonious statement of the whole Christian faith."[35]

Only in the second step does Carmody express her allegiance to a type of feminist theology which is qualified by moderate present-day feminist sensibilities. Carmody is "intrigued by the prospect of exploring the divine mystery anew from the perspective of feminist appreciation of Christian orthodoxy."[36] Although she points out that "the rule of men which has prevailed in most of the Christian churches in most historical periods has worked to the neglect of women's rights, freedoms and joys,"[37] she does not contemplate that such kyriarchal injustices and exclusions also have shaped the very discourses of Christian orthodox theology.

Instead, the author reinscribes the gendered dualisms of the tradition — religious/secular, church/world, Christians/feminists — into the very fabric of her construction of a Christian feminist theology. This re-inscription significantly likens her asymmetric dualistic frame of reference to a harmonious marriage in which tensions exist. By portraying Christianity and feminism as two independent partners, Carmody implies that Christians are not feminists and feminists seem not to be Christian. It is, of course, correct to say that the "orthodox" malestream tradition to which her first allegiance is sworn is not feminist. But by the same token it cannot be said of feminist theology that it is not orthodox, since *as Christians,* feminist theologians are committed to work for a theological vision that can motivate feminist struggles for justice and liberation for wo/men.

Since so-called radical feminists have indicted Christianity as through and through patriarchal, Carmody seeks to avoid their "either leave — or accept" alternative by resorting to the theological notion of the "full humanity" of wo/men, a concept which has been much problematized in feminist theory. However, she does not discuss this feminist critique but simply states as a faith conviction: "Observation, historical study, cultural analysis, and years of probing Christian faith have convinced me that the sexes are fully equal in this presence of humanity, both in its flaws and its graces."[38]

Because Carmody seeks to avoid the reinscription of the dualistic opposition Christianity-feminism which she ascribes to radical feminism, she resorts to an all-too-easy harmonization of kyriarchal forms of Christianity and feminist theology. Yet such a strategy leads not just to tensions between orthodoxy and feminism but to further violence against those wo/men who are not willing to adopt the kyriarchal lens of traditional "orthodoxy." To theologically relate "feminist" and "Christian," either in an antagonistic or complementary way, means to continue to construe feminist theology in a dualistic fashion. How then can one avoid re-inscribing this dualism that feminist theology seeks to overcome? Feminist theology, I have previously argued, must not be theorized within the western gender framework. Rather it must displace this epistemological gender frame with a critical analysis of wo/men's multiplicative oppressions. In a world of oppression in which domination is ideologically justified by a series of dualistic oppositions and turned into hegemonic "common sense," one is only able to avoid a dualistic malestream frame of reference if one does consciously seek to subvert and displace it.

I suggest that one must replace the western gender discourse, with its asymmetric dualisms — male-female, culture-nature, society-religion, church-world, subject-object, orthodoxy-heresy — with the systemic-theological alternative: *kyriarchy-basileia* [reign or commonweal of G*d] which names the conflict between the system of multiplicative oppressions and radical democratic equality/power, between male ecclesiastical hierarchy and the discipleship of equals. However, this conflictive alternative must not be construed as dualistic dichotomy, because the *basileia*, i.e., G*d's intended world, free of oppression and dehumanization, is already incipient historical reality. It becomes realized again and again in the emancipatory struggles of wo/men who are inspired by the radical democratic vision of full equality, freedom, dignity, and well-being for everyone.

How then can feminist theology be conceptualized as a critical theology of liberation within such a theological socio-political conflictive alternative? In order to approach this question, one needs to look more carefully at the standard definition of theology as "faith seeking understanding," with which even liberal[39] and liberation theologians[40] work. Yet, if one looks at this definition from a critical feminist perspective, it becomes immediately clear that this formula does not suffice. While this traditional understanding of theology seeks to avoid fideistic anti-intellectualism, it does not specifically name the subject who does theology. As newly speaking subjects in theology, feminist theologians are not just concerned with understanding but with changing kyriocentric theology and kyriarchal church into the discipleship of equals.

For that reason, I prefer the active meaning of the literal sense of theology in Greek [*theo-legein*]. Theology can be construed either as object of faith and inquiry, as word and teaching about God [*theo-logos*] or it can be conceptualized as activity, as speaking of the Divine. In a liberationist feminist understanding, theology is not just a verbal product and datum that needs to be explicated. Rather theology is an ongoing activity and process that explores how Christians can and should speak about G*d in very particular kyriarchal situations and ever-changing socio-political contexts. In short, from a critical feminist perspective, theology is best understood as the activity and practice of "naming the Divine." As such an intellectual-spiritual practice, feminist theology seeks to critically analyze and change the ways Scripture, traditions, and malestream theologies speak about G*d. It seeks to do so in the interest of all wo/men, especially those struggling at the bottom of the kyriarchal pyramid of oppressions for survival and well-being.

Such a conceptualization of theology as the practice of "doing theology" is best understood as positioned *within* the reality and vision of the basileia, which stands in conflictive tensions to the reality and ethos of kyriarchy. However, one must be careful not to construe this conflictive alternative as a dualistic opposition. Instead one must theorize "theologizing within the horizon of the basileia"[41] as a transforming process *within* kyriarchal structures. Consequently, a critical feminist theology has the task to problematize again and again all theological language and its conditions of "speaking" or "theologizing."

If Sophia, the divine power of liberation, is revealed in the emancipatory theologizing and struggles within the horizon of the basileia, then one cannot speak of G*d either as utterly transcendent or as totally immanent. Although G*d is "beyond" oppression, G*d's revelatory presence can be experienced *within* the struggles against dehumanization and injustice. The Divine is to be renamed again and again in the experiences of struggling for the change and transformation of oppressive structures and dehumanizing ideologies. G*d is to be named as active "power of well-being in our midst." Thus feminist theology becomes sophialogy, a speaking of and about Divine Wisdom, whose name oscillates between Divine transcendence and human immanence. It is S/he who accompanies us in our struggles against injustice and for liberation, just as s/he has accompanied the Israelites on their desert journey from slavery to freedom.[42]

Conclusion

I would like to conclude this introduction to feminist theology as a critical theology of liberation by invoking the images of two foresisters: that of the African[43] philosopher Hypatia and the Syrophoenician woman. Hypatia (ca. 370–415 c.e.), a philosopher, scientist, and professor at the university, was lynched by a Christian mob in the streets of Alexandria in Egypt.[44] Her story, together with that of the Syrophoenician woman, marks the dangerous discursive space of feminist theological studies. Hypatia's name signifies the misogynist violence provoked by the intellectual work of wo/men, whereas the image of the Syrophoenician bespeaks wo/men's agency and courage.

In my book *But She Said*, I have argued that feminist scholars in theology and religion are like the woman from Syrophoenicia who, according to the gospels, enters the house where Jesus stays and breaks through the cultural "masculine" tendency to separate and isolate, to draw exclusive boundaries. Wo/men have entered the house of religious studies and theology from which we were excluded for centuries. Yet, wo/men's theological silencing and exclusion is only one side of the story. The other side is the "dangerous memory" of wo/men's religious agency as prophets, teachers, and wise women not only in Christianity but also in Judaism, Islam, and nonbiblical religions. Both sides of the story must be held together, if wo/men should find their intellectual theological voices today.

The Greek woman outsider who moves into the house in order to engage Jesus, the teacher, in a debate about inside and outside for the sake of her daughter's welfare, emerges as a paradigm for the feminist theologian. Mention of this wo/man calls forth the names of other wo/men of Wisdom who throughout the centuries not only have been victims of kyriarchal religion but also have shaped and defined biblical and other religions, although historical records either do not mention them or refer to them as marginal figures. The mere names of wo/men prophets, religious leaders, and wise women which have survived in anti-heretical or colonial records indicate that wo/men always have been religious leaders, teachers, and theologians.

As mystics, missionaries, witches, medicine wo/men, prophets, heretics, and shamans, wo/men always have shaped religious symbol-systems and created emancipatory communities of theological reflection. It is this theological tradition of wo/men who, as messengers and apostles of Divine Sophia, have gathered around Her table all the excluded, marginalized, and dehumanized which feminist liberation theologians seek to reclaim today.

This table of Divine Wisdom provides spiritual food and drink in our struggles to transform the oppressive structures of church and society that shackle our spirits and stay our hands. This spiritual struggle for a different church and world of justice, equality, and well-being does not turn us into idealistic dreamers but gathers the *ekklēsia* of wo/men as a movement of those who in the power of Wisdom seek to realize the dream and vision of G*d's alternative community, society, and world, of justice and well-being for everyone. As the contributions to this book indicate, a Catholic Christian feminist theology is inspired and compelled by Her gospel of liberation.

NOTES

1. I have resorted to this way of writing wo/men in order to destabilize the essentialist notions of woman and indicate that from the perspective and positionality of wo/men who are multiply oppressed, the term is also inclusive of disenfranchised men.

2. Anna Julia Cooper, *A Voice From the South*, 1892; republished in the Schomburg Library of Nineteenth-Century Black Women Writers, New York: Oxford University Press.

3. I owe this expression to the feminist sociologist Dorothy Smith.

4. In my book *Jesus: Miriam's Child, Sophia's Prophet: Critical Issues in Feminist Christology*, New York: Continuum, 1994, I have switched from the orthodox Jewish writing of G-d which I had adopted in *But She Said* and *Discipleship of Equals* in order to indicate the brokenness and inadequacy of human language to name the Divine to this spelling of G*d, which seeks to avoid the

conservative malestream association which the writing of G-d has for Jewish feminists.

5. In a similar fashion, the volume *Feminist Theology from the Third World: A Reader,* edited by Ursula King and also published by Orbis Books, gathers a variety of theological voices. However, King — a white European feminist — not only selects the articles of third world wo/men but also frames and thereby defines third world Feminist Theology theoretically and theologically. Since I reject such a method of appropriation, I have limited my selection for the most part to articles which I have thematized or solicited as a board member and co-editor of *Concilium.*

6. See my introduction to *Feminist Theology in Different Contexts,* Orbis Books, 1996, which was edited by Mary Shawn Copeland and myself.

7. My co-editors responsible for the Feminist Theology issues over the last ten years have been professors Mary Collins, OSB, Anne Carr, RSM, and Mary Shawn Copeland. I invoke their names here because I want to express my special appreciation and thanks to them for what they have done for *Concilium* and especially for their collegial collaboration and creative insights.

8. The following thematic issues have appeared: *Women Invisible in Theology and Church, Concilium:* T. & T. Clark, 1985, co-edited with Mary Collins; *Women, Work, and Poverty, Concilium:* T. & T. Clark, 1987, co-edited with Ann Carr; *Motherhood: Experience, Institution, Theology, Concilium:* T. & T. Clark, 1989, co-edited with A. Carr; *The Special Nature of Women? Concilium,* Philadelphia: Trinity Press, 1991, co-edited with A. Carr; *Violence Against Women,* Maryknoll, N.Y.: Orbis Books, 1994, co-edited with M. Shawn Copeland, and *Feminist Theology in Different Contexts,* Maryknoll, N.Y.: Orbis, 1996, co-edited with M. Shawn Copeland, all of which have found in all seven language areas of *Concilium* a very receptive and enthusiastic readership.

9. In my book *But She Said: Feminist Practices of Biblical Interpretation,* Boston: Beacon Press, 1992, I introduced the term *kyriarchy,* i.e., the rule/reign of the Lord/master/father/husband, to explicate that patriarchy is not just a dualistic male dominance but an interstructured social system of multiplicative structures of oppression. Since antiquity this system includes not just sexism/heterosexism but also racism, class exploitation, and colonialism as basic structures of wo/men's and disenfranchised men's oppression. Kyriarchy is the counter system to radical democracy.

10. See, e.g., Carol P. Christ and Judith Plaskow, *Womanspirit Rising: A Feminist Reader in Religion,* San Francisco: Harper & Row, 1979; Judith Plaskow and Carol P. Christ, *Weaving the Visions: Patterns in Feminist Spirituality,* San Francisco: Harper & Row, 1989; Marianne Ferguson, *Women and Religion,* Englewood Cliffs: Prentice-Hall, 1995.

11. For this section, see my article "Feminist Studies in Religion and a Radical Democratic Ethos," *Religion and Theology* 2, no. 2 (1995), pp. 122–44.

12. See, e.g., the report of Laura Flanders, "'Stolen Feminism' Hoax: Anti-Feminist Attack Based on Error-Filled Anecdotes," September/October issue of *Extra* (1994).

13. See for instance bell hooks, *Feminist Theory: From Margin to Center,* Boston: South End Press, 1984; *Talking Back: Thinking Feminist/Thinking Black,* Boston: South End Press, 1989; and *Yearning: Race, Gender, and Cul-*

tural Politics, Boston: South End Press, 1990; Paula Giddings, *When and Where I Enter: The Impact of Black Women on Race and Sex in America*, New York: W. Morrow, 1984; Cheryl A. Wall, ed., *Changing Our Own Words: Essays on Criticism, Theory, and Writing by Black Women*, New Brunswick: Rutgers, 1989; Henry Louis Gates, ed., *Reading Black: Reading Feminist*, New York: Meridian, 1990; Patricia Hill Collins, *Black Feminist Thought: Knowledge, Consciousness and the Politics of Empowerment*, Boston: Unwin Hyman, 1990; Joanne M. Braxton and Andree Nicola McLaughlin, eds., *Wild Women in the Whirlwind: Afro-American Culture and the Contemporary Literary Renaissance*, New Brunswick: Rutgers University Press, 1990.

14. Whereas third world women's *theological* discourses seem more and more to reject the self-designation feminist, third world feminist theorists refuse to abandon the term feminism for three reasons: First, they argue that the term evokes a long tradition of political struggles; second, they urge third world feminists to participate in setting the agenda and shaping the practices of global feminism; third, they insist on constructing a model of feminist theorizing that is inclusive, widens their options, and enhances their understanding. Cf., for instance, bell hooks, *Talking Back*, pp. 181f.; and Cheryl Johnson-Odim, "Common Themes, Different Contexts: Third World Women and Feminism," in *Third World Women and the Politics of Feminism*, ed. Chandra Talpade Mohanty, Ann Russo, Lourdes Torres, Bloomington: Indiana University Press, 1991, pp. 314–27; cf. also P. H. Collins, *Black Feminist Thought*.

15. For this term see Ada María Isasi-Díaz, "Mujeristas [Roundtable]," *Journal of Feminist Studies in Religion* 8 (1992), pp. 105–26.

16. The work of Katie Geneva Cannon has been path breaking in developing womanist theology and ethics. See her new book, *Katie's Canon: Womanism and the Soul of the Black Community*, New York: Continuum, 1995. See also Cheryl J. Sanders, ed., *Living the Intersection: Womanism and Afrocentrism in Theology*, Minneapolis: Fortress, 1995 and the various hermeneutical contributions on womanist, mujerista, and Asian/African or Latin American liberation hermeneutics in Elisabeth Schüssler Fiorenza, ed., *Searching the Scriptures: An Introduction*, New York: Crossroad, 1994.

17. See, for instance, Barbara Smith, ed., *Home Girls: A Black Feminist Anthology*, New York: Kitchen Table: Women of Color Press, 1983; bell hooks, *Feminist Theory: From Margin to Center*, Boston: South End Press, 1984.

18. For this expression see bell hooks, *Feminist Theory*.

19. For a overview of the terminology and problem of defining patriarchy see V. Beechey, "On Patriarchy," *Feminist Review* 3 (1979), pp. 66–82; G. Lerner, *The Creation of Patriarchy*, New York: Oxford University Press, 1986, pp. 231–41; and the literature discussed by Christine Schaumberger, "Patriarchat als feministischer Begriff," in Elisabeth Gössmann a. o., ed., *Wörterbuch der feministischen Theologie*. Gütersloh: Gütersloher Verlagshaus, 1991, pp. 321–23.

20. See Deborah K. King, "Multiple Jeopardy, Multiple Consciousness: The Context of Black Feminist Ideology," *Signs* 14, no. 1 (1988), 42–72. Patricia Hill Collins, *Black Feminist Thought*, pp. 225–30, speaks of race, class, and gender as three distinctive but interlocking systems of oppression as part of one overarching structure of domination. What I have named as "kyriarchy"

she calls "matrix of domination." A better expression for either "patriarchy" or "matrix of domination" might be "patrix of domination."

21. For an extended argument see my book *But She Said: Practices of Feminist Biblical Interpretation,* Boston: Beacon Press, 1992; for a similar but different argument see also Lois McNay, *Foucault and Feminism,* Boston: Northeastern University Press, 1992, pp. 116–56.

22. Since the expression "New Testament" is intertwined with and bespeaks Christian supersessionism and anti-Judaism, I use "Christian Testament."

23. See R. Kübler, *Schattenarbeit: Charlotte von Kirschbaum — Die Theologin an der Seite Karl Barth's,* Cologne, 1987.

24. For documentation see also the whole issue of *Concilium* on Women, Work, and Poverty.

25. See my analysis "We Are Still Invisible: Theological Analysis of the Study of Women and Ministry," in Doris Gottemöller and Rita Hofbauer, eds., *Women and Ministry: Personal Experience and Future Hope,* Washington, 1981, pp. 29–43; reprinted in my book *Discipleship of Equals.*

26. For bibliographic documentation of this section see my book *Discipleship of Equals: A Critical Feminist Ekklesia-logy of Liberation,* New York: Crossroad, 1993.

27. See especially the work of Mary Elisabeth Hunt, *Fierce Tenderness: A Feminist Theology of Friendship,* New York: Crossroad, 1991.

28. Throughout its twenty-year history, the Women's Ordination Conference in the U.S. has insisted on the ordination of women to a new priesthood in a renewed church. It therefore has denounced the exclusion of women from ordination as a structural sin and explored the meaning of ordination in the church as a discipleship community of equals. To construe this creative — albeit conflictive — tension as opposition and dualistic either-or choice, as recent press reports on the 1995 WOC anniversary celebration have done, is to misunderstand the theological stance of WOC.

29. For a comparative study of the women's ordination question see Jacqueline Field-Bibb, *Women Towards Priesthood: Ministerial Politics and Feminist Praxis,* Cambridge: University Press, 1991.

30. For an overview of Catholic theology see Francis Schüssler Fiorenza, "Systematic Theology: Tasks and Methods," in Francis Schüssler Fiorenza and John Galvin, eds., *Systematic Theology: Roman Catholic Perspectives,* vol. 1, Minneapolis: Fortress, 1991, pp. 1–88.

31. Francis Martin, *The Feminist Question: Feminist Theology in the Light of Christian Tradition,* Grand Rapids: Eerdmans, 1994, mistakes this assertion as modernist individualism and charges that the "feminist question" is not properly theological because its starting point is feminist consciousness and "does not have as its basis the teaching of revelation and expects to be modified by it." However, he overlooks that a Christian feminist consciousness is always already shaped and informed by biblical faith.

He argues that feminist theology is methodologically deficient because it is not "*from* Revelation." Because it allegedly "does not have a biblical view of God," it is in his view also deficient in its content (pp. 408f.). However, this criticism begs the question because at issue is *not* revelation but the androcentric and kyriocentric language and conceptualization of revelation and its interpretation in malestream tradition and theology.

32. Martin overlooks this shift in the central question of theology. At stake in feminist theology is the question of who is responsible for the dehumanizing and oppressive historical effects of Christian Scriptures, traditions, theologies, and church practices — elite clergymen or G*d. Because he overlooks this shift from the modern question of whether G*d exists raised by secularization to the liberation theological question as to "how" to speak of G*d without legitimizing dehumanizing oppression, he condemns feminist theology as being indebted to the modern rationalism of the European Enlightenment. However, one has the suspicion that such a misapprehension is dictated by his desire to trivialize and marginalize feminist theology as not being theo-logical in the proper sense.

33. Denise L. Carmody, *Christian Feminist Theology*, Cambridge: Blackwell, 1995, p. ix.

34. Ibid., p. 6.

35. Ibid., p. x.

36. Ibid., p. 11.

37. Ibid., p. xi.

38. Ibid., p. 5.

39. See, for example, Rebecca S. Chopp and Mark Lewis Taylor, eds., *Reconstructing Christian Theology*, Minneapolis: Fortress, 1994, p. 12: "Theology is quite literally language and knowledge about God. More important, perhaps, is a historical perspective that shows Christian theology to have two related senses: as 'faith seeking understanding' and as the 'scientific understanding of God.'"

40. See Clodovis Boff, "Methodology of the Theology of Liberation," in Jon Sobrino and Ignacio Ellacuría, eds., *Systematic Theology: Perspectives from Liberation Theology*, Maryknoll, N.Y.: Orbis Books, 1995, p. 2.

41. For the centrality of the basileia, the "reign of G*d," as a formal and material principle of liberation theology see, for instance, Jon Sobrino, "Central Position of the Reign of God in Liberation Theology," in Jon Sobrino and Ignacio Ellacuría, eds., *Systematic Theology*, pp. 38–75.

42. See *Wisdom of Solomon* 10:1–21.

43. For this emphasis see Cheikh Anta Diop, *The Cultural History of Black Africa*, Chicago: Third World Press, 1990.

44. See the entry on "Hypatia" in Jennifer S. Uglow and Frances Hinton, eds., *The International Dictionary of Women's Biography*, New York: Continuum, 1985, p. 234.

PART I

CLAIMING OUR OWN
THEOLOGICAL VOICES

1

For Women in Men's World

A Critical Feminist Theology of Liberation

ELISABETH SCHÜSSLER FIORENZA

> This is a poem for me
> and women like me
> we who live in men's worlds
> like the free spirits of birds in the sky... [1]

Feminist writers and poets explore the experiences of women in androcentric culture and patriarchal society. They seek for a new voice, a "common language" that could express the meaning and significance of women's lives and could articulate the religious experience of "trying to be in our souls."[2] In 1896 Alice Meynell, who was one of the greatest English poets of her time but is virtually forgotten today — likened such a woman thinker to the biblical figure of the Good Shepherd: "She walks — the lady of my delight — a shepherdess of sheep." She guards the flock of her thoughts "so circumspect and right: She has her soul to keep."[3] In a similar vein the black poet Ntozake Shange ends her choreopoem *"for colored girls who have considered suicide/when the rainbow is enuf"* with an affirmation born out of the exploration of black women's pain and oppression: "i found god in myself... & i loved her fiercely."[4]

Just as feminist poets, so also feminist theologians seek to articulate what it means that women have found God in our soul — soul not understood as over and against body and world but as religious and spiritual self, as the feminist vision of self-affirmation and freedom lived in men's worlds and expressed in the oppressor's language. Within the patriarchal context of Christian religion women's spirit has continued to explode from time to time proclaiming truth and justice. However, for the most

3

part such articulations of women's spiritual experiences were swallowed up by historical forgetfulness and covered up by androcentric language.

For the first time in Christian history we women no longer seek to express our experience of God's Spirit within the frameworks of androcentric spirituality but attempt to articulate that we have found God in our soul in such a way that this experience of her presence can transform and break through the traditional frameworks of androcentric theology and patriarchal church. For the first time in Christian history women have achieved sufficient theological education and economic-institutional independence to refuse to be just the objects of men's theologizing and to become the initiating subjects of theology and spirituality.

We Christian women have begun to formulate our own theological questions, to explore our own Christian history, and to chart our own spiritual visions. The theology which we have learned has left us out, the history of the Church is not written as women's history, and the clerical-patriarchal structures of Church identify it as a men's church.[5] In her article "In the Shadow of the Father" Hildegunde Wöller has articulated this alienating experience of women studying theology: "Theology and life remained unmediated in myself. A dream plagued me several years: again and again the same dream: I came home and found in my bed a child about whose existence I had known nothing and whom I had forgotten. It was starved and frozen to death. Nobody had heard it crying. I felt innocent."[6] Only when she attempted the journey inward to take care of the lost child did she realize that the Gospel addressed her self. But when she began to communicate this experience those whom she had called her "theological fathers" did not understand her and labelled her religious experience of self "dangerous, subjective, or irrelevant."

Feminist Theology

Feminist theology is often misunderstood as a genitive theology, as the theology *of Woman*. It is misconstrued as "feminine" theology, a theology that perpetuates the cultural-religious stereotypes of femininity and masculinity. Establishment theologians usually qualify feminist theology as "so-called," as a somewhat dubious and academically suspect enterprise. Such prevalent and often deliberate misrepresentations of feminist theology are, of course, not accidental. By qualifying feminist theology as "Woman's" or as "feminine" theology it can be restricted to women who are marginalized, trivialized, and considered of no importance in a patriarchal church and society. While the "pro-feminine" expressions in theology are lauded, the characterization "feminist" is labelled "radical, abrasive, fanatic, and unwomanly." Naturally such a misrepresentation of feminist theology invites its rejection as a "particularistic" theology restricted to a tiny minority in society and church — militant women — with whom no "real" woman should want to be associated.

The early feminists assumed that the intellectual frameworks as well as the contents of academic education and scientific knowledge available to men but not to women were valid, true, humanistic, and objective. If women just could overcome their exclusion from academic institutions and the professions they could fully participate in the production of human knowledge and art. One of the first to question this assumption was Virginia Woolf, who insisted in *Three Guineas* that women must raise the question whether they should join the "processions of educated men."[7] They had to decide under what terms and conditions women should join them and to inquire where the processions of the sons of educated men would lead them. The feminist studies movement within the second wave of the women's movement has explicitly addressed these questions.

The resurgence of the women's liberation movement has not just revived women's political struggles for equal rights and full access to academic institutions but also inaugurated an intellectual evolution that engenders a paradigm shift[8] from an androcentric world-view and intellectual framework to a feminist comprehension of the world, human history, and Christian religion. While androcentric scholarship takes *man* (male) as the paradigmatic human being, feminist scholarship[9] insists on the reconceptualization of our intellectual frameworks in such a way that they become truly inclusive of women as subjects of human scholarship and knowledge on the one hand and articulate male experience and insights as a particular experience and perception of reality and truth on the other hand.

Thus feminist scholarship throws into question the dominant cultural mind-set articulated in male language, classical male texts, scholarly frameworks and theories of men that make invisible, marginalize and trivialize women. Such an androcentric world-view perpetuates a popular scientific consciousness that declares women's experiences, cultural contributions, scientific knowledge, and artistic or religious expression as less valuable, less significant, or less worthy than those of men. Feminist studies challenge male symbolic representations, historical interpretations, and our habitual consciousness of sexism as a classificatory given in our language and thought-world. They point to the interaction between language and society, sexual stereotypes and economic exploitation, gender and race as social constructs and political oppression, to the interface of sexism, colonialism, and militarism in Western society. Sexism, racism, colonialism, and militarism are thereby unmasked as constitutive of the language of oppression in our society,[10] a language that is declared as value-neutral and objective in academic discourse.

However, it must be noted that Feminist Studies articulate the feminist paradigms in different ways and with the help of varying philosophical or sociological-political analyses.[11] While, e.g., liberal feminism insists on the autonomy and equal rights of the individual, socialist or Marxist feminists see the relationship between social class and gender within Western capitalism as determinative of women's societal oppression. Third world feminists in turn insist that the interactions of racism, colonialism, and sexism are defining women's oppression and struggle for liberation.[12] Such a variety of analyses and theoretical perspectives results in different conceptions of feminism, women's liberation, and of being human in the world.

Such a diversity in approach and polyphony in feminist intellectual articulations is also found in feminist theology and in feminist studies in religion.[13] It is therefore misleading to speak of feminist theology as such or of *the* feminist theology without recognizing many different articulations and analyses of feminist theologies.[14] These articulations do not only share in the diverse presuppositions and theoretical analyses of women's experiences but also work within diverse theological frameworks, e.g., neo-orthodoxy, liberal theology, process theology, evangelical theology, or liberation theology. As theological articulations they are rooted in diverse ecclesial visions and political-religious contexts. I have defined my own theological perspective as a critical feminist theology of liberation which is indebted to historical-critical, critical-political, and liberation-theological analyses and is rooted in my experience and engagement as a Catholic Christian woman.[15]

A Critical Feminist Theology of Liberation

Such a feminist theology conceives of feminism not just as a theoretical world-view and analysis but as a women's liberation movement for societal and ecclesial change. Patriarchy is not just a "dualistic ideology" or androcentric world-construction in language, not just the domination of all men over all women, but a social-cultural-political system of graded subjugations and dominations. Sexism, racism, and militaristic colonialism are the roots and pillars of patriarchy. Although this patriarchal system has undergone significant changes throughout its history it survives as "capitalist patriarchy"[16] in modern societies. It has found its classic Western definition in Aristotelian philosophy which has decisively influenced not only Western political philosophy and legal systems but also Christian theology.[17]

Patriarchy defines not just women as "the other" but it also defines subjugated peoples and races as "the other" to be exploited and dominated in the service of powerful men. It defines women not just as "the other" of men but also as subordinated and subjected to propertied men. It conceives of women's and colored peoples' "nature" in terms of their "function" for patriarchal society which, like the patriarchal household of antiquity, is sustained by female and slave labor. Women of color or poor women are doubly and triply oppressed in capitalist patriarchy. Patriarchy however does not just determine societal structures but also the hierarchical male structures of the Church,[18] which supports and often sustains the patriarchal structures of society that specify women's oppression not just in terms of race and class but also in terms of heterosexuality and motherhood. The right-wing backlash against the women's movement in society is legitimated and fuelled by a patriarchal Church and theology. Over and against capitalist patriarchy in society and Church, feminist theology insists that the victimization and dehumanization of the "poorest and most despised woman on earth" exhibits the full death-dealing powers of patriarchal evil while poor and third world women's struggle for survival and liberation expresses the fullest experience of God's grace and power in our midst.

Feminist theology therefore challenges all forms of liberation theology to take their preferential "option" for the poor and oppressed seriously as the option for poor and third world women because the majority of the poor and exploited today are women and children dependent on women for survival. As the African theologian Amba Oduyoye has pointed out:

> It is not simply a challenge to the dominant theology of the capitalist West. It is a challenge to the maleness of Christian theology worldwide, together with the patriarchal presuppositions that govern all our relationships as well as the traditional situation in which men (male human beings) reflected upon the whole of life on behalf of the whole community of women and men, young and old.[19]

Insofar as feminist theology does not begin with statements about God and revelation but with the experience of women struggling for liberation from patriarchal oppression its universal character comes to the fore in the voices of women from different races, classes, cultures, and nations.[20] Insofar as the primary theological question for liberation theology is not "How can we believe in God?" but "How can the poor achieve dignity?" the hermeneutical privilege of the poor must be articulated as the hermeneutical privilege of poor women. Liberation theology must address the patriarchal domination and sexual exploitation of women.[21] Moreover a critical feminist theology of liberation must articulate the quest for women's dignity and liberation ultimately as the quest for God.

Toward a Whole Theology

Feminist theology in the U.S. has insisted on the importance of "wholeness" as a basic category in theology:[22] the integration of body and soul, world and Church, earth and heaven, immanence and transcendence, female and male, nature and human technology. Elisabeth Moltmann-Wendel has pointed out that the category of "wholeness" did not play a role in German academic theology but is found in the religious expressions of women in the last 100 years or so.[23] A feminist theology of liberation strives for the overcoming of theological dualisms but at the same time insists that a "whole theology" is only possible when the structures of hierarchical domination in theology and Church are overcome.

As long as women suffer the injustice and dehumanization of societal and religious patriarchy, a feminist theology must remain first and foremost a critical theology. It must theologically name the alienation, anger, pain, and dehumanization of women engendered by patriarchal religion. At the same time it must articulate an alternative vision of wholeness by exploring women's experiences of survival and salvation as well as by assessing Christian texts, doctrinal traditions, moral injunctions, ecclesiastical pronouncements, and ecclesial structures in terms of women's liberation from patriarchal exploitation and oppression. A whole theology will only then become possible when the root of dualistic theology consisting in the contradiction between the liberating-inclusive vision of the Gospel and the cultural patriarchal structures of the hierarchical Church are overcome. How difficult it is for women to sustain this hope of the Gospel over and against their own experience of patriarchal oppression is articulated in the following lines of a poem written by a Catholic feminist during a workshop on feminist theology:

> My mother Mary was like the original Mary in many ways.
> When she was just a little girl
>   she submitted to being raped by her father
> When she was married
>   she submitted to being beaten by my father
> When she had emotional problems
>   she submitted to shock treatment by her psychiatrist

When she was physically ill
  she submitted to surgery by her surgeon.
Now she is dead — I hope God is not a father.

Mary died when she was 70 in 1979.
I held her hand and told her that she would be free
  when she stopped breathing Our Father's air
Her last breath was a long gasp —
  followed by a look of peace
The kind she had when she rocked me.
Now she knows her heart is not a liar.
She has escaped Our Fathers.
Please God, let it be true.[24]

The pain and anguish that patriarchal liturgies and androcentric God-language inflict on women can only be understood when theologians and ministers realize the patriarchal dehumanization of women in our society and Church.

Therefore a feminist theology that conceives of itself as a critical theology of liberation must sustain a creative but often painful tension. In order to remain feminist and faithful to women's experiences it must insist that Christian theology, biblical tradition, and the Christian churches are guilty of the structural sin of sexist-racist patriarchy which perpetuates and legitimates the societal exploitation and violence against women. Patriarchal religion and theology perpetuate and legitimate rape, wife-battering, child-abuse, sexual exploitation of women, second-class citizenship, and many more injustices against women. At the same time a critical feminist theology of liberation must be able to show that Christian faith, tradition, and Church are *not* inherently sexist and racist, if it wants to remain a Christian theology. In order to sustain this creative tension such a feminist theology has to move critically beyond androcentric texts, traditional teachings of men, and patriarchal structures by centering on the historical struggle of self-identified women and women-identified men against sexist-racist-militarist patriarchy and for liberation in the power of the Spirit.

Such a feminist theology does not ask for the integration of women into patriarchal ecclesial structures, nor does it advocate a separatist strategy but it works for the transformation of Christian symbols, tradition, and community as well as for the transformation of women. It does not derive its liberating vision from a special feminine nature nor from a metaphysical feminine principle or divinity. In exorcising the internalized sin of sexism as well as in calling the whole Christian Church to conversion feminist theology reclaims women's Christian "birthright" of being

Church, fully gifted and responsible members of the "body of Christ" who have the power to articulate our own and our sisters' religious life. As women-church we celebrate our vision and power for change, we ritual-ize our struggles, we articulate our own theological insights, and share our strength by intellectually and spiritually nurturing each other. At the same time we remain fully aware that the church of women is always the *ecclesia reformanda* in need of conversion and "revolutionary patience" with our own failures as well as with those of our sisters.

To advocate as the "hermeneutical center"[25] for a feminist critical the-ology of liberation women's liberation struggle in society and religion, to speak of the *ekklēsia* of women, does not mean to advocate a sepa-ratist strategy or to mythologize women. It means simply to make women visible as active participants and leaders in the Church, to underline women's contributions and suffering throughout Church history, and to safeguard women's autonomy and freedom from spiritual-theological patriarchal controls. Just as we speak of the church of the poor, the churches of Africa or Asia, of Presbyterian, Anglican, or Roman Catho-lic churches without relinquishing our theological vision of the universal Catholic Christian Church, so it is also justified to speak of women-church as a manifestation of the universal Church. Since all Christian churches suffer from the structural evil of sexist-racist patriarchy in var-ious degrees, the church of women is a truly ecumenical movement that transcends traditional "man made" denominational lines. As a feminist movement of self-identified women and women-identified men, women-church defines its commitment in and through solidarity with women who, suffering from the triple oppression of racism, sexism, and poverty, nevertheless struggle for survival and human dignity.

I have refrained here from defining feminist theology either in terms of the traditional *topoi* of theology (God, Christ, church, sacraments, an-thropology, moral theology, etc.)[26] or in terms of an academic religious studies approach. Both approaches are valuable and necessary, but they attempt to chart new visions and roads with the old maps of ecclesias-tical or academic theology. Certainly, feminist theology could not have been born either without the women's movement for the integration of women into Church ministry and academic theology or without the plu-ralism and autonomy of liberal theology. Nevertheless, a critical feminist theology of liberation cannot remain within the paradigm of the "equal rights" movement and the paradigm of liberal theology, but it must call for a paradigm shift in theology and ecclesial self-understanding.

As a theology by and for women committed to the feminist lib-eration struggle, its theoretical explorations and methodological ap-proaches must be critically evaluated in available theological-spiritual-institutional resources for women's liberation struggle in society and

Church. Feminist theology therefore does not define itself primarily either in terms of traditional theology or ecclesial spirituality but in terms of women's struggle against societal, cultural, and religious patriarchy. As a critical theology of liberation, feminist theology challenges therefore all androcentric forms of liberation theology to become more consistent and universal in the "option for the oppressed," the majority of whom are women. At the same time as it unmasks the pretense of theology committed to the *ekklêsia* of women as the gathering of free and fully responsible "citizens," feminist theology challenges the ecclesiastical theology of seminaries and Divinity Schools to abandon their clerical particularistic self-understandings and become a theology for the whole Church.

In short, such a feminist theology is not limited to women's interests and questions, but understands itself as a different way and alternative perspective for doing theology. At the same time it insists that the androcentric-clerical theology produced in Western universities and seminaries no longer can claim to be a Catholic Christian theology if it does not become a theology inclusive of the experiences of all members of the Church, women and men, lay and clergy. Finally, it cannot claim to be a liberative theology proclaiming the "good news" of salvation, if it does not take seriously its call to become a theology for the poor — women, men, and children — a theology subversive of all forms of sexist-racist-capitalist patriarchy. The feminist Catholic poet and social activist Renny Golden expresses this challenge to all establishment theology and churches so well:

> . . . Our freedom is your only way out.
> On the underground railroad
> you can ride with us or you become the jailer.
> Harriet Tubman never lost one entrusted to her
> Neither will we.[27]

NOTES

1. From Sandra Maria Esteves, "For Tulani," in *Ordinary Women: An Anthology of Poetry by New York City Women,* New York, 1978, p. 44.

2. Carol P. Christ, *Diving Deep and Surfacing: Women Writers on Spiritual Quest,* Boston, 1980.

3. Beverly Ann Schlack, "The 'Poetess of Poets': Alice Meynell Rediscovered," *Women's Studies* 7 (1980), pp. 111–26, 113f.

4. New York, 1976, p. 63. See also Carol Christ in the work cited in note 2, pp. 97–117.

5. See the articles in *Frauen in der Männerkirche,* ed. B. Brooten and N. Greinacher, Munich and Mainz, 1982.

6. Hildegunde Wöller, "Im Schatten des Vaters," in *Frau und Religion: Gotteserfahrungen im Patriarchat,* ed. Elisabeth Moltmann-Wendel, Frankfurt, 1983, pp. 174–77, 176 (my own translation).

7. V. Woolf, *Three Guineas,* New York and London, 1966, pp. 60–63.

8. See Thomas S. Kuhn, *The Structure of Scientific Revolutions,* Chicago, 1962; Elizabeth Janeway, "Who Is Sylvia? On the Loss of Sexual Paradigms," *Signs* 5 (1980), pp. 573–89.

9. See, e.g., S. Harding and M. B. Hintikka, *Discovering Reality: Feminist Perspectives on Epistemology, Metaphysics, Methodology and Philosophy of Science,* Studies in Epistemology 161, Boston, 1983; L. F. Pusch, *Feminismus: Inspektion der Herrenkultur,* Frankfurt, 1983.

10. See H. Bosmajian, *The Language of Oppression,* Washington, 1974; S. Trömel-Plötz, *Frauensprache — Sprache der Veränderung,* Frankfurt, 1982.

11. See D. Griffin Crowder, "Amazons and Mothers? Monique Wittig, Hélène Cixous and Theories of Women's Writing," *Contemporary Literature* 24, no. 2 (1983), pp. 117–44, who underlines these differences in her discussion of French and American feminism.

12. See, e.g., S. A. Gonzales, "La Chicana: Guadalupe or Malinche," in *Comparative Perspective of Third World Women: The Impact of Race, Sex and Class,* ed. B. Lindsay, New York, 1980, pp. 229–50.

13. See A. Barstow Driver, "Review Essay: Religion," *Signs* 2 (1976), pp. 434–42; C. P. Christ, "The New Feminist Theology: A Review of the Literature," *Religious Studies Review* 3 (1977), pp. 203–12; *Womanspirit Rising: A Feminist Reader in Religion,* ed. C. P. Christ and J. Plaskow, San Francisco, 1979, pp. 1–17.

14. See C. Halkes, *Gott hat nicht nur starke Söhne: Grundzüge einer feministischen Theologie,* Gütersloh, 1980; E. Gössmann, *Die streitbaren Schwestern: Was Will die feministische Theologie?* Freiburg, 1981.

15. See my articles "Feminist Theology as a Critical Theology of Liberation," *Theological Studies* 36 (1975), pp. 605–26; "Towards a Liberating and Liberated Theology," *Concilium* 15 (1979), pp. 22–32: "To Comfort or To Challenge?" *New Woman, New Church, New Priestly Ministry,* ed. M. Dwyer, Rochester, 1980, pp. 43–60, and my forthcoming "Claiming the Center" in *Womanspirit Bonding.*

16. See Z. R. Eisenstein, *The Radical Future of Liberal Feminism,* New York, 1981, for an analysis of "capitalist patriarchy."

17. See my "Discipleship and Patriarchy: Early Christian Ethos and Christian Ethics in a Feminist Perspective," in *The American Society of Christian Ethics: Selected Papers,* ed. L. Rasmussen, Waterloo, 1982, pp. 131–72 for a review of literature.

18. See my "We Are Still Invisible: Theological Analysis of 'Women and Ministry,'" *Women and Ministry: Present Experience and Future Hopes,* ed. D. Gottemöller and R. Hofbauer, Washington, 1981, pp. 29–43 and "Emanzipation aus der Bibel," *Evangelische Kommentare* 16 (1983), pp. 195–98.

19. "Reflections from a Third World Woman's Perspective: Women's Experience and Liberation Theologies," in *Irruption from the Third World,* New York, 1983, pp. 246–55 and p. 250.

20. See especially M. Katoppo, *Compassionate and Free: An Asian Woman's Theology*, New York, 1980; E. Tamez, *The Bible of the Oppressed*, Maryknoll, N.Y., 1982.

21. See especially also J. Grant, "Die schwarze Theologie und die schwarze Frau," in *Frauen in der Männerkirche*, ed. Brooten and Greinacher, pp. 212–34; "Black Theology and Black Woman," in *Black Theology: A Documentary History*, ed. Wilmore and Cone, New York, 1979.

22. See especially Nelle Morton, "Towards a Whole Theology," in *Sexism in the 1970s*, Geneva, 1975, pp. 56–65.

23. *Frau und Religion*, ed. E. Moltmann-Wendel, pp. 31ff.

24. From an unpublished poem "My Mother Mary" by Joan Wyzenbeek read at the workshop "Womanspirit Bonding," Grailville, 1982.

25. For a fuller development of such a feminist hermeneutics see my book *In Memory of Her: A Feminist Reconstruction of Christian Origins*, New York, 1983, especially pp. 3–95, 343–51.

26. For such an approach see C. J. M. Halkes, "Feministische Theologie: Eine Zwischenbilanz," in *Frauen in der Männerkirche*, ed. Brooten and Greinacher, pp. 158–74, and the excellent work of R. R. Ruether, *Sexism and God-Talk: Toward a Feminist Theology*, Boston, 1983.

27. From a poem entitled "Women Behind Walls for the Women in Cook County Jail and Dwight Prison," by Renny Golden, in Golden and Collins, *Struggle is a Name for Hope: Poetry*, Worker Writer Series 3, Minneapolis, 1982.

2

Women's Voices
in Latin American Theology

MARIA JOSÉ F. ROSADO NUNES

The first time I said, "You're wrong" to a great theologian friend of mine, I was shocked at myself; I thought it couldn't be me talking. It was not the first time I had thought differently from him on some aspects of theology, but I had never dared to express my disagreement. I had taken a leap forward in life . . . I had moved from being an echo to being a voice.
— Elsa Tamez, *Las mujeres toman la palabra*, 1989

Introducing the Subject

Feminine courage has been very quiet on our continent, in the ecclesial sphere and even more so in that formerly absolutely forbidden to women: theology. In the seventeenth century, from 12 November 1651 to 17 April 1695, a most extraordinary woman lived in Mexico: Sor Juana Inés de la Cruz, whom Beatriz Melano Couch has called "the first woman theologian in the Americas, North or South" (Couch, 1985, 51, 54).

Despite the three centuries that have elapsed since her death, one element in her life story has become contemporary, or sadly "modern," as Octavio Paz says. At the end of her life, Sor Juana was forced to abandon her intellectual work, to get rid of her library and to spend her nights in "penance and disciplines." The "conversion" imposed on her by the Holy Office was in fact her humiliation and confession of defeat. This was the upshot of the daring of this seventeenth-century woman, who defended women's, and particularly religious', right of access to full knowledge. How can we not recall the "invitation" to study and the "silence" imposed on Sister Ivone Gebara, on the eve of the twenty-first century, when read-

14

ing Octavio Paz's words on Sor Juana: "Her fate as a writer castigated by prelates sure of the truth of their opinions reminds us, men of the twentieth century, of the destiny of free intellectuals in societies dominated by orthodoxy and ruled by bureaucracy" (Paz, 1982, 629). This is also the moment to recall the cases of Leonardo Boff in Brazil, Uta Ranke-Heinemann in Germany, and so many women prevented in our time from teaching in theology schools or from attending courses reserved for the clergy, whose names we do not even know.

Women's Voices in Latin American Theology

The 1960s to 1980s saw a great mobilization of women in Latin America. In the struggle for civil rights, faced with a situation of growing poverty under dictatorial military regimes, in urban and rural popular social movements, the women of the continent stood out for their intense participation in politics. In the religious sphere, in the Catholic and some Protestant churches, the period was marked by the formation and spread of base church communities (CEBs) and of the discourse that legitimized them, liberation theology. Large numbers of Catholic women were involved in the project for forming a "church of the poor."

It was in this socio-ecclesial context that women in Latin America started producing theology. The same process that mobilized Catholic women — lay women of the popular classes and religious — to form base communities, eventually also integrated some women in the process of working out theology. This access to theology came about, though, only in the 1980s, being therefore later than women's involvement in the base communities and the rise of liberation theology, which began to find its voice in the 1960s and 1970s.

Women theologians' first publications appeared in specialist pastoral reviews or in collective works of liberation theology. These formed the sphere of reference for women's theological thinking. From 1979 on, various meetings and seminars were organized on a continent-wide scale, bringing women from the Christian churches together. The first of these was held in Mexico, in a place particularly significant for women: close to Tepeyac. There, on the sacred mountain Tonantzin, the Goddess-Mother consoled the Aztec people oppressed by the white European invaders (Nauta and Goldewijk, 1987, 8ff.).

In the final document produced by this meeting, after assessing the base communities and liberation theology, the participants accentuated the situation of oppression in which women lived in the churches and in society as a whole. They noted the absence of "a specific contribution from a women's viewpoint" in theological work, and urged the active participation of Latin American women, as intellectual agents within the popular process. Various other meetings followed: in San José in 1981, Managua in 1983, Bogotá in 1984, Buenos Aires in 1985, Oaxtepec in 1986. These meetings brought together women from different Christian confessions, encouraged and supported by international ecumenical bodies, such as EATWOT (Ecumenical Association of Third World Theologians).

The theology produced by women in Latin America, and more specifically in Brazil, has its own special characteristics, stemming from the social and religious context in which it is worked out. It is, first, work that reflects the hegemonic position in the Catholicism of the period, of sectors engaged in discourse and pastoral practice aimed at "those excluded from society," generally termed "the poor." Women theologians did not evolve their own methodology; following liberation theology, they started from the option for the poor and engagement in a praxis of liberation. If, however, women originally appeared — or disappeared — among the generality of the "people," the discourse of women theologians gradually came to tackle the specificity of the situation of poor women. Several of their texts indicated women's poverty as the material for the act of "doing women." In a surprising innovation, on becoming agents of the process of doing theology, they take as the object of their theological activity the situation of those who are excluded among the excluded: the women of the poor classes. Their work thus differs from that of male theologians, who deal with "the poor" without reference to the distinctions that the fact of being men or women — as that of race — imposes on the way poverty affects these social categories and the way they experience poverty.

Besides the characteristic of engagement with the daily experience of women "of the people," there is a second distinguishing feature of women's theology, at least in Brazil: the creation of ample opportunities for women theologians to meet and discuss among themselves. In 1985, the first national reunion was held on the subject of "women's theological work in the Christian churches." Several others followed. Christian women, theologians, pastors and pastoral agents in the base communities meet regularly to discuss relevant aspects of faith "from the women's angle." Besides this, gains are being made in the institutional sphere, with study groups and other bodies multiplying in theological colleges and universities. A "feminist chair" has been instituted in IMES (the Methodist Institute of Higher Education) in São Bernardo do Campo, as a result of representations made by an organized group of women theologians. The formation of such groups is part of women's struggle for recognition of their right of full access to all areas of learning and intellectual speculation. This is an important political advance, by no means confined to theology. Over the whole country, innumerable centers for feminist studies have been established over the past few years.

A third characteristic of women's studies in the theological field is their development in the area of biblical studies. Countless publications on "women of the Bible" seek to rescue the outstanding female figures in the "history of salvation," showing how important their presence and actions were in the development of the "people of God." Biblical studies, though, are not limited to this recovery of outstanding female personages; they rather concentrate on a broad reinterpretation of the whole of the sacred books in a sense favorable to women, revealing them as protagonists, in the full sense, in "saving action."

A Feminist Theology?

Classifying the theology produced by women in Latin America as "feminist" raises a number of questions.[1] Some women theologians themselves find this nomenclature debatable. Taking a stance very close to that of "leftist" tendencies, they regard feminism as a "bourgeois" and "first-world" movement, so questioning its applicability to our situation. Or they see women's movements in our part of the world as so specific to the situation of the third world that "feminist" is an inadequate designation. This discussion is not confined to the feminist movement, as such, in Latin America. There are groups that identify themselves as definitely "feminist," while others call themselves "women's movements."

Nevertheless, among women theologians closest to the feminist groups, this discussion is posited in a different form, and they speak of the need to develop their own theological discourse, one that addresses the questions raised by the feminist movement more directly. Gathered at the Fourth Feminist Conference of Latin America and the Caribbean, in 1987, these women, most of them active in base communities and women's organizations, took part in a workshop on "Feminism and the Churches." The final document they produced includes an analysis of the patriarchy operative in church institutions of the region and a proposal for ways ahead, to be worked out by women themselves, in terms of theology and worship. They said: "We need to overcome the fear of developing our own theology; we need to interpret and systematize our own experiences in our Christian communities" (Nauta, 1987, 12). They then stress the positive contributions made by the churches of Latin America in the field of human rights and struggles for social justice, and the significance of liberation theology in overcoming situations of injustice and affirming "the power of the poor to transform society." Therefore, they add, "we protest against the fact that liberation theology has not dealt with the specific oppression of women to a significant extent; for this reason, we consider urgent the development of a feminist liberation theology."

The U.S. theologian Beverly Harrison also stresses this ambivalence in liberation theology. After affirming the solidarity of feminists with liberation theologians, for whom theology is a reflection on praxis, she declares: "But we must also say to the Latin Americans that every time you sniff power, whether in ecclesiastical hierarchies or theological associations, and every time you express what you have to say in relation to that power, women are invisible in the way you speak . . . " (in Biehl, 1987, 92–3). The Peruvian theologian Rosa Trapasso follows the same critical line: "It seems to me that liberation theology does not go far enough in questioning the basic roots of oppression, in a society such as that of Peru." And she points to the reasons for this failing: "Since liberation theology is generally run by male theologians, it does not question the prevailing *machismo* in the structures of society, which limits its capacity for contributing effectively to changing it . . . this model can be broken only by a will to examine the sin of sexism in the Church and a critique of the patriarchal structures that lie at the root of oppression in society" (in Nauta and Goldewijk, 1987, 6 n. 7). It is not without significance that this theologian's words were relegated to a footnote in the book in which they appeared, and that she was presented as a dissonant voice in the chorus of Latin American women theologians, many of whom "do not wish to set themselves up in opposition to men theologians or their discourse" (*id.*, 4). A Brazilian woman theologian also affirms, without referring directly to liberation theology, that: "Women theologians (in Latin America) mostly work on material produced by men and furthermore do not dare to criticize this material from a feminine standpoint, so as not to lose the ground they have won" (Gebara, 1989, 920).

So the different postures adopted by women theologians in Latin America show, on the one hand, their strong links with liberation theology and, on the other, the problems raised by this linkage. On the methodological level, what allowed "women's experience" to become part of theological discourse was the breakthrough achieved by liberation theology, tying theological reflection to the experience of faith communities rather than to dogmatic discourse. "We know that no one would pay attention to us, or hear what we are saying, if there had not been a large number of protests made by men theologians against the prevailing theological paradigms" (Harrison, in Biehl, 1987, 72).

The methodological evaluation of "reality" undertaken by liberation theology made it possible for women theologians to use the concrete experiences of women as a "hermeneutical key" for re-reading the Bible and religious traditions. Despite this, a problem arises when we try to define this "women's experience." "In the mystique/policies put forward by progressive Latin American currents, women have still not broken through in their likeness and difference. The breakthrough of the poor has still not really viscerally integrated the breakthrough of women," says Ivone Gebara. In utilizing Marxism as "an instrument for analysing reality," liberation theology has not come to incorporate the critique made by social feminists — which can also be said, in general terms, of most theology produced by women in Latin America. This means that tackling problems related to the domination and exploitation of women in contemporary societies is often modelled, in many of these texts, on a reductionist class analysis. Social relationships are stratified, with sexual relationships, like those between races, being subordinated to class relationships.

This type of analysis produces political proposals — and pastoral practices — in which "struggles" are classified as "general" or "specific" with one subordinated to the other. The latter are taken to include women's and race struggles. Overthrowing capitalism, as the existing political and economic system, is made the "priority" task. "Women are generally told that the process of social change requires priorities and strategies. And they then have to wait at the end of the line for their liberation. And in the end, as Ruether states, they have to disappear, serving other struggles than those specifically their own" (Biehl, 1987, 93).

In effect, establishing hierarchies in overcoming inequalities means postponing other emancipations, until "basic needs" have been satisfied. And yet, defining what is understood as "basic needs" and what is "the main struggle" is a political task and should involve everyone, if an excluding definition is not to consolidate particular forms of oppression. In one center for feminist studies, there was a humorous poster saying: "If men got pregnant, abortion would be a 'basic right.'"

The words of two Latin American women theologians show the different positions held in the female theological milieu with regard to this question. One says: "From this perspective, I can then identify fully with the struggle for life, with the struggle for a radical change aimed at affecting not sexual oppression but also, in the first place, class and racial oppression and exploitation" (in Tamez, 1986, 166). The other states: "The change that comes through political and economic structures is very limited. Without confronting the problems of patriarchy and hierarchy — which continue to oppress people on the basis of race, sex and class — there is little possibility of advance in the direction of a more just society" (in Nauta and Goldewijk, 1987, 16–17). While the first hierarchizes the oppressions suffered by the female population, the second stresses their links with other forms.

The difficulty some women theologians find in undertaking the discussions with Marxism referred to above is perhaps owing to the critical position adopted by men theologians with regard to feminism. "It is because of Latin American theology," says one woman theologian, "that I cannot impede the struggle of Latin American women by *misrepresenting* them on the lines of First-World feminism" (Tamez, 1986, 166: my italics). Just as in left-wing circles, so in Christian ones there is a value classification of the feminist movement. There is a "bad feminism," for which there is no place in Latin America, "against men." This feminism informs a "radical" theology, critical of the exclusion of women from positions of power in the church, preoccupied with problems involving sexuality, reproduction, or violence against women. Such questions are "without interest" for women "of the people," involved as they are in the daily struggle for survival, one way and another, gaining their "voice" in the church through the base communities.

The "good feminism," a gentle critic of ecclesial institutions, is the one that can be assimilated by traditional theology, as it can by liberation theology. This is because theology, by incorporating the "women question," can keep women precisely as a "topic." "Women" in a social or ecclesial setting come to be treated as chapter headings or the subject of "specialized" books. In other words, the "question" or "subject of women" is incorporated only when it does not rock the already-established theological foundation, whether traditional or liberational. Men accept a certain openness and dialogue provided that the basic ways of looking at the world remain those "that they themselves produce" (Gebara, 1989, 920). Recent books of theology — or of associated disciplines such as pastoral practice or catechesis — can deal with systematic theology or other subjects that seem to have nothing to do "with women" by ignoring the "subject" and producing a totally "gender-neutral" (or "race-neutral") discourse. Theology "about women" is delegated to women, as if it were of interest only to this "specific" group, while men continue to produce a supposedly "universal" theology.

So, besides the "economic reductionism" mentioned above, a certain "biological essentialism" pervades a good part of Latin American theological output. Constant references to the "exceptional qualities" of women do nothing except confirm a supposed "feminine nature." Two Brazilian women theologians, Nancy C. Pereira and Tânia V. Sampaio, commenting on what liberation theologians say about women's theological work, draw attention to this problem. According to them, classifying women's theological work as closer "to life" in its actuality and poetry, as opposed to men's "abstract" and "rational" discourse, can actually reinforce the notion that rational discourse is a male preserve — "competent" discourse — while "tender and affective" discourse is female. They ask: would not the type of contribution made by women rather "result from their condition as oppressed and removed from more rational and abstract intellectual development?" (in Tamez, 1989, 110–11).

One of the criticisms made by women social scientists of liberation theology is precisely its reduction of socially constructed sexual categories — gender — to biological characteristics. One of the indicators of this referral of women to biology is their removal to "feminine essence," to what is "different," "mysterious," to a sphere hovering beyond what is properly "human," i.e., masculine, already explained by science and therefore without "mysteries." One might ask here: what sort of social or market acceptance would there be for a book titled *The Masculine Secret of the Mystery?* This enclosure of women under "specific" headings comes up against the feminist theologians' endeavor to deconstruct and reconstruct theological discourse in its totality. "We are not seeking simply to be incorporated in androcentric theological or intellectual work," says Fiorenza, "but have come to see the need to redefine and transform all intellectual institutions and academic disciplines, if we want them to allow women to participate as subjects and not as objects of university research and theological science" (in Rosado Nunes, 1987, 27).

Feminist theologians deny the "universal" pretension of existing theology, pointing to its "particular" character, i.e., the fact that it is made from a male point of view and is therefore exclusivist. "Recourse to the experience of women thus explodes like a critical force, revealing classical theology, including its named traditions, as being based on the experience of men rather than on universal human experience" (Ruether, 1983, 13). They propose a re-working that would allow the inclusion not only of women, but also of non-whites, non-Westerners. Breaking patriarchal structures requires, according to them, a radical change of "paradigms." Borresen speaks of a "real revolution affecting all human speech about God. This would be the most profound paradigm-shift known in the history of Christian doctrines," transforming not only "human verbalizations on the divine, but also the symbol system" (in Rosado Nunes, 1987, 27). It is not, then, a matter of integrating women into a society and a church in which the masculine still prevails as a norm, but of radically altering patriarchal structures, which depend on a misogynist legitimation and an androcentric view of reality.

The problems of linking feminist theology with liberation theology appear again on another level: that of critique of church structures. The base communities and the "Mothers' Clubs" linked to them are certainly contributing, to an extent unknown in the history of Catholicism, to ensuring the "protagonism of poor women" within the church itself and within Brazilian society. The developments of this process, with the creation of autonomous groups of women within the base communities, or as breakaway groups from them, are thereby pointing up the limitations of church action in relation to the female population (Rosado Nunes, 1991). The inclusion of poor women in pastoral practice and ecclesial discourse is not, on its own, a guarantee of gain in terms of women's exercising autonomy in thought and action or of winning space within the institutional power structure. Socio-historical analysis of the process of integrating the female population on ecclesial projects shows, at least in the case of Brazilian Catholicism, that this tends more towards defending institutional interests in maintaining and even reinforcing the existing social and religious power structures than truly to taking women's concerns on board. It could not be any other way, given the absolutely masculine nature of religious power in the Catholic Church.

The constitutional dynamic of the so-called "Church of the Poor" is no different. Recent inquiries reveal the lack of linkage between the base communities and the direct interests of women. "I have never met or heard speak of a single Mothers' Club that had been formed with the intention of helping women to raise their own consciousness, or to act politically, as women," says Sônia Alvarez. And she goes on: "Besides this, the strategy of conscientization, so central to 'mixed' groups such as the base communities, is rarely undertaken in Mothers' Clubs linked to the church, except in those formed on the initiative of the women themselves" (Alvarez, 1990, 23). Latin American theological discourse often exalts the "participation" of women in the communities, without critically considering the ambivalence of this process. They are incorporated into a process that is not theirs, which they have not helped to plan, even if they can derive certain advantages from it.

Furthermore, the "restorationist policies" (Benedetti, 1990) that have been gaining ground over the past few years in the Catholic Church, as evidenced from strict control of theological output to the "re-clericalization" of base groups — communities and parishes —, show the difficulties inherent in any attempt to invest lay people with real power in the Catholic Church. Now, any change in the status of lay people in the Catholic Church affects its female adherents in a radical manner, since all Catholic women, including religious, are excluded from access to the priesthood, are lay. And even "more than lay men," since the internal laws that regulate the workings of the church — the Code of Canon Law — exclude them, explicitly, from functions which, in certain circumstances, are delegated to lay men in the community. "Women are not, then, lay people, properly speaking, meaning people who enjoy the full rights of the baptized," writes Zimmermann (in Rosado Nunes, 1987, 30).

This means that any discourse that contains a proposal to include women effectively in Catholicism must necessarily subvert its present structures, by affecting the main pillar on which they rest, the clergy-lay distinction, with its attribution of sacred power to the former and the dispossession of the latter. A discourse that truly includes women presupposes a critique of the patriarchal structures of society — and of the church — and, therefore, presents itself as a discourse that deconstructs the power of men, in all social spheres, including the religious and symbolic. In this sense, it goes beyond the simple "addition" of women to existing discourses and proposes the reformulation of the whole discourse. This is because there is no way of speaking of "women" without immediately speaking of "men," once they define one another as socially constructed categories. Now, liberation theology arose in the context of a church that was being innovative in the field of pastoral practice, politically confrontational against military dictatorship, in the case of Brazil, and allying itself, at least partially, with sectors of society working for radical change. At the same time, power within the Catholic Church institution shifted to the sector of the hierarchy that defended institutional innovations, on the level of discourse and practice, by proposing a degree of democratization of internal structures. So, in contrast to what happened in other Latin American countries, in Brazil the establishment of base communities and the elaboration of the theological discourse that legitimized and stimulated them were not carried out in opposition to the hierarchy. On the contrary, it was in agreement with the hierarchy that the "Church of the Poor," or "Christianity of Liberation," as it has been called (Lowy, 1988) was born. This does not, however, mean that there have not been some conflicts.

The strategy of working with the hierarchy, adopted by most radical groups and resulting from experience of earlier conflictive experiences that left a bad memory — such as the dismantling of Catholic Action in the 1960s — is connected with the fact that most theologians are members of the clergy. Besides this, there are elements in the church history of the Catholic ecclesial institution in Brazil that explain this tendency to avoid rather than aggravate conflicts. Such a situation means that criticism of the patriarchal structures of the church is minimized, or at least set aside as inconvenient, because of internal institutional arrangements. It is not uncommon for existing conflicts with Rome to be invoked as justification for the impossibility of opening up a new flank in the battle by raising polemical issues relating to the "question of women" in the church. For reasons that are not difficult to appreciate, the hierarchy reacts very strongly to any questioning of the ecclesial structure or the way it functions. Discourse revolving around the poor was partially assimilated by the institution and even incorporated into official discourse, though often in a sense differing markedly from that meant by liberation theologians, while theoretical and practical proposals for changes on the organizational level are found unacceptable. The condemnation of Leonardo Boff's *Church: Charism and Power*, and present difficulties with pastoral practices that invest lay men in the communities with symbolic and organizational power, are some indications of this state of affairs.

Finally, the theological output of Latin American women raises another question: that of its relationship to the feminist theology produced in the United States and Europe. This originated in the 1960s, closely linked to women's struggles in feminist movements and taking a critical stance in relation to the exclusion imposed on women inside the church institution. Mary Daly, with her *The Catholic and the Second Sex* (1968), can be considered its first representative in the Catholic camp. But in the 1950s, theological reflection had already been linked to the feminist movement in discussion on the ordination of women. This feminist theological writing was, however — and still is — difficult to find in Latin America (Taborda, 1990, 312 n. 4). The Brazilian edition of *Concilium* introduced us to the thinking of several of these women, who published articles in the review. Elisabeth Schüssler Fiorenza's *In Memory of Her: A Feminist Theological Reconstruction of Christian Origins* was the first weighty work of feminist theology to be translated in Brazil, nearly ten years after its original appearance in English.[2] So this field of theological endeavor could become a point of reference for Latin American theology written by women only after considerable delay and to a somewhat restricted extent. Such a situation is indicative of the balance of power between women and men in the work sphere, in that of the dissemination of knowledge and inside institutions. Publishing houses here are run by men, and they did not consider U.S. and European feminist theology worth translating, despite its volume, importance and the lively polemic aroused by its original-language publication. This theology was often discounted on grounds of its "first world" character. Seen as remote from the concerns of Latin American women, it was ignored as a reference point for theological work in the third world.

In this way, male theologians became the main interlocutors for Latin American women theologians. They have till now been the champions of women's work, bestowing on them the legitimacy of their work as theologians. They have also been mainly responsible for women's appointments to academic posts, since, at least in Brazil, theological studies are confined to confessional universities, governed by clerics.

Even on the level of relations with Latin American feminism, there is a certain imbalance. Dialogue with feminists is recent, at any rate in Brazil. Opportunities for discussion between women theologians and women engaged in feminist work are only just beginning to be organized. This lack of contact stems from the histories of feminist struggles in the country as a whole and those of women within the Catholic Church, which have apparently run mostly on parallel lines, crossing only in conflictive situations. For Catholic women, the feminist camp was simply not "their" camp. Still today, despite the vitality and originality of feminist movements on this continent, their claims and struggles have not yet been made the object of theological reflection, at least on the part of Christian women. Despite this, it seems that the last few years have seen a growing openness of women theologians to dialogue with feminists. On various occasions for theological-pastoral discussion — meetings, seminaries and the like — feminists are being invited to take part. This is also leading to a breaking down of barriers and prejudices held by feminists about women with a place in church institutions.

On the base level in the church, however, women of "the people" are increasingly identifying with feminist discourse and practical proposals. The present situation — socio-political as well as ecclesial — encourages this coming together and recognition of common interests, even if differences are not entirely annulled. And it is perhaps precisely this movement of women on the fringes of society toward feminism that is awakening in women theologians suspicions of the possibilities such a coming together might offer in terms of the content and methods of a theology "of women," or "for women," or "feminist" — and why not?

In Conclusion

This article has dealt with the theological work undertaken by Christian women in Latin America, particularly in Brazil. It has not taken any particular study as a starting point, still less claimed to be an exhaustive examination of their work. My aim has been much more modest: I have sought to analyze the social and ecclesial conditions that have permitted the rise of this form of theological discourse in this part of the world, going on to outline some of its characteristics and the difficulties faced by women in producing it.

I should point out that reasons of lack of space and time have forced me to deal in the singular with both theology — feminist and liberation — and feminism, whereas both contain, as various analyses have shown, several currents. Without traducing this plural — or whatever one calls it — reality, I have tried here to establish connections and divergences, to state problems and to raise questions applicable, to a more or less general degree, to these different forms of discourse. As a Brazilian poet put it: "I am not waiting for the day when all men [and women!] will agree: I just know of some pretty harmonies without a last judgment" (Caetano Veloso, *Fora da Ordem*).

Translated by Paul Burns

NOTES

1. A recent thesis studies the theological production of women in Brazil: "Feminismo do sagrado — O dilema 'igualdade/diferença' na perspectiva de teólogas católicas," Rio de Janeiro, 1995.

2. See my criticism of the omission of the phrase "In Memory of Her" from the title of the translation in *Mulheres e Deuses*.

BIBLIOGRAPHICAL REFERENCES

Alvarez, Sônia E., 1990, "Women's Participation in the Brazilian 'Peoples Church': A Critical Appraisal," in *Feminist Studies* 16, no. 2.

Benedetti, Luiz Roberto, 1990, "O impasse entre o politico e o religioso nas CEBs," in *Perspectiva Teologica* 58.

Biehl, João Guilherme, 1987, *De Igual para Igual: Um Diálogo Critico entre a Teologia de Liberação e as Teologias Negra, Feminista e Pacifista*. Petrópolis.

Couch, Beatriz Melano, 1985, "Sor Juana Inés de la Cruz: The First Woman Theologian in the Americas," in J. and E. Webster, eds., *The Church and Women in the Third World*, Philadelphia.

Lowy, Michael, 1988, "Marxisme et théologie de la libération," in *Cahiers d'Etude et de Recherche* 10.

Nauta, Romic, 1987, "Latin American Women's Theology," in *Exchange* 48.

———, and Berma Klein Goldewijk, 1987, "Feminist Perspectives in Latin American Liberation Theology," in *Exchange* 48.

Paz, Octavio, 1982, *Sor Juana Inés de la Cruz o las Trampas de la Fe*, Barcelona.

Rosado Nunes, Maria José Fontelas, 1987, "Igreja Católica e Poder Feminino," in *Comunicações do ISER 27*.

———, 1991, "Eglise, sexe et pouvoir. Les femmes dans le catholicisme au Brésil — Le cas des communautés ecclésiales de base," doctoral thesis, École des Hautes Études en Sciences Sociales, Paris.

Ruether, Rosemary Radford, 1983, *Sexism and God-Talk: Toward a Feminist Theology*. Boston and London.

Taborda, Francisco, 1990, "Feminismo e teologia feminista no Primeiro Mundo: Breve panorâmica para uma primeira informação," in *Perspectiva Teologica*, 58.

Tamez, Elsa, 1986, *Teólogos de la liberación hablan sobre la mujer*, San José, Costa Rica.

———, 1989, "Las mujeres toman la palabra," in *Diálogo con Teólogos de la liberación*, San José, Costa Rica.

3

Weaving a Strong Web

Feminist Theo/alogizing in an Australian Context

ELAINE WAINWRIGHT

Feminist theology for women in Australia is not something one can find primarily in books. It occurs, rather, in the daily, urgent, sometimes desperate exploration, reassessment and recreation of meaning which women are continually making in their lives. In this sense, feminist theology is the collective and individual pool of women's experience which is continually growing and changing as we act it out in our lives and interpret for ourselves and each other in our conversation.[1]

These words of Marie Tulip's opened the first issue of *Women-Church,* an Australian Journal of Feminist Studies in Religion, inaugurated in August 1987. They represent her assessment of Australian "feminist theology" at that time and indicate that Australian feminist theologians have been latecomers to the international dialogue. Geographical isolation from the major centers and networks of this dialogue has been one contributing factor. Isolation of individual scholars in academic institutions resistant to feminist approaches to both religion and theology is another.

In the intervening years since 1987, feminist theology in Australia has, however, begun to assume a public face. It is being undertaken by individuals and small groups in centers separated from one another by the distances that characterize this vast and sparsely populated land of Australia. Its locations, too, are multifarious: study, ritual and spirituality groups; in homes and other spaces, some of which are women's spaces; in religious studies and theology departments in universities; and in theological schools. Communities of resistance are thus being formed as women and men are beginning to recognize that theology can only be done in truth when it is as inclusive of women's experience as it is of men's; and are undertaking feminist theologizing in these contexts. The strong web which such networking is beginning to create across our land provides an image of the complexity and the diversity of feminist theologizing and feminist religious thought and practice within the Australian context in recent years; and of the exciting and new stage that the future holds.

Weaving the Web

Two recent Australian publications — *Claiming our Rites* and *Freedom and Entrapment*[2] — are indicative of some of the characteristics of this emerging new reality imaged as a web. They are both collections of essays and hence represent a broad sweep of Australian feminist scholars who are in critical dialogue with a range of religious traditions including the Christian theological tradition.

The origins of the two collections were in the fields of religious studies and Christian theology respectively, but the appearance of a number of contributors in both volumes indicates the networking that exists among Australian scholars across these fields. Indeed, the web encompasses feminist scholars, feminist thinkers in studies in religion, Christian theology, spirituality and spiritualities, and the history of women and religion in Australia. Such webbing has not been without tension, as differences among women have emerged in terms of their positioning of themselves in relation to patriarchal religions, new spiritualities, experience and tradition. It is, however, very visible in the contributions to *Women-Church* across its sixteen editions since 1987 and in the newly established network, Women Scholars in Religion and Theology, whose first directory appeared in 1993. It would be difficult and indeed undesirable to isolate a small part of this web and call it feminist theology distinct from the experience, thinking and writing that is emerging from these interconnected fields.

Two factors have contributed significantly to this characteristic of feminist religious thought in Australia. The first is small numbers and the dispersion of women scholars across the nation, which makes networking an important political strategy. The second is the lack of support for gender studies in religion in Australian universities[3] and for feminist studies in theology in its theological schools. Indeed, many scholars have been able to introduce one or two units into the course offerings across various institutions,[4] and advanced degree research students have been able to undertake research in these fields, but there is at present no institutional support for or recognition of gender or feminist studies in religion and theology as an area of specialization across our vast continent. The establishment of such centers will be a significant political breakthrough.

Australian women's unique cultural experiences, like those of their sisters across the globe, have become a powerful source for a new spiritual, theological and religious imagination, and a number of small journals have been the vehicles for women's reflection upon this experience. *Magdalene,* which was produced by Sydney women from 1973 to 1987, gave voice to "a wide range of women's experience and their reflection on it in a context of meaning which assumes a feminist religious possibility."[5] *Women-Church,* as already noted, had its origin in 1987, when *Magdalene* finished publication, and its co-editors, Hilary Carey and Erin White, wrote in the inaugural "Editor's Introduction" that they hoped that this journal would "encourage the widest possible range of views and serve as a stimulus for further thought both about the divine and the particular journeys in religion taken by Australian women."[6] Their hope has indeed been more than realized as this magazine links women across the continent and stimulates reflection, discussion and debate. July/August 1989 saw the first publication of *Voices from the Silence,* a National Ecumenical Women's Journal in which "the most silent and silenced of our sisters could be heard."[7] Even more recently, *Sounding Sophia,* the publication of the Sophia feminist spiritual center in Adelaide, provided another avenue for women's religious and theological reflection on their experience.

Australian women's literature is providing another source for the Australian feminist theological and religious imagination. Veronica Brady, long time Associate Professor of English at the University of Western Australia, has consistently drawn upon Australian literature, but predominantly its male authors, as her theological source.[8] Her article in *Freedom and Entrapment,* however, sees a shift in focus to Australian women's writings[9] and together with Elaine Lindsay's contribution to *Claiming our Rites*[10] begins to redress the absence of women from discussions of Australian spirituality. Lindsay, in fact, allows the spirituality of the Australian novelist and mystic Barbara Hanrahan to speak through her own writing. This reflects her current doctoral research *Rewriting God: Spirituality in Contemporary Australian Women's Fiction,* and points to the intersection between literature, spirituality and theology in the lives of a number of Australian women in a way which gives expression to unique Australian characteristics, especially relationship to the land, a significant factor shaping history and national identity. Lindsay provides a hint of this when she says that "instead of adding to the sorry line of explorers and battlers who parade through malestream spirituality, Hanrahan wrote new myths set in domestic Australia, celebrating the courage needed to stay fresh and alive to the possibilities of each day."[11]

Those Australian feminist theologians and religious scholars whose sources are ancient and contemporary texts within both Christianity and other religious traditions are participating in a feminist interpretative project which is international and multivocal.[12] As a result, they share the concerns of and are in dialogue with feminist scholars around the world engaged in the task of re-reading the grand narratives of not only Western religions but indigenous and Eastern religions as well. For the purpose of this essay, however, I will highlight the emerging contribution Australian feminist scholars are making to the re-interpretation of Christianity, since this is the dominant religious affiliation within Australia, the most recent Australian Bureau of Statistics citing that affiliation at 74% of the population.

Australian feminist biblical scholars are only in recent years beginning their contribution to the international dialogue. Dorothy Lee's article in *Claiming our Rites*[13] questions the impact for women's spirituality of beginning the interpretation of the sacred text with a hermeneutics of suspicion. In that same volume, I take account of Mary Daly's and Rosemary Radford Ruether's critique of androcentric christology and begin a re-reading of the Matthaean characterization of Jesus.[14] Veronica Lawson's essay in *Freedom and Entrapment* gives a taste of her doctoral research, which approaches the question of the genre of Luke-Acts from a feminist perspective.[15] Advanced research in biblical studies and many aspects of Christian theology is being undertaken by a number of students around the country. Most particularly, however, it is through courses in theological colleges and universities, publications in local journals and participation in workshops in many centers that women are weaving a strong web of reclamation of the biblical and Christian tradition across the continent.[16]

Maryanne Confoy, one of the editors of and contributors to *Freedom and Entrapment,* has taught for a number of years at one of Australia's theological colleges. From her perspective of personal development and ministry formation, she wrote recently of the "tremendous demands" which the Australian system makes on its faculty members.[17] These demands are often greater on the small number of women teaching theology because of a lack of mentors, possible marginalization among a predominantly male faculty, additional workload if they wish to teach feminist studies in religion and theology, and the added demand of study for those still seeking the qualifications necessary to maintain their positions. Perhaps those demands will be lessened as the many women currently undertaking advanced degrees across the broad spectrum of theology, spirituality and religion take their places in theological colleges, universities, spirituality centers and other centers of learning. Communities of resistance within theological colleges may be further strengthened as women enter strategic positions in the wake of Dorothy Lee's recent appointment as Professor of New Testament at The Uniting Church Theological Hall in Melbourne. These are signs of hope for the future strengthening of the web of resistance.

This web is, however, very fragile in a number of places. The editors of *Claiming our Rites* noted that studies in religion is a peculiarly "Western" activity and that "the absence of a paper of Aboriginal authorship in this collection is itself a marker of the limits of a field dependent on conventions which constrain to the point of exclusion."[18] The very title of Anne Pattel-Gray's contribution to *Freedom and Entrapment,* "Not yet Tiddas (Sisters): An Aboriginal womanist critique of Australian Church feminism," suggests that theology, too, is no stranger to the same type of exclusion when undertaken, as it has been in Australia, by predominantly white women of European descent.[19] The spirituality of indigenous Australian women is, however, not only being expressed but also heard and recognized by other Australians through their literature, their music and dance and their art.[20] The challenge remains for Australian feminists to allow the "theoretical and practical space" for the voices of Aboriginal women to be heard in their "difference and dissent." Likewise, Australia's geographical location on the edge of the Pacific rim and the southern tip of Asia has largely been ignored in feminist theological discourse and it opens up an area of dialogue for the future.

The lack of institutional support for feminist studies in religion and theology in Australia indicates, however, that the voice of women generally in all the "difference and dissent" is being excluded from Australian theologizing. The significant impact of this exclusion on the history of these studies has not, however, always been recognized. In the beginning of the current women's movement, Barbara Thiering was a public voice for the movement's impact on Australian women's practice of religion, especially Christianity.[21] The personal testimony of women who were students in her courses at the University of Sydney indicates that she inspired many who would become political activists in their churches, especially the Anglican church. She herself, however, was marginalized by that church. Other stories of the genderization of Australian churches have likewise been told.[22] As Australian women appropriated feminism and its impact on theology and religion by way of the publications from the United States of America and Europe which reached these shores during the 1970s and 1980s, they became more aware of their virtual exclusion from the path of theological education unless they were training for ministry in those denominations which ordained women. Many women turned, therefore, to other disciplines — philosophy, literature and sociology.

These women have taken religion and religious traditions into the universities as research topics in a variety of disciplines, leading to a strengthening of the secular and religious in those institutions. In Australia generally, this bond has not been strong, and Australian feminist studies and feminist critical theory have given little or no attention to religion and theology. The relationship has not, however, been hostile, as the debate — Is it worthwhile for women to pour their energies into a feminist movement within Christianity? — at the first conference of the National Foundation of Australian Women indicated. There are signs that another strand of our web might be strengthened as Australian women become more competent in the analyses of theological and religious traditions using multi-disciplinary perspectives, and as women's studies departments become more secure within Australian universities. The dialogue between Australian feminists shows signs of becoming more diverse so that it will include religion and theology. This expanded vision can only strengthen feminist theologizing in Australia and ground it more firmly in its geographical location.

Lack of ecclesial support for Australian women's theologizing has, on the other hand, led to the development of strong political networks of women within the three major Christian denominations and ecumenically across these denominations. These networks have become the locations of some of our most significant feminist theologizing and strategizing. Within the Catholic tradition, and particularly during the 1970s and 1980s, women in religious congregations had been given the opportunity for theological education, often overseas, where they were influenced by feminist theologians in the United States and Europe. This led them, through the Conference of Major Superiors of Women and Men Religious, to initiate the WATAC (Women and the Australian Church) project, which began with a survey of the roles of women in church and society but was intended to be a consciousness-raising activity for all in the Catholic Church. The organization, through a varied history, continues today as a grass-roots women's group within the Catholic tradition providing the space in which women can explore their theological and spiritual traditions.[23] Much of the feminist energy of Anglican women in Australia during the 1980s was directed to the Movement of the Ordination of Women (MOW), both its political strategies and theological and spiritual underpinning.[24] Their goal was attained at the end of 1992 with the ordination of women in a number of Australian dioceses.[25] The Uniting Church women who had access to ordination in their tradition only recently established FUN (Feminist Uniting Network). From the first National Conference on Women in the Uniting Church in Australia in 1990[26] came the Last Supper Project, which commissioned a painting of the Last Supper which would include women, highlighting another expression of women's theologizing. Also from the project has come the book *A Place at the Table: Women at the Last Supper,* which explores artistic and theological aspects of the theme.[27]

One significant point of focus for Australian feminist theology has been the biennial conference, organized by the above groups with Sydney Women-Church since 1989. They symbolize the ecumenical nature of feminist theology in Australia with the degree of co-operation in local centers reflecting the ecclesial history of the states or cities in which groups are located. This ecumenism is also visible in The Australian Feminist Theology Foundation, established in 1992 as a strategic action to encourage feminist theology and support it financially; to challenge patriarchal structures, theology and practice; to develop inclusive and participatory liturgy; and "to promote feminist theology as a rigorous, analytical and intellectual pilgrimage of significance for the whole community."[28]

Conclusion

Australia's ecclesial and national histories, its geographical location, dispersion of peoples across a vast land and, no doubt, many other factors, have meant that only recently have Australian feminist theological voices been raised aloud in the public arena. The brief resonances of the small number of these voices that have been heard in this article indicate that Australian feminist theologians and religionists stand on the edge of new possibilities for the future. They will be challenged to provide the space for differences among women — ethnic, racial, socio-economic, denominational, sexual orientation and many others — to be heard theologically both in dialogue and dissent. The future will also call for a strengthening of the web linking women in their dispersion across vast distances of this continent and into the Pacific and Asia. The institutionalization of Australian feminist theology and studies of religion without their co-optation into patriarchal structures will require skillful political strategies so that energies can be concentrated. Local sources will inform a more specifically Australian feminist theology, while the addressing of international religious and theological concerns will continue. The weaving of a strong web across this continent has begun. Its fragile strands need to be strengthened and its connections with the wider global network developed, but there are many who will undertake these tasks.

In an article such as this, I am aware how the limitations of space prevent a real acknowledgment of the breadth and strength of the strong web of Australian feminist theology. So I would like to dedicate the article to all those women engaged in Australian feminist theology who are contributing and will contribute in so many different ways to the weaving of a much stronger web for the future.

NOTES

1. Marie Tulip, "Dimensions of Feminist Theology in Australia," *Women-Church* 1, 1987, p. 4.
2. Morny Joy and Penelope Magee, eds., *Claiming our Rites: Studies in Religion by Australian Women Scholars,* Adelaide, 1994; Maryanne Confoy and Dorothy Lee, eds., *Freedom and Entrapment,* Melbourne, 1995.
3. As noted by Joy and Magee, *Claiming our Rites* (n. 2), p. xii.
4. Alan Bayley, "Women and Religion Courses in Australia," *Australian Religion Studies Review* 1, no. 1, 1988, pp. 53–60; Erin White, "Webbing," *Women-Church* 3, 1988, p. 5. There has been no recent survey, and the numbers and extent of course offerings would certainly have increased significantly.
5. Tulip, "Dimensions of Feminist Theology" (n. 1), p. 4.
6. Hilary Carey and Erin White, "Editor's Introduction," *Women-Church* 1, 1987, p. 3. The contribution of Erin White and Marie Tulip to Australian feminist theology is also evident in their co-authored book, *Knowing Otherwise: Feminism, Women and Religion,* Melbourne, 1990.
7. Sandra Brown, "Voices," *Voices from the Silence* 1, 1989, p. 1.
8. Veronica Brady, *A Crucible of Prophets: Australians and the Question of God,* Australian and New Zealand Studies in Theology and Religion, Sydney, 1981; and *Caught Up in the Draught: On Contemporary Australian Culture and Society,* Sydney, 1994.
9. Veronica Brady, "Every Christian in Her Own Place: Women's Writing and Theological Understanding," in *Freedom and Entrapment* (n. 2), pp. 63–78.
10. Elaine Lindsay, "A Mystic in Her Garden: Spirituality and the Fiction of Barbara Hanrahan," in *Claiming our Rites* (n. 2), pp. 19–36.
11. Ibid., p. 30.
12. The number of contributions to the two recent publications that belong in this category are too numerous to detail here.
13. Dorothy A. Lee, "Reclaiming the Sacred Text: Christian Feminism and Spirituality," in *Claiming our Rites* (n. 2), pp. 79–98.
14. Elaine Mary Wainwright, "Wisdom Is Justified by Her Deeds: Claiming the Jesus-Myth," *Claiming our Rites* (n. 2), pp. 57–78. See also, *Towards a Feminist Critical Reading of the Gospel according to Matthew,* Beihefte zur Zeitschrift für die neutestamentliche Wissenschaft 60, Berlin, 1991; eadem, "The Gospel of Matthew," in *Searching the Scriptures,* vol. 2: *A Feminist Commentary,* ed. Elisabeth Schüssler Fiorenza, New York and London, 1994, pp. 635–77.
15. Veronica Lawson, "Scraps of Sustenance for the Journey out of Patri-

archy: Acts 1:1–14 in Feminist Perspective," in *Freedom and Entrapment* (n. 2), pp. 149–64.

16. The work of Christine Burke, *Through a Woman's Eyes: Encounters with Jesus*, Burwood, Victoria, 1989, makes a significant contribution to this process.

17. Maryanne Confoy, "Women's Impact on Theological Education," in *Discovering an Australian Theology*, ed. Peter Malone, Homebush, NSW, 1988, pp. 147–61.

18. *Claiming our Rites* (n. 2), xx.

19. *Freedom and Entrapment* (n. 2), pp. 165–92. I have added the translation of "Tiddas" to the title for international readers.

20. By way of example see Sally Morgan, *My Place*, Freemantle, 1987; Miriam-Rose Ungunmerr-Baumann, *Australian Stations of the Cross*, Melbourne, 1984; Rosemary Crumlin and Anthony Knight, eds., *Aboriginal Art and Spirituality*, North Blackburn, Vic., 1991.

21. Barbara Thiering, *Created Second? Aspects of Women's Liberation in Australia*, Adelaide, 1973; and eadem, ed., *Deliver Us from Eve: Essays on Australian Women and Religion*, Sydney, 1977.

22. Margaret Ann Franklin, ed., *The Force of the Feminine*, Sydney, 1986; Margaret Ann Franklin and Ruth Sturmey Jones, eds., *Opening the Cage: Stories of Church and Gender*, Sydney, 1987.

23. Angela Coco, "Women and the Australian Church: Project or Proclamation," B.A. Hons. Thesis submitted to the Department of Studies in Religion at the University of Queensland 1991, studies the movement and its history.

24. See Muriel Porter, *Women in the Church: The Great Ordination Debate in Australia*, Ringwood, Vic., 1989, as one insight into this story. The local and national magazines of MOW also contain the stories and the theology of this long struggle.

25. In the subsequent year a new organization, Ordination of Catholic Women (OCW), came into existence and held its first conference in Canberra in 1994 just months after the May 1994 papal letter *Ordinatio Sacralis*.

26. Elizabeth Wood Ellem, ed., *The Church Made Whole*, Melbourne, 1990, is a publication of proceedings.

27. Judi Fisher and Janet Wood, eds., *A Place at the Table: Women at the Last Supper*, Melbourne, 1993.

28. Summarized and quoted from the brochure of the Foundation.

4

Between Colonialism and Inculturation

Feminist Theologies in Africa

TERESIA M. HINGA

Introduction

In 1989, approximately seventy African women met in Ghana with the aim of initiating a forum through which they could research, analyze, and reflect upon their experiences in the tremendous variety of contexts in which they live. After suitable debate and deliberation, this group decided to call itself "The Circle of Concerned African Women Theologians."

Whereas it would be inaccurate to claim that before 1989 an African women's theological voice was absent in Africa,[1] the 1989 meeting was a turning-point in the emergence of a more formal and probably more systematic "feminist" theology on the continent. Through this convocation and its consequent activities, the diverse struggles of African women and how these have been shaped and influenced by the historical, religious, cultural and theological milieux in which they live become more crystallized and visible.

An analysis of the goals[2] of this circle of women, then, becomes a viable framework through which to describe the nature and direction of the feminist theological voice in Africa, a voice which two decades ago was conspicuous by its absence. Our task here is to highlight the key features of this nascent theological voice.

The Clues in the Name and the Will to Arise

Perhaps the best place to start our analysis is to examine more closely the implications of the very title the women chose to designate them-

36

selves. What clues does the name "The Circle of Concerned African Women Theologians" give us for understanding the nature and the direction of the women's theological voice in Africa? Several points are pertinent here.

First, we note that the women seem to have deliberately avoided labeling their project "feminist," despite the fact that feminist theology had already been flourishing under that label in the West for at least a decade. The significance of the seeming avoidance of the label "feminist" becomes clear when we consider that, by definition, feminist theology is contextual, seeking to give analytical weight specifically to the experiences of women and the injustices they suffer particularly because of sexism. Despite the commitment by feminists to make the experiences of women the primary source and rationale for their theology, it is also recognized that there is no such thing as "generic women" whose "generic experiences" can become the subject-matter of "generic feminist theology." Women's experiences are so diverse that to speak of a monolithic feminist theology is seemingly absurd.[3]

The awareness of the problem implicit in thinking of feminist theology as monolithic led African women to conclude that their experiences are sufficiently different from those of women elsewhere to warrant a distinct analysis and a distinct label.[4]

The women also seem to have been careful to include the term "Africa" in their self-designation, drawing attention to two aspects of their project. First, they insisted that the cultural context from which they speak and to which they speak is itself distinct from other cultural contexts, particularly the Western one, and that this distinct cultural context shapes their theological agenda significantly. Second, they pointed to their distinct history as Africans, a history which has been irrevocably marked by colonialism. The inclusion of the term Africa then was their attempt to name the cultural and social-historical location which is the springboard for their theology.

The significance of the term African in the women's self-definition becomes even more poignant when we consider that the primary concern of African women has been their lack of voice in theological as well as in other discourses. This situation has largely been attributable to the legacy of imperialism and paternalism that has characterized the relationship between Westerners and Africans. The assumption for a long time has been that Africans are to be guided, represented and spoken on behalf of, since they are either unwilling or unable to do so for themselves. African women have been double victims of this legacy, since even when it is considered viable to listen to Africa, the voice of African women is still unheard, since it is assumed that their voice is included in that of men. It is the injustice implicit in this enforced silence that led Oduyoye, the pioneer and leading African feminist theologian, to lament: "As long as men and Western strangers continue to write exclusively about Africa, African women will continue to be represented as if they were dead!" (Oduyoye and Kanyoro, 1992, 10).

Considering this injustice, then, part of African women's struggle is against the imperialism implicit in the efforts of others, particularly Westerners, to represent them, a struggle which they share with male theologians. For African women, however, their critique of Western paternalism includes the critique of Western women insofar as they, too, may presume to speak on their behalf. African women insist that the right to speak for themselves is a necessary condition for their emancipation and must be respected by all. As Ifi, a leading African feminist, insists: "African women can ignore historical and cultural differences only at their own peril in view of the damage done already by colonialism and still being inflicted by neo-colonialism and Western feminist imperialism" (Ifi, 1987, 8).

Realizing also that years of forced silence may in fact have led women to become entrenched in apathy and seeming acquiescence with the various oppressions, African feminist theology today is both a protest against the forced silence, and also a wake-up call to African women to rise and fight against the forces of injustice that surround them. The commitment to speak and act for themselves is well captured in the title of their first book, *The Will to Arise*, comprising papers discussed in the 1989 convocation. In her introduction to the book, Oduyoye interprets the title as symbolic of the women's vision of themselves. As she put it: "*The Will to Arise* is the voice of African women theologians. It is grounded in the challenges of scripture and results from a new wave of change. African women reading the scriptures have begun to see that God's call for them is not passive. It is compelling and compulsory. It is a call to action and wholeness that challenges the will and the intellect" (Oduyoye and Kanyoro, 1).

The third pertinent aspect of the women's description of their project is their insistence that they are a circle of concerned African women. This drew attention to the fact that contrary to stereotypes of African women as either unaware or indifferent to their oppression, they are conscious, capable and willing to deal with issues of moral concern. It is such concerns that they consider a challenge both to their will and their intellect as they consciously and conscientiously strive to analyze the web of oppression[5] under which they live. Not only are the women aware of the issues confronting them and the continent as a whole, but they also feel compelled to act towards the resolution of these issues.

One can infer, then, that though the African women have not given themselves the technical title of "feminists," they are nonetheless involved in a project that is similar to that of women in other contexts, particularly in the third world. As Ursula King remarks in the Introduction to her anthology of feminist theology from the third world, African women's theology is a feminist theology which puts emphasis on praxis and action. It sees theology as an ongoing process and is committed to life, justice, and freedom from oppression. It is not theology as reified but is primarily concerned with concrete issues of life as experienced.

African Women's Theological Concerns

What then are the concrete issues that concern African women as feminist theologians?

The foregoing analysis reveals that the primary concern of African women is their desire to break out of their enforced silence. Claiming their right to speak for themselves, the women began the process of naming their pain, and isolated various areas of concern; however, they prioritized the analysis of the implications of religion and culture for their lives. Thus, the goal for the first phase of their project would be to "concentrate efforts on producing literature from the basis of religion and culture to enrich the critical study of religion in Africa" (Oduyoye, 1990, 1). Consequently, the circle embarked on a sustained, systematic research and publication initiative, focusing on the critical analysis of the impact of culture and religion in their lives.

This project addresses several dimensions of the problem of religion and culture in Africa. First, there is the issue of diversity. To speak of religion and culture in Africa is to speak of at least three major heritages, namely, indigenous African religion, Christianity and Islam. These have, either cumulatively or independently, significantly influenced the definition of women in Africa. In analyzing the impact of culture and religion on their lives, African women have had to reckon with the diversity of concepts and interpretations of womanhood that are implicit in these traditions.[6] It is this cultural pluralism which made it methodologically imperative for the women to adopt what they called a dialogical approach. Their aim was not only to ensure a more inclusive forum that would respect this essential pluralism of the continent, but also to set an example of how best to deal with the issue of cultural diversity which often occasions conflict in Africa. Thus, as they argued: "The circle is designed to focus on the three main religions in Africa: it will be a symbol of Africa's recognition of the necessity of the dialogical approach to religious and cultural plurality in Africa and the practical consequences it has for peace in our communities" (Oduyoye, 1990, 2).

Second, in navigating their critical route through the issue of religion and culture, the women also have to deal with the historical reality of cultural imperialism implicit in the imposition of the Western way of life in Africa, particularly the imposition of Western religion. Here, African women are engaged in a two-pronged struggle. On the one hand they are fighting along with African men against such cultural imperialism and are therefore critical of agendas and proposals made by Westerners about the viability or otherwise of aspects of African culture.[7]

At the same time, however, aware that African culture itself is not immune to sexism, the women's critique is also addressed to African men who tend to idealize it. Some men accuse women of raising false alarms about the alleged oppression and sexism in Africa, while others accuse African women of uncritically imitating disgruntled Western women who in turn are stereotyped as unnecessarily belligerent, anti-men and anti-family, attitudes which are considered un-African and therefore unworthy of self-respecting African women.

Such attitudes of trivialization and denial are not only found in the secular society in Africa but are also manifest in the church and even in emerging "third world" theologies of liberation. Indeed, it is the experience of such trivialization of their plight within the established theological forums which led initially to what has been referred to as the irruption of women.[8] The women's critique is therefore legitimately directed to African male theologians for thus participating in the silencing of women: In the women's words:

> What Third World theology says to Western theology is that their voices must be heard because experiences vary...it is this same word that African women say to African men theologians...we live in the same continent but...there are many Africas...the Africa of the rich and the Africa of the poor...the Africa of men who command and that of women who obey....To all we wish to say that a new factor has arrived on the theological scene in the form of African women who write theology and who have covenanted to articulate the concerns of women...all who call themselves prophetic theologians of Africa will have to reckon with this! (Oduyoye, 1990, 41).

While the immediate occasion for the outburst of women was the use of sexist language in theological forums, the women perceived this as a symptom of a broader problem of sexism and patriarchy even in African cultures. Realizing this, using a critical feminist hermeneutics of suspicion which refuses an *a priori* idealization of any culture, African women embarked on a systematic evaluation of African culture in the light of sexism.[9]

Third, although most of the women involved in the circle are Christians, their critical hermeneutics of religion and culture also involves them in an analysis of the decisively ambiguous impact of Christianity in their lives. On the one hand they have noted that Christianity has participated in the oppression of women, since it has functioned to legitimize colonialism, racism and sexism. On the other hand, it is noted that many African women have appropriated for themselves the gospel of liberty implicit in Christianity as a strong motivating force in their struggle for liberation.

Recognizing the practice of injustices in church and society as a sinful betrayal of the vision of Jesus who laid a foundation for a human society characterized by equality, freedom and justice, African Christian women see their task as a prophetic one of unmasking and challenging such sinful practices and structures of injustices. Thus, they see no contradiction, as some Western feminists do, in being both feminist and Christian.

The women's critique of Christianity also involves them in a critical re-reading and re-evaluating of the role of the Bible as a source for Christian theology. Again, here they differ from some of their Western sisters, who see the Bible as so irredeemably warped by patriarchy that it is useless as a resource for women seeking liberation from sexism. While rejecting sexist and patriarchal exegeses and hermeneutics as sinful, women have continued critically to read the Bible and reflect upon it for inspiration and as a theological resource.

We may conclude, therefore, that a primary concern of African women's theology is to voice their protest against sexism and its roots in religion and culture. This protest is initially two-pronged, since it is directed at both African religion and culture and Christianity.

Conclusions: The Enduring Challenges

While the above is a summary of key themes in the emergent African feminist theology so far, it is not an exhaustive account, since African feminist theology is a theology still en route. Thus it would be premature to say that we have captured all that it could become! Suffice it here in conclusion to highlight some of the enduring issues and challenges which the women have courageously committed themselves to address, despite the many odds facing them.

First, African women have committed themselves to create a theology that is not just about women but is also of women. Now, considering that the majority of African women are so embroiled in daily struggles for survival as to make their involvement in "formal" theology impossible, the circle of theologians must be consistent in its efforts to include the experiences of the so-called grass-roots women in their theological agenda. The enduring challenge is for the women theologians to resist privileging experiences of elite women as normative for theology. They must also guard against the danger of silencing the masses of women by an *a priori* presumption to speak on their behalf. This necessitates constant dialogue with all women, whatever their social status. Only then can the emerging theology become genuinely representative, echoing the concerns of all women, despite the bewildering variety of their experiences.

Second, emerging African feminist theology so far is largely a product of Christian women, particularly from the mainstream missionary churches. Considering, however, that Africa is not a cultural or religious monolith, the Christian women's voice is not the only possible theological voice there. The evolving African feminist theology is then challenged to honor its commitment not to privilege Christianity at the expense of other religious traditions. Thus it must consider the insights and experiences of non-Christian women, particularly Muslim women, since Islam is a major force in African women's lives. It will also need to take seriously the experiences of African women, who, undeterred by Christian propaganda against African religion, continue to practice forms of African spirituality as healers, priestesses and prophetesses. African feminist theology must also take the experiences of those who do their theology on the fringes of Christianity. This includes the multitudes of women members of independent churches, many of which, it will be remembered, started in protest against the marginalization of Africans and their spirituality by missionaries and their theological discourse, and were often dismissed as heretical or culpably syncretic. Given the women's commitment to a dialogical approach to the issue of religious pluralism, African feminist theology may thus be compelled to shift from the prevailing christocentric model of theology in order to do justice to the variety of African women's spiritualities and religious experience.

Third, although in this first phase of their project women are primarily engaged in a legitimate feminist critique of religion and culture in Africa, it is also important to remember the equally urgent issues of survival that the African women are facing. For African feminist theology to avoid the danger of reification, it has to be consistently engaged with issues of women's political empowerment and economic justice, issues that are at the root of many of the problems that African women continue to endure. Since African women's theology is committed to play an advocacy role on behalf of women, it is challenged to persist in seeking practical solutions to the many problems that women face. Such a visible and unwavering engagement with issues of women's survival will be a significant measure of the continued credibility of feminist theology as it evolves on the continent.

Last but not least, though African feminist theology is context-specific and focused, for reasons discussed earlier, the question persists as to the relationship African women perceive themselves to have with other feminist theologians elsewhere. Here, it seems, the women think it possible to envisage a future marked by their genuine solidarity with all those of good will who strive for a more just global community. Their enduring commitment and challenge is to bring practical gifts and contributions to the process of healing and reconstruction, not only of their battered continent but also of a battered world.

NOTES

1. For details of events that led to the crystalization of the women's theological voice, see Mercy Amba Oduyoye, "Reflections from a Third World Perspective: Women's Experience and Liberation Theology," in King, 1994, pp. 22–33.

2. The Circle of Women committed themselves initially to a seven-year research and publication project. They planned to convene again in 1996 to take stock of their achievements and map out future strategies. For details of the Circle and its goals, see Oduyoye, 1990, pp. 1–7.

3. The issue of the diversity of women's experiences and its implications for the global feminist project is the subject matter of Spelman, 1988.

4. Similar conclusions have been reached by Black women in North America, who call their version of theology "womanist," while Hispanic women have labeled theirs "Mujerista theology."

5. The phrase "web of oppression" is used in African feminist discourse to describe the multiple and interlocking levels of oppression that they face as result of racism, classism, colonialism and sexism, a situation similar to that of all so-called "third world women."

6. Consider, for example, the difficulties women may face in their attempt at critical evaluation of the practice of polygamy, given that this practice is considered legitimate in Islam and African religion, while it is outlawed in Christianity.

7. See, for instance, the heated controversies surrounding the interpretations of practices like polygamy and female circumcision as discussed, for example, in the preface to Ifi, 1987, and compare this with Oduyoye, 1990, p. 45.

8. For details of the events that led to the irruption of women see Oduyoye in King, 1994, pp. 23ff.

9. See the essays in the Circle's first anthology, *The Will to Arise*.

BIBLIOGRAPHY

Ifi, Amadiume, 1987, *Male Daughters and Female Husbands: Gender and Sex in African Society*, London.

King, Ursula, 1994, *Feminist Theology from the Third World: A Reader*, Maryknoll, N.Y.

Oduyoye, Mercy Amba, 1990, *Talitha Qumi: The Proceedings of the Convocation of African Women Theologians*, Ibadan.

Oduyoye, Mercy Amba, and R. A. Kanyoro, eds., 1992, *The Will to Arise: Women, Tradition and the Church in Africa*, Maryknoll, N.Y.

Spelman, E. Vicky, 1988, *Inessential Woman: Problems of Exclusion in Feminist Thought*, Boston.

5

South Asian Feminist Theory and Its Significance for Feminist Theology

GABRIELE DIETRICH

Some Relationships in Need of Clarification

The present article tries to address itself to some significant concepts and issues of South Asian feminist theory and to explore their relevance for feminist theologizing. In this, no attempt can be made to be comprehensive or representative for the South Asian countries. Being located in South India, my main experience relates to India, especially the South, and up to a point Sri Lanka. Pakistan and Bangladesh are only marginally dealt with, though certainly the major debates overlap the boundaries of countries.

To come to grips with the relationship of secular feminist theory and feminist theology, some peculiarities of the region need to be taken into account.

First of all, feminist theology is socially visible only in the south of India as well as Sri Lanka, where larger Christian minorities form part of the population. Even then, feminist theology has not been perceived by the women's movement as a discipline putting forward serious methodological issues. Nor has secular feminist theory been perceived much in feminist theology. The reasons for this are not far to seek. All the South Asian countries have religious majority cultures which gravitate in different degrees towards establishing the majority culture as a state religion. Even India, though technically still a secular state, has gone far along the way of becoming a "Hindu nation."

Second, "women's studies" has become established as an academic discipline, in the wake of the two decades after International Women's Year. However, feminist theory is not necessarily predominant in such academic departments, as they tend to shun the in-depth analysis of

patriarchy and focus much more on "gender studies" and empirical research about women. In India, some of the theological colleges like TTS,
Gurukul and recently UTC have departments for women's studies, but
women here often find it difficult to uphold a feminist perspective within
the extremely male dominated faculties and student bodies. The difference and connection between women's studies and feminist theology is
often unclear. Independent institutions like the Center for Society and
Religion, Colombo, have made an impact on the Catholic Church up to
a point by putting forward feminist theology, and on the Catholic side
in India groups like WINA (catering to laywomen) and WORTH (formed
by religious sisters) have generated discussions and materials. WORTH
in particular has done serious work in discussing Western theological
positions and analyzing Hindu mythological materials.

Third, despite the fact that women's studies often lack feminist teeth,
and feminist theology either draws on Western imports or tends to remain entirely experiential or narrative, there is a significant ferment
created by a body of theoretical debate which is located and rooted
mainly in the activist scene of the women's movement. These debates
surface, for instance, in the bi-annual meetings of the Indian Association
of Women's Studies (IAWS), which gives room for activists as a matter of
principle and in activist conferences and workshops, some of which are
international within the region.

Fourth, what this body of debate means for feminist theology needs to
be examined. This is not easy, as feminist theology in South Asia has not
clarified itself much in its relationship to liberation theology in general
or dalit theology in particular, despite having a commitment to the poor
and oppressed. The present article only outlines some of the significant
issues and concepts raised, without being able to outline in any detail the
theological methodology which would be adequate to respond to these
issues and conceptualizations.

Some Key Issues and Related Concepts

The Concept of Feminism Itself

There is controversy about the concept in the first place. Often it has
been suggested by liberal as well as Marxist critics that feminism is in
itself a "Western" concept which cannot be directly applied in Asia.[1] This
has partly to do with the fact that feminism emerged in some of our countries as a reaction to certain aspects of party politics, especially of the
Left. For this reason, for the generation of feminists who became active
in the late 1960s and early 1970s it was connected with the vision of

a new economic order, human relations with nature, a classless society. This means there has been a strong socialist feminist mainstream in South Asia. In more recent years, the question of peasants, dalits and women and ecology got connected. For this reason, not only did the question of patriarchy, caste and class get addressed in an integrated way, but the overall question of transformation of society was ever-present. Therefore, the question constantly needs to be addressed whether the basic demands relate only to what one would put under the label of equity feminism or whether a fundamentally different type of development is envisaged. In other words, are we addressing questions of equal rights only or are we envisaging a fundamentally different perspective on each and every issue and aspect of society? A more liberal type of equity feminism has in some ways been integrated by the state in the wake of the U.N. Decade of Women. This approach can also be found in many NGOs which work on gender awareness and gender justice and often co-operate closely with the state. On the other hand, the need for much more fundamental transformation is strongly felt by unions in the informal sector, dalits, adivasis, peasants and some of the ecological movements. Obviously, all of this is theologically relevant. This debate helps us to see more critically what is happening with respect to women in the churches.

The South Asian churches have up to a point addressed themselves to questions of women's ordination and gender-just language; they also unavoidably have to address the problem of mass poverty in their midst, and much of feminist theology has a definite option for the poor. However, the barriers between dalit theology and feminist theology have not been broken down. As large parts of the dalit movements have a perception that feminism is a middle-class, upper-caste urban phenomenon, dalit theologians also insist on the primacy of caste discrimination, and do not work out the connection between caste and patriarchy very clearly. In contrast to this, over the past five years the women's movement has begun very seriously to address caste and communal issues, and autonomous organizations of dalit women are coming forward strongly. This is a learning process which has not yet been reflected in the perceptions of church and theology.

Ecology and Control over Resources — Production of Life

In South Asia, there is an intensive thinking process going on over the ecological question. This has to do with resistance against big dams (e.g., Sardar Sarovar on the Narmada, Tehri dam in Garhwal, Mahaveli in Sri Lanka) as well as with movements to save the forest and protect the rights of forest dwellers, and with the survival struggle for water. In 1990 the National Forum of Fishworkers (NFF) in India organized the

coastal march Protect Waters, Protect Life all along the eastern and western coast of India. Massive agitations against foreign licensing have been
going on, and prawn cultivation is a main target of protest.

As Bina Agarwal has been pointing out,[2] the Indian experience has
thrown up a different kind of perspective, which she terms feminist
environmentalism as opposed to a more Western-inspired formulation
of ecofeminism, which is closer to concepts of "deep ecology." While
ecofeminism in the West has tended to focus on the close nexus between "women" as a general category, the Indian debate has brought
forward much more in depth the class reality of poor peasant women
who are marginalized by the hegemonic development process. In brief,
the following ingredients can be identified:

> An alternative approach, suggested by feminist environmentalism,
> needs to be *transformational* rather than welfarist — where devel-
> opment, redistribution and ecology link in mutually regenerative
> ways. This would necessitate complex inter-related changes such
> as in the *composition* of what is produced, the *technologies* used
> to produce it, the *processes* by which decisions on products and
> technologies are arrived at, the *knowledge-systems* on which such
> choices are based, and the class and gender distribution of prod-
> ucts and tasks.[3]

This means that a transformational ecofeminism or feminist environmentalism need to go in detail into alternative economics. It raises the
question of what is produced, how and for whom, how is it processed and
marketed and the organizational aspects required for alternative patterns of production, as well as the movements which will have to fight the
forces of the state, which pushes the hegemonic ecologically destructive
development model.

This kind of approach is fairly close to the writings of Maria Mies
and Vandana Shiva, who have made a wide impact in the international
debate, basing themselves on the Indian experience.[4] However, their
conceptualization is considerably more sweeping in connecting women's
subsistence production with a spirituality of reconciliation with Mother
Earth and a scathing criticism of Western science and technology as
patriarchal and colonial. We have therefore been accused of ecological
myth-making.[5] Some of this criticism raises the question how caste/
class aspects are worked out in their approach, and how much the
scathing critique of Western individualism is warranted in the face of the
fact that the patriarchal culture in the communities involved in struggles to save the forest dominates the movement as well and suffocates its

feminist aspiration. Again, the need to raise organizational questions is imperative.

This has been done in exemplary ways by Chhaya Datar[6] in her position paper for the RC 32 Session 16 and 17 at the International Sociology Congress in Bielefeldt in July 1994. Chhaya very clearly distinguishes between two fundamentally different strategies among feminists. One integrates women into the "mainstream" characterized by growth orientation, consumerism, hi-tech, emphasis on market, centralization of market forces, emphasis on women's participation in public life. The other redefines development, which is forced upon women's activity in survival and subsistence economy, sharing of natural resources, production for basic needs as opposed to wants, security of food and shelter, decentralized production and marketing processes with democratic participation. This envisages alternative technology characteristic of an agriculture focused on a post-heavy industry production process and decentralizes rural industries based on developed artisanal skills and local resources.

A crucial conceptualization in which some of these attempts are summed up is that of the "production of life" rather than production for profit. In the South Asian workshop on Women and Development in January 1989, in which twenty-three prominent women activists from the countries of the region came together, this was formulated as follows:

> "Production of Life" includes not only the bearing and rearing of children but also the basic sustenance of life in subsistence production, household labor, informal sector, basic ecological activities which preserve forest cover, water systems, energy and the ozone layer. We prefer this concept to the traditional Marxist conceptualization which sees these basic life-processes as "re-production," while "production" is seen as extended production for the market and for accumulation of capital. We affirm the production of life as the basis of all other economic processes. It is obvious that a struggle which puts production of life at the center is by definition anti-capitalist, anti-imperialist and critical of mechanistic solutions which modern, Western science and technology may try to offer as a panacea for the ecological breakdown of the planet. It is also profoundly different from the development concepts which have been followed by actually existing socialism. This relates us to the whole feminist ecological debate which tries to redefine "productivity," "work and leisure," Gross Natural Product v. Gross National Product, parameters of work input and participation, relationship between the unorganized and organized sectors, need-based v. want-based production, and so on.[7]

This also presupposes a deep connection between nature and women's bodies, women and health and government policies on sensitive issues like forest, water, health and population.[8]

What does all this imply for feminist theology? It will not require only integration of caste/class perspective with patriarchy, but also a creation theology which relates itself to the whole process of human labor. Besides, while Asian theologies have been more cosmological and focused on the inter-connectedness of all forms of life, as well as spirituality, the feminist ecological experience compels us to look into the concrete circumstances in which the natural balance is disturbed, access to water, soil and means of survival undermined, etc. Thus, ecological theological reflection needs to also include the critique of mammon, the consumerist middle-class ethos of the churches, the sharing miracles as connected to food security, water as a common property resource, the Earth as God-given and therefore not private property, the critique of administrative hierarchies, the integrity of the good creation as opposed to bio-technology, sex determination and female foeticide, the symbolisms of the seed and the tree of life as opposed to the activities of multi-national seed companies and deforestation.

The Question of Religion, Communalism, Fundamentalism

Feminist theology in South Asia finds itself in a situation where Christianity itself is a small minority religion vis-à-vis a state which either promotes a state religion or, as in India, gravitates towards increasing assertion of the majority culture. Not only that, women of the region are divided by religious family laws! Because of the overwhelming presence of patriarchal religion in women's lives, there has been a tendency in all the South Asian countries to view religion as a destructive and oppressive force.

As I have worked out much more extensively elsewhere,[9] an incisive debate on the possible liberating and sustaining aspects of religion first arose in the national conference of the autonomous women's movements held in Bombay in 1986. This opened up the possibility of taking cognizance of feminist Christian theology. However, such interaction did not take place, partly because of the latent majority communalist implications of the secular women's movement itself. This point was forcefully driven home by Flavia Agnes, a feminist lawyer, at the conference of the National Association of Women's Studies in Yadavpur in 1991, where she characterized the underlying majority communalist assumptions in the secular women's movement and, for the first time in the history of the IAWS, made public reference to Christian liberation theology/

feminist theology as a tool of cultural liberation in a plenary session of the association.

The ensuing debate was heavy and emotion-charged, as it confronted all the participants in great depth with their religious identity and community. However, the focus did not shift to the methodology of dealing with religious texts or symbols, e.g., the question of women reappropriating their religious heritage in a radical perspective. The reasons for this are not far to seek. From the late 1980s onwards, with the increasing spread of communalism and fundamentalism in India, much to the consternation of the women's movement, women were seen to join more actively the ranks of communal and fundamentalist organizations, even though these were blatantly patriarchal. Not only that, women were also seen not only tolerating but themselves actively inflicting violence on other women belonging to the minority community. It became necessary to examine why for women the communal identification, though patriarchal, seemed to harbor more promise than the solidarity of the women's movement. The reasons are largely twofold. In general, the communal organization enables women to participate in public life with the support of the menfolk and elderly women of their community. As far as the minority community is concerned, especially among themselves, the fundamentalist organization becomes a vehicle of political assertion which safeguards the very right to survive and to fight for political sovereignty. For the sake of this right, even restrictive dress codes and norms of behavior become acceptable,[10] as has been seen among the militant movement for the independence of Kashmir. For the majority community, the communal organization becomes a vehicle of asserting relative independence even in dress and life style, a place where identity can be found and asserted and an ideological vehicle to channel aggression and national pride.

Paola Bacchetta has made this semi-Fascist brand of women's liberation strikingly visible in her research on women in the RSS.[11]

Such observations raise some serious questions about the ways feminist theology in India goes about inculturation. The tendency is to respond to the influence of Western feminist discourse on Goddess religion and to have recourse to female prototypes in the Hindu pantheon. For example, Catholic sisters have to cope with a thoroughly patriarchal environment and theological discourse tends to speak in terms of Shakti, Saraswathi, Mariamma, etc., as feminine expressions of the divine and to analyze mythologies according to how they empower or subordinate women.[12] This does not call into question the connotation of such symbols in the upsurge of Hindu majority communalism. Empowerment within a potentially Fascist framework may be very injurious to the women's cause. We are also compelled to examine the problem that solidarity with Muslim women is by definition excluded in such symbolism. How can such political appropriation and distortion be dealt with?

There is no one clear answer to this question, since *any* religious symbolism can be distorted by oppressive political appropriation, as the history of Christianity itself amply shows. However, a partial answer lies in the awareness of the social origin and functioning of such symbols historically and in the present day with respect to the life worlds of the different religious communities, channels of communication, formation of ideology and relationship to the larger systems of society which make an impact on these life worlds.

This leads us back to the perception of the social structures and the life worlds in which religious expressions are culturally embedded. It is interesting to note that on the whole, most feminist organizations in India have been extremely reluctant and restrained to draw on goddess symbolism because of the above-mentioned political constellation.

At the same time, there has been sustained interest in the exploration of women bhakti saints. The Indian magazine *Manushi* celebrated its ten years of existence with a special issue on women bhaktars. This interest has been more systematically worked out in a deeply significant study by Parita Mukta on Mirabai, the early sixteenth-century saint of Rajasthan who was devoted to Lord Krishna and who, in the strength of his love, not only rejected the authority of her husband, the ruler of Chittoor, but the whole martial, casteist, feudal ethos of the Rajputs, which was deeply inimical to women and people of lower castes. Mirabai, opting out of the privileged life at the court of Chittoor, had to cope with attempts to murder her and was facing severe social ostracism. Taking to a Chamar (leather worker) guru, Rohidas, the oral tradition of her songs became the medium of value assertion for artisanal castes, peasants and dalits, especially in Saurashtra, where Mira had migrated. She becomes part of

> a group of the underprivileged who are tied to each other by a distinct set of values that affirm a simple life uncorrupted by wealth and privilege. It is a group which deems that the good, the just, cannot flow from those exercising power and force. The members of this group are tied to each other by a system of morality and a system of values which uphold a community of the minds and hearts, held together by a sharing of common purpose. In the Mira bahkti, the tension and the power of these values is provided by the fact that Mira had to fight hard to retain her affiliation to a life of simplicity.[13]

This study of Parita Mukta is theologically significant in a number of ways. She does not analyze the written texts of Mira bhakti but traces Mira through the medium of the orally transmitted culture of the communities, to whom the bhajan sessions are an affirmation of an identity and a way of life. Tracing the tradition in specific caste groups, she identifies the aspects of production, legitimation and motivation. Thus, she works out an ethos of frugality in the artisanal and peasant classes which blatantly challenges the legitimacy of the hegemonic patriarchal family and caste values of the Rajputs and in this transmits an ongoing motivation for protest and assertion, for an alternative social identity up to the present day.

This is not only significant as a methodology of research which is directly relevant for theologizing, but also forcefully affirms an ethos which is diametrically opposed not only to the traditions of feudalism but also to the values of consumerism, competition, reification and cultural nivellation which spread like wildfire in the wake of the new economic policies. We are very close here to some of the essential values of the Jesus community. Parita Mukta also shows concisely how the same tradition of Mira bhajans was blunted and deprived of its anti-patriarchal and anti-family sting by Gandhiji during the freedom struggle and how finally Mira today is being commercialized through movies and comic strips by the middle classes. However, this in no way takes away the forcefulness of the social protest of the poor bhajniks, but on the contrary accentuates it. Far beyond deconstruction or reconstruction of mere texts, and far beyond a merely biographical narrative approach to the person of Mira, we find a reconstruction of the ethos and the life world of the community of bhajniks to whom the very organization of the bhajan sessions becomes a medium which constitutes identity and social affirmation.

The Question of Violence: Domestic, Communal, Economic, and Direct Warfare

In South Asia, we have been forced to face the question of violence in an integrated way which does not allow us to draw neat boundaries between domestic violence, public rowdyism, communal and caste violence and ethnic warfare. This means that violence against women and other forms of violence which involve the whole communities must be analyzed in all their interlinkages.

On the one hand this has been made visible in the biographies of some of our most outstanding feminists; on the other, it has also gone into the conceptualizations of different movements. Within the brief space available, only a glimpse can be had of the depths of the overall problematic.

During the 1970s, when the rape question catapulted the Indian women's movement into action, the scourge of domestic violence was first made visible in very explicit ways by Flavia Agnes, who was then with

Forum Against Oppression of Women.[14] She not only exposed her own biography as a battered wife to the public but contributed a great deal through writing and speeches towards tackling violence against women. She later became a lawyer to assist women to fight violence on their own. During the 1990s, she has moved into work against communal violence and significantly contributed to organizational work during the Bombay riots after the destruction of the Babri Masjid in Ayodhya in December 1992. The organizations which supported her, i.e., the Forum as well as the Lawyers Collective and later Majlis, a legal cultural organization, have gone deep into the overall connections between the different forms of violence. Discussions on the interconnections between the different forms of violence have also taken place over the years in the magazine *Manushi.*[15]

These observations link us back with the painful events in Sri Lanka over the past twenty years, where military and ethnic violence has taken a heavy toll on the social fabric. One of the most outstanding contributions to feminist theory and praxis has come from Rajani Rajasingham, a doctor and human rights activist of extraordinary courage and integrity. She devoted her energies to the social reconstruction of the Tamil community in Jaffna, not least by co-founding the University Teachers for Human Rights (UTHR) and later the Poorani Women's Center. The book *The Broken Palmyra,* which she co-authored with Rajan Hoole, K. Sridharan and Daya Somasundaram, gives a meticulous documentation of the violence not only of the Sri Lankan Army and the IPKF but also of all the Tamil groups. It was this insistence not to apply double standards which made her a target of the LTTE and cost her her life.[16] In her meticulous accounts of violence Rajani also analyzed the role of women within the militant groups, their relative empowerment in the armed struggle, their compulsion to uncover human rights violations, the chauvinistic tendency to push women into the role of "brave and valiant mothers," and the tendency of Tamil society to disown such women all the same. Most significantly, despite the extensive documentation of atrocities, women do not appear as victims in this account, but as those who have questioned, braved the guns and protected the community. In this attempt to assert life, ethnic boundaries are transcended and state power stands exposed side by side with the Indian army and the Fascist tendencies within the LTTE and other groups.

We are facing a situation here where traditional Marxist positions, which locate patriarchy mainly in the relations of production, and a radical feminist approach, which would focus more on the autonomy of patriarchal violence, are transcended. On the one hand, the role of the state in legitimizing and perpetuating violence becomes overwhelmingly clear, while at the same time, the violent structure of the life world, the day-to-day social structures of survival, of culture, of language, of communications, become painfully visible. Gail Omvedt has traced such connections in the debates emerging out of dalit movements and peasant movements in Maharashtra.[17] Vandana Shiva has brought out the connection between the state, technocratic development policies and communalization of politics in her book on the Punjab situation.[18]

The recent upsurge of mass movements against alcoholism has made the linkage between domestic violence, a construction of the life world and policies of the state visible in a different way.

Why and how are these connections theologically relevant? Christian feminists in the region are facing the challenge to address themselves fully to the politics of transformation which connects the violence of the hegemonic development concept, ethnic, caste and communal violence eroding the social fabric and militarizing political life with the "ordinary" day-to-day violence against women in their daily life world. This requires a shift of emphasis from the attempt to achieve equal rights, empower women, especially poor women, etc., towards an in-depth analysis of the root causes of deepening poverty and a theory of human needs which redeems the fall of the good creation in the light of table-fellowship for all. This cannot be an abstract postulate, but needs to be a very conscious process of the reorganization of society itself, in which feminist theologizing needs to locate itself and take part.

The Organizational Question

In each and every part of this article, confronting the organizational question has become imperative. It will therefore be helpful to look at the organizational question in some more detail and to spell out some of the more important aspects. In an earlier article entitled "The World as the Body of God," I tried to theologize directly on women's experiences in the slum-dwellers' and fish-workers' movements.[19] While I got the feedback that these theological reflections were inspiring and directly accessible because of their immediate and virtually poetic quality, it was also pointed out to me that it was not self-evident why reflection on people's movements should be of crucial theological importance. In the following some attempt is made to clarify the connections.

Life World — Systems — People's Movements[20]

In traditional societies, the horizon of interaction was dominated by the coherence of life worlds which were mediated by local languages and cultures, and in which legitimacy was reinforced by religious beliefs and rituals. While the state would superimpose systems of administration and commerce, this would leave the social structures largely untouched. Such non-interference can be observed even in the colonial policies of the British Raj, where the day-to-day culture of survival, the family, the caste system and the religious life remained largely untouched. However, with the onslaught of modern science and technology and electronic communications, these systems of the state, the multinational corporations, international media, and the international monetary system have permeated daily life and rapidly dissolved the social structures of the life world. While this has sometimes led to a certain weakening of traditional patriarchal structures, it has invited and reinforced more efficient modernized forms of colonial and neo-colonial patriarchy and has also dissolved structures of traditional solidarity which safeguarded survival and cultural cohesiveness, despite the costs of patriarchal, caste-, class-, and age-based inequalities.

While historically people's movements have taken the shape of religious reform embodied in peasants' movements, and later of artisanal guilds and trade unions, the present-day situation catalyzes movements into new shapes and into more crucial positions. They depend on the life world for recruiting membership and also empower the life world to renew itself and to resist the onslaught of totalitarian systems and social disintegration. Without the interaction of progressive social movements, the life world will either easily disintegrate — as has happened in many Western countries — or it will fossilize into rigid patriarchal and chauvinistic forms which project religions, ethnic or caste-based community identity at the cost of women, children and all democratically minded sections. Without drawing on the traditional solidarities of the life world, movements will become culturally uprooted, ideologically abstract and out of touch with the humanistic contents of day-to-day survival. This also implies that the struggle for an alternative economy which is implied in the struggle for the hegemony of production of life over production for profit will have to be located in the interaction between life world and social movements.

Family — Caste — Community

In the present situation of economic and political crisis, the organizational forms of the life world face an identity crisis and a crisis of legitimation. Families are torn apart under the impact of the hegemonic development concept; caste identities, evened out by industrialism and city life, get reaffirmed in violent clashes in villages, in the unavoidable struggles about reservation and even in the organizational processes of the dalit movements. Religious community, under the pressures of the scarcity of resources and the onslaught of the media, takes on more and more communal connotations. Movements are cast in-between.

The women's movement, with its bitter experience of patriarchy and scathing critique of the family, finds itself at times in the same boat as the forces of modernity which dismantle the family. At the same time, women's subsistence survival base is destroyed by these same forces and women end up as sex objects and prostitutes.

The dalit movements, avowedly out to dismantle the caste system, find themselves reinforcing caste and getting split among each other along caste lines; finally they can end up being co-opted by communal forces. Communalization of politics reinforces an aggressive patriarchal structure, but at the same time offers free spaces for women to find a semblance of emancipation with the blessing of the religious community and a protected kind of identity.

Opening the debate on each of these issues and at the same time allowing the life world to reorganize itself creatively, without traditionalist pressures but also free from atomizing individualism, is a vital task for the survival of our humanness.

The Role of the State

In the process outlined above, the role of the state has to be put in question afresh. In the post-independence period of South Asia, for a while there was a hope that the state might be able to safeguard and strengthen democratic spaces. This hope has undergone severe strains under conditions of military regimes, emergency and civil war. All of this has affected the life worlds of daily survival and women's spaces in society very adversely. After the U.N. decade on women, even now the South Asian states have not signed the Convention on Elimination of All Forms of Discrimination against Women (CEDAW). At the same time, the state co-opts people's movements and women's movements to implement its own development programs. Feminists are using such spaces, while at the same time the resource situation deteriorates and the daily survival struggles of women are getting harsher. The state is abdicating more and more of its responsibility for infrastructure and social welfare, and at the same time taking an active part in the communalization of politics.

Nobody can do theology in a neutral space any more. We are in the middle of the survival struggle, the co-optation, the communalization of politics. Concern for priority, survival rights, freedom of religion, much of this may appear as a lost cause before long unless our interventions are forceful.

Conclusion

Facing the issues and conceptualizations outlined above will require new theological methodologies which we can only start to think of. As some of us have pointed out earlier,[21] we will need a combination of the conceptual and the narrative. While the secular women's movement in its attempt to analyze culture and religion could benefit from some of the hermeneutical debates on biblical texts, Christian feminists need to widen their perception of feminist social analysis in order even to locate themselves successfully in the first step on the hermeneutic circle. The spaces for intercultural sharing of women's faith and aspirations have to be opened up not only within church and theology but within the life world of daily interaction and in the day-to-day reality of women's survival struggles.

NOTES

1. Kamla Bhasin and Nighat Said Khan, *Some Questions on Feminism and Its Relevance in South Asia,* Kali for Women, 1990.

2. Bina Agarwal, "The Gender and Environment Debate: Lessons from India," *Feminist Studies* 18, I, 1992, pp. 119–55.

3. Ibid., p. 151.

4. Vandana Shiva, *Staying Alive,* Kali for Women, 1988; Vandana Shiva and Maria Mies, *Ecofeminism,* London, 1991.

5. Cecile Jackson, "Radical Environmental Myths: A Gender Perspective," *New Left Review* 210, pp. 124–40.

6. See her discussion paper submitted to RC 32 at the Bielefeldt International Sociology Congress, July 1994.

7. "Pressing Against the Boundaries," Report FAO, New Delhi, 1989, p. 54.

8. Vandana Shiva, ed., *Minding Our Bodies: Women from the South and North Reconnect Ecology and Health,* Kali for Women, 1993.

9. "Women and Religious Identities in India after Ayodhya," in *Against All Odds,* ed. Kamla Bhasin, Ritu Menon, and Nighat Said Khan, Kali for Women, 1994.

10. See Shiraz Sidhva, "Dukhtaram-e-Millett: Profile of a Militant, Fundamentalist Women's Organization," in *Against All Odds* (n. 9), pp. 123–31.

11. Paola Bacchetta, "'All our goddesses are armed,' Religion, Resistance and Revenge in the Life of a Militant Hindu Nationalist Woman," in *Against All Odds* (n. 9), p. 153f.

12. Margaret Shanti and Corona Mary, eds., *We Dare to Speak,* Worth Study Series, 1, 1994.

13. Parita Mukta, *Upholding the Common Life: The Community of Mirabai,* London, 1994, p. 91.

14. See Flavia's *My Story ... Our Story of Rebuilding Broken Lives,* Bombay, 1984.

15. See, e.g., Madhu Kishwar, "Safety Is Indivisible: The Warning from Bombay Riots," and Flavia Agnes, "Behrampada — A Besieged Basti," in *Manushi* 74–75, January–April 1993.

16. *The Broken Palmyra*, Claremont, Calif., 1990. See also John Merrit, "The Battle for No Man's Land," *The Observer*, 29 April 1990, pp. 46ff.

17. Gail Omvedt, *Violence Against Women: New Movements and New Theories in India*, Kali for Women, 1990.

18. Vandana Shiva, *The Violence of the Green Revolution: Ecological Degradation and Political Conflict in Punjab*, Dehradun, 1989.

19. Gabriele Dietrich, "The World as the Body of God," *Journal of Dharma* 18, no. 3 (1993).

20. Some of the conceptual framework used here is taken from the Frankfurt school of sociology and its discussion on systems theory. My colleague David Rajendran has applied some of this to Indian people's movements in his doctoral research. I draw partly on discussions with him.

21. See Margaret Shanthi, "Towards a Feminist Theology," and Gabriele Dietrich, "On Doing Feminist Theology in South Asia," *Kristu Jyoti* 6, no. 2, June 1990.

6

Hunger for Bread and Roses

Toward a Critical-Feminist Theology of Women's Work

CHRISTINE SCHAUMBERGER

"Bread and roses" was the demand of the women workers who went on strike in the textile factories of Lawrence, Massachusetts, in January 1912 against starvation wages and child labor, and at the same time for their right to all beauties of life. Inspired by this demand of the striking factory workers, the feminist song "Bread and Roses" talks about the experience of hunger ("Hearts starve as well as bodies"), recalls the memory of "unnumbered women dead," women with "their ancient cry for bread," and conjures up the vision of justice in labor and pleasure:

> "No more the drudge and idler—ten toil where one reposes—
> but a sharing of life's glories: bread and roses, bread and roses."

Ideas and facts of liberation in feminist theology should surrender to the spell of this hunger for bread, art, love and beauty, this remembrance of the sufferings and longings of dead women, and this vision of justice in labor and pleasure. Although more and more women are piecing the feminist movements into an ever stronger worldwide web, women still hunger in hearts and bodies, are still deprived of creative work in solidarity for "life in abundance" and of a just division of this abundance: "our powers expended daily on the struggle to hand a kind of life on to our children."[1]

Now as ever, women are forced to wage a daily struggle for their own survival and that of their dependents, at the expense of other women and the basis of our life: "where can we find a place which does not, while providing us with a living, at the same time attack and undermine the basis of our biological life on this earth?"[2]

We women can only liberate ourselves if we undertake theoretical and practical labors, if we "dig," to bring to light the buried and forgotten ex-

60

periences, life stories, efforts, longings and destructions of women, if we "go," to leave our "natural" place in the patriarchal order, have new experiences, to change our personal, material conditions of life, our feelings and ideas, and the world. The process may be step by step, but with each step we shall give form and radical energy to our visions.

"...Go Ever Further, Dig Ever Deeper":[3] On the Difficulty and the Necessity of Making Women's Work and Women's Poverty Visible in Feminist Theology

Most essays in feminist theology stress their basis in women's experience, very few explicitly discuss women's work.[4] Many feminist theologians seem to see women's work not as a "specifically theological," but as a "pre-theological" issue. But as long as feminist theology is not rooted in women's real and varied experiences of work and exploitation, and does not consider women's struggles at work not to be cheated of the fruits of our labor, an essential area of women's lives and hopes, and so a large part of women themselves, remain invisible.

The tendency to exclude, or simply to forget, women's work in feminist theology has many causes. First, it is of course a sign of the all-embracing and ever-present power of patriarchy that we only occasionally succeed in challenging and — with great effort — overcoming androcentric perceptions. Feminists have maintained a constant tradition of criticizing the androcentric division of life into the private sphere and the public sphere (politics and jobs), the polarization and ranging in hierarchies of man and woman, culture and nature, reason and emotion, spiritual and material, and the academic division of labor which does not consider reality as a whole, but only in fragments. The definition of women's productivity in creating and maintaining life as "nature" in contrast to men's work, which is defined as a cultural achievement, the definition of the private as the woman's sphere, while the public sphere is the man's — with religion relegated to the private sphere — is based on this fragmenting approach. So too is the description — and from a feminist viewpoint devaluing — of science, professional work and politics as men's business and the domestic sphere as a woman's world untainted by destructive male politics. Its effects are also felt when feminist theologians treat the conditions, results and rewards of women's work as problems which, while important, are not in themselves religious and theological issues. When feminist theologians fail to attach theological relevance to women's work and women's poverty, the feminist critique of male theology makes no difference to their acceptance of the male definition of what theology "really" is and leaves them still within the confines of the theology they criticize.

There is a second reason for the invisibility of women's work in feminist theology. This is the practical employment situation of feminist theologians. It is hard enough to venture into imagining and desiring models of women's liberation, but in the world of work our liberation seems to face even greater obstacles from so-called "material pressures" and inherent laws in working life. The more hopeless and inescapable our work prospects seem, the greater our temptation to exclude women's work from theological analysis and reflection, to save ourselves from falling from flights of intellectual feminism on to the hard ground of facts. What feminist theologian can "afford," in the sense of keeping herself alive, to work consistently and uncompromisingly on feminist theology so that practice and theory coincide in her personal and in her working life? By accepting the feminist goal of total liberation from patriarchy we set ourselves such high ideals that many of us live with a constant "bad conscience." In our practical working lives we are torn:

- between the basic need to earn enough money to survive, the threat of unemployment and the basic need to refuse to be skivvies for the destructive purposes of patriarchy;
- between the strategy of bringing about fundamental changes in social and Church institutions and the need for independent foundational work under our own control;
- between the pressure of deadlines and production created for the women's movement by the policies of the dominators, and the longing for enough time to rethink everything from the bottom up;
- between the need to continue with feminist and theological work in all its forms, to keep "digging" and "going," demanding our right to do nothing, "to enjoy life," and the fear that those we love and feel responsible for will be let down, and that commitment to feminist theology is turning us into "unnatural mothers, daughters and friends."

"It is a great balancing act for women to cope with these multiple contradictions and to try again every day to live here in the present situation and at the same time to turn it in the direction of a feminist utopia."[5] But if feminist theology has no roots in the everyday life of particular women, with its contradictions, it is no different from the male theology it criticizes in that it remains idealistic theology with no dialectical relation to the social reality of women and to the political praxis of the women's movement, which takes its cue from the reality of work.

Third, making an issue of women's work confronts White feminist theologians with the fact that we have so far generally been expressing the experience of a small group of women, separated in particular by their working conditions, from most women.

> Like Virginia Woolf, I am aware of the women who are not with us here because they are washing the dishes and looking after the children. Nearly fifty years after she spoke, the fact remains largely unchanged. And I am thinking also of women whom she left out of the picture altogether — women who are washing other people's dishes and caring for other people's children, not to mention women who went on the street last night in order to feed their children.[6]

Through the women's movement we have finally learned to say "we" as women, but the subject of women's work and women's poverty brings discomfort back into this feeling of togetherness. Women's working conditions, their position in the international labor market, wage rates for women, the forms of pressure on them to do particular jobs, their exclusion from other jobs and selection for different sorts of work in reality divide women from each other. They also help to play women off against each other: working women consumers against the women producing for the world market in "third" world factories, "first" world women who are "really doing all right" against the hungry women of the world who are still "underdeveloped," the "bourgeois" feminists against lower class women, "whose men are oppressed," the "emancipated" against the "non-working" housewives, the women with alibis against the women "who just don't make enough effort," the "abnormal" women against "proper" women.

> But our strength consists in seeing the differences between women as fruitful and facing up to the distortions which are our innocent inheritance, but now we have to be corrected by *us*. If through our anger with each other we come to have real insight into our differences, our consciousness of these differences can turn into a consciousness of power. Anger among like-minded people produces change, not destruction. Unease and feelings of being lost, which often appear in the process, are not fatal, but a sign that we are maturing.[7]

We have to grapple with the divisions among women, the connections between women's work and these divisions and the function of these divisions in maintaining the power of patriarchy. It is essential if we are to break the mystifying universalizing discussions of "women" which still dominate feminist theology and focus on a particular image of women, not the variety of real women. It is essential if we are to have our goal women's liberation which — since women may at any moment lose all privileges because of being women, not because of their performance at work — is directed at the liberation of the poorest and most invisible women. "Our struggles can have meaning and our privileges — however precarious under patriarchy — can be justified only if they can help to change the lives of women whose gifts — and whose very being — continue to be thwarted and silenced."[8]

"The Impossible Competing with the Possible": Women's Work as an Inspiration and Irritation for Feminist Theology

Seeing the World as a Whole

In turning its attention to women's work, feminist theology finds its critique of theology and the Church strengthened. It is not only forced to remember that the oppression and exploitation of women's productivity has been legitimated as a punishment for sin, and the ceaseless work of women is dismissed as less valuable than contemplative absorption. In addition it is forced to realize how far the outlook of currently dominant theology fragments human life, and the effect this fragmentation has on women's work.

The sphere of private life, which in West Germany is regarded as the women's sphere, has become the principal theater of privatized religion, and women the "preferential" agents of this religion. And on top of the burden of work, and the lack of recognition of most of their work, women are also told to give up, for the sake of "love," careers, financial independence, self-fulfillment through a job, and then to feel "happy." They are made to bear the burden of creating and sustaining families as "islands of Christian virtue,"[9] and "undamaged world," in the face of a hostile society and destructive working conditions. This is regarded as their real vocation, irrespective of any other work. Women are bound to fail in this task: "where Christian love is lived only in the family, it soon becomes impossible even there."[10]

Because concepts such as "love" and "nature" are used to make women's work invisible, feminist analysis of that work and its function in a society based on work is an important tool for feminist theology in its attempt to break theological dualism and patriarchal structures of domination in Church and society.

However strange terms such as "human production" and "work as relationship" may be in a world in which work is defined as the total opposite of love in order to conceal its exploitative nature, it is nonetheless important to stick to such concepts in view of the confrontations and battles to come. It is important because such terms, conversely, are a critique of a world in which "work," in the usual sense of the word, is not only defined, but also practiced, as something totally beyond the bounds of love. The recognition and insistence of the present women's movement that love is also work, an activity which involves toil, demands concentration but is also productive, life-sustaining, vital to life, the insistence that without this work no society could exist, these ideas are the essential precondition for a radical criticism of dualism.[11]

Our fragmented life cannot be restored by giving special status to "female" spheres and putting together the separate fragments to make a whole. The longing for wholeness requires a complete transformation and surpassing of all these individual spheres. Nor can an integrated life be created by "individual" and "political" change which move along in parallel without connection. The demand for life to be a whole instead calls for a redefinition of "individual" and "political."

The feminist desire for wholeness also prevents feminists from being satisfied with a "feminist" science within the corset of the traditional division of labor. It is no longer enough for us to investigate "women in the Bible." We go further, and try to discover the details of the work and lives of particular women — including those of whom nothing is said — and ask what conversion, discipleship, healing and repentance mean in these situations for women, i.e., what they changed in practice.

We no longer regard the description "sinner" as a moral label, but as a description of a situation in work and life. We examine the character and function of prostitution of women's work, and the poverty of women condemned to (forced) labor as prostitutes. We are not content to point proudly to our foresisters in early Christian history, but try to find out what sort of work, for example, Lydia the dealer in purple, did and how, and what social and economic consequences this work had.

Nor can we be content any longer to ask what a theological principle or a theological model "has to do with women's experiences"; we go further and investigate what relevance a theology shows in the different actual work situations and lives of women, whether it contributes to theological analysis and reflection on this situation and provides a stimulus to liberating change. For example, what is the meaning of the theological proposition that religion is a break from the everyday routine in relation to housework, which requires women to be available "round the clock"?[12]

As Elisabeth Schüssler Fiorenza has shown, wholeness cannot be created while the roots and manifestations of dualism persist.[13] As long as patriarchy rules, the feminist insistence on perceiving the world as a whole has a primary critical function. It exposes and mourns the fragmentation of our perception, and measures and condemns the sufferings of women for the sake of the ideal of an integrated life by our insistence that I can and must relate the "I believe in the resurrection of the dead" to the mill-workers of Lawrence, the mothers of "Bread and Roses."

Feminist Theology: Opium, Valium, or Food?

Feminist theology needs to look carefully at women's work and poverty for another reason, to avoid the danger that it might have an effect on women similar to that of the theology currently prevailing in bourgeois society. It must beware of distracting them from the guilty record of theology and the Church, giving a theological gloss to the present situation (and the higher status now given to the despised feminine), or comforting them out of the situation with intoxicating utopias which have no real effect on everyday working life. A feminist theology which allows people to forget the painful reality of women and encourages women in a feeling of happiness seems to make survival easier.

In such a case it may have the effect of opium, makes possible flight into a "different" world, a world of women, in which the domination of patriarchy seems to be broken, but has the effect that — compared with these "different" worlds of women, either imagined, or to some extent independently created by women — changing the existing situation seems hopeless and in the end irrelevant. This separate world of women then becomes the center of feminist life, and the dominant "normal" world a foreign land, from the influence of which feminists should withdraw more and more.

These worlds of women are important, and break new ground in challenging the dominant, accepted pattern, and create an awareness that different life is desirable, "realistic" and liberating. But an exclusive concentration on these autonomous worlds of women without a critical and transformative purchase on what remains "normal" life for most women in patriarchal structures, and without any intention of destroying or changing what are recognized as patriarchal structures, leaves untouched the domination of patriarchy over all women — including those who are experimenting with independent and liberated living.

Alternatively, feminist theology may be like valium if it comforts women by making them forget the pain of the dehumanization and destruction of women by the effects of the history of work dominated by men and the forcing of women into "women's work." A feminist theology which raises the status of despised femininity, portrays womanhood as a better, undamaged form of human existence, and women's activities such as "mothering" as more valuable than men's work acts like valium (which, not by accident, is prescribed to so many women for "disturbances at work") in making oppressive and exploitative working conditions for women more bearable, "calms" pain, anger, and unrest at injustice and at the same time enables women to continue their pre-ordained women's work under the same conditions.

Feminist theology must become a food, a life-support.[14] Not only must it make possible material survival; it must also encourage women to overcome the destruction of life and possibility to which they contribute through their work for patriarchy. It must awaken a hunger for a liberated, whole life and the longing for the possibility of decent, life-giving work, share it with other women and nourish it — not kill it — scare people out of the accustomed acceptance of the life of working women and goad them into change, transformation — and destruction.

To give our theology substance as food, feminist theologians must take sides (self-) critically with women's struggles at work, especially those of poor "Third" World women. It must focus on the real situations of women at work, be analytic with the cognitive interest to make visible the causes and underpinnings of patriarchal domination. It must be visionary in its following of the promise present in the still to be reconstructed history of women in the Bible, a promise of equality, justice, liberation and wholeness. Such an approach to feminist theology starts with an awareness and reflection on specific work experiences of women, but does not exalt them theologically; instead, by keeping a deliberate distance it attempts to get a broader view.[15] Seen through "strange" eyes, from a distance, the "obvious," the daily routine is thrown into sharper focus and revealed as not obvious, but changeable and in need of change. Ways of achieving such a distance in order to transform the obvious include:

- seeing things from the point of view of the most invisible and poorest women and their situation at work;
- looking at the social history of women's work in one's own context and in a different one;
- using the tools of feminist sociological and historical analysis of women's work;
- recalling and inventing visions of liberated and liberating work;
- taking an active part in feminist political activity.

These new viewpoints will lead to a feminist reworking of the whole of theology. It has to start with the trivial things of women's everyday life, since it is here that the dominant religion most massively brings about the oppression of women in the attitudes learned by and expected of women in the bourgeois world: giving up personal development and

direction, accepting the status quo, conforming to prevailing expectations, seeing oneself as a powerless victim, attempting to heal the injuries
caused by patriarchal domination by private "love," the patience which
underpins domination and is expressed in the constantly heard comments: "I don't complain," "We all have our cross to bear," "There is
nothing to be done," "You just have to put up with it." Feminist theology
criticizes the forcing of women into triviality, and the way the Church's
preaching proclaims modesty, endurance and putting up with this triviality as Christian female virtues. It recalls that "normality" does not
necessarily have the last word, that the "impossible" can come to pass,
that existing limits can be transcended, that the last shall be first.

Feminist attempts at liberation operate in the tension between the
most exact possible appreciation of the banality of women's everyday
lives (as supermarket cashiers, housewives, mothers, daughters, girl-
friends, neighbors, voluntary parish workers) and the call for unlimited
justice, the right to creative work and life in abundance. A critical feminist theology of women's work needs feminist visions of liberation, not
as a consolation, but as "the strongest telescope, that of finely honed
utopian consciousness, needed to penetrate what is closest to hand,"[16]
and to bring about changes which transcend limitations. "In the conflict
of the impossible with the possible we expand our possibilities. The important thing, it seems to me, is that we create it, this tension by which
we grow, that we head for a goal, even if it retreats as we approach it."[17]

Translated by Francis McDonagh

NOTES

1. Adrienne Rich, "Hunger," in *The Dream of a Common Language,* New
York and London, 1978, pp. 12–14.

2. Christa Wolf, "Ein Brief," in *Mut zur Angst: Schriftsteller fur den Frieden,*
ed. Ingrid Krieger, Darmstadt-Neuwied, 1982, pp. 152–59, quotation from
p. 155.

3. Adrienne Rich, "Women and Honor: Some Notes on Lying," *Heresis* 1,
no. 1 (1987) (translated from the author's German).

4. In contrast women's work is one of the topics most studied by feminist
social scientists and historians. For studies which focus on the worldwide connections between women's oppression, poverty and exploitation, see Claudia
von Werlhof, Maria Mies, and Veronika Bennholdt-Thomsen, *Frauen, die Letzte
Kolonie,* Reinbek, 1983; Claudia von Werlhof, *Wenn die Bauern Wiederkommen:
Frauen, Arbeit und Agrobusiness in Venezuela,* Bremen, 1985.

5. Editorial, *Beiträge zur feministischen Theorie und Praxis* 15/16, 5–6,
quotation p. 5.

6. Adrienne Rich, "When We Dead Awaken: Writing as Re-Vision," (1971) in

On Lies, Secrets, Silence, New York 1979, London, 1980, p. 38. The reference to Virginia Woolf is to *A Room of One's Own.*

7. Audre Lorde, "The Uses of Anger," *Women's Studies Quarterly* 9, no. 3 (1981). Translated from the German.

8. Adrienne Rich, ibid.

9. J. B. Metz, "Messianic or Bourgeois Religion?," *The Emergent Church: The Future of Christianity in a Postbourgeois World,* New York, 1981, p. 7.

10. Ibid.

11. Christel Neususs, *Die Kopfgeburten der Arbeiterbewegung oder Die Genossin Luxemburg Bringt Alles Durcheinander,* Hamburg, 1985.

12. For essays in feminist theology designed to make the work and poverty of women theological issues, see, e.g., Elisabeth Schüssler Fiorenza, *In Memory of Her: A Feminist Reconstruction of Christian Origins,* New York, 1983; *Bread Not Stone: The Challenge of Feminist Biblical Interpretation,* Boston, 1984; Luise Schottroff, *Unser Erbe ist Unsere Macht! Warum die Erinnerung und die Purpurhändlerin Lydia für uns frauenbefreiende Kraft hat* (1987).

13. See Elisabeth Schüssler Fiorenza, "For Women in Men's Worlds: A Critical Feminist Theology of Liberation," in *Concilium* 171 (1/1984), pp. 32–39.

14. I am here drawing on ideas of Ingeborg Bachmann, who compares poetry with bread, and Audre Lorde, who calls eroticism a food.

15. On the concept of cognitive distancing, see Ferdinand W. Menne, "Rekonstruktion der Familie: Kognitive Distanzierung angesichts der Verstrickung in Alltagsgeschichte(n)," in *Geschichte der Familie oder Familiengeschichte?* ed. Anneliese Mannzmann, Königstein, 1981, pp. 57–53.

16. Ernst Bloch, *Das Prinzip Hoffnung* I, Frankfurt, 1974, p. 11.

17. Ingeborg Bachmann, "Die Wahrheit ist dem Menschen Zumutbar. Rede zur Verleihung des Horspiel-presies der Kriegsblinden," *Die Wahrheit ist dem Menschen Zumutbar,* Munich, 1981, pp. 75–77, quotation from p. 76.

7

Critical Theologies for the Liberation of Women

M. SHAWN COPELAND

By now, it is neither controversial nor polemical to state that the thorough-going critical hermeneutical, epistemological and praxial commitment of theology to the radical liberation of women insinuates a major paradigm shift in reflection on religion and its role and significance in various geographic, social (i.e., political, economic and technological) and cultural sectors. On the one hand, since these theologies are concerned with much more than the domination of women by men, they liberate reflection on religion, advance its criticality and vitality, restore its seriousness and authority. These critical theologies, whether they stem from the experiences of Aboriginal, African, Asian, Caribbean, European, Indian, Latin American, North American, Pacific Basin subjects, entail certain common fundamentals: women's experiences form the point of departure, ideology critique as well as critique of all forms of patriarchy, explicit identification of hermeneutical location, social analysis and praxial resistance to kyriarchal oppressions. Moreover, these theologies overcome the aleatory distantiations of modernity — secular from sacred, private from public, objectivity from subjectivity, thought from feeling, theory from praxis. They expose the elaborate prevarications that mask the massive atrocities that have come to define the last five hundred years of human history. On the other hand, these theologies resist reductive, leveling, binary or totalizing world-views or systems that purport to impose any utopian solution to the maintenance and transmission of religious and societal oppression. These critical theologies instigate the emancipation of women's subjugated and violated bodies and knowledges; discredit reified and hegemonic ontological signifiers; interrogate and engage common and different religious, social and theoretical sites of struggle.

These critical theologies affirm black, brown, red, yellow, white women in all their diversities, histories and cultures, even as they problematize those diversities, histories and cultures as well as those interconnecting cognitive, moral, religious, social praxial relations among and between these women at all points and in all sites of struggle. As the exercise of rationality in theology, such interrogation, engagement and problematization is extended through the notion of *difference*, which has increasingly displaced the notion of *sisterhood* as a key theoretical tool in critical feminist theologies.

For nearly two decades, "sisterhood" characterized the principal project of the global women's movement, yet the most basic denotation of "sisterhood" remains conflictual and inflammatory. Freighted with patriarchal familial ideology, "sisterhood" intimates the nurturant and reproductive roles of women within that family as well as women's feelings of connection and loyalty to other women growing out of shared experiences of oppression.[1] At the same time, "sisterhood" is aligned with the bourgeois individualism that granted "the passage of a few middle class women into the public sphere," congealing not only *differences* in social class between them and working-class women, but crucial *differences* of social location as well. Thus "sisterhood" evades broad-based, differentiated efforts toward the kind of social transformation that effects justice for all human persons.[2] The Aboriginal womanist theologian Anne Pattel-Gray captures the ambiguous and failed story of sisterhood across different racial, cultural, ethnic, religious, sexual, political, economic and philosophic borders when she writes,"Not yet Tiddas."[3] *Not yet sisters.* Thus, it is difficult and painful for diverse critical theologies committed to the radical liberation of women to speak univocally, *to speak in or under one voice.* These theologies require differentiated understandings and pluri-voiced speech. Indeed, "difference" resists and contests any tendency toward a smothering maternalistic "ma-'am-stream feminist theology." Here, "feminist" functions (as it always has in *Concilium*'s Feminist Theology series) to pluralize, to destabilize, to dismantle, to problematize any propensity to asphyxiate or suppress difference in critical theologies committed to the radical liberation of women.

I

Feminists have come to insist that the absence of considerations of difference weakens any form of feminist discourse; at the same time, this option for a pluralist rather than unitary understanding of women has fostered rich and provocative complication. Within the wide and fluid borders of critical feminist theologies, what is meant by difference? What praxial and philosophic interpretations lie behind that use? What is mediated in the analytical use of the notion of difference? What does the multiplicity invoked by difference contribute to the tasks of interdependence, collaboration and solidarity among critical feminist theologies? Insofar as religious, cultural, and geo-social (i.e., geo-political, -economic, and -technological) structures divide, how can and does difference empower?

Logical and Espistemological Difference

Several inter-related issues are posed in consideration of logical and epistemological difference. First, the use of difference in critical feminist theologies neither intends nor adverts to what deconstructionists mean by the play of *difference.* Jacques Derrida in *Of Grammatology* makes *difference* basic: it displaces, intervenes, disrupts. *Difference* resists what is invariable, yet it dissolves the tendency to absolutize dimensions of specificity or particularity in reality. Eve Sedgwick contends that the "analytic move [deconstruction] makes is to demonstrate that categories presented in a culture as symmetrical, binary oppositions actually subsist in...more unsettled dynamic tacit relation."[4] Symbiosis, affiliation and interdependence can be detected in difference. Second, behind the commonsense use of difference lie derogation and indirection; thus, any positive epistemological charge of difference may be subverted by logical opposition. Difference insinuates not merely variance, but deviation, division, discrepancy, discord, incongruity, incompatibility, inconsistency, anomaly, contrariety, aberration and misunderstanding. When such disaffirming and antagonistic intention suffuses consciousness, use of difference as a tool risks capitulation to the unitary, to the uniform, to the powerful — even to the feminist as unitary and powerful. In critical feminist theologies, the use of difference must include struggle, although not struggle for individualism or intrapsychic fulfillment or singularity or, even, separateness. Rather, difference carries forward struggle for life in its uniqueness, variation and fullness; difference is a celebrative option for life in all its integrity, in all its distinctiveness. Italian feminists apprehend this most clearly in their refusal to take equality as the conceptual opposite of difference. Rather, Italian feminists maintain that "difference is an existential principle which concerns mode of human being, the peculiarity of one's own experiences, goals, possibilities and one's sense of existence in a given situation and in the situations one wants to create for oneself."[5] This clarification recollects not only the colonial juridical history of the notion of equality and its invasive role in the cultures of women (and men) of the two-thirds world, but also its rigid reign over social class relations.

Third, the notion of difference in critical feminist theologies raises the problems of understanding experience. Because experience is such a general notion, speech about experience wants precision, filling out, explanation; the very generality of experience may undermine the concrete. It is preferable to speak of patterns of experience and, on this account, to distinguish several patterns — biological, psychological, dramatic, aesthetic, artistic, practical, social, intellectual, mystical. At the same time, critical feminist theologians must be wise in the apprehension and use of experience as a category of analysis. To confine difference chiefly to the world of immediacy, i.e., the world of sensible experience, is to limit experience to the "already-out-there-now" and to condemn the human subject to the "already-in-here-now." On this position, what is to be known is obvious, seen and extroverted, but it can be known *really* and only by the subject who is having the experience. Such confinement of difference renders understanding of an "other" and her experience impossible. Consequently, some of the deepest concerns of some critical feminist theologians are disconnected from the concerns of other and different feminist theologians. Some women protest, while other women more or less consciously acquiesce to the assertion: the experience of some particular woman or group of women cannot be understood or judged or critiqued by other and different women. An isolating relativism as well as a pernicious pluralism vitiates the ground for understanding, reflection and judgment; for evaluation, deliberation and praxis. Still, this situation presents critical feminist theologies with a distinctive epistemological challenge: to reject the ocular, totalizing, pornographic myth that knowing is taking a look, critical knowing is taking a second and good look. Critically interrogated, difference, in and of experience, prompts these theologies to probe and name experience; to understand what is common and singular and different; to question, to test insights, to judge.

Fourth, critical feminist theologies do not reject local thinking; they use logic to debunk stereotypes; to expose ideology; to demystify systems, structures and processes that divide and oppress. These theologies take up their stand for truth at the feet of poor white, yellow, red, brown, black women. From this point of departure, critical feminist theologies insist that truth is never independent of cultural, social and historical conditions. For these theologies, the search for truth is motivated by the deepest concerns of all those who transgress the definitions of "so-called acceptable" women — especially poor women and lesbians who embody "indecent difference."[6] Thus, the experience, insight, understanding and judgment of poor, oppressed and marginalized women stand as normative in any critical feminist theological formulation.

Fifth, in the search for meaning and value, critical feminist theologies interpret scriptures and scriptural traditions within different religious,

historical, cultural and geo-social situations. Because these critical theologies recognize the possibility of arbitrarily cutting off questions in the
search for truth, they are alert to the danger of conceding difference,
while, simultaneously, levelling difference through toleration, through
indifference to difference. In a critical epistemic, difference stands as
"a fund of necessary polarities between which creativity can spark like
a dialectic."[7] Thus, difference is both a source of understanding and
a deterrent to the more or less conscious choice to identify and substitute partial or provisional or probable truth as truth exclusively,
comprehensively.

Consider the writing of histories. Critical feminist theologies reject
"big" histories of male dominance and supremacy, meta-narratives of
phallo-macho-centric conquest. These theologies affirm "large-scale empirical narratives" that introduce local complexifying accounts which recover lost traditions and practices of female agency, creativity and resistance; narratives that reclaim female-centered practices mislabelled as
natural; narratives that "revalue previously derogated forms of women's
culture."[8] When these large-scale and local narratives engage one another dialectically, they counteract any tendencies to distort or to de-
ceive. To give careful attention to local narratives helps to prevent
large-scale ones from solidifying into "quasi-meta-narratives"; to give
careful attention to large-scale accounts helps to prevent local ones from
"devolving into *simple demonstrations of difference.*"[9]

Still, what has been said about the confrontation of critical feminist theologies with male dominated histories must be repeated from
the standpoint of women in poor, marginalized and oppressed communities. Critical feminist theologies must reject "big" histories of female
achievement and prominence. These "gyne-centric meta-narratives" often overlook the complicity of societally privileged women in fabricating
spurious identifies for men of oppressed and marginalized groups: the
black man as sexual beast, the red man as savage animal, the brown
man as indolent, the yellow as inscrutable. Such gyne-centric meta-
narratives often ignore the complex relations of power between privileged
and non-privileged women in sites of domination and oppression. Yet,
precisely because they are *plural,* critical feminist theologies invite large-
scale empirical narratives that will explore women's interactions across
intersecting lines of difference in religion, philosophy, race, culture, ethnicity, history, geo-social situation, class and sexual orientation. These
narratives are further complexified by local and particular accounts
that recover, restore and revalue women's lived lives. When these large-
scale and local narratives of women's lived lives engage one another
dialectically, they controvert any tendency to stifle, to manipulate, to
betray.

II

Difference in critical feminist perspectives does not permit some relative situation in which the privileged sit comfortably repentant beside the oppressed. Difference challenges us to overcome the societal conditioning that would have us ignore our differences or treat them with suspicion or contempt, arrogance or conceit. Difference challenges us to reject the reproduction of kyriarchal thinking. Difference instigates a new pedagogy by which to educate ourselves critically about ourselves, about "other" and different women (and men), about our inter-relations in situations of domination and oppression. This dialectic rescinds and criss-crosses those borders or structures erected to divide, to segregate, to disempower. Such dialectical analysis not only trespasses borders but unmasks those women (and men) in whose interest and for whose material profit those perimeters have been constructed and guarded. It is in the range and seriousness of sustained plural dialectical encounters that difference gains real authority and pushes through false pedantic antitheses as well as totalizing hegemonic world-views. In this process, not only are new knowledges and resources unleashed for all women (and men), but new obligations emerge. What is at stake both for poor, oppressed and marginalized women (and their communities) and societally privileged women (and their communities) is authentic praxis in the context of recognizing, grappling with, learning and celebrating difference. As Audre Lorde observes, "In our world, divide and conquer must become define and empower."[10]

Praxis and Difference

Critical feminist theologies institute a paradigm shift in theology; integral to that shift is epistemological rupture or a new way of grasping and affirming truth. Given their critical orientation, those feminist theologies that assume the epistemological task of contesting androcentric, imperialistic and subjugating knowledges have a further challenge to social praxis. Even as praxis is a vital site of difference, difference stakes out another site for praxis.

In Christian terms, knowledge does not lead to power, but to responsibility. Since these critical theologies consciously intend what is true, what is just, they call for a social praxis that does not simply reproduce the present intellectual, cultural, or geo-social situation. These theologies promote and support efforts, beginning at the feet of poor, oppressed, and marginalized women, to critique, purify, and transform those situations. Critical feminist theologies are wary of all forms of contrivance, coercion, or instrumentality in the struggle for liberation. These theologies never oppose social to personal praxis; rather, personal praxis finds authentic viability in the geo-social domain. The woman (and man) active in history, in the geo-social situation, realizes herself (or himself) in new, wholesome, redemptive patterns of intersubjective, communal, geo-social relations. At the same time, the woman (and the man) active in history creates new, wholesome, redemptive intersubjective, communal, geo-social relations.

Difference and Moral Authenticity

Since critical feminist theologies intend to produce and reproduce what is true — in word and in deed — these theologies recognize an ethics of thinking, that is, truth is a way of being. It is painfully the case that the moral state of a theologian does not determine the quality of her (or his) theologizing. But critical feminist theologians acknowledge the inescapable moral relation *between* what they think and speak and write and the nature of relations they form with other women (and different women). For instance, most white European and North American feminists have come to understand critique as a fundamental gesture of theology. Yet, how is it that most white European and North American feminist theologians so often perceive themselves as shaping (or, at least, unconsciously assume themselves to be shaping) the theoretical script and stage for the theologizing of "other" and different women in whose oppression they have historically participated and from which, even now, they continue to benefit? How is it possible that truly critical white European and North American feminist theologians expect their work to constitute the primary source of tradition of thought for "other" and different women doing theology? Is it possible that truly critical white European and North American feminist theologians overlook self-criticism? Or, can truly critical womanist theologians simply impose their theological analysis as the primary source or tradition of thought for other black women doing theology in other and different geo-social situations? Is it possible that truly critical womanist theologians overlook self-criticism? Or, can truly critical minjung theologians refuse to embrace the punished and despised lesbian? Is it possible that truly critical minjung theologians overlook self-criticism? Hegemony is always a possibility, even for the oppressed. This is why we must heed Audre Lorde's caution to continual self-criticism; this is why we must be humbly, critically, attuned to our own moral and theological praxis, lest unconsciously we appropriate the attitudes, spirit, sensibility and tools of the master.[11]

Perspectival Differences

Perspectival differences in critical feminist theologies can never be identified exclusively with the specificity of social location, i.e., differences in religion, culture, race, ethnicity, social class, sexual orientation. Rather, perspectives emerge from critical inquiry, understanding, reflection and judgment on social location. Insofar as critical feminist theologies stress complexity, understand differences in social location and grasp their own differing formulations as provisional and probable, they are perspectives. While the proper subject of critical feminist theologies is women's experiences, there can be no cheap fusion of perspectives, no indifference to the ways in which women are globally implicated, often, but not always, through no fault of their own, in the oppression of other women (and children and men). North American and European feminists must consider the impact of their daily material living on the lives of the women (and children and men) of Africa, Asia, the Caribbean, Latin America, the Pacific Basin. At the same time, socially privileged women within Africa, Asia, Latin America and the Pacific Basin must confront their co-optation in the structures that oppress poor and marginalized women (and children and men) in their geo-social situations. White European and North American women must analyze how, in their particular geo-social situations, systemic and structured racism (in its multiple forms, e.g., anti-Semitism, anti-black) erases nationality or citizenship, reducing "other" women (and men) to simple biological physiognomy. In erasure, difference is made dangerous. European and North American women need to scrutinize, for instance, just how homophobia is sedimented in consciousness and deforms thinking. Through bias, the different are rendered a danger. At the same time, women of poor, oppressed and marginalized communities living within Europe and North America must confront their complicity in structures and institutions that assault other women (and children and men) in other oppressed and marginalized communities living in that same geo-social situation. Perhaps what is more important, women of oppressed and marginalized communities living within Europe and North America must reckon with the ways in which they have been co-opted, not only by the structures of domination, but by the destructive experience of being dominated.

III

This issue of *Concilium* explores difference as a model for understanding and expressing a new situation in theology. This chapter has interrogated some of the implications and consequences of difference in critical theologies committed to the radical liberation of women. It remains to inquire about the future of difference. What are the possibility and future of difference? What future will difference make for critical feminist theologies?

First, in as much as critical theologies committed to the liberation of women stem from real struggles to profess a living faith in a genuine God of hope and love, they call for deep-going conversion, not only of the theologian, but also of her cultural and social community, especially her religious community. Christian experience has long confirmed Audre Lorde's assertion that "without community there is no liberation."[12] But authentic community is a product neither of geography nor of the suppression of differences. Rather, authentic community emerges in the strenuous effort to understand common and different experiences; to interrogate those differences, commonalities and interdependencies rigorously; to reach common judgments; to realize and sustain interdependent commitments. As community in difference is a hard-won achievement, so too is difference in community. Such interdependence is reached only through deep-going conversion and serious, honest conversation — speaking with head and heart and flesh; listening with head and heart and flesh.

Second, when difference is grasped as "a fund of necessary polarities," then interdependence is no longer threatening. It is important to distinguish interdependence from assimilation or absorption and loss. "Pour your pitcher of wine into the wide river. And where is your wine? There is only the river."[13] How poignantly the Aboriginal poet Oodgeroo conveys the anguished ambivalence of an ancient people who, though forced to surrender much that they love, passionately defend their roots and revere their difference!

> We are different hearts and minds
> In a different body. Do not ask of us
> To be deserters, to disown our mother,
> To change the unchangeable.
> The gum cannot be changed into an oak.[14]

Assimilation disguises those latent possibilities of domination in difference that not only intimidate the formation of community with the coerced uniformity but menace the crucial role that difference plays in the self-constitution of identity.

Difference is the authentic context for interdependence. Authentic interdependent engagement of women (and men) of different histories, cultures, stories and races; of different gifts, strengths, aptitudes and skills, empowers women (and men) to envision and forge new relations, to draw new courage to decide, act and be. Authentic interdependent engagement of women (and men) of different religious, cultural, historical and social situations initiates new fields for differentiated social and cognitive praxis on behalf of social justice in the concrete. The interdependence of difference is a crucial condition for realizing our very full humanity.[15]

Third, solidarity is crucial to the future of difference, the future of the interdependence of difference, indeed, to the future of humanity. Unlike coalitions, those transitory aggregates that conjoin solely to manipulate advantage, rather than change or transform structures of oppression, solidarity is less self-interested and less pragmatic. Unlike partnerships, corporate relations fabricated and sustained through monetary transactions, solidarity opens us to new and creative possibilities in human relations. While much less intimate than friendship, solidarity insinuates cohesion, bonding and interdependence. Insofar as solidarity is something to be achieved, it moves us on to something larger than, yet constitutive of, ourselves. Solidarity, then, is a practice. It extends the ground on which we may stand with other women (and children and men) who may be different in culture, history, religion, race, social class, sexual orientation, but without whom we have no future. Solidarity is both the result and the cause of practically intelligent collaborations that bring about new mediations and through which we are made new.

In the practice of solidarity, we recognize again the contingency of justice in our world: that is, justice is not necessary, things could be, and often are, otherwise. Yet, in as much as critical feminist theologies are Christian, solidarity is crucial in realizing and celebrating the future of difference. Indeed, solidarity is a basic and fundamental gesture of theology. It could not be otherwise, for the incarnation is God's own radical act of solidarity, God's act of love, hope, and life enfleshed in Jesus. And is this not the task of authentic Christians of different histories, cultures, times and places — to enflesh love and hope and life wherever love and hope and life are fragile.

NOTES

1. Elizabeth Fox-Genovese, "The Personal Is Not Political Enough," *Marxist Perspectives* 2, Winter 1979–80, pp. 94–113; see also Nancy A. Hewitt, "Beyond the Search for Sisterhood: American Women's History in the 1980s," in *Unequal Sisters: A Multicultural Reader in US Women's History,* ed. Ellen Carol DuBois and Vicki L. Ruiz, London and New York, 1990, pp. 1–14; Bonnie Thornton Dill, "'On the Hem of Life': Race, Class and the Prospects of Sisterhood," in *Class, Race and Sex: The Dynamics of Control,* ed. Amy Swerdlow and Hannah Lessinger, Boston, 1983, pp. 173–88; Hester Eisenstein and Alice Jardine, eds., *The Future of Difference,* New Brunswick, 1985; Virginia Fabella, *Beyond Bonding,* Manila, 1993; Chandra Talpade Mohanty, Ann Russo, and Lourdes Torres, eds., *Third World Women and the Politics of Feminism,* Bloomington and Indianapolis, 1991; Stanlie M. James and Abena P. A. Busia, eds., *Theorizing*

Black Feminisms: The Visionary Pragmatism of Black Women, London and New York, 1993; Gayatri Spivak, *In Other Worlds*, London and New York, 1987; Iris Marion Young, *Justice and the Politics of Difference*, Princeton, 1990.

2. Fox-Genovese, "The Personal Is Not Political Enough" (n. 1), pp. 97–98.

3. Anne Pattel-Gray, "Not Yet Tiddas: An Aboriginal Womanist Critique of Australian Church Feminism," in *Freedom and Entrapment: Women Thinking Theology*, ed. Maryanne Confoy, Dorothy A. Lee, and Joan Nowotny, North Blackburn, 1995, pp. 165–92.

4. Eve Kosofsky Sedgwick, *The Epistemology of the Closet*, Berkeley, 1990, pp. 9–10.

5. Paolo Bono and Sandra Kemp, ed., "Introduction: Coming from the South," in *Italian Feminist Thought*, Oxford, 1991, p. 15.

6. Alessandra Bocchetti, "The Indecent Difference," in *Italian Feminist Thought*, pp. 148–61 (n. 5); cf. Luce Irigaray, "Sexual Difference," in Toril Moi, ed., *French Feminist Thought: A Reader*, Oxford, 1987, pp. 118–30.

7. Audre Lorde, "The Master's Tools Will Never Dismantle the Master's House," in *Sister Outsider,* Trumansburg, 1984, III.

8. Nancy Fraser, "False Antitheses: A Response to Seyla Benhabib and Judith Butler," in Seyla Benhabib, Judith Butler, Drucilla Cornel, Nancy Fraser, *Feminist Contentions: A Philosophical Exchange*, New York and London, 1995, pp. 62–63.

9. Ibid., p. 62, emphasis mine.

10. Lorde, "The Master's Tools Will Never Dismantle the Master's House," in *Sister Outsider* (n. 7), p. 112.

11. Ibid., pp. 110–13.

12. Ibid., pp. 112.

13. Oodgeroo, "Assimilation — No!," quoted in Kathie Cochrane, *Oodgeroo,* St. Lucia, Queensland, 1994, p. 74.

14. Ibid.

15. Nancy Hartsock, "Difference and Domination in the Women's Movement: The Dialectic of Theory and Practice," in *Class, Race and Sex: The Dynamics of Control* (n. 1), pp. 166–67.

PART II

NAMING THE STRUCTURES OF WOMEN'S OPPRESSION

8

Women, Work, and Poverty

ANNE CARR

The working situations of women across the world, despite the best efforts of many, is only part of the global picture. Nevertheless it opens a window on the grim reality of women's lives and work today. It enables a glimpse that is revealing, frightening, and demanding in its moral and theological implications for the Church. For it demonstrates the poverty-ridden plight of so many women and their children as the poorest of the world's poor. The situation of women in their work is often, globally and systemically, one of misery, degradation, despair. This is particularly true in the third world, but it is shockingly the case in the undersides of the first world as well. It is a situation which calls upon Christians everywhere, but especially those of us in more privileged contexts, for attention, analysis, and active transformation.

From the emerging electronic sweatshops of North America to the enforced prostitution of women who sell their bodies for sheer survival in Asia, from the plight of women of color who are the field workers in Africa and the domestic workers in Latin America, the United States, and South Africa to the homeless women and children everywhere, there is a chilling similarity in the patterns and taken-for-granted structures of women's lives and work. They are patterns and structures of patriarchy, domination, and exploitation that demonstrate the problems of sexism at its worst, especially as it is interstructured with racism and classism. These patterns are deeply ingrained in the economic, political, and social fabric across the world and they have been made more complicated by the multi-national character of the work of the poor today. And they are deeply ingrained in the home and the Church as well as the other institutions of society.

The facts of some of the concrete situations of women and their work reveal the way in which the domination of patriarchy extends from the home to other institutions. It is the traditional patriarchal structure of the home which is in place when it is taken for granted by women and men alike that work in and for the household — cleaning, washing, ironing, mending, cooking, shopping, care for the children, the sick, the elderly, and men — is the responsibility of women alone and further, that this labor is inferior, unvalued, unrecognized and uncompensated. The woman who say she is "just a housewife" and thinks that she does not "work" because she is not part of the paid labor force has absorbed the messages of patriarchy in her own debased self-image. The same understanding of women's inferiority is extended to situations where a woman does work outside the home and receives minimal compensation for her labor, usually performing the most menial and underpaid occupations, and suffering loss of community connections because of the expectation of almost total availability to her employers. In effect, many women have two jobs, and struggle to balance the demands of each. If the woman is a mother, her workday is sixteen hours in comparison with the eight-hour workday of the average father. And neither liberal nor Marxist-socialist theory adequately accounts for her work with an economic concept that fits the reality of women's lives. Empirical evidence from one recent survey shows that women today simply get less sleep as they rise earlier and retire later each day in their effort to accomplish the work demanded by their positions, one paid and the other unpaid. While in more affluent situations some privileged women work outside the home for personal meaning and fulfillment, they still do double work. And more often it is the case that women must use their labor, their very bodies, to obtain money for the economic survival of their children, their parents and extended families, and themselves. They are often the heads of single-parent families: it is women and their dependent children who are the poorest of the poor.

Even in the relatively affluent countries of Western Europe and North America, where infant mortality is low and really few starve, there are the public poor, the wanderers, the homeless, and the "hidden poor" who are mostly women. There is the new category of women who work in the home, without contract, minimum wage, or any benefits or security, and the large group of "welfare women" who find themselves unable to escape the vicious circle of life-long dependence on public aid. For these women there are too few jobs, or only jobs for which they are unqualified or over-qualified. Many of these are divorced and responsible for young children; many — young and old — have never been married. These "welfare women" are forced to open their private lives to government inspectors, to submit to the indignity of being informed on by neighbors, to suffer in the cold because they cannot pay gas and electric bills in the winter, to spend the hours of the day in searching for the cheap goods of survival. They are viewed by society as objects of pity, or as lazy, defrauders, profiteers, sluts. Few of these women go to church, especially if they have been divorced. They are uncomfortable because the climate of the churches is so middle class that they are forced to hide the real facts of their situation.

In this context, so aptly described as "the feminization of poverty," some women labor under the triple burden of race, sex, and class as these biased structures interconnect in their lives. In addition to their debased position as women, intrinsically inferior to men because of their sex, women of color find their capacities underdeveloped — they are often illiterate — and their opportunities unjustly constrained because of their race and their socio-economic status. In the stark examples of South Africa and Latin America and, in a frighteningly similar way in the United States, these women are consigned to the task of supporting affluent white men, and by extension, white women in the elitism of their ruling social, political, and economic positions. The labor of these poor women of color, generally unprotected by law or union, reveals the commoditization of individuals, in all their human capacities and desires, into the masses of cheap labor required by contemporary forms of capitalism.

The patriarchal structures which are embedded in home and society and which are at the source of the denigration of women's labor are, sadly, nowhere more evident than in the churches. Far from embodying a prophetic leadership, the world-wide churches lag far behind many societies in their attention to women, to the patterns of women's lives and work, and the full incorporation of women into the work of the churches for the coming of the commonwealth of God. Women do much of the work in the churches but it is often on a volunteer or unpaid basis, and in limited roles which do not engage their full talents. And where there is movement toward the full recognition of women, there is the threat of schism and further fracture of unity: ecumenism is used as an argument against the ordination of women. Though women represent more than half the constituency of the churches, their leadership is still for the most part invisible. Where the issue of the male-female relationship has been discussed, as at the World Council of Churches meeting in Sheffield in 1983, it is still overshadowed by the attention given to other, more "theological" issues. The result is that some women seek elsewhere for a form of Church that enables their sense of dignity and respect, while nuns and lay-women are forced to compete with one another as they seek adequate remuneration for their work in and for the Church, and lesbian Christians are denied their rights in the Church as well as their rights to a decent livelihood in civil society because of ecclesiastical strictures.

In the social teaching of the Church, not only historically but still in the present, there is clear evidence of the dualistic and patriarchal theological anthropology that is rooted in an outmoded Aristotelian biology and Greek philosophy. It is explicitly expressed in the theologies of Augustine and Thomas Aquinas and underlies the traditional view that holds that men represent the transcendence of the human soul or spirit, while women represent human carnality or immanence. Men thus have the priority as being creators of culture in the public realm while women are rightly confined to "nature" or the private realm of family life. The theological norm is represented by the male, and by the supposed "complementarity" of male and female in the heterosexual unit. This theology reinforces the several pressures under which women struggle to balance the responsibility for the family with the necessity of outside earning, encourages their irresponsibility of men toward women and children, and has long been criticized by feminist theology. But feminist thinkers are approaching this problem in new ways today.

Feminist theology may have emerged from middle-class sources, as it was begun and developed by privileged, university-educated women in North America and Europe. But it soon became critical, not only of the patriarchal frameworks of the academic theology but self-critical in its perceptions as well. As it sought to integrate the insight of Black and Latin American liberation thought, it quickly came to recognize its need to envision the solidarity of *all* women in the transformation of the churches, the whole of theology, and of society. In its effort to participate in the work-struggle of women everywhere but especially in the third world, it has become more concrete, more analytical, more visionary. Thus feminist theology today searches for those "strategies for solidarity" which seek to unite women, and never to divide classes or races, in the common Christian task of transformation.

Feminist theology is rightly critical of a theology of servanthood which, as one of our authors claims, can only be encouraged and realized when there is an equality of power, in the Church, in the home, in society. The recently espoused "option for the poor" that the Church has adopted in several official documents necessarily becomes, in feminist perspective, an option for poor women, for the "other," and for a new order of justice and love in society. Feminist theology, with its concern for reciprocity and mutuality, for human wholeness and peace, recognizes that the vast sums of money spent for arms only serve to increase militarism, nuclearism, and ecological destruction while denying the chief Christian and moral criterion for any society — its treatment of the poor in its midst. And, as our survey shows, the poorest of the poor are women and the children who are dependent on them.

To attend to the facts and figures of women's work and poverty, to give voice to poor women everywhere but especially in the third world, to analyze the structures and systems within which most women live and work, and to envision a transformed social order in which there is free and freeing work — "bread and roses" for everyone — these are the urgent tasks of a critical, Christian feminist theology. Far beyond merely representing a peripheral issue to the "real" work of the Church, this theology struggles to become a genuine means towards new life for women. For the credibility and the very reality of the Church as the bearer of the message of Jesus, as the living sign of salvation in the world in its service of the poor, depends on the transformative knowledge and practice of Christians everywhere in the dynamism of concrete history. This transformative knowledge and practice can demonstrate that the impossible can be realized, that "the last can become the first," that the Christian vision can become real in the reality of women's lives and work in the world.

The standard posed in the scene of final judgment in Matthew's gospel, "For I was hungry and you gave me food; I was thirsty and you gave me drink; I was a stranger and you made me welcome..." (25:35) remains the standard which Christian feminist theology applies to itself, to the Church, and to Christians everywhere today.

9

Uneven Development, Capitalism, and Patriarchy

NANTAWAN BOONPRASAT LEWIS

Many have long understood prostitution to be a personal issue. Prostitutes are women who are promiscuous sexually, and are greedy for money. It is best understood as a social issue from a moral perspective, namely, men exploit women's bodies for their sexual desire and women are abused by brokers, brothel owners, pimps, and police. Few would want to seriously question or explore the crucial role of our social and economic structure nationally and internationally, as well as our cultural-religious values articulated by men and the social treatment toward women that has been inflicted on them and or that has caused them to be in this profession. In the past decade, a rapid increase in the number of women who enter into prostitution, particularly in the Philippines, Korea, Taiwan, and Thailand, compels concerned scholars to examine the root cause and offer analyses and suggestive solutions to this situation. Not all of us, however, see a connection between uneven development, capitalism, and patriarchy as crucial factors conditioning aggravated degrees of exploitation of female labor in Asia, as well as the rest of the third world. It is my suggestion that unless this deadly connection is fully dealt with, the feminization of poverty will continue to worsen women's well-being. A closer look at a prosperous growth of prostitution in Asia helps to illustrate this argument.

Victims without Crime: Transnational Tourism and Prostitution

In her well articulated article, Thanh-Dam, citing recent studies (Cohen, 1982; O'Grady, 1981; Stol, 1980; Bond, 1980; Ech and Rosenblum, 1975), observes that "there seems to be a strong correlation between the development of the tourist industry and the rise of prostitution in the Third World."[1] Her observation is drawn from the development of transnational tourism taking place in Asia and other parts of the third world during the last two decades, and an alarming number of young women entering the sex entertainment business as prostitutes or under a facade of hospitality girls, masseuses, cocktail girls, waitresses, and hostesses. Statistics show that from 1974 to 1980 the number of Thai women in sexual service in Bangkok rose from 426,908 to between 500,000–700,000 women.[2] Director Lucina Aldez of the Bureau of Women and Minors of the Ministry of Labor gave an estimation of 100,000 women being employed in the "hospitality business" in Manila.[3] Korean women reported that the number of prostitutes, both attached and not attached to Kiseang House, given by officials as approximately 15,000 women is two or three times lower than the actual number of women in the profession.[4]

The rapid growth of prostitution can be best understood when one examines the development of tourism in the third world countries which during the last decade have been enjoying foreign currency brought in by the tourism industry. It is estimated that the number of tourists arriving in Southeast Asia alone increased twenty-five times between 1960 and 1979.[5] According to Robert E. Wood: "Underdeveloped countries did not simply stumble into tourism as a promising way to earn foreign exchange."[6] The encouragement and initiation came from abroad. A study of Green and De Boer (1976, 103–22) reveals that tourism development is a subject under consideration by a number of United Nations agencies. International financiers, including bilateral and multilateral aid agencies including the World Bank Group showed enthusiasm toward the idea. The chief reason for this is explained by Wood as follows:

> Tourism is classified as an export, but the rapid growth of demand for it contrasts sharply with the declining of stagnant demand for many of the basic exports from underdeveloped countries. The declining terms of trade from most of their exports have encouraged a search for other exports more able to hold their own on the world market. With world demand growing rapidly, tourism has appeared a strong candidate.[7]

To many third world governments, the welcoming of tourism is seen as, in Thanh-Dam's words, "a way of earning the badly needed foreign exchange which other development strategies have failed to provide."[8] In critics' eyes, however, the incentive behind the encouragement of international financiers is an expansion of a new form of economic imperialism imposed on third world countries by giant corporations in the first world in the name of development strategy. Their criticism is derived from the way tourism industry is operated. Its operation demonstrates a strong relation between the World Bank Group and private enterprises. The growth of mass tourism has involved an introduction of the "package tour," advanced technology in air transportation, the vast difference of income and currency exchange between the first and the third world. Tourism development has turned out to be a joint operation among transnational airlines, their franchise hotels, tour agencies, and credit card companies, with a large profit going back to the first world.

Given that the dynamics of operation in the tourist industry are as described, it is no surprise that in the late 1970s there was a twenty percent increase in tourism in the countries of Southeast Asia, and the growth is steady. Interestingly, the majority of these tourists are male. For example, it was reported that among 667,000 Japanese who paid a visit to South Korea in 1978, ninety percent of them were men.[9] So were eighty percent of 200,000 Japanese tourists who visited Thailand in 1979.[10]

The connection between sex tourism and economic development in third world countries is obvious. Male government officials in the ASEAN (Associations of Southeast Asian Nations), for example, see "prostitution" as a good incentive to induce foreign currency. A mayor of a notorious city for foreign tourists in the Eastern Seaboard of Thailand once said in a newspaper interview (*Depthnews*, 1 April 1982) that: "We accept prostitution as a part of the development process." Speaking at a national conference of provincial governors in October 1980, the then Thai Deputy Prime Minister Boonchu Rojanasathian urged the governor to join the government in the national tourism effort by developing scenic spots in their provinces as well as encouraging sex business as an inviting incentive.[11] In South Korea, the Park administration was criticized by ex-President Mr. Yun Po-Sun for making a business of selling Korean women's bodies to Japanese men as a national policy for accumulating foreign exchange.[12]

Poverty and Prostitution as Women's Livelihood: The Women's Stories

While Asian countries are enjoying the flow of foreign currency, prostitution has consequently been transformed into a transnational business with demanding markets in Japan, Singapore, Hong Kong, and Western European countries, in particular West Germany, the Netherlands, and Sweden.[13] In the Thai case, at one point, the figure of cash flow in this business is larger than the national budget of the country.[14] Nonetheless, this phenomenal amount of cash flow is deceiving in respect to what the women receive. Like their foresisters in the business, little of the money generated in the business goes into their hands. A larger portion of it finds its way to tourist agencies, hotel and club owners, tour operators, pimps, job brokers, police and other groups involved. Neumann reports that in the Philippines, one night with a woman would generally cost the men about $50. The amount is broken down among club owner ($15), tour operator ($15), local guide ($10), Japanese guide ($10). The women who put their bodies to work receive between $4.25–$5.75 from the owner's share.[15] This situation is similar in Thailand, Korea, and Taiwan.

It has been pointed out in several studies (Neumann, 1979; Pongpaijit, 1982) that most women who choose prostitution do so as a means of survival. As Lindsay correctly assesses: "Women choose for the same reason some choose factory work or clerical work: it is one of the few jobs that women are allowed...."[16]

The stories some of these women share are astounding in terms of how much their fate is determined by "poverty." Neumann gave an account of a hospitality girl in the Philippines:

> Olga, 18, was first taken to work in a bar as a go-go dancer when she was 14 by her mother. Her beauty was regarded as an asset by a family plagued with poverty in Samar. She lost her virginity the first night of her employment at Le Beau two years ago. "I am ashamed to work in that place, but I do because of financial reasons."[17]

While doing a study on prostitution in Chiang Mai, northern Thailand, a city notorious for sex tourism, my students and I came to learn of the unfortunate life of young women in different brothels there. One of them was Lāa.

Lāa is an eighteen-year-old, good-looking young woman, with a fourth grade education, who has been working at a local brothel. Like many of her friends in the brothel, she comes from a poverty-stricken rural town nearby. Her parents are poor farmers. Her wage for eight hours of working in the field was fifteen Baht ($1=27 Baht). While working in her village, a neighbor persuaded her to go to work in Bangkok with a promise of better working conditions and pay as a house servant. In Bangkok, the then sixteen-year-old girl discovered that she was to work as a prostitute. Lāa worked in Bangkok for a year and a half before returning home. She did not like the hardship of her work. Additionally, she was given no choice of customers and was confined to the brothel at all times. She was however able to return to the village. Back in the village for a few months, a neighbor offered to help her find a similar job in Chiang Mai. Not being able to find employment with competitive pay, Lāa went back to work in a brothel again.

As tragic as it is, Lāa's story is not unique. It is a life lived by most women in northern Thailand. The ultimate reason for being in this profession is sheer need. As a researcher on prostitution succinctly puts it: "Virtually all prostitutes are driven into it by economic necessity, not by enjoyment of their work."[18]

Sexual Division of Labor

While most theories attribute the worsening exploitation of female labor in Asia as fundamentally caused by the failure of their respective governments' policy on national development and Western economic imperialism, sexual division of labor plays a crucial role in both supporting and perpetuating exploitation. Traditional values embedded in all societies in Asia and most human societies, define women's role in terms of their relations as wives or sex partners of men and of mothers of children while men's roles are defined in terms of public functions to which prestige, power, and authority attach. These role definitions have come to give gender identity for women and men and thus a standard by which their full adulthood is judged.

Such traditional gender role definitions historically create the sexual division of labor which puts women in the domestic sphere, assuming the sole function of reproduction, and naturally places men in the public sphere of production. This results in the infliction of a double bondage for women: domestication and social retardation.

The domestication of women involves women not only in being responsible for household work which is economically invisible but also in being sexually attractive to men. The latter allows our societies to tolerate and accept the commoditization of women's bodies in the sexual business. As Khin Thitsa points out, to some women, this sexual implication enables them to "grasp their own selves in their situations, and learn to exploit to the fullest degree women's 'natural' position as sexual provider for/of men, the female body as an object and territory for men to use, in order to gain (as women normally attempt to through virginity, marriage, and monogamy) material security."[19]

From another perspective, however, although prostitution is cleverly used by women as a strategy for survival and a better opportunity to have more control over the proceeds of their work, even a larger part of their return is harvested by other agents involved, so that it still contributes to women's subordination to men. Furthermore, as other studies about women indicate, prostitution serves not simply as a way of rejecting traditional customs and norms of what a moral woman is, but, as Thanh-Dam states, "it also reflects female social retardation which renders women ill-equipped for absorption into other productive spheres when abandoning their traditional productive roles."[20]

Parent-Daughter Relationship: Peasants' Culturally Appropriate Means for Survival

As this study has discussed, the majority of women in prostitution enter this profession because of their impoverished economic situation. Most of them justify their work by arguing that they have to support their parents and siblings. The poverty-stricken situation of the family is their major psychological defense mechanism used to appease the difficult feelings and the guilt arising from working in a profession which is culturally and morally condemned by society.

A sixteen-year-old Filipina gave her account of how she ended up working as a hospitality girl. "My boyfriend in the province took me and then left. I was ashamed and we are very poor, so I left with a friend and came here. I send some money to my family. . . . "

Remittance of income to help parents building a house, buying a piece of land to cultivate, or supporting siblings' education gives the women a gratifying attitude toward their work.

Economic hardship is also a justifying reason for parents in persuading, encouraging, as well as accepting prostitution as a career for their daughters.

During a field study in northern Thailand, my students and I were able to trace the path back to a village from which most of our case study prostitutes came. We discovered that there were many fewer young women than men in the village. With widespread poverty in the area and no effective solution to it, either parents have to make a deal with brothel owners or prostitute brokers in exchange for a considerable amount of cash or give a blessing to daughters who personally decide to follow the short-term economically prosperous path of their sisters. Rumor has it that a family celebrates the whole week when a daughter is born. A female infant is a parent's future financial security. Daughters bring more money to a family than sons as they later work as prostitutes. When being asked of their concern for the village's notorious reputation, most villagers humbly decline their moral judgment on both parents and daughters on the ground that the women's livelihood as prostitutes benefits their family's well-being.

The story may strike some of us as being immoral. Questions can be raised in terms of how such practice is communally accepted. Nonetheless, the case of a particular village in northern Thailand demonstrates the dynamics of moral behavior in the economics of subsistence. That is, in a situation in which their existence is in suspense, peasants will yield to the principle of safety-first for their survival. Prostitution, exploited as it is, has become the best solution and option available for their economic hardship. The parent-daughter relationship is culturally appropriated to serve such an interest. Unfortunately, this appropriation is done at the expense of women's well-being.

Will There Be a Rainbow Tomorrow?: Women's Quest for a Better Future

The study thus far attempts to suggest an analysis of women's situation in an Asian setting through a discussion of prostitution in the region. The picture looks grim as it unravels webs of women's oppression inflicted on them through economic injustice (capitalism), male dominant culture and tradition, and a patriarchal social structure, to name a few factors. A realization of how we contribute to deposit layers of oppression in a global horizon is a sign of a rainbow for women's future. Our sisters' struggle is surely *our* struggle. As bluntly and succinctly put by Lindsay:

> To survive within those structures, all of us, all the time, in some way or another, sell ourselves to men . . . and even if we manage to survive financially in the counterculture, we contribute to the image of a free and benevolent society that tolerates its nonconformists, an image that is a useful tool in the preservation of patriarchal power. To say that some of us don't sell ourselves is like saying that some of us don't breathe polluted air; it simply isn't possible. Our degradation may be more successfully disguised in one occupation than in another, but it is always there. . . . [21]

A question which is put before us is simply whether we acknowledge it and do something to change it, *together.*

NOTES

1. Truong Thanh-Dam, "The Dynamics of Sex Tourism," *Development and Change* 14 (1983), p. 533.

2. Committee on Long-Term Women Development Planning, "General Condition of Women in Sexual Business," *Report on the Study for Long-Term Women Development Planning* (1982–2006), pp. 15–4 (in Thai).

3. A. Lin Neumann, "Hospitality Girls in the Philippines," *ISIS International Bulletin* 13 (1979), p. 13.

4. "A Report from South Korea," *Asian Women Liberation* 3 (1980), p. 11.

5. Robert E. Wood, "The Economics of Tourism," *Southeast Asia Chronicle* (June 1981), p. 2.

6. Ibid., p. 3.

7. Ibid.

8. Thanh-Dam, the article cited in note 1, p. 546.

9. Yayori Mastui, "Economy and Psychology of Prostitution Tourism," *Asian Women Liberation* 3 (1980), p. 8.

10. Marie Fuwa, "Thailand Year of Tourism," *Asian Women Liberation* 3 (1980), p. 22.

11. Matichon, 18 October (1980) (in Thai).

12. Matsui, the article cited in note 9, p. 8.

13. For more information on the European connection in transnational prostitution, see *ISIS International Bulletin* 13 (1979).

14. *Bangkok Post*, 9 March (1982), p. 10.

15. Neumann, the article cited in note 3, p. 14.

16. Karen Lindsay, "Madonna or Whore," *ISIS International Bulletin* 13 (1979), p. 5.

17. Neumann, the article cited in note 3, p. 15.

18. *Thailand Update*, March–April (1982), p. 9.

19. Khin Thitsa, "Women and Development in Southeast Asia," Occasional Papers, Centre of SE Asia Studies, University of Kent at Canterbury (September 1983), pp. 40–41.

20. Thanh-Dam, the article cited in note 1, p. 539.

21. Lindsay, the article cited in note 16, p. 4.

10

African-American Women
and Domestic Violence

DELORES S. WILLIAMS

Black women's experiences with violence have ranged far beyond their homes. Historically, African-American women have suffered violence in three domestic contexts. In contra-distinction to international environments, black women have met with violence in the domestic context of North America. They also experienced violence working in the homes of white female and male employers in the United States. And they suffered violence in their own homes and communities.

In their writings and personal testimonies, black women have revealed the various strategies they used to deal with this violence. They have resorted to legal procedures. Some of them have used public rhetoric and polemic to try to motivate other groups in the society to do something about the violence black women experience. Some have used home-spun folk remedies to threaten those who attempt to violate them. Some black women have told their stories to each other and therefore shared ways of confronting violence.

This essay will describe the violence black women have experienced and do experience in each of the three domestic contexts. Brief mention will be made of the strategies some black women have used to deal with this violence. Finally I give attention to what I believe to be a primary contributor to the perpetuation of the abuse black women have experienced in the three domestic contexts.

The aim of the essay is not to romanticize black women's way of dealing with domestic violence. Nor do I mean to suggest that *all* African-American women are successful in their struggle with abuse. An alarming statistic released in July 1993 on New York television discourages romantic and stereotypical notions about black women being so strong they can confront and survive all abuse. The news person reported that last year in America forty-eight percent of the deaths of black women under forty years old were due to economic violence, i.e., violence in black women's homes. But any discussion of African-American women's experience with violence in their homes and communities must take seriously the long history of national violence directed toward black women and black men.

Beginning with Slavery

Public violence to black women's bodies began early in American history when auction blocks were established for the sale of black slaves. During sales, black women were often stripped to the waist so that their breasts could be examined and other parts of their bodies could be viewed by potential buyers in order to speculate about the childbearing capacity of female slaves. Buyers had no concern for the violation this public inspection of black women's bodies inflicted upon black women's spirits. Neither did buyers care that their rough handling of black women's bodies often bruised the women. There were also public places where recalcitrant slaves were taken to be beaten if their masters deemed a beating necessary but did not want to do it themselves. Black women were not exempt from this kind of treatment.

After slavery, when reconstruction ended (1877), the Jim Crow laws were passed in the South, making segregation of the race legal. Some black women experienced public displays of violence at the hands of white people enforcing these laws. One such woman was Ida B. Wells, who was traveling by train in Tennessee in 1884. Sitting in the car designated first class, Wells was approached by the conductor who told her she would have to move to the car assigned for colored people. She refused to move, for she had been sold a first-class ticket. With the affirmation of the white passengers, the conductor brought in a baggageman, who helped him drag Wells out of the coach. Wells responded to this violence and humiliation by suing the railroad. In the circuit court she won her suit. But in the state supreme court the railroad won its appeal, mainly because it falsified the evidence.

Other forms of violence in the domestic precincts of the American South affected black women and black men. Lynching of black people by white mobs was widespread in the South after reconstruction until the waning of the 1960s civil rights movement. While black men have been lynched in large numbers, black women were also lynched. Ida B. Wells' essay "Lynch Law," written in 1893, contains a passage describing the lynching of black females by white mobs:

The women of the race have not escaped the fury of the mob. In Jackson, Tennessee, in the summer of 1886, a white woman died of poisoning. Her black cook was . . . hurried away to jail. When the mob had worked itself into lynching pitch, she was dragged out of jail, every stitch of clothing torn from her body, and she was hung in the public court-house square in sight of everybody. . . . The husband of the poisoned woman has since died a raving maniac, and his ravings showed that he, and not the poor black cook, was the poisoner of his wife.[1]

Wells also tells of " . . . a fifteen year old Negro girl . . . hanged in Rayville, Louisiana in the spring of 1892 on the same charge of poisoning white persons. There was no more proof or investigation of this case than the one in Jackson."[2] Then there was the case of "A Negro woman, Lou Stevens . . . hanged from a railway bridge in Hollendale, Mississippi, in 1892. She was charged with being accessory to the murder of her white paramour, who had shamefully abused her."[3] In an address at Tremont Temple in Boston in 1893, Wells told her audience that when lynchings occurred "the power of the state, country and city, the civil authorities and the strong arm of the military power were all on the side of the mob and lawlessness."[4]

Wells devoted much action and public rhetoric to exposing the violence done to black women and black men in the domestic United States. She concluded that lynching was " . . . a national crime and requires a national remedy."[5] Wells left posterity an extensive and thorough record of America's history of lynching black people, women and men. Public murder of black women and men did not end with the nineteenth century. In the latter part of the twentieth century one of the most shocking lynchings, affecting the life of a black mother, occurred when her fifteen-year-old son Emmitt Till was lynched by Southern white men.

Today in America violence done to black women takes many forms. Though lynching at the hands of a mass of white people is no longer common, there is the brutality and even death that black women have experienced at the hands of policemen. A few years ago in New York an old black woman, Mrs. Eleanor Bumpers, was killed by policemen who rushed into her home and shot her when she allegedly came at them with a knife. Then, there is the violence in the African-American community caused by drugs made easily available to black people by forces outside the black community. African-Americans do not have the amount of money needed to supply the huge amount of drugs flooding the black community. This financing comes from beyond the community from non-black people who have large cash flows. The effect of these accessible drugs in the community has been widespread murder and other forms of violence affecting African-American women and their children.

Not only have black women had to confront violence done to them on a national scale. They also have a long history of experiencing violence in white homes where they have worked as domestics from slavery to the present.

Violence in the Work-Place

The slave narratives of African-American women are replete with testimonies of the violence slave women suffered in the homes of slave owners. Two kinds of physical abuse were most common. Female slaves were often stripped of their clothes and physically beaten by their slave owners. Also, they were often sexually assaulted by the males who owned them. Mary Prince's slave narrative tells of a slave woman who " . . . was stripped naked, notwithstanding her pregnancy, and . . . tied to a tree in the yard." The slave master " . . . flogged her as hard as he could like, both with the whip and cow-skin, till she was all over streaming with blood. He rested, and then beat her again and again. . . . "[6] Physical beating was common treatment for "naughty," defiant or "high-spirited" slave women.

Many testimonies of slave women and slave men tell about female slaves being sexually harassed and/or raped by their owners and other white men. In her narrative *Incidents in the Life of a Slave Girl*, Linda Brent describes the ingenious method she devised to prevent her sexual violation by her slave master Dr. Flint. She hid in a crawl space under her grandmother's roof for several years. Slave women had no control over their bodies; therefore they were violated at will by their white male slave owners. Wives of slave owners often contributed to this by violating the dignity of female slaves. The owners' wives stigmatized slave women for the sexual misconduct their husbands, the slave owners, directed toward female slaves. They referred to these slave women as concubines, which suggested that slave women had a choice in the matter. Mary Boykin Chesnut's *A Diary from Dixie*, beginning its entries in 1861, resorts to this practice as the author laments the sexual relation between slave masters and slave women. Chesnut claimed: "Under slavery, we [i.e., white women] live surrounded by prostitutes [female slaves]. . . . Like patriarchs of old, our men live all in one house with their wives and their concubines." She goes on to say that " . . . the mulattoes one sees in every family partly resemble the white children. . . . My disgust . . . is boiling over. Thank God for my country women, but alas for the men."[7]

Though the violence black women experienced in the homes of their slave owners was more brutal, the violence black women experience today in the homes of the white people for whom they work is no less insulting. In his collection of urban narratives *Drylongso*, the anthropologist John Langston Gwaltney includes the testimony of a black domestic worker who has to resort to protective measures to discourage her female employer's husband from sexually harassing her. The black woman finally used a black folk remedy to discourage the advances of this man. She says "I had to threaten that devil [her male employer] with a pot of hot grease to get him to keep his hands to hisself."[8]

The abuse some African-American women suffer in their homes at the hands of their male partners has much to do with the way in which many black men perceive black manhood and the threats to it.

Manhood, Opportunity, and Control

In the 1940s the African-American male novelist Richard Wright wrote the novel *Native Son*, which projected a clear view of what Wright took to be the condition of manhood among rank-and-file, poor black males living in large urban ghettos. This book was a great success in the black community partly because of the image it projected of black manhood: oppressed, afraid and enraged. Bigger Thomas, the protagonist, was a poor black young adult living on the South Side (the ghetto) of Chicago. Inadequately educated, a school drop-out, jobless, living in one rat-infested room with his mother, brother and sister, Bigger was consumed with fear and rage. This fear and rage was manifested in "bullying" conduct which ultimately ended in Bigger murdering two women: a rich young white woman and his black girl friend Bessie. The white woman was murdered accidentally; Bessie's murder was willful and brutal. It represented Bigger's effort to gain the sense of power and control he could not exert in the white world but could exert in the ghetto through his behavior as a bully. In his daily life, Bigger was trapped in a racist world that offered him no opportunity for advancement or self-realization.

The insight to be drawn from Wright's depiction of Bigger Thomas is that black men in American society are denied access to the legitimate avenues of quest and conquest which are thought to lead to the possession of manhood in the social world of America. Most black women are denied access to the financial resources in America which help men in their economic quest to found and head corporations, to secure adequate economic resources in order to provide for themselves and their families. They are denied the jobs and the kind of education that lead men to the top of the economic ladder.

Inasmuch as black men are denied access to some of the highest status-granting quest and conquest routes, some black men begin to re-gard black women as the arena of conquest. Conquering black women's bodies sexually becomes the object of this quest and the means of dem-onstrating strong black manhood. Black teenage pregnancies often result from this black male way of proving manhood through the conquest of black women's bodies. Fundamental to this notion of quest and conquest (as indicative of manhood) involving black women's bodies is the idea of male control of female. And this control must be publicly demonstrated in order for a man "to be a man" in the estimation of his male peers.

This was clearly indicated in the African-American rebellion of the 1960s, when some of the black nationalists declared that a woman should walk six paces behind "her" man, thus indicating that he was "the boss." It is no wonder that many black men during the 1960s and 1970s rebellion proudly repeated the declaration Eldridge Cleaver made in his book *Soul on Ice:* "We shall have our manhood or the earth will be razed in our attempt." If secured, this manhood would be about the business of subordinating and controlling African-American women.

When black women refuse to be the object of this conquest, when they refuse to allow black men to control them, domestic violence in the home can occur. In her book *The Habit of Surviving*, Kesho Yvonne Scott records Marilyn's story-telling of teenage pregnancy, of her effort to return to school, of the ensuing struggle with her husband

> Bobby [who] reacted. He saw school as a threat to him somehow. He expected me to do everything in the house, study when he wasn't home... my grades started to slip, the fighting started, and all the talk about being a poet and writer... seemed like such a distance away. I stopped the fighting because I took everything in the house and broke it.... He quit beating me. But I was already beat. So... I quit school. Trapped again.[9]

Certainly drugs, mental problems and experiences of abuse as chil-dren may cause some black men to resort to violence in the home that injures or kills black women. But Constance A. Bean makes a point that applies to all men, black or white, in patriarchal society. These kinds of societies sanction men's feelings that they have the right to control their families, including the women. The men feel "...that their male image depends on their ability to dominate and control...." Bean points out that "the law often reflects male privilege, including the view that the... [abused] woman must somehow have been at fault for what happened to her."[10]

With regard to African-American women, there are additional reasons that might account for the violence they continue to experience in the three domestic contexts of nation, work-place and personal abode. One of the most serious contributors to this violence is the discourse about the origin and the nature of the Negro (female and male) that began in the nineteenth century in North America.

Human or Beast?

The anti-black literature that circulated in America from the time of the Civil War (1863) until 1925 did much to convince the American public that the Negro — female and male — was a different order of species than "man" (meaning white people). The Ariel controversy, beginning in print in 1867 with the appearance of a pamphlet entitled *The Negro: What Is His Ethnological Status*, raised these questions:[11] "What is his [Negro men and women] Ethnological Status? Is he the progeny of Ham? Is he a descendent of Adam and Eve? Has he a Soul? Or is he a Beast, in God's nomenclature? What is his Status as fixed in God's creation? What is his relation to the White race?"[12] Using the Bible to provide proof for the insulting response given to these questions, Ariel concluded that the Negro was not descended from Ham because Ham was white. Interpreting the identity of the "passengers" in Noah's ark, Ariel argues:

> As the negro is not the progeny of Ham...and knowing that he is of neither family of Shem or Jepheth, who were white, straight haired, etc., and the negro we have now on earth, is kinky-headed and black, by this logic of facts we know, that he came out of the ark, and is a totally different race of men from the three brothers. How did he get in there, and in what station or capacity? We answer, that he went into the ark by command of God; and as he was neither Noah, nor one of his sons, all of whom were white, then by the logic of facts, he could only enter it as a beast, and along with the beasts.[13]

According to Ariel, the Negro female and male came out of the ark as beasts, and as beasts they had no souls, were not human and therefore were not the descendants of Adam and Eve.

Accounting for the present appearance of the Negro as an improvement upon the beast who came out of the ark, Ariel says:

> We will begin with the cat. The cat, as a genus of species of animals, we trace in his order of creation through various grades — cougar, panther, leopard, tiger, up to the lion, improving in each graduation from the small cat up to the lion, a noble beast...we take up the

monkey, and trace him likewise through his upward and advancing orders — baboon, orang-utan and gorilla, up to the negro, another noble animal, the noblest of the beast creation.[14]

According to Ariel, all the human beings who went on board the ark, i.e., Noah and his family, had white skin with the physical features of white people. Thus white people could not be of the same species as black people. God ordained that "man" and "beast" belonged to two different orders of creation. "Ariel" was but one of the pamphlets appearing during this period committed to proving Negroes were beasts.

These anti-black arguments helped to mold an American consciousness about the Negro that even today regards black people as beasts, female and male. Therefore, black women (and black men) can be abused and treated like animals rather than like humans. Since Ariel and other anti-black material used the Bible to substantiate their claims, they advanced their argument that God gave humans (read white people) control over all beasts, for this is recorded in the creation story in Genesis. So God intended white people to rule over or control black people. Since black women and men were animals, white people or humans could treat black people in any way that helped maintain white control. It is not hard to imagine that black women and black men experienced all kinds of violence and abuse as these "human" white people tried to maintain their God-ordained control.

Neither is it surprising that American legal and judicial officers have historically reacted with vengeance when blacks abused or killed whites, but responded in a passive, indifferent or "lukewarm" way when whites abused or killed black people. According to this skewed mythology about white human and black beast, the legal system could not act in any other way if its judges believed in the order of creation in the Bible as interpreted by such "intelligent" agents as Ariel.

The violence African-American women have experienced in their homes at the hands of their male partners raises several questions when one considers the existence, nature and popularity of the Ariel literature and controversy. Does the black male "control mentality" that incites the violence males inflict upon black women have kinship with the "control mentality" of white people (thought by Ariel to be human) that inflicts violence upon black people (thought by Ariel to be beasts)? Have some black men, in their violation of black women, internalized this Ariel view of humanity and beast, appropriating humanity for themselves and beasts for black women? Does the African-American community need to turn its attention to the re-definition of black manhood so that black women will be freed from violence in their homes and communities?

In the final analysis African-American women must defend themselves against the violence they are likely to experience in the three contexts of nation, work and home. One of the ablest defenses is a united sisterhood dedicated to securing the life, health and well-being of black women. If it is true, as Toni Morrison says, that African-American women have no one to defend them and may have invented themselves, it is altogether fitting and proper for black women to protect their invention. They must use all their resources — God, church, school, education, politics — to survive and help each other survive.

NOTES

1. Ida B. Wells, "Lynch Law in All Its Phases," in Darlene Clark Hine, ed., *Black Women in United States History*, vol. 15, Brooklyn, New York, 1990, p. 197.

2. Ibid., pp. 197–98.

3. Ibid.

4. Ibid., p. 176.

5. Ida Wells, "Lynching: Our National Crime," *National Negro Conference: Proceedings*, New York, 1909, pp. 174–79.

6. Mary Prince, "The History of Mary Prince, A West Indian Slave," in Henry Lewis Gates, Jr., ed., *Six Women's Slave Narratives*, New York, first published London, 1731, p. 7.

7. Mary Boykin Chesnut, *A Diary from Dixie* (1905), Cambridge, Mass., 1961, pp. 21–22.

8. John Langston Gwaltney, *Drylongso*, New York, 1980, p. 150.

9. Kesho Yvonne Scott, *The Habit of Surviving*, New Brunswick and London, 1991, p. 30.

10. Constance A. Bean, *Women Murdered by the Men They Loved*, New York, 1992, p. 44.

11. This controversy got its name from the author's pseudonym, which was given as Ariel.

12. For the complete text of the Ariel controversy and other anti-black literature during this period see John David Smith, *Anti-Black Thought, 1863–1925*, vols. 5 and 6, New York.

13. Ibid., p. 20.

14. Ibid., pp. 22–23.

11

Conquered and Violated Women

JULIA ESQUIVEL

The *Conquistadores*

All men. In the fullness of their physical force and driven by a great ambition, gold and glory. Some petty nobles; the majority poor, with no name of note in Spain and no possibility of winning one at home.

Almost all with some military rank, owners of weapons more powerful than those of the warriors of this continent. Two important factors in their superiority were horses and gunpowder. The psychological effect of both was perhaps similar to that produced by bombers or unarmed peasant populations in some counter-insurgency wars today. These two weapons turned them into creators of terror. They used them as a source of strength, strategic deception and even myth.

They regarded the task of subduing, subjugating and enslaving as a favor to the inhabitants of the New World. This certainly drove them to make the continent Spanish and seal this achievement with religion. Severo Martínez says:

> This means that the arms struggle was only a means, a device for achieving economic subjugation, and that this last aim was the decisive element in the conquest. And it can also be shown that evangelization was a third phase, the ideological subjugation necessary, like the military phase, for the consolidation of the economic conquest.

When *conquistadores* reached here, they thought that they had reached the riches and products of the orient, and this belief blinded them. Many of them did not realize when they arrived that they were looking at the *other face of the world.*

105

As a result, when they arrived, they invented the "Indians," although the people of these lands already had names. When they realized their mistake they did not correct it. In creating the Indians they reinforced the ever-growing advantages of their domination over them. Severo Martínez says again:

> This means that when the social group of the creoles began to develop and defend the prejudice of their Hispanic superiority — a basic prejudice in the ideology of the group — the determining factor in their effective superiority over the Indians was not Spanish descent in terms of flesh and blood, but the inheritance of the conquest in terms of wealth and political power. Enjoying very favorable conditions of life, they were able to farm and develop all the capacities which had not been able to develop among the Indians.

The imposed identity of "Indians" and its whole burden of submission, dependence and servitude grew during the consolidation of the conquest, the so-called colonization. With it grew the power and wealth of the invaders and their descendants, and conversely the underdevelopment of the "Indian." Frantz Fanon gets it exactly right when he says that "Colonialism cannot be understood without the possibility of torturing, raping and killing." They had no limits.

The Women

In order to get an idea of the significance of the treatment of Indian women during the conquest and colonization we need to spend a little time to understand how European women were treated in this period. When the Spaniard arrived, there were differences between one people and another; it was not a homogeneous world. Women are not treated exactly alike in all societies. Although some of them enjoyed a certain freedom, and even a degree of social authority, the great majority lived under male tutelage, in patriarchal and authoritarian societies. They were prepared to be conquered. They were familiar with submission to the male as a condition for survival. Conquest and domination by the Spaniards increased their defenselessness, because, like the land and the gold, they became the property of the victors. Their bodies became land to be conquered because they had been the property of men who waged the war. All wars, and especially wars of conquest, bring with them the violation of women. By virtue of this fact men think and feel that they become stronger by invading and possessing women's bodies. The act of taking the women of the defeated men affirms them in this sense of power.

The defeat, the capture or flight of the men places the women in a situation of vulnerability and defenselessness such that opposition on their part to the will of the victor can bring more prolonged sufferings, not just for them, but also for their children. The woman thus feels obliged by these circumstances to remain silent and submit to save her life and those of her children. If she remains subject to one man, or the first passes her on in turn to different men, her situation is so complex that in order to stay alive she almost has to deaden her senses. Many had children by one or several Spaniards.

The accounts of the Spanish chroniclers talk much more about the booty, the war itself, Christianization, and relatively little of the Indian women. The little they do say is to do with physical abuse of women as subjects of sexual pleasure and also as servants or slaves.

"Official" concubinage was given the name *barraganería,* and in order to be admitted to it the woman had to be baptized first. Indian patriarchal tradition allowed and encouraged Indian men to give daughters of nobles to the Spaniards to seal an alliance, as occurred in Europe, and they also offered women temporarily as a sign of hospitality, as they offered food or gifts.

The women were almost always abandoned when their owner married a Spanish woman. Cortez married some of his captains to women he had raped. Examples are the daughters of Moctezuma, and Malintzin, a slave used as a "tongue," that is, Cortez' translator and interpreter. She came to be indispensable to him since she spoke three languages. She was exceptionally beautiful. The woman's life shows very well that even the women who lived with Spanish men for relatively long periods were never treated as equals, any more than the Spanish women. Like the "Indies," the Indian women were taken, used and their individuality and culture were ignored.

Malinnalli Tenepal was known as Malintzin or Malinche, the origin of the word *malinchismo,* to be a traitor, a collaborator with the enemy, the one in power. Malinnalli was the daughter of the chief Xaltipan. She was stolen in time of war by Ollinteutli, chief of Olutla, who offered her to the captain Juan de Grijalva, who commanded the Catholic king's fleet which sailed from Cuba to Yucatan in 1518. The girl was thirteen years old and of cheerful disposition. She was brought richly dressed, accompanied by Ollinteutli's chiefs and maidens singing wedding songs.

No sooner on the boat than she was baptized by the priest Juan Díaz. That same night, when the boat started back for Cuba, she was raped by Grijalva. When they reached Cuba, Grijalva rejoined his wife and gave the girl to Alonso de Hernández Portocarrero, who was related to the nobility. Malintzin lived with her new owner for some time, and learned Spanish, as well as speaking Náhautl and Maya. The expeditions which came and went from Cuba, and her knowledge of Spanish, enabled her to begin to understand in her own way the spirit and ways of these Christians. Later Portocarrero took her with him to Cozumel and other parts of the continent. She saw battles and massacres, always as the property of Portocarrero and subject to the plans and decisions of men.

As a result of the difference between the *conquistadores* and the accusations against Cortez, Cortez sent Portocarrero to Spain as procurator to defend him against the charges made against him. Portocarrero was imprisoned in Spain and Cortez took over Malintzin for his sexual caprices and to use her as a "tongue." Noticing that the captains and officers were coming up to talk to her, Cortez isolated her completely, ordering that no one should talk to her and appointing Juan de Arteaga to keep watch on her day and night, even when she attended to the needs of nature. These events gradually changed the cheerful character of the young woman. She lived like this the whole time. Cortez made her pregnant, and when he discovered this, he married her to Juan Jaramillo on the expedition to the Hibueras when Jaramillo was unconscious as a result of a drinking bout. When he came around, he objected to "such a great lord transferring his obligations to him," but nevertheless profited from the situation. Though Cortez had ordered her to be married, Malintzin had to stay at his side all the time, during all the expeditions and battles, to be his "tongue." She was always watched by Arteaga.

When the conquest was largely secure, Cortez was obliged to leave for Spain to defend himself against innumerable charges and demands before Charles V, and, with Jaramillo's agreement, stole Malintzin's little son from her. The boy was born on the unsuccessful expedition to the Hibueras in a very difficult situation for Malintzin. She brought him up on her own until the age of four, until he was taken up from the house in which she lived with Jaramillo. Malintzin also had a daughter with Jaramillo. When this daughter was two, five days before the trial of Cortez before the Residency was due to begin, at which Malintzin had been told she would be called as a witness, Malintzin was murdered in her house with thirteen knife-blows at dawn on 24 January 1529. Jaramillo robbed Malintzin's daughter of all her mother's property when he married the Spaniard Beatriz de Andrade.

It was very common for Indian women of high rank, daughters of kings and chiefs, to be taken and used sexually by the *conquistadores*. They were then given to officers and later to common soldiers. They were treated as objects and nullified as human beings.

According to the researcher Otilia Meza, from whose book I obtained these details:

And Hernando Cortez, to whom she had been an excellent "tongue" as well as concubine, never recognized her valuable help, which had brought him so much of glory, and his ingratitude reached such a pitch that he shamefully forged her name on the famous lying "Cartas de Relación" which he wrote to Charles V, informing him that "an Indian woman had married Xuan Xaramillo and given him as a dowry the villages of Olutla and Tetiquipaje in the province of Coatzacoalco. He then gave Malinalli the village of Kolotepec, in Mexico the mansions of Jesús María and Medinas, the gardens of Moctezuma in Chapultepec and a plot of land in San Cosme."

For the sake of these lands, and for the prestige of being Cortez' "friend," Captain Jaramillo did the *conquistador*'s bidding, and was probably an accomplice in, if not responsible for, Malintzin's death.

This story is just one example among many.

And they took them, picked out the most beautiful, those with light brown complexions. Some women, when they were taken, smeared themselves with mud and wrapped an old, torn cloak around their hips and put a rag as a shirt over their busts; they dressed in old rags. And on all sides the Christians probed. They opened their shirts, rubbed their hands all over them, over their ears, their breasts, their hair (Sahagún).

And [Cuauhtemoc's] martyrdom began. He bore it with dignity, in silence. His young wife, Tecuichpo — Cotton Tuft — daughter of Moctezuma, suffered the fate reserved for women prisoners of war. Cortez raped her and gave her to his soldiers, then took her back again and later made her pregnant (Héctor Pérez Martínez, *Cuauhtemoc*).

And some chiefs ... did not waste time. They did not abandon their wives and children, but went to great lengths to put them in safe-keeping near the houses, on the other canal. ... And then too the women fought in Tlatelolco, throwing lances. They dealt blows at the invaders; they were dressed as warriors (*Visión de los vencidos*, Anonymous chroniclers of Tlatelolco).

The admiral gave me a most beautiful Caribbean woman, and as she stood there naked, as is their custom, I felt a desire to go with her. I tried to carry out my desires, but she would not consent, and attacked me in such a way with her nails that I wished I had never started. But when I saw this I took a rope and beat her, and she screamed. Finally we reached such a state of agreement that

I can tell you that she was brought up in a school of whores (Letter of Michele de Cunco, 1492, quoted in Todorov, *La Conquête d'Amérique*).

The powers established in the course of these 500 years, and the armies and police forces — sometimes trained by so-called developed countries — use methods no different from those used by the *conquistadores*. The Indian people in the interior of our countries still live in states of defenselessness and vulnerability which makes them easy victims of abuses of power.

The ferocity in the massacres and the cannibalism goes with an unrestrained sexual violence and a machismo which makes the woman into an animal to give the soldier pleasure, and afterwards, when she's no more use, she can be murdered. Sometimes we've seen the soldiers queue up to rape a girl, and afterwards she was like a rag. And our brothers who survived the massacre and have gone back to the macabre scene of the events found our women naked or with their skirts up (*Guatemala: Government against the people*).

When they rape a girl or a woman, they line up and go one after another. Then, when they've all had their turn at raping the poor woman, they kill her (Indigenous from the war zone of Huehuetenango).

And we too have realized that the army has taught the soldiers to be arrogant and take liberties with women, and rape them, even in peace-time. We've found this in the capital: they practice on our sisters who work as domestics in their houses. The violence is accompanied by this arrogance, although sometimes they use deceit or flattery to get their way (Tribunal Permanente de los Pueblos, Sesión de Guatemala: *Genocidio en Guatemala*).

Answer: After it was all over, then . . . and they shut the door on us in the court, and after they had shut the door, since the window has one, two, three small holes, we were looking. Well, they went in and took our wives out of the church. They took twenty, some took ten. They went in groups among the houses, and then they started ra-, they started raping the women there in the houses. They finished raping them, and then they shot the women and then, after they'd killed them they set fire to the houses.

Question: So they raped them and afterwards killed them by shooting?

Answer: Yes, and finally they set fire to the houses and the houses all burned down. They went in among, among the houses and went in groups of fifteen or ten, the soldiers went with the women. They'd go in groups of ten or maybe fifteen, twelve soldiers. First they raped them, then they killed them...

Question: In groups they...

Answer: In groups, yes in groups. They went with them, with our wives. And all our children, like the women...were shut in the church...and they were crying, our poor children, they were screaming, they were calling us, but in the end they died (*Masacre de San Francisco: la muerte de las mujeres*, Huehuetenango, Guatemala, 17 July 1982).

Abuses committed by police and soldiers were daily events in Guatemala in the 1980s.

The Challenge

Jewish exegesis offers us a very important way of reading the story of the creation of human beings as male and female. The reading suggested is: "he took one of the sides" instead of "one of the ribs."

If Adam is alone, it is not because the man-woman couple does not exist, but because the couple is in a situation in which the future pairs do not know each other and are unable to dialogue.

This myth of the Hermaphrodite is both a biological and a psychological reality. We have already said that every human being is the seat of a double polarity: they are at the same time male and female, in their genes and in their psychological make-up....In the ancient world and in the middle ages the women used to be shown behind the man. Only the man could really see the future; the woman's view was blocked—all she saw was the man.

Yes, exactly, alongside. It's true that for many centuries in most civilizations the place of the woman was behind the man, rather than alongside.

The midrash, I think, takes us beyond that. It teaches us that God did not want to create the woman behind the man, or alongside him. He wanted something deeper for human beings, a face-to-face sexuality. The woman should be in front of the man, facing him, "shining face to shining face..."

God placed the woman in front of Adam, facing him, because she is his future (Eisenberg and Abecassis).

In the Song of Songs there is a developing process of this experience of meeting which leads to this "face to face." The expressions the two use, man and women, are a journey of discovery full of marvelous reciprocity. Throughout the poem there is a series of searches, absences, meetings, which again and again keep giving rise to the experience of wonder in the presence of the other person who is completely equal and yet different. This wonder reminds us of Adam's first reaction to Eve, "This is bone of my bones and flesh of my flesh!" Before Eve appeared in front of him Adam had been unable to find real companionship. He had had enough time to see, reflect and realize that it wasn't in human nature to behave like the animals. Among them the male is controlled by the rhythm of the female's coming into heat. Both basically responded to a biological programming.

The man, in contrast, suffers an absence; he is alone. It is something bigger, more than biological necessity. He yearns for a companion to fill this emptiness. His complete fulfillment depends on his being able to love and be loved. His desire cannot attain full satisfaction; for the sexual relationship to be human, it must be a relation of love.

The rabbis interpreted the creation of Eve in terms of the separation of the two halves of the Hermaphrodite, with the clear intention of comparing them to the two sides of the Tabernacle or the Temple. Both were the site of the presence of God. In this way they were saying that God is present in the union of man and woman.

Instinctive possession, merely to satisfy a bodily need, expels God from the relationship, that is, drives out the possibility of loving, of fullness. It also produces divorce as the death of the relationship. Reducing the woman to the instrument of animal satisfaction was what the *conquistadores* did, and there were no controls on it. The same spirit is encouraged today by the consumer society.

Neither the discovery nor the conquest has ended in Latin America. It has not been possible to have an authentic discovery because of the conquest and the spirit of the conquest alive today in the policies of the great powers. Our true human and cultural identity has been constantly distorted since the coming of the *conquistadores*. We have passed from one servitude to another, exposed to pressures and inventions by economic, political and military powers trying to dominate us. Under these conditions women have been invaded, colonized and raped, if not in their bodies, then in their personalities and in their identities, as so many testimonies of Indian women bear witness. The Indian peoples have had to adopt an attitude of submission in order to survive, and adopt a form of resistance which disguised their true nature. Very often this resistance took the form of revolt, always in unfavorable conditions, such as flight to the remotest parts of the jungles and mountains to save their lives and preserve a minimal space of freedom until today.

The plea of Esther, the young Jewess chosen to satisfy the desires of King Ahasuerus, expresses this attitude of submission in order to save one's life while waiting for a favorable moment to secure freedom. In her outburst she lets her true identity escape:

> You have knowledge of all things,
> and you know that I hate honors from the godless,
> that I loathe the bed of the uncircumcised,
> of any foreigner whatever.
> You know I am under constraint,
> that I loathe the symbol of my high position
> bound round my brow when I appear at court (Esther 4:17u–w).

Like Esther, our peoples are prisoners of an identity and a destiny imposed by the powerful of the earth. Those who decide our destiny, from within or without, sometimes do not know our geography or our languages, far less our aspirations for life and freedom.

We women and peoples of Latin America have so far been only beginning to understand how vital it is for us to understand who we are and where we are coming from if we are to be able to choose what to believe and how to live. As long as "the stronger" does not attain a truly human balance which enables him to recognize us as bone of his bone and flesh of his flesh, there will not be true humanity. Man-woman will be the image and likeness of God when we obtain this equality in difference, flourishing in a creative, fruitful harmony, in the couple and in the relationships of all peoples and societies. The clay of our beings as persons and peoples, molding itself freely in genuine encounter, in mutual discovery and reciprocal respect, will make possible the impossible.

The prophet drowns our hope with light:

> On every lofty mountain, on every high hill
> there will be streams and water-courses, on the day of the
> great slaughter
> when the strongholds fall.
> Then moonlight will be as bright as sunlight
> and sunlight itself be seven times brighter
> — like the light of seven days in one —
> on the day Yahweh dresses his people's wound
> and heals the scars of the blows they have received (Isaiah 30:25–26).

In the Maya cosmogony as in so many others, the sun corresponds to the male and the moon to the female. The prophecy says that the instant we achieve equal brightness, the brightness will be perfect; the people's wounds and scars will be healed. With this healing will come what is now impossible: irrigation channels and streams will water the highlands, and they will be able to become farmland, these *altiplanos*, now semi-barren, to which the Indian peoples of America were pushed out. Equality of access to true development will make both the male aspect and the female aspect shine, and will enrich both, without detriment to either. This maturing will mark the *kairos* for the rising again of true life on the earth as the home of all.

Translated by Francis McDonagh

BOOKS CITED

Baudot, G., and Tzvetan Todorov, *Relatos Axtecas de la Conquista*, Consejo Nacional para la Cultura y las Artes, Mexico, 1990.

Castillo, Bernal Díaz de, *Historia de la Conquista de la Nueva España*, Mexico, 1964.

Coll, Josefina Oliva de, *La Resistencia Indígena ante la Conquista*, Mexico, 1988.

Eisenberg, Josy, and Armand Abecassis, *Et Dieu créa Eve: A Bible Ouverte II: Présences du Judaïsme*, Paris, 1979.

Falla, Ricardo, SJ, Centro de Investigación y Acción Social de Centroamérica (CIASCA).

———, *Masacre de la Finca San Francisco, Huehuetenango, Guatemala, 17 julio 1982*, Copenhagen 1983.

Historia General de las Cosas de la Nueva España, Mexico, 1989.

Lafaye, Jacques, *Los Conquistadores*, Mexico, 1988.

Meza, Otilia, *Malinalli Tenepal, la Gran Calumniada*, Mexico, 1988.

Peláez, Severo Martínez, *La Patria del Criolla*, Costa Rica, 1985.

Tribunal Permanente de los Pueblos, Sesión de Guatemala, Madrid, enero de 1983: *Genocidio en Guatemala*.

12

To Bear Children for the Fatherland

Mothers and Militarism

MARY CONDREN

The words of one of the closing addresses to women at the Second Vatican Council have never ceased to give me pause for thought. "Women of the entire universe, you to whom life is entrusted, it is for you to save the peace of the world." On the face of it, these were noble sentiments, a recognition of the place of women in Catholic theology. But the context in which they were spoken belies, and radically undermines, the sentiments expressed. For women had hardly been allowed to speak at this event, even on the subject of saving the world.

The statement epitomizes the double jeopardy into which women have been placed in Western culture. On the one hand, women are expected to become the repositories and safeguarders of morality, a position uniquely accorded to them by their experience of mothering. Yet when women try to extend their moral consciousness into the wider political or religious world where it may have serious effect, their "femininity," the basis upon which their superior moral stance appears to rest, is said to all but disappear.

The dilemma was nowhere better expressed than in recent years in Ireland with the "Peace Women." When thousands of women marched through the streets of Ireland crying "peace" their leaders were awarded the Nobel Peace Prize. When the same women, realizing there could be no peace without justice, set out to develop a concrete program of action to address social inequity, their support dwindled to a trickle. They had become "political"; they had lost their "peace" platform, and for all intents and purposes, they may as well have lost their honor.

In recent years, the enormity of the nuclear threat has generated many new studies of warfare and of the complex role played by gender politics.

Is there a relationship, natural or otherwise, between women and peace? Is this relationship one that can be used to bring about peace, or is it simply a foil to disguise and even legitimate the death-dealing of modern statecraft? Why, for instance, do nations devote so much of their financial and cultural resources to the preservation of the war machinery and so little to institutes devoted to the study of peacemaking? If wars are indeed waged for the "defense of women and children," why is so little public money spent on rape crisis centers who deal on a daily basis with the ongoing war against women and children waged by patriarchal sexual attitudes and practices? There are some very curious contradictions around the issue of women, peace, and defense, that need much further exploration.

While in the thought of the Vatican and certain strands of the feminist movement women might be "natural" pacifists, historically, the evidence on the role of women in warfare is ambivalent. While it would be true to say that women have seldom, if ever, initiated war, in the animal kingdom there is no fiercer animal than a mother protecting her young. In the major European wars women have worked in the ancillary services in roles ranging from nursing to concentration camp supervisors. In contemporary warfare, especially in those of "liberation," women play an active part as combatants, and indeed today the question is often raised as to whether women's liberation should automatically make them liable for conscription and combat duty.

Quite aside from their actual roles in warfare, women have played a variety of symbolic roles. Women have acted as "pretexts for war," "recompense for allies," "valuables" that need to be defended, guarantors of "the warrior's rest and recreation," nurses and cheerleaders, "miracle mothers," "wistful wives," "treacherous tramps," and "co-operative citizens." Women's role on the battlefield has been so all-pervasive that the contemporary theorist Nancy Huston has commented that if women were not "present in their absence" on the battlefield, *nothing would happen there worth writing about.*[1]

Mothers of soldiers traditionally have taken pride in seeing their sons march off to war as though their willingness to fight proved their manhood. Some mothers support their son's military involvement on the grounds that the military will "take care" of their sons, especially those the women found hard to discipline.[2]

Even where they are not actively involved in war efforts women play a role as the "witnesses" to men's heroism. Women have acted as "mirrors" reflecting back to men double their original size.[3] As Tacitus wrote,

> Close by them, too, are those who are dearest to them, so that they
> hear the shrieks of women, the cries of infants. They [women] are

to every man the most sacred witnesses of his bravery — they are the most generous applauders. The soldier brings his wounds to his mother and his wife. . . . [4]

Perhaps women's greatest act of witness to men's warrior deeds lies in her act of mourning. From the earliest times the "mourning" of women has played a crucial role in warfare. When the ancient religious rites of Greece were abolished in favor of those of the state, the only rites remaining to women were the women's wail, left to "accompany the fall of the victim in the great blood sacrifice."[5] When one of the hunger strikers in Ireland died several years ago a fellow republican prisoner wrote a tribute to his wife:

> . . . she despaired not. She bore the pain and took comfort from the fact that Joe was faithful and he fought. In sharing the grief of Goretti McDonnell we share in the grief of every bereaved Irish mother or wife. From time immemorial, from their courage we draw new strength.[6]

And even though women rarely *invent* war tales, throughout the ages and through various ancestral rites, they have acted successfully as transmitters of the heroic deeds of men.[7]

Participation in warfare has conveyed very dubious "benefits" to women. In medieval times, women's right to hold property was made conditional upon her willingness to "defend" herself.[8] Similarly, although many early suffragists were anti-war, they also were quick to recognize the benefits women's participation in warfare had brought to them, including the enfranchisement they had sought for so long.[9]

War also provides an escape valve when the inherent violence of patriarchal social relations threatens to overspill, allowing this violence to escape temporarily and "emigrate" without destroying the sexual relations of those societies in which it is situated. For men it offers an escape from "civilization," in which all the pent-up hostility against the "Other" in their lives can be directed at alternative enemies abroad. Women can temporarily lose their quality of "Otherness" in warfare, enter the public world and reject the stifling domesticity to which their role as men's "Other" has confined them.[10]

Given the evidence, we must conclude that women are not "naturally" pacifists. Nevertheless, their involvement in warfare, at whatever level, represents a profound tragedy. For warfare, more than any other institution, plays a powerful role in the generation of symbolic capital for patriarchal culture in which their self-interest as women is constantly and radically undermined.

Patriarchal societies thrive on the establishment of dualisms; between men and women, the sacred and profane, and between the public and the private. These dualisms do not come naturally, but must be maintained through periodic exhortations, philosophical discourse, and ritual. Warfare provides the occasion for all three.

Throughout warfare and the training of soldiers, the hatred of women and what they represent plays a major role in enabling soldiers to forge their identities. Soldiers are often insulted by their commanding officers with such epithets as "vagina-face," "used sanitary napkin," "abortion," or "miscarriage." Indeed one of the central tactics of warrior training is the questioning of a soldier's manhood, which he will then go to any lengths, usually violent, to defend. For men do not just become "men," they become "Not-Women."[11]

The world of a soldier is essentially a "barracks community," where as far as possible any traces of women's influence are eliminated.[12] Ideally the barracks community is homosexual. Plato held that homosexual lovers would be invincible, and he regretted that it was not possible to turn cowardly soldiers into women.[13] Even the peace-loving Wilfrid Owen spoke of women with a certain contempt. As he wrote in one of his letters to his mother: "All women, without exception, *annoy me*."[14]

In the most explicit initiation rites of tribal warriors, some young men actually step on their mother's bellies in a gesture signifying their initiation or individuation. Some soldiers talk of their "freedom" from the "stuffiness" of drawing rooms, or the restraints of civilization represented by women, while in one of his marching songs, A. E. Housman sings happily: "Woman bore me/I will rise."

It has even been argued that the patriarchal discourses generated during the First World War were a direct response to the early suffragist movement, the first serious threat that patriarchal social relations had experienced, and that had threatened the "manhood" of the society, a threat that had already found expression in an increased incidence of violence against, and male resentment of women.[15] In the discourses of the major world wars "manhood" and "nationality" are almost synonymous. As Patrick Pearse wrote at that time, echoing sentiments to be found throughout Europe: "bloodshed is a cleansing and sanctifying thing, and the nation which regards it as the final horror has lost its *manhood*" (emphasis added).[16]

During warfare the male can successfully project his fear of women, or fear of the insecurity of his manhood, onto a superior male represented by the government. Men's social identity is forged in the sacred world of battle, a world that becomes sacred because it is freed from the polluting influences of women. Men who would otherwise be doomed to social inferiority or ignominy, and those who identify with them, can through their warrior efforts be elevated to hero status transcending, even for the moment, class and economic barriers, and becoming, through their willingness to sacrifice, automatically superior to the other half of the human race.[17] Ideally, however, for manhood to be equated with sacrality, wars will be fought on behalf of God, or certainly with God "on their side."

In the legitimating efforts of states war veterans, and the cult of the war-dead, now play a powerful symbolic role. Monuments to the "Unknown Soldier" who "gave his all" now, throughout Europe, replace those once erected to the dead Christ "who died for all." The sacrifices of war often now replace sacrifices on the altar.

The gendered split between the sacred and the profane is paralleled by the split between the public and private life. The ancient Greeks and their contemporary followers such as Kant and Hegel, decided that women were a decided impediment to the life of the *polis*. Women, they argued, were incapable of transcending their particularistic interests, too rooted in the care of their families to sacrifice themselves for the "Common Good." Only men are considered capable of achieving the degree of ethical abstraction necessary to see the whole, and the proof of their ethical consciousness was their willingness to lay down their lives. Indeed according to Immanuel Kant, "perpetual peace" would be the greatest threat to ethical consciousness, while Georg Wilhelm Friedrich Hegel's master/slave paradigm of the state and the need for constant "transcendence," could lead to nothing less than perpetual warfare.

In the ideal patriarchal state women would inhabit only the domestic world. Warfare, according to political philosophers, is fundamentally incompatible with self-love or with the protection of one's own self-interests. As Mary O'Brien argues, according to political philosophers, women could not become part of the state because of their "unheroic and irrational objection to the slaughter of their own children."[18] But in the last analysis, patriarchal ethics depend upon perpetual warfare for their continued existence.[19]

Given the multitude of roles that women play in war, the seeming benefits to be derived therefrom, and yet the overwhelming evidence of the role of warfare in generating symbolic capital for the continuing oppression of women, how can we begin to talk about the relationship between women and peace, or must women forever bear children for the fatherland? Faced with the overwhelming threat of nuclear destruction we have little choice but to maintain that there is such a relationship, however tenuous. But given the historical manipulation of this relationship, we also have to maintain that, far from being "natural," the relationship is one that must be worked at, labored over, and extracted like a screaming newborn from the morass of contemporary sexual politics.

The myth of the "natural" peacefulness of women has carried with it several implications. First, logically, if women are "naturally" pacifist then nothing in their social conditions, or conditioning, needs to be changed. Not surprisingly, this situation suits those who wish to maintain the patriarchal *status quo.* Second, the ideology of women's "natural" pacifism has historically served to maintain the myth of women's powerlessness. Third, women's moral purity has been gained, and now is maintained, at the cost of its political effectiveness. Let us examine each of these in turn.

Quite apart from the symbolic and actual roles women play in warfare, feminist theorists are now seriously proposing that maternal practice "is as conducive to battle as to peace."[20] In particular, the cult of motherhood with its attendant ideology of self-denial and sexual repression, far from encouraging social equilibrium, may be doing precisely the opposite. Women's lack of a clearly defined "self-interest" leaves them in a moral vacuum. On the one hand, their selflessness confines them to the home, the world of domestic decision making, and on the other, on the one occasion where they are allowed to enter the political world in times of war, their selflessness is then expended on the profoundly selfish adventures of nationalists and patriots. Not taking responsibility for, or having any clear articulation of, their erotic or other needs, these can then be exploited in the service of the war machine. Like some of the early suffragists they confuse the "national interest" with their own, preventing the international bonding and co-operation of women on terms that would genuinely support their self-interests as generators and sustainers of the human race and defenders of human life.

The cult of motherhood carries with it the myth of women's powerlessness. In turn, this prevents women from studying the kinds of power we do have and reduces us to a condition of moral imbecility in the use of that power. The myth of women's powerlessness and selflessness, in particular, prevents women from coming to terms with the profoundly political nature of child rearing practices.

Feminist theory is increasingly finding correlations between rigidly defined sex roles and institutional violence.[21] Hierarchical societies depend crucially on their boundary definitions and a premium is, therefore, laid upon male aggression enabling, as it does, these boundaries to be maintained. In turn, the more boundaries need to be maintained, the more this will be reflected in child rearing practices.

Recent studies of the childrearing involved in such persons as Adolf Hitler, and contemporary terrorists, indicate clearly that their early childhood experiences of violence predispose such future adults to violence and revenge, either on their own children, or on society at large. In some cases, such as that of Hitler, the need for revenge is insatiable and the need to redress childhood traumas wreaks future havoc on the social world.[22]

While Hitler may be an extreme example, other evidence now indicates that even the more "normal" childrearing practices can have devastating impact on the social world. In particular, women who buy into the myth of their own powerlessness, who have no sense of self-worth, become incapable of conferring an enabling form of recognition upon their children that would allow them successfully to individuate. Their female children will usually react to this by emulating their mother's behavior, thereby passing it on to the next generation. Their lack of self-esteem makes them particularly prone to becoming "co-dependents" of substance abusers, and vulnerable to the physical and psychological abusiveness of the submission/domination syndrome.[23]

Women's loss of self also produces misogynistic sons who, in the process of their own separation from their mother, and faced with the "non-being" of their mother's femaleness, desperately define themselves as "Not-Women," and search furiously for a compensatory, revengeful, and exaggerated male identity that often finds violent expression.[24]

The myth of women's moral purity has been gained, and is now maintained, at the cost of its political effectiveness. Keeping women out of the life of the city, seemingly powerless, and pathologically "unselfish," has been the most effective way of ensuring their loss of control over that which has traditionally been most precious to them: the lives of their own children. This moral purity is vitiated at its source.

In return for the unquestioning acceptance of the myth of women's moral purity, and the myth of women's powerlessness, women receive "protection." It is precisely the nature of this protection that women need to suspect and criticize, given that the discourse of "protection" is operative throughout and legitimates the war machine, and its daily equivalent: rape.[25]

There is then no essential relationship between women and peace, and those who argue there is, are usually engaging in manipulative and mystifying rhetoric designed to maintain the sexual *status quo*. In addition, they are often guilty of indulging in false compensation practices such as the idealization of "true womanhood," or the claim that the real object of their warrior enterprises is protection of the "motherland."

Any discussion of women's role in peacemaking, therefore, must arise, not from an idealist or theological category as to woman's "true nature," but must come from the praxis of women's lives. Several theorists have recently proposed one way forward as the systematization of "maternal thinking," in order to extrapolate from women's roles in the private world, based on "preservative and attentive love," to the public world.[26]

Feminist theorists stress the dangers inherent in this enterprise, the dangers of inauthenticity, and in particular, the danger of establishing a new idealism. "Maternal thinking" is a "moral activity rather than a virtue achieved."[27] It is at once a spiritual practice, akin to non-violence training, and an attempt to develop on a par with the Marxist analyses of production, an epistemology of the policies of reproduction and its effect on the public and private world.

As the feminist movement has claimed from the beginning, "the personal is political," and perhaps now for the first time in human history these traditional dualisms can be reconciled with the aid of a theology that is respectful of the real roles women and men play in the world and of the political and theological consequences arising therefrom.

NOTES

1. Nancy Huston, "Tales of War and Tears of Women," *Women's Studies International Forum* 5 (1982), pp. 275.

2. Linda Rennie Forcey, "Making of Men in the Military: Perspectives from Mothers," *Women's Studies International Forum* 6, no. 6 (1984), pp. 478, 484.

3. Judith Hicks Stiehm, "The Protected, the Protector, the Defender," *Women's Studies International Forum* 5, nos. 3/4 (1982), p. 370.

4. Cited in Mary Beard, *Women as Force in History*, 1947; New York, 1972, p. 289.

5. Jean Pierre-Vernant and Pierre Vidal-Naquet, *Tragedy and Myth in Ancient Greece*, Sussex, 1981, p. 16.

6. Cited in Eileen Fairweather et al., *Only Our Rivers Run Free: Northern Ireland: The Women's War*, London, 1984, pp. 101–2.

7. Huston, "Tales of War," p. 275.

8. Mary Condren, *The Serpent and the Goddess: Women, Religion and Power in Celtic Ireland*, San Francisco, 1989, p. 64.

9. Betty Rozak and Theodore Rozak, eds., *Masculine/Feminine: Readings in Sexual Mythology and the Liberation of Women*, New York, 1969, p. 98.

10. Jean Bethe Elshtain, "Woman, Mirror and Other: Toward a Theory of Women, War and Feminism," *Humanities in Society* 5, nos. 1/2 (1982), p. 39.

11. See Nancy Jay, "Gender and Dichotomy," *Feminist Studies* 7, no. 1 (1981), pp. 38–56.

12. See Nancy Hartsock, "The Barracks Community in Western Political Thought: Prolegomena to a Feminist Critique of War and Politics," *Women's Studies International Forum* 5 (1982), pp. 283–86.

13. Sara Ruddick, "Preservative Love and Military Destruction: Some Reflections on Mothering and Peace," in *Mothering: Essays in Feminist Theory*, ed. Joyce Trebilcot, Totowa, N.J., 1984, p. 253; Plato, *The Laws*, Harmondsworth, 1970 ed., s. 944.

14. Wilfrid Owen, *Collected Letters*, ed. Harold Owen and John Bell, London, 1967, p. 274. Cited in Caryn McTighe Musil, "Wilfrid Owen and Abram," *Women's Studies* 13 (1986), p. 60.

15. Roszak and Roszak, *Masculine/Feminine*, p. 95.

16. Patrick Pearse, *Collected Works: Political Writings and Speeches*, Dublin, 1924, p. 99.

17. See Nancy Jay, "Sacrifice as Remedy for Having Been Born of Woman," in *Immaculate and Powerful: The Female in Sacred Image and Social Reality*, ed. Clarissa Atkinson et al., Boston, 1985, pp. 283–309.

18. Mary O'Brien, *The Politics of Reproduction*, London, 1981, p. 148.

19. Jo-Ann Pilardi Fuchs, "On the War Path and Beyond: Hegel, Freud and Feminist Theory," *Women's Studies International Forum* 6, no. 6 (1983), p. 566. See also, Edith Wyschogrod, *Spirit in Ashes: Hegel, Heidegger and Man-Made Death*, New Haven, 1985.

20. Ruddick, "Preservative Love," p. 255.

21. Riane Eisler, "Violence and Male Dominance: The Ticking Time Bomb," *Humanities in Society* 7, nos. 1/2 (1984), pp. 5–6.

22. See Alice Miller, *For Your Own Good: Hidden Cruelty in Child-Rearing and the Roots of Violence*, trans. Hildegarde and Hunter Hannum, New York, 1984. *Am Anfang war Erziehung*, Frankfurt am Main, 1980.

23. See Jessica Benjamin, *The Bonds of Love: Psychoanalysis, Feminism and the Problem of Domination*, New York, 1988.

24. Nancy Hartsock, *Money, Sex and Power: Toward a Feminist Historical Materialism*, Boston, 1985, pp. 169, 177. See also Nancy Chodorow, *The Reproduction of Mothering: Psychoanalysis and the Sociology of Gender*, Berkeley, 1978; Dorothy Dinnerstein, *The Mermaid and the Minotaur: Sexual Arrangements and Human Malaise*, New York, 1977.

25. Jean Bethke Elshtain, "On Beautiful Souls, Just Warriors and Feminist Consciousness," *Women's Studies International Forum* 3, no. 4 (1982), p. 342.

26. Sara Ruddick, "Maternal Thinking," in *Mothering: Essays in Feminist Theory*, ed. Joyce Trebilcot, p. 221.

27. Ruddick, "Preservative Love," p. 239.

13

Poverty and Motherhood

MERCY AMBA ODUYOYE

The juxtaposition of poverty and motherhood is so strange as to be almost offensive. Granted this response is the result of socialization and may be dismissed as the internalization of domesticating cultural norms. In this contribution I do not wish to debate this issue nor go into the economic discussions that link motherhood with population control and the debates on abortion, planned parenthood and responsible parenthood, as all these affect men as well as women. I therefore do not wish to link them to motherhood. What I am offering is a testimony which I believe will find resonance in many African women's souls.

I am Ghanaian and an Akan with both my parents and their parents on both sides belonging to mother-centered groups. *My* political and economic status in Akan structures depends on who my mother is. I am who I am because of who my mother is. I have no biological children but I am the first of my parents' nine children. Any Akan daughter will tell you what that means. I have not experienced motherhood but I know what "mothering" means. I have accompanied my mother through her motherhood. Motherhood has not made my mother poor. *My mother is rich.* She has a community of people whose joys and sorrows are hers. I am rich because I have a community and hold a special place in it. I am not a mother but I have children.

To many ears this sounds folkloric, a glorification of a culture, sublimation of instincts and many such explanations. For me this is life. The Akan proverbs below are not just sayings, they are the heart of the wisdom by which the Akan live today and can be a guide even for the management of the political unit called Ghana. Mothering is a religious duty. It is what a good socio-political and economic system should be about if the human beings entrusted to the state are to be fully human, nurtured to care for and take care of themselves, one another, and of their environments. Biological motherhood embodies all of this for the Akan as for many African peoples. One proverb observes: "When you catch a hen her chickens are easily collected." Children are disoriented and fall easy prey when mothering is absent or inadequate. Another proverb puts it more emphatically: "When mother is no more, the clan is no more." It is the presence of a mother that keeps the Akan family together in that social system. "A child may resemble the father, but a child belongs to the mother." With such a high premium on biological motherhood and mothering as a principle of human relations and the organization of the human community, to associate motherhood with poverty will need a very careful analysis and detailed substantiation. Mothering, biologically or otherwise, calls for a life of letting go, a readiness to share resources and to receive with appreciation what others offer for the good of the community.

There are several folktales of periods of famine depicting the sacrifices of mothers in order to save their children and many proverbs that crystallize in a few words what motherhood demands of women. "The tortoise does not have breasts, but she feeds her children." "However inconvenient the path to the nest the brooding hen will get to the eggs." So women in Africa exercise motherhood against all odds. The quality of a sense of duty and fulfillment and achievement that must go with this determination to see another person become human, cannot be associated with poverty of understanding about the value of humanity. It may be exercised in the midst of abject lack of material goods and that makes it all the more a marvel that women continue to mother. Scarcely ever does one find a deliberate choice of childlessness among African women and furthest from our understanding of life is to make that choice for economic reasons.

The Penalty of Motherhood

Dramatic change in the economic basis of life in Africa is what has led to the association of women with poverty. The system makes women poor by deliberately excluding them from what generates wealth. Mothers fall easy prey to this new approach to community life that is more individualistic and competitive. When children were seen to belong to the whole family, indeed the whole community, being poor was not necessarily the result of having children. Today it can be a cause. When a nation acts as a mother to its citizens the education, health and well-being of children are in the national budget and mothers are treated as contributing to the "assets" of the nation. What is a nation without people to make it great? It seems such a trite observation but children do not "belong" only to parents, children are assets of the whole nation. Poverty is put together with motherhood when women are penalized by state, religion and culture for becoming mothers. In cultures that do not understand the African concept of family and mothering, a woman who bears her traditional responsibility of mothering, including carrying financial responsibility for children of the family (even if they are her mother's children), is penalized because of Western ideas of adoption. She is considered "single" when her home is full of human beings to be nurtured and loved. The survival of these children depends on her industry and doing this has nothing to do with biology. But with it is an indispensable aspect of the mothering that human life needs in order for human community to be humane and creative.

In some Western societies, women with children who are not attached to men are penalized in all sorts of ways, while in others women have to prove they have no men in order to get state assistance for their children. The criteria is not the welfare of women and children but their relation to the androcentric laws by which most of humanity is ordered and governed. These androcentric legal provisions have difficulty recognizing mothers as heads of households but choose to invent names like "single mothers," suggesting they have stepped outside the norm of submitting to male authority. There are no single parents (men or women) in Africa, as such persons are recognized as integral to the African family. Women-headed homes of modern times have been created by the exigencies of migrant workers who are prevented by the laws of the countries where they give their labor and pay taxes from bringing in even those closest to them, spouse and children.

In Africa the instabilities of war and disruptions of natural disasters, economic and political mismanagement often result in the disruption of whole communities and inexorably propel women into the situation of having to parent their children single-handedly. Stateless and homeless, they struggle to care for the people who have survived with them. The global economic order that operates a hierarchy of persons is able to turn a blind eye to certain categories of human beings deemed dispensable. There are people whose welfare is theirs alone, but whose labor when they sell it, is bought for wages that cannot sustain life. Their salaries are determined by how much debt their governments have to pay, what structural adjustments are being made and how determined the governments are to pay the cut-throat interest on loans they borrow from the loan granting nations in order to feather nests of "experts" and "advisors" from the same countries. The whole family suffers, but the traditional expectation that women will be more caring and more compassionate puts the burden of the situation on women. They give until they have nothing more to share but their poverty.

The Impoverishment of Women

The impoverishment of women in Africa is an aspect of the impoverishment of the third world which has remained undisclosed or ignored until women themselves made their voices heard. Whatever poverty women as mothers struggle with cannot be understood apart from the real poverty-maker, power, the inability to influence the decisions that condition one's life.

Knowledge is power, and women are kept ignorant of how and what political, military and economic arrangements are arrived at. Women are kept ignorant of what the drugs they take, or are made to take, do to their own bodies and to the environment. The sources and the processes of the food they cook and put before their families are often not revealed and if they are, the economic and political milieu of the producers are not made known. Even when the agricultural and industrial processes involve women, women become peripheral to the actual decisions, they are "farm hands" and "robots" on assembly lines. The whys and wherefores are not made known to women. Why would women submit to radiation, Depo Provera, sex selection and other hazards of contemporary reproductive technology and genetic engineering that invade and violate their bodies and therefore impoverish their sense of personhood by treating them as objects of research and experiments? In most countries it is women who are exploited in this genetic technology.

In Africa socio-cultural impoverishment is more evident as Western technological culture intensifies its claim to be *the* human culture and imposes its norms of what is legal and ethical on the rest of the world. Women in Africa do not fall into the category of the under-employed, if anything they are over-employed as none can claim a 40–hour week. That they are unpaid as statistics have it for women globally does not need to be debated, but over and above this is the phenomenon of being taken for granted, of not having one's labor enter the statistics of the national production. Their labor goes undocumented and therefore in the contemporary way of looking at government spending, women are not numbered among producers and therefore are not recognized as entitled to consume any social service. When one speaks of the impoverishment of women in Africa, one is referring to persons whose physical labor is used to fetch them enough sustenance for themselves and their families, but who can no longer cope because the market value of their products has fallen or the land that they used to deploy has been appropriated by governments or acquired by those who have big money for more "profitable" enterprises. Such "profits" do not profit women in Africa and states impoverished by international economic injustice that no longer have the means to sustain women's welfare are the poorer for this.

In West Africa women continued their traditional economic activities of farming, food processing "fast food," making and marketing of household requirements and long distance trade as a parallel to the Western economic institution that absorbed the labors of West African men in what is known as the "modern sector." Women's development in West Africa has followed this line and more and more supplementary income-generating activities have been created. Women's economic impoverishment has led to a burst of creativity in domestic survival strategies. Creativity in this area is sustained by the hope that the situation will change for the better.

On the level of traditional cultural demands however, little has changed and it would appear there is no hope for changes that will restore what is dignifying for women and remove the cultural obstacles to women's humanity. The impoverishment of women that has resulted from the joint effects of Western Christianity and Islam, Arabic and African cultures is still being overlooked. In conflicts of cultural values, women's culture and women's welfare have always taken second place. The real roots of the impoverishment of women, socially and economically, are to be found in the materialistic Western culture with its androcentric laws and perspectives, for these reinforce African ones and together suppress and often eliminate women's welfare from their provisions.

I have heard pronouncements during population debates that tend to assume that only African and other southern cultures value children and put the onus on women (married women, that is women whose attachment to men is socially approved) to provide care for them. This however is not the case, as the biotechnology that makes surrogate motherhood and *in vitro* fertilization possible is beginning to tell another story. Men everywhere are capable of demanding babies of their wives rather than adopting and "mothering" one that needs parents. Scientists exploit women's bodies for these experiments which require loans which the men may not even help to repay. There are cases outside Africa where mothers have been deprived of land by husbands and then thrown out with their children to fend for themselves. The Asante proverb *eba a eka oni* "when it happens (i.e., when children get into trouble) it affects the mother," can be illustrated in many cultures.

The androcentric world needs to have a continual flow of human beings, to carry patriarchal names and other naming systems. The androcentric world needs children to be born and socialized into citizens who will even lay down their lives for their country. This androcentric world expects women to be the producers of human beings, but the experience of women is that their own development and perception of humanness and the human community have to be set aside in order to be "good women" serving the system. Material and economic poverty are the experience of many women. Material and economic poverty are the experience of many mothers. What makes the latter thoroughly unacceptable is that the system often shields the fathers from the "poverty" that could be associated with their paternity.

A Child Belongs to the Mother

The mother-centered Asante who say a child belongs to the mother also say a child is the mother's until it is born, then its welfare becomes a community responsibility. The mother-to-be however is protected by the community. She is aided by taboos that will ensure safe delivery and guarantee the health of the mother. Inability to transform this ancient wisdom into modern socio-economic terms is what is at the root of the economic impoverishment of women. The impoverishment of mothers, therefore, is an indication of the inability of human social thinking to match our technological development. Human relations and development of norms of community life lag behind economic systems. Women have fallen victim to this human poverty of spirit which puts profits before people and interests before production. In the hierarchy of human needs reproduction of the human species has a very low priority, hence motherhood is not prized. State and other institutions have not found a way of mothering the human community, only women and biological mothers continue to see this mothering of the human race as a sacred duty. Being poor, women make their communities rich, they guarantee the survival of their families in the face of all odds. The many television pictures of mothers in famine and refugee situations tell the story more vividly than words.

God's Economy

In planning how the earth's resources could be managed to sustain all creation, God was generous from the beginning. In the beginning all was good, for all was of God. The interdependence of all creation was built into the beginning and there were no "trespasses" and trespassers for all appropriated only what was necessary for survival and none was or felt exploited. Few such communities may be found in human history.

Exploitation among human beings are only matched by human exploitation of the rest of nature. Exploitation of women by human community is mirrored by the exploitation of the humanity of mothers in families and in society through social norms and legal provisions. What we need to turn our attention to, therefore, is the poverty of the human spirit that ignores that humanity of women as persons in God's image and mothers as co-creators with God and imitators of God's management of creation.

In a mother's economy, abundant life and comfort for others precede her own comfort. Injustice to mothers arises from economic management which does not provide for a mother's well-being and comfort beyond her needs as a child-bearer. Even then all is done for the sake of the child. Are mothers human in their own being or cared for only insofar as they perform the biological function of child bearing? The injustice done to women generally and specially to mothers has often been described as the injustice we do to the generation to come by our wanton exploitation of the earth.

As World Bank and International Monetary Fund prescriptions bite harder into the economy of the third world, so the face of poverty becomes clearer and clearer. When a poor country has to export more to already rich countries, it takes land from the poor, especially women, to grow what the North needs, not what mothers in the South need to feed children. When governments cut spending, schooling and health care fall on families and all work triple-time just to be able to feed the children — so mothers eat last. When wages and salaries are frozen so that a month's earnings only provide food for five days, husbands and children eat first. When foreigners buy their investments to put into "productive" ventures they grow for export, they weave and sew for export, they assemble for export and employ men, young women and lastly women with children; all of whom are paid unjust wages that bear no relation to transportation costs and rising food prices.

The anti-baby economy of the North is preached in the South, through these economic measures and quite overtly, since at least in one African country young women can only get employment in the formal sector if they can show that they are on an anti-motherhood drug. So the message is clear, if you do not want to be poor or become impoverished do not become a mother. In God's economy, the human being is a necessary and integral part. God gave the management of the earth to the Earth-beings that God created. Managing has become exploiting, except where mothers are concerned. To cope with the survival of the people whose well-being depends on her, a mother spends all her meager wages, does extra work, or stops wage-earning if home-nursing is what is needed.

In Africa women will continue to do all these things and more in order to be mothers. They may not have many children to fill the earth but the deliberate no-child solution is not an option. The solution lies in better management of creation, the earth, the human community, the nation and the home by both women and men, rich and poor, North and South. The increasing impoverishment of human communities in the South cannot be reversed by calling attention to motherhood. Mothers in Africa know poverty, but for them the solution is a challenge to which they respond in innovative ways. The survival of the human race is a human responsibility, not just that of mothers. Motherhood gives our race the guarantee of survival. Mothers are not only to be honored, they are to be empowered.

14

The Rape of Mother Earth

Ecology and Patriarchy

CATHARINA HALKES

This essay consists of three parts: the shift from an organic vision of the earth, nature and the universe to a mechanistic way of looking at things in which nature is regulated by external factors and matter is merely something dead and lifeless; theological reflections on the effect of Gen. 1:26–28 and some impulses for a renewed theology of creation; and some notes on patriarchy, feminism and ecology.

From Organic Vision to Mechanistic Interpretation

Of old, people experienced their world, nature, the earth and the entire universe as holy, as an interconnected reality that was both *fascinosum et tremendum*. There was a mysterious order to be experienced in the change of day and night, of ebb and flood, of sun and moon, of the seasons. In all ancient cultures and religions this mystery of ordered organization and fruitfulness is symbolized in the image of the Great Mother. The well-known student of comparative religion Gerardus van der Leeuw wrote of the figure of the mother: "There is nothing more sacred on earth than the worship of the mother, which leads us back to the deepest secret in our soul, the relation of mother and child. She is the most mysterious figure of God."[1] God the Father, the masculine God, is a newcomer; the son as hero and redeemer is earlier. This Great Mother exists under many figures and many names: she is the world mother, the queen of heaven, and mother of earth. As late as the palaeolithic period this latter image involved the entire universe and did not then include any sexual polarization: human beings thought of themselves then as being in her lap, which provided them with both security and food. But later this image could be used in a more restricted sense, of mother earth as opposed to heaven as masculine and paternal, with the two sexes being symbolized: the seed of heaven was poured into the womb of the earth in the form of dew or rain and fertility was thus guaranteed.[2]

To put it another way, the fundamental metaphor that linked the individual human being, society and the universe was that of an organism which expressed the mutual dependence that was present in every sphere. The earth was experienced as a living organism, sensitive with all regard to all human activity. In all its organic vitality it was compared with the human body and in particular with the female body, whose womb fed all life and provided what was needed.

Because human beings gradually no longer felt themselves to be enfolded by the Great Mother but regarded themselves as living *on* the earth, a certain distancing from the earth arose which led to debate about the admissibility of intervention in her body. Not only in classical antiquity but up till the end of the Middle Ages voices of dissuasion and warning were to be heard, for example with regard to mining, which uses technology to capture more artificially from mother earth the precious treasurers which she keeps hidden in her lap and allows to grow organically. This intervention is then seen as procuring an abortion.[3]

The Indian understanding of life, which has always been opposed to interventions that are literally incisions in the body of mother earth, thus existed in our own culture too. Miners have long brought offerings and sought forgiveness in their prayers for penetrating the womb of the earth.

Debate in this field from classical antiquity onwards centered round three subjects: the lawfulness of violating the earth and bringing to light what it had been holding and preserving hidden away; the "ecological" consequences of, for example, felling trees, deforestation and the pollution of rivers; and finally opposition to greed and male lust.

We must however acknowledge that over against the positive image of nature as a kind and nourishing mother there was also a negative image: nature as savage, wild, unpredictable and ungovernable, capable of causing violence and chaos. This image too was experienced as "feminine" and slowly began to obtain more influence. Up to the sixteenth century the positive image of mother earth prevailed: it called for respect and restraint with regard to human intervention. But then the expansive delight in enterprise, in commerce and technology asserted itself and the tension between the experience of nature as worthy of respect and nature as untrustworthy became too great. The image of mother earth had to give way to that of nature as "wild" and asking to be tamed. Norms and values thus shifted.

Through the victory of a more mechanistic way of looking at the world as a whole the mastering of nature came more and more into focus. The warnings mentioned above (including those of the Roman Pliny) against greed were thus explained, but in order to understand those directed against lust it is necessary to establish that the female body still always provided the image of nature. John Donne (1573–1631) wrote in his elegy "To his mistris going to bed":

> Licence my roaving hands, and let them go,
> Before, behind, between, above, below.
> O my America! my new-found land. . . . [4]

Lust and physical love for the human body are associated with the shafts and pits in which the miner sought his gold. And this America is then the symbol and reality of the newly discovered country with its "wild" tracts of land and people, its "virgin" forests: it can be conquered, raped and exploited and the killing of its inhabitants provides the blood to fertilize its soil.

Finally there is the image of nature as means of escape from work that continually occupies people more and more. That is represented by a nymph in idyllic pastoral surroundings, already unveiled but wholly passive, ready to comfort tired men.

In and through the revolutions that characterize the seventeenth century we also see the transition from an organic metaphor of the mother who feeds and protects to the metaphor of a machine, a mechanism, an external factor, applied by man to conquer her either in her passivity or in her "wildness" and to rob her of her riches. [5]

This marks the start of the "masculine birth of time," the title of an early work by one of the founding fathers of the new empirical physical sciences, Francis Bacon, Lord Verulam (1561–1626). In his expressive language the association of nature with the passive female body becomes more than clear.

In *De dignitate et augmentis scientiarum* Bacon writes:

Neither am I of opinion in this history of marvels that superstitious narratives of sorceries, witchcrafts, charms, dreams, divinations, and the like, where there is an assurance and clear evidence of the fact, should be altogether excluded. . . . Howsoever the use and practice of such arts is to be condemned, yet from the speculation and consideration of them . . . a useful light may be gained, not only for a true judgment of the offenses of persons charged with such practices, but likewise for the further disclosing of the secrets of nature. Neither ought a man to make scruple of entering and penetrating into these holes and corners, when the inquisition of truth is his whole object.[6]

One of Bacon's posts was that of attorney general at the time when King James VI was intensifying the laws against witches. He knew very well what was meant by inquisition. Carolyn Merchant summarizes his views as follows, citing his *Novum Organon* and *The Great Instauration:*

> The new method of interrogation was not through abstract notions, but through the instruction of the understanding "that it may in very truth dissect nature." The instruments of the mind supply suggestions, those of the hand give motion and aid the work. "By art and the hand of man," nature can be "forced out of her natural state and squeezed and moulded." In this way, "human knowledge and human power meet as one."[7]

Even in his earliest work we come across the now well-known words: "I am come in very truth leading to you nature with all her children to bind her to your service and make her your slave."[8]

In complete agreement with the social transformations aimed at restoring women to be a psychic and reproductive resource once again, Bacon developed the power of language as a political instrument in order to reduce "feminine nature" to a resource for economic production. He called the union of science and nature "a chaste and lawful marriage" in which the power of "the man" and the passivity of "the woman" found expression.

After the development of the empirical natural sciences the rationalism of the new thought must also be mentioned. Descartes was the great father of this. The human intellect alone now became the *res cogitans* and all the rest — nature, the universe, the corporeal and material world — became merely *res extensae*, extension, the object of the knowing intellect. Nature thus became mind-less, spirit-less, and human beings through their rational knowledge could become its *maitres et possesseurs*. The dualism between man and nature that thus arose is obvious: nature was seen merely as extension and the mind that perceived it was without extension.

Of course with this brief description of the thought of Bacon and Descartes I am not doing justice to the importance of their work. All I am concerned with here is the down-grading of nature and, in the case of Bacon, the association of nature with domination of the female element. Western philosophy and natural science from now on began developing in a direction which on the one hand has led to impressive results and on the other has caused the alienation of man from nature and ultimately has been at the expense of mother earth and the entire environment.

Towards a Renewed Theology of Creation

It is striking that not only philosophers followed this path but that theologians, too, wholeheartedly agreed with this development. We see this become apparent particularly in the views of the theology of secularization. Here are just a few examples: "All technology expresses dominion over things and thus over nature. The ancient mythical saying: 'Subdue the earth' has been fulfilled by technology" (Tillich, 1927). A. van Leeuwen has as the main theme of his *Christianity in World History* the idea that "the cosmic tree that represents the living universe," image of ontocracy, must give way before technocracy, the fruit of Judaism and Christianity. Levinas too advocates the destruction of all "sacred groves."[9] Both anxiety about becoming fascinated by nature (the tree of life) and the work-ethic play their part here in the thinking of predominantly Protestant theologians.

Only through the ecological crisis has the idea been awakened that the Christian theology of creation has been insufficiently developed and has insufficient powers of expression. This deficiency is expressed in the implicit criticism of the ancient nature-religions contained in the biblical accounts of creation whereby creation becomes understood merely as "separating" and the figure of the mother has disappeared. As a result the covenant, particularly in Protestant theology, has gained priority over creation. Karl Barth (and many after him) regards creation as the "external ground" of the covenant and the covenant as the "internal ground" of creation. What is internal is the essence, what is external the periphery. In this way creation becomes merely the start of the history of the covenant and can only be understood on the basis of the covenant, and thus on the basis of history.[10] (Barth was later to adopt a somewhat modified position.)

Not only was human nature of small worth in the Protestant confession of faith but there was also a strong ambivalence with regard to nature as a whole. Catholic theology remained more positive in this respect and recognized God's traces in creation. In Vatican II's pastoral constitution *Gaudium et spes* there is strong emphasis on human responsibility for the whole of creation. It is striking that of recent years Protestant theologians are making up this lost ground, as is shown by important works by among others Moltmann, Liedke, and Altner.[11]

In the third place the interpretation of "subduing the earth," "dominion" in Gen. 1:28, has been an obstacle in reaching a better understanding of our responsibility with regard of the whole of creation. Being made in the image of God was thought to consist of ruling like God over the earth and this ruling was seen in the patriarchal sense as domination. Bacon and Descartes were believers who thought that when human beings had fuller knowledge they were also in a position to rule in this way: knowledge is power.

A new theological approach is marked by important elements which can make the theology of creation stronger and more complete. Here I can only mention them without developing them:

1. Creation is not merely "separating" but is also the ordering of what exists and the giving of creative impulses. This is developed above all in process theology.

2. Creation is a theological category of its own, intended for *all* men and women and for the whole world. It should not be regarded as a category derived from the covenant.

3. In usual talk of the six days of creation the sabbath is totally forgotten, the day pre-eminently of release from work. "And God rested from the work of his hands and saw that it was good." This points to a more contemplative attitude in which God, humankind and the world are linked to each other.[12]

4. Alongside God's action of redemption and liberation which has had all the emphasis, we must also bring God's action of blessing back into our attention. The psalms are full of it. The emphasis thus falls also on what may be called the durative aspect of God's action that keeps everything in being and protects it. In addition the cyclical aspect of creation, of birth, growth and decay, regains its proper value.[13]

5. In place of the completely transcendent monotheistic God, almost separated from "his" creation, more attention is now being paid again to the aspect of relationship in the internal life of the Godhead, the *perichoresis* of the three divine persons, the communication and solidarity both internally and externally and thus also with regard to creation and the world. The Godhead becomes more cosmic and its immanence in our world is expressed and recognized. Jürgen Moltmann in particular is compelling on this panentheism.

6. In the language of image and metaphor with which a new metaphorical theology is concerned, the metaphor has been developed of the world as the body of God (compare the Church as the body of Christ), an image which intensifies our involvement in and responsibility for this world that God has created and increases the worth of our corporeality.[14] It is perhaps significant that the writers referred to here are women who, as is also shown by many publications from the field of feminist theology, are concerned to resist polarization, dualism and separation in order to ask for attention to be paid to connectedness and inter-relationship, be-

tween God and the world, God and human beings, and human beings and creation.[15]

7. Finally a transition can be detected from an anthropocentric (or rather in fact an androcentric) theology of creation to an ecological one which has as its starting point the interdependence of everything that lives and moves throughout the whole of creation.

Patriarchy, Feminism and Ecology

It is particularly the last two points that bring us to the third section of this essay. My position is that as long as patriarchy endures an ecology that leads to real change is impossible.

In this context I define patriarchy in a broad sense and understand by it: (a) the organization of society as a pyramid, with those in power and authority at the top and underneath a structure depending on a chain of command and obedience; (b) the mentality that is the consequence of this thinking of power as domination and regarding men (mind) as superior to women (body); (c) striving for progress and mastery, if necessary at the expense of others — "inferiors," women, other races and regions, nature itself.[16]

What is involved in patriarchy is not in the first instance individual men but a social system that is dominated by men (the fathers). It concerns the social construction of reality (the building up of society) — the significance, value and judgments that are applied to what is happening in society (the culture of civilization) — and finally it concerns a constructed symbolic universe, a "sacred canopy" which expresses the way in which people think about religious and cosmic reality and how they project their values and norms on to this background. For this reason the feminist protest against the image of God as Father was necessary because the dominant culture had developed this image according to its own ideal and had made it subservient to that.

Before theology reacted to the ecological crisis two new movements had come into being and taken the lead: the ecological movement and the new women's movement, feminism. Both shared an egalitarian perspective: the ecological movement developed an ecological ethic which depended on the mutual interrelationship between humankind and its environment; the feminist movement had as its primary aim to liberate women from the alienation that had been imposed on them so that they could reach an authentic understanding of themselves to make them aware of their own roots and personal experiences. Because of this it was able to catch sight of the fate of all other marginalized groups, declare its solidarity with them and finally in this way realize their inter-relationship with the whole of creation.

Environmental problems are ultimately societal problems and form a sub-section of a particular social system. Hence they can only be grasped in the light of the historical development of that society. It is not technology but society itself that is the problem, its culture, the values and norms that it has established, and the economy that it operates. It is the dominant culture or civilization itself that has allowed science and technology, originally means of amassing knowledge for the benefit of all, to become independent and almost impossible to pin down or come to grips with.

For women it is necessary to dig down to a deeper layer in these matters because it is a matter of social problems. Precisely because we have been excluded from culture we have acquired experiences which are now relevant: perseverance, patience, solidarity with daily and other cyclical rhythms, and above all facing up realistically and soberly to the way things are going. All this does not form part of our "feminine nature" but is the result of the way patriarchy assigned roles to us and made us invisible for so long.

Now that we realize this properly we can shake off the possible internalization that has been the consequence of this, rise up and take our place as people who contribute to the culture of our society and who moreover want to go on living in connectedness and association with nature.

The ecological movement and the women's movement are therefore most profoundly subversive, offering a critique of the dominant culture and wanting to bring about its transformation. What in fact is involved here is a protest against unbridled progress that pays no attention to the consequences; a protest against the lethal rivalry in which people begrudge each other life; a protest against the aggressive style of action in the world economy without regard to the number of countries in the third world that are the victims of this; a protest against the exploitation of the earth, of the environment, without listening to the warnings these are giving; a protest against the dominant linear way of thinking that pays no attention to the rhythm of the cyclic life of nature and humankind; and finally it involves a protest against the impossibility of coming to grips with the political and economic powers thanks to their abstract language that is designed for concealment, thanks to their complex financial arrangements and the enormous scale these are on, and thanks to their life-sapping bureaucracy.

Of course it makes sense for these movements — and I include the peace movement here too — to exercise pressure "from below" and thus to gain power through influencing people, through making people aware and through protest. But we shall need to look further and develop strategies for a "grassroots," for an economy with a human face, and for a spirituality of compassion that reaches out to all who are marginalized, including the environment. It is a question now of "eco" and no longer of "ego."[17]

Only one answer is possible, not only to the question of how we can survive but above all to the fundamental question of how we can live with each other in another way and reach a convivial society. The answer is: when patriarchy disappears; when it gives up its practices of power and thus the oppression of innumerable people; when it abandons war as an instrument of conquest and as a means of solving differences; and when it gives up its mental pictures, its thinking in stereotypes, particularly where women are concerned.

Women are still always associated with "nature," with their body, with their womb; and men with culture, power, and conquest. Men have been socialized so profoundly that they are afraid of their body, of nature, of decay and of death. They project all this on the female body. While men have for ages been the masters of our reproductive capacity, the danger is now not imaginary that in an excessive technological application of science they may once again make themselves the masters of the woman's womb, see the procreation of children as a medical matter (hence "culture") and set the tone once again.

Whenever women today take part in science and technology they can only contribute to the fall of patriarchy if they do not adapt or compromise but remain loyal to their own presuppositions.

On the basis of this kind of attitude co-operation is conceivable between all who form part of the ecological and women's movements: an arena for men and women to listen to each other and by working through the ecological problems to touch the roots of our true humanity: to remain true to nature, to listen to it and thus to create an ecological culture in which there is room for everyone and everything.

Ultimately patriarchy is not something predestined but a historical phenomenon. It arose at some time; it can also disappear again. And it is now the time for that. . . .

Translated by Robert Nowell

NOTES

1. G. van der Leeuw, *Phänomenologie der Religion*, 3d ed., Tübingen, 1970, pp. 86f.
2. Cf. Jürgen Moltmann, *Gott in der Schöpfung*, 2d ed., Munich, 1985, pp. 300ff.

3. Carolyn Merchant, *The Death of Nature*, San Francisco, 1980, p. 7.

4. Quoted in Merchant, *The Death of Nature*, pp. 40–41.

5. Ibid., chapter 1, *passim.*

6. Quoted in ibid., p. 168.

7. Ibid., p. 171.

8. Francis Bacon, *The Masculine Birth of Time*, ed. and tr. Benjamin Farrington, Liverpool, 1964, p. 62, quoted in ibid., p. 170.

9. Cf. Hans Achterhuis, "De boom des levens: mythe of realiteit?," in Hans Achterhuis et al., *Over bomen gesproken*, Baarn, 1985, pp. 113–44.

10. Gerhard Liedke, *Im Bauch des Fisches — Ökologische Theologie*, 5th ed., Stuttgart, 1989.

11. Moltmann, *Gott in der Schöpfung;*, Gerhard Liedke, *Im Bauch des Fisches*, Stuttgart, 1979; G. Altner, ed., *Ökologische Theologie*, Stuttgart, 1989.

12. Moltmann, *Gott in der Schöpfung*, pp. 281–98.

13. Claus Westermann, *Der Segen in der Bibel und im Handeln der Kirche*, Munich, 1968.

14. Sallie McFague, *Models of God*, London, 1987, pp. 59–91; Grace Jantzen, *God's World, God's Body*, Philadelphia and London, 1984.

15. Cf. also, Dorothee Sölle, *To Work and to Love*, Philadelphia, 1984; Carter Heyward, *Our Passion for Justice*, New York, 1984.

16. Cf. Gerda Lerner, *The Creation of Patriarchy*, New York and Oxford, 1986. For a comprehensive bibliography see Catharina J. M. Halkes, . . . *En alles zal worden herschapen*, Baarn, 1989.

17. Charlene Spretnak and Fritjof Capra, *Green Politics*, Santa Fe, N.M., 1986.

15

Option for the Poor as an Option for Poor Women

IVONE GEBARA

The reflections I present here are bound to be colored by my being a Latin American woman, my way of life, my situation as an intellectual and by what my eyes see, my senses feel and my mind connects. Of course my approach is limited. I simply want to say how we are involved in the announcing of the Gospel to the poor in our own lives as Latin American women.

Opting for the poor is not something general and abstract but historical and particular. That is to say that in different cultures and countries the poor have to be identified and historically situated as those from among whom something new can arise, something bound up with the restoration of life and the coming of justice. I think this historical sense of the poor was always present within the movement of Old Testament prophets, within the Jesus movement and within several Church movements from apostolic times on. The word "poor" has always had a particular reference. We can find it in the history of the Jewish people and other peoples who believed in the God of life. The poor are the widows, orphans, the sick, foreigners and prisoners. We must not escape into theories or endless justifications to hide from this reality. We must simply look at the lives of those who live on the edge of society and become aware of their sufferings.

Today, too, faith requires that we learn to identify the poor who are among us and, possibly, the poor we are. In this sense the word "poor," even though it refers primarily to a social group deprived of material goods, can be expanded to include an impoverished culture, voiceless minorities without rights, groups seeking elementary recognition in society. Women are included in this expansion of the term poor. This does not in any way detract from the fundamental question of class struggle in Latin America or mean that we have lost sight of the problem of strikers, or those men, women and children in all kinds of want. It is merely to look at one particular aspect of the problem of the oppressed.

Women's attainment of historical self-awareness and readiness to act on it is one of the "cultural revolutions" of our time. Hence it is also a "theological revolution" struggling to happen in spite of difficulties of all kinds. I want to make three points which I think are important to begin discussion on the option for the poor woman as an option for the poor.

Woman's Option for Herself

We live in a world in which external appearances seem to be regarded as the most important thing. What do we mean by external appearances? We do not just mean that we live in a consumer society luring all of us rich or poor to identify ourselves by what we eat or wear, clothes, jewels, etc. . . . We must go deeper, to the level of our deepest self. Who we are, what kind of world do we want to create, what kind of relationships do we want? We are talking about a woman's option for herself as a first step towards changing the existing structures in the society in which we live.

Saying a woman should make an option for herself might sound silly at first. If we are women, how can we choose to be women? This question echoes the one Nicodemus asked Jesus: "How can one be born again?" (John 3:4). There is no ready-made answer. We have to start with the basic: accept the reality of being a woman, that is to say, make what we are our own, be reborn by an act of deep acceptance of our being with its own history made up of choices and non-choices since the beginning of our lives. It is very difficult to be reborn as a woman. It is a conversation, a coming around to oneself. It is like going back into our mother's womb to rebring our being as a woman to the light of day.

It seems to me that not enough attention has been paid to this aspect during these recent years of women's historical consciousness-raising and discovery of her increasingly important role in our societies. In Latin America we have mainly stressed the participation of women in various popular organizations and women's organizations to fight for our rights. Often women get caught up in these movements and in the hurly burly of militant action fail to turn inward upon themselves. In my opinion this leaves an emptiness, which over the course of time, has visible consequences at the level of the social struggle. If there has been no self-reflection the struggle can become purely external. This inward looking is a deep acceptance of the wonder of the self, body and mind, in its harmony and contradiction. It means working on ourself, fighting from within the false images we have acquired of ourselves. All this effort, linked to a wider social struggle, can make new creatures of us, new women who have listened to our deepest inner voice telling us to accept and welcome ourselves first and foremost simply as women. This is a difficult journey which we are not too keen to embark on, for at first sight it may seem pointless, not producing any change because everything goes on within us and the real struggle is out there. This attitude reveals a split between our deep self and our outward self, as if we could choose between one or the other aspect of our being. Our lives are a dichotomy, a lack of unity — though of course this unity is always difficult to maintain for every human being at every stage of life.

There is no ready-made formula for rebirth or rediscovering or creating this unity of the self. There are some poor women whose lives have attained this unity at an extraordinarily deep level. With the help of happenings, meetings, sufferings and joys in their own lives, they have been able to discover the wellspring of unity in themselves. This means that discovering one's personal unity does not mean you necessarily have to belong to a certain social class, even though your social class will have an effect on the way in which you theoretically formulate or verbally express this unity. What more can we say about this source of unity? It is difficult. It is mysterious, it seems to be closer to intuition and poetic feeling, beyond saying. You have to have "groped" it to realize its importance and value to every human struggle, and particularly for the women's struggle now at the end of the twentieth century.

Self-acceptance and welcoming, rebirth of the self as woman, the creation of one's own personal unity, feeling one's center, are incomplete, fragmentary and poor expressions to describe this first step towards oneself in order to be more open to others. "To love others as oneself" is a key phrase for Christians and also for others. It tries to show how love of others is not distinct from love of self or love of self from love of others. They are two poles of the same loving movement and one cannot develop fully without the other. I should like to say even more about it and describe the experience in more detail. But it seems to me that it is not something one does once and for all. It is a continual movement of our whole being and at every stage of our life we are invited to renew it. We are always at risk of becoming alienated from ourselves, split off from what we are, distracted from our true self, becoming lost in the contradictions of our society.

In saying this I am thinking in Latin America of the Indian woman who must get back to her roots, which have been disturbed since the time of colonization, I am thinking of the Black woman who has to bear the racial prejudices of the Whites who brought her people from Africa, I think of poor single mothers, prostitutes from choice or necessity, women abandoned by husbands, immigrants for various reasons, and I also think of intellectuals like myself. We are all invited to be reborn, accept our roots, discover and love ourselves in spite of present suffering and oppression. This love of self is a personal act even if others help us to find it or to start looking for it. Each one of us has to say 'I want to be healed' in order to cast out the hundreds of demons that bind us down and hold us captive to ourselves, to others and the social structure of our time.

Option for ourself is a personal act but is not a solitary one. It also means being open and welcoming to others. Which takes us on to our second point.

Option for Others

This echoes a question put to Jesus: "Who is my neighbor?" or who should I be a neighbor to? In other words, this is love's second pole, love of others.

According to the Gospel this second pole cannot be reduced just to people near us, our own family. It must be expanded to include "those who have fallen by the wayside," to those others whose sufferings call for justice, pity and love. Opting for others has the same source as opting for oneself. The reborn self, which has rediscovered its roots, finds itself in a particular history with all kinds of other people who also need to be reborn collectively, to rediscover themselves as a human group, as a society with a history and its own roots. The self seeking rebirth cannot be reborn effectively unless it strives to help others be reborn too.

In the option for others, the other is collective, that is to say it means option for a human group in distress, a group whose human integrity is diminished, either by our various societies or by the Church. In Latin America this collective is the poor with many faces: workers, peasants, beggars, abandoned children, lost young people and others. They are men and women but now we need to single out the women.

The poor woman today is the poorest of the poor. She is the other: bleeding and burdened, housewife, mother, daughter, wife. She is both subject and object of our option for the poor. There is a considerable literature on the double or triple oppression of women: at home, and in her female condition. I do not want to go over this, just to touch upon one aspect of this reality which I think fundamental to the women's liberation movement today. This is women's collective power, a power which is beginning to be recognized and used in various popular organizations in a special way by women themselves. This is a sign of the times!

What is this power? It takes many historical forms and no doubt there is both positive and negative mixed in it. That is human life. Any action, expression or feeling is always a mixture of positive and negative.

All human striving contains these two forms of energy, which are indispensable to the evolution of nature and history. I will try to describe
this power in its positive aspect, merely pointing out that this side will
never be found in its pure state, as if it had been chemically isolated in
a laboratory.

First and foremost, this power is *resistance*. For the last twenty years
in Latin America women's resistance has taken the form of defending life
and refusing to submit to social and political forces organized for death.
Women have broken out of the purely domestic sphere and engaged in
demonstrations against dictatorial regimes, all kinds of authoritarianism, all kinds of sexual and racial discrimination, raising of food prices
and for other social struggles. They have realized that the struggle for
their own and their children's lives also takes place outside the four
walls of home. Women shout and march in the streets demanding freedom for political prisoners, respect and justice. Some call it collective
hysteria, others call it lack of judgment. But those who have understood what it means to fight for life with all their strength call it a gift
of the Spirit.

In poor districts of Latin American cities women resist in order to survive. In order to survive you have to find the means each day, get food for
the children, particularly if there is no man to help support the household. Women resist in the country to have land for planting, living and
struggling for justice with many other comrades.

Resistance is also expressed in collective ways of working at various
crafts, sharing responsibility for production and selling and also sharing
the profits. This becomes more than a work initiative because these small
organizations become cells for personal and communal change. Within
these cells women dare to talk about themselves, about social and political organizations or disorganization. They have the freedom to reflect,
agree or disagree and then their consciousness, lulled by the clatter of
plates and pans, begins to awaken. It finds words and feels the urge to
reorganize this world differently.

Thus this power becomes *creativity*. Of course we could say that resistance and creativity are not confined to women's power. Perhaps I need
to say more about these terms to make the sense in which I am using
them clearer. I am talking about a form of resistance and creativity which
is expressed in a special way among women. They are trying to express
the changes in human relationships which have come about recently and
which can be considered as unique in history as they have occurred at
the end of the twentieth century. In this sense when I speak of creativity
I mean women's new place in our societies. I am not therefore saying this
is the only way in which the word can be used, but I am using it with a
special reference to particular events and experiences.

By their conversion to themselves, to others and to history, women have become able:

- by their way of behaving to help change patriarchal attitudes in force among us. They are still there but consciousness of change is becoming stronger and stronger;
- to challenge the status of "destiny" accorded to the hierarchically organized family with the man at the top;
- to begin living more equally with men and even change certain aspects of the masculine role. They have become aware of the value of housework, never previously recognized as work, and have fought for it to be given proper recognition and status.

This creativity is a way of re-creating the world at various levels, to the extent that we can now talking about a "before" and "after" the awakening of the historical consciousness of Latin American women.

Finally, women's power is *freedom*. It seems pointless here to discuss the different meanings of the word freedom. I am using it here in an almost symbolic sense, beyond conceptual difficulties. I am taking about a breath of fresh air blowing through our whole being enabling us to live differently. I am going to limit my use of the term freedom to the religious sphere because we have used the term creativity with a wider scope.

Talking about women's freedom, especially poor women in Latin America, means talking about God differently. It goes beyond the mere concept, although this is often a useful tool.

By a significant number of women God is no longer seen in the image of a man, father, husband or son, but as Spirit, breath of life, energy refusing to be locked in a box. The women's liberation movement is a movement of theological creativity and freedom, that is, a search for God, for the fulfillment of divine signs, recognition of a miraculous presence in women's lives. A woman worker trying to share with her friends what God meant to her said: "It's like a force preventing me giving in to the wickedness of the capitalist system. It is a life in me which reminds me of the spirit that was in Jesus driving him to struggle against evil." This is a living theology learned from everyday life, woven from the experience of one woman and many others, who today in the various base communities and popular movements or elsewhere have the courage to speak of God in their own way, without being afraid they are getting him wrong, because they are convinced that the God of Jesus, the God of Mary, is more than an idea, theory or law.

The power called freedom for many women is like being pregnant with the Spirit. Their vision of God derived from their own lives goes way beyond the one imposed by our macho culture. God is, he is in us and we live with him in all the originality of our female being, our history, questions and limits. He is the power, the energy driving us towards ourselves and towards others to seek for something new, something greater than ourselves, but which will come upon this finite earth.

Option for a New Future of Justice and Love

Although my third point is made separately, it is contained within both the first and second points. Love of self and love of others create a new present and a new future.

If we look at the whole history of the poor in Latin America, particularly over recent years, we may well ask, why speak of a new future, when for most countries the number of poor people has increased, the distressed and needy have multiplied, injustice of every sort is eaten and drunk by the poor with their daily bread and water. How can we sing of our hope for justice, our longing for love in exile from our self and our country? We have more reasons to weep than to laugh for joy! Nevertheless we hope for a new future and this hope is the breath of life to us. It gives our lives direction, meaning and weight. The desire for a better world, a new world, another world is part of being human. This desire is an unquenchable thirst. The women of Latin America are fundamentally concerned with this thirst.

By their resistance in various popular movements they have shown their capacity to love life and to keep hoping in spite of suffering and poverty. They have managed to live lives of sharing and solidarity among themselves and with others, however scanty their resources. They have spread warmth and tenderness to counter the institutionalized violence of our societies.

At the level of a theology which is not systematically expressed, these are the "signs of the Kingdom," signs telling us we must go on hoping in spite of the temptation to despair. On the whole people representing religious power find it difficult to accept these signs. They are not codified, they escape ecclesiastical control, which insists that everything must be in accordance with the rubrics to be in accordance with God. The representatives of religious power feel sure they know God's will for men and especially for women. But God's love cannot be confined. It is found in unexpected places. He shuddered in Mary's heart making the babe leap in Elizabeth's womb. He made Mary Magdalene cry and filled her with joy and tenderness. His love takes hold of a woman's whole being and is expressed in many ways.

Similar things happen today among Latin American women. They experience quite a few "visitations" of love in the course of the year, quite a few annunciations of the signs of justice in their daily struggle for life and their rights. All this is a sort of *theopraxis*, encounter with God in life, experience of God in the events that go to make up daily living.

This love surpasses the law of any doctrinal systemization. It simply appears in the experience of living. It is there, often nameless, mixed up with all sorts of behaviors like yeast in dough. When the dough is ready, you cannot take out the yeast and put it back in a box. This is what God's love is like among women.

If hope is vital for human beings, it is not something that exists in advance ready-made. It has to be sought, nourished, shared, supported, made actual through signs in order to remain true and strong.

Women are the nightwatchers of hope, waiting for the dawn. They are certain that when night is over the bright sun will shine and that even in the middle of the night there are often twinkling stars.

Translated by Dinah Livingstone

16

Paternalistic Religion

DOROTHEE SÖLLE

One of the names with which the Jewish-Christian religion refers to God is "Father." This symbolic attribute obviously has practical implications for people today. What are these implications? I am not concerned here with the way this symbolic representation originated in history, nor with its original meaning. I want to look at how it operated in history, and what happened once it was established.

The editors of this issue, two gentlemen who thank eleven other gentlemen for their "valuable suggestions and indications," came out with some composite terminology which can only be translated into English by "Father-God" or "God as Father" *(Vatergott)* and a "Culture of Obedience" *(Gehorsamskultur).* Both these expressions annoy me intensely, and my objections can be formulated in three questions:

1. Did this obedience only create and determine a "culture" — or did it simply lead to a barbaric situation?

2. Can the word "father" still mean "God" when we have learned that God and liberation are mutually inclusive concepts?

3. Which exactly are the elements in the fatherhood symbolism we cannot do without?

The answers to these questions cannot ignore history and subjective experience.

Personally, I can see them only as a German, a woman, and as somebody who tries to be a Christian at the end of the twentieth century. As such I refuse to deny my national, sexual and socio-economic identity.

This reaction springs from the fact that theological jargon does indeed distinguish the God of philosophy from the God of Abraham, Isaac and Jacob but then has nothing to say about the God of Sarah, Rebecca and Rachel. The "fathers of the faith" are reflected in the idea of the "Father in heaven," but the "mothers of the faith" are left in a limbo of obscurity: they are somehow "prehistoric," unremembered, forgotten, in fact, repressed. This repression not only affects the 51 percent of mankind who, as a result, never found their theological voice. It also has had a catastrophic effect on the theologians who are part of the other 49 percent, particularly in the way they express themselves.

The ignoring of the female component of the soul, the running down of everything that has a feminine flavor about it, has done more damage to the way theologians speak and write than any assault from the secular world. This purging and impoverishing process has led to the repression of the emphatic "wholeness," "awareness" and "integration" which marked the language of the gospel.

What is called scientific theology is usually conveyed in a language devoid of a sense of awareness. It is unaware of the emotions, insensitive to what people experience. It has no interest and no appeal; it has a dull flatness because it leaves no room for doubt, that shadow of the faith. One has only to read the male theologians' commentaries on Eve's conversation with the serpent in paradise which make it appear as if any intellectual and sexual curiosity is something of the devil. Who would bother to have a conversation with that kind of serpent?

Any theology that wants to communicate with real people must, however, use a language that shows awareness, brings them and their problems into the dialogue, and is forceful. This grows from practical experience and leads to a change in being and behavior.

At present the current language of scientific theology only very rarely achieves this quality of being truly alive. When it manages this at all, it does so in a roundabout way, in opposition to the academic establishment which pursues the male-inspired ideals of neutralism, of being above party-line and emotions, and whose energy is aimed at making the problem go away. The student is trained in how not to say "I" when speaking scientifically. It reveals already a certain subversive talent when theologians (unfortunately mainly white men) rediscover a way of dealing with their subject which shows awareness, is emotionally rich and understands the individual.

I

The deepest difficulty I have with a culture based on obedience is linked with my national identity.

The history of the people I belong to has been slanted by a key event which occurred in this century. This event twisted language, words, ideas and images precisely because it was central, a "key" event. Because of this, words and ideas have acquired an irrevocably different meaning. Because of this these words and ideas have lost their original innocence. As one concerned with communication who has faced life after that event I neither can nor want to forget this fact. This means I cannot overlook the fact that a given poem uses words which embody their own historical development. Thus star, smoke and hair still meant something different in German even as late as 1942 from what they came to mean after the greatest crimes and calamity in the history of my people.

My first serious doubt about a "Christian culture of obedience" is whether obedience is not precisely one of those ideas which are no longer valid after the holocaust.[1] The question how deeply the conditioning of the Christian mind to an attitude of total obedience prepared the ground for Nazism is a matter for historians. For theologians the fact that Eichmann, who was enrolled in the German YMCA by his parents, constantly stressed obedience, as did Rudolf Hosz, whose father destined him for the priesthood, should be enough to rob this concept of all its theological innocence. Nor does it help to make a distinction between the "true" or "proper" obedience to *God* and obedience to *man*. Can one want and develop an attitude towards God which one criticizes in people in their attitude towards men and institutions?

Should obedience necessarily lead to a barbaric situation? This question is much wider than its mere connection with historical Nazism. Today "obedience" is seen in terms not of charismatic leaders but of the "market forces" of the economy, the use of energy and growing militarization. It is true that the technocrats have long ago taken over the inheritance of the priests. But even in the new situation where obedience is preferably spoken of in terms of "the rules of the game," the structural elements of authoritarian religion persist and the remaining traces of religious education prepare the increasingly a-religious masses for an obedience from which all personal features, based on trust and sacrifice have vanished.

This new computerized obedience has three structural elements in common with the old religious obedience:

a. acceptance of a superior power which controls our destiny and excludes responsibility for our own fate;

b. subjection to the rules of this power which needs no moral legitimation, say, in love or justice;

c. a deep-rooted pessimism where man is concerned: the human being, incapable of death and love, is a powerless and meaningless creature whose obedience feeds precisely on the denial of its own innate potential

The main virtue of an authoritarian religion is obedience and self-abrogation is the center of gravity, in contrast with a humanitarian religion, where the chief virtue is self-realization and resistance to growth is the cardinal sin.[2]

From the point of view of social history such an authoritarian concept of religion affirms society and has a stabilizing influence on its prevailing tendencies. In such a context authoritarian religion discourages any willingness to aim at great emancipation and a critical attempt to rise above the established realities, also — and particularly — when these trends base their arguments on religious grounds: God's love and righteousness are less important than his power.

Authoritarian religion leads to that infantile clinging to consolation which we can observe in the sentimentality of religious art and the history of devotionalism. But this goes together with a compulsive need for order, a fear of confusion and chaos, a desire for clarity and control. And when religion is dying out it is precisely this rigidity which survives; it is the authoritarian bonds which mostly persist in a life that is understood as dominated by technocracy. The Milgram experiment showed that a vast majority of the ordinary people included in the research were quite prepared, under scientific direction, to torture innocent fellow humans with electric current, which is precisely what happens in a "culture" of obedience. Obedience operates in the barbaric ethos of fascism, Nazism or technocracy.

II

The late Erich Fromm distinguished between humanitarian forms of religion and authoritarian ones. The historical Jesus, early Buddhism and the mystics of most religions display the kind of religion which is not repressive, not based on one-sided and asymmetric dependence but operates with a force which springs from the inner life. It is precisely here that one begins to question the social-psychological implications of the father-symbol.

Why do people worship a God whose supreme quality is power, whose interest lies in subjection and who fears equality?

Theologians, accepting such a being, to be addressed as "Lord" and not content with just power, are bound to ascribe omnipotence to it.

The main objections of a developing feminist theology to the existing kind of theology are directed against phallocratic fantasies and the worship of power. Why should we worship and love a being which not only fails to rise above the moral level of past, male-dominated culture but even turns it into an establishment?

May I put this in terms of my own theological development? My objections to the divine "super-power" began to make themselves felt when I was in Auschwitz. I published my first book, called *Ein Kapitel Theologie nach dem Tode Gottes (A Chapter of Theology after the Death of God)* in 1965. There I followed Bonhoeffer, and was radical and christocentric. God himself, whether acting or speaking, cannot be experienced by man. So we should cling to the non-dominant, powerless Christ who has nothing to persuade and to save us but his love. His very powerlessness constitutes an inner-personal authority; not because he begot, created or made us are we his, but simply because his only power is love, and this love, without any weapons, is stronger than death itself.

My difficulties about God as Father, begetter, ruler and the manager of history grew as I began to understand more clearly what it means to be born a woman, and therefore "incomplete," and so to have to live in a patriarchal society. How could I want power to be the dominant characteristic of my life? And how could I worship a God who was only a male?

Male power, for me, is something to do with roaring, shooting and giving orders. I do not think this patriarchal culture has done me any more damage than other women. It only became constantly more obvious to me that any identification with the aggressor, the ruler, the violator, is the worst thing that can happen to a woman.

Moreover, the father-symbol cannot have the same fascination for those who will never be a "father." Even power replaced by mercy, or the kind and gentle father, does not solve the problem. A kind slave-owner may well be loved and respected by his slaves.

Yet, feminine piety is and will be a kind of "Uncle Tom" piety. But when women are subjected to functions and an obedience which have been laid down by males with regard to a God who is assumed to have fixed all this in "nature," then women's potential is destroyed and they will never achieve the full status of human persons. No "father" can liberate us, women, from the history of my people and the sexism of today's culture. So: can the father-symbol still adequately represent what we mean by "God?"

When one understands that anything we say about God is bound to be symbolic, then any symbol which presumes to cover the absolute must be relativized. God does indeed transcend our speech but only if we do not lock him up in our human symbols.

I quite agree that "father" is one way in which we can talk about God but when this way is forced upon us as the exclusive way, then we confine God in the prison of this symbol.

Because of this sort of enforced language all other symbolic expressions which people have used to convey their experience of God are repressed or at least considered as of lesser value. It is true that Paul VI attracted widespread attention when he once said that God was at least as much "mother" as "father." But in religious practice we are still far from having achieved this relativization of symbolic speech. When once we began a service in the church of St. Catherine in Hamburg with "In the name of the Father and the Mother, the Son and the Spirit," there was a fierce argument whether this kind of language should be allowed. Changing the sacred language of the liturgy is one way of escaping from prison and so is seen as a threat. Four women together pronounced the blessing: "May God bless you and watch over you. May She let the light of her countenance shine upon you, and may She grant you peace."

This shows the way in which everywhere women, aware of their situation, are groping for a solution. This wish for another way of presenting God, for other symbols and expectations, is important for those who feel themselves offended, humiliated and disgusted by the culture in which we live. It is not the male who is the first victim of the sexism which has molded the language of theology.

The relativization of such an absolutized symbol as "father" is the least we can ask for. Other symbols can be used for God. We can address God as "mother" or "sister," if we want to confine ourselves to family terminology. But it seems to me that symbols taken from nature are in any case much clearer because they are innocent of any authoritarian implication.

Theological language could get rid of the streak of domination if it looked at the language of the mystics.

"Source of all that is good," "life-giving wind," "water of life," "light" are all symbols of God which do not imply power or authority and do not smack of any chauvinism. There is no room for "supreme power," domination, or the denial of one's own validity in the mystical tradition. It often explicitly criticizes the lord-servant relationship and it has been superseded particularly by the mystics' inventive use of language.

In this tradition religion means the experience of being one with the whole, of belonging together, but never of subjection. In this perspective people do not worship God because of his power and domination. They rather want to "drown" themselves in his love which is the "ground" of their existence. There is a preference for symbols like "depth," "sea," and those referring to motherhood and to nature at large. Here our relationship to God is not one of obedience but of union; it is not a matter of a distant God exacting sacrifice and self-denial, but rather a matter of agreement and consent, of being at one with what is alive. And this then becomes what religion is about. When this happens solidarity will replace obedience as the dominant virtue.

III

Are there any elements in this father symbolism applied to God which a liberating theology cannot do without? Is a personalist terminology here preferable to other possible symbols? Do we need to explain the relationship between God and man through this father symbol?

In a patriarchal culture the father represents the dependence of the individual. It is rooted in the biological fact that the young of the human species are begotten and need care and protection for a long time. But does our protracted childhood justify a religious language which is essentially based on the parent-child relationship? And is the underrating of the mother in this relationship, as if it is only the father who provides the original begetting and survival, not an additional emphasis on the authoritarian element in this relationship? In Judaism the father-image is based on his function as head of the family, with definite legal, religious, pedagogical and economic power.

The father is judge, priest, teacher and controls the means of production.

Whoever lives in this culture and addresses God as father has personally experienced these various ways of being dependent, and for a woman this experience is still much more acute. Only gentleness and compassion, the other feature of the father symbol can make this dependency tolerable.

This linking of absolute authority with mercy is the main characteristic of God as father. Everywhere paternal kindness and judicial power constitute the two poles which determine the father-image. But when the accumulation of power based on this combination of biology with sociology is collapsing and rapidly becoming a thing of the past, does this not also deprive any religious exaggeration of these functions of any rational foundation? Is there then something in the father-image we cannot do without?

It seems to me that at the core of all feminist philosophy or theology there lies this matter of "dependency." Do we need a liberating concept, a central value, which women themselves should discover? Or are there ways of being dependent which simply cannot be ignored? Is it a good thing to make oneself emotionally independent, or would this only lead us to the position of the male with his superficial ties who would not dare attack the ideologized independence of the male heroes? What does it mean anthropologically to be dependent? What does it mean in social life? The area covered by this inter-feminist debate is also the area where decisions have to be made in theology. Is this dependency only a repressive inheritance from the past or is it part of the simple fact that we are "created"?

We have not made or planned ourselves nor have we chosen our own place in history or geography. Our whole life is inserted between a "before" and an "after"; we are essentially integrated in this process, and we can only tear ourselves out of the implied relationships at our own peril. Ontologically we are not and never are alone. There is a "one world" which we have to believe in; there is a universal "wholeness" and a universal purpose.

Is it not possible that addressing God as father expresses precisely this interdependence? One of the texts by Simon Dach (1605–59) set to music by Johann Sebastian Bach runs as follows:

> Though master, only through thy power,
> Brought to the light by thee,
> Through thee my life is still in flower,
> My years and months through thee to be.
> Thou knowest when I have to leave
> This vale of tears. And where,
> Or when my life will end.
> Thou, Father, knowest: Thou art there. (Freely translated)

Here the "power" of the Lord, called "Father" in the last line, accurately shows that it refers to the power to beget, create, sustain, and in the end, terminate life. We have no control over either our birth or our death. So, to address God as father means that life and death are not left to the contingencies of our existence. To see the world as creation means to see it as well willed, planned, and "good." If speaking of God as father helps us not simply to face our transiency as something to overcome, but to affirm our dependency and to accept our finite and creaturely condition, then there is no reason why we should not do so. Symbols taken from family life can be liberating if they interpret our dependence theologically as expressing our trust in father and mother.

Symbols for God, taken from family life and speaking of God our father and God our mother can be liberating, not because they cushion the inimical and oppressive features of patriarchism but because they integrate us with nature and the human family. Then calling God "father" is no longer a matter of sociological exploitation, of fixing people in predetermined social roles and endorsing a false dependency; it will no longer be used to turn childlikeness into infantilism. It will rather enable us to have confidence in that life which transcends our own lifetime. It will never even lead us to trust Brother Death.

Translated by T. L. Westow

NOTES

1. For what follows, see my critique of the Christian ideology of obedience (first published in 1968) in D. Sölle, *Phantasie und Gehorsam: Überlegungen zu einer künftigen christlichen Ethik,* 8th ed., Stuttgart, 1978 (English translation *Beyond mere Obedience*).

2. Fromm made his basic distinction between humanitarian and authoritarian religion in his *Psychoanalysis and Religion,* New Haven, 1950.

PART III

THE THEOLOGICAL CONSTRUCTION OF WOMEN'S SILENCE

17

Breaking the Silence —
Becoming Visible

ELISABETH SCHÜSSLER FIORENZA

Women are not only the "silent majority" but we are also the "silenced majority" in the Roman Catholic Church. Throughout the centuries and still today the authority of the apostle Paul has been invoked against women's preaching and teaching in the Church: "The women should keep silence in the churches. For they are not permitted to speak but should be subordinate..." (1 Cor. 14:34) and "Let a woman learn in silence with all submissiveness. I permit no woman to teach or to have authority over men; she is to keep silent. For Adam was formed first and then Eve; and Adam was not deceived but the woman was deceived and became a transgressor" (1 Tim. 2:11–14 RSV).

To quote these well-worn biblical phrases again might be for some readers like pouring water into the Tiber or the Charles River. Yet women's theological silence in the Church is still reinforced. As recently as last May during the visit of Pope John Paul II in the Netherlands Professor Catharina Halkes, the leading Roman Catholic feminist theologian in Europe, was forbidden to address the pontiff. Although women can study theology, we only rarely become professors at influential theological schools and faculties. We are excluded from preaching and articulating Church policy or doctrine because we are not admitted to the episcopacy or the college of cardinals. No feminist theologian speaks with official "teaching authority," no one of us belongs to an international or papal theological commission, no one serves as "perita" of a bishop or an episcopal Synod, and only very few — if any — of us are acknowledged as "theological authorities" in our own right. Theological textbooks and discussions, theological debates and controversies, and even liberation or political theologians ignore out theological work.[1]

This deliberate or unconscious silencing of women in the Church engenders our ecclesial and theological invisibility. Although women are the majority of people still going to church and of those joining religious orders, the Church is officially represented by males only. Although the Church is called "our mother" and referred to with the pronoun "she," it is personified and governed by fathers and brothers only. Therefore, whenever we speak of the Church we see before our eyes the pope in Rome, bishops or pastors, cardinals and monsignors, deacons and altar boys, all of whom are men. Eucharistic con-celebrations, televised bishops' conferences, the laying on of hands in the ordination rite are manifestations of the Church as an "old boys' club." No wonder that many Christians believe that God is a male patriarch and that the male sex of Jesus Christ is salvific.

Women *as Church* are invisible neither by accident nor by our own default but by patriarchal law that excludes us from Church office on the basis of sex. (Such discrimination on the basis of sex is generally acknowledged today as sexism.) The present policy and official theology of the Roman hierarchy still enforces the New Testament injunction "women should be silent in all the churches" and seeks to legitimate such policy theologically. The Vatican statement against the ordination of women argues that women do not have a "natural resemblance" to the maleness of Christ.[2] This argument, however, implies either that women cannot be baptized because in baptism Christians become members of the (male) body of Christ or that we do not remain women because those baptized have been conformed to the "perfect male." In any case, such a theology denies the universality of incarnation and salvation in order to maintain and legitimate the patriarchal structures of the Church.

Feminist theology seeks to unmask the oppressive function of such a patriarchal theology. It explores women's experience of oppression and discrimination in society and religion as well as our experiences of hope, love and faith in the struggle for liberation and wholeness. As a critical theology of liberation[3] it articulates as its core problem how androcentric language, theoretical frameworks, and theological scholarship function to sustain and perpetrate patriarchal structures in society and Church. In short my thesis is: *the silence and invisibility of women is generated by the patriarchal structure of the Church and maintained by androcentric, i.e., male-defined theology.* Since patriarchy is often used interchangeably with sexism and androcentrism, it becomes necessary to clarify here first the way in which I use these terms as basic analytic categories. Androcentrism or androcentric dualism is a world construction in language, mindset, or ideology that legitimizes patriarchy, whereas sexism, racism, and classism are structural components of a patriarchal societal system of domination and exploitation.

Societal and Ecclesiastical Patriarchy

An understanding of patriarchy solely in terms of male supremacy and misogynist sexism is not able to articulate the interaction of racism, classism, and sexism in Western militarist societies. Therefore, I suggest that we do not understand patriarchy in the general sense as a social system in which *all* men have power over *all* women but in the classical sense as it was defined in Aristotelian philosophy.[4] Aristotelian political philosophy was concerned with the relationship between rulers and ruled in household and State. Aristotle did not define patriarchy simply as the rule of men over women but as a graded male status system of domination and subordination, authority and obedience, rulers and subjects in household and State. Wives and children, slaves and property were owned and at the disposal of the freeborn Greek male head of the household. He was the full citizen and determined public life. The patriarchal relationships in household and State according to Aristotle are based not on social convention but on "nature." He therefore insisted that the discussions of political ethics and household management begin with marriage which he defined as "the union of natural ruler and natural subject." Slaves and freeborn women, Aristotle argued, are not "fit to rule" because of their "natures" which he in turn had defined according to their socioeconomic functions.

The classics scholar Marilyn Arthur[5] has elaborated that the articulation of the polarity between the sexes and of the difference in the male and female nature is not explicit in the writings of the Greek aristocratic period but only emerges with the introduction of Athenian democracy. While in aristocratic society family status more than gender roles defines the situation of women, in Athenian democracy the political and legal structures of the State prescribe women's subservience and exclude freeborn women from citizenship. Thus explicit articulation of the specific "natures" of the subordinate members of the household is occasioned by the contradiction between the social-political structures of Athenian democracy restricting full citizenship to free propertied male heads of households on the one hand and the democratic ideal of human dignity and freedom articulated in the middle-class democracy of the city-state on the other hand.

In other words, a philosophical justification of sociopatriarchal roles as based on distinctive human "natures" of slaves and freeborn women is necessitated by a socio-political situation where the equality and dignity of *all* humans is articulated but their actual participation in political and social self-determination is prohibited because they remain the economic and sexual property of freeborn male heads of the households. Androcentric legitimizations become necessary whenever a different social or religious order becomes possible.

Feminist political philosophers[6] have shown that the same contradiction between democratic ideals and social-patriarchal, political-legal structures characterizes modern Western society. Aristotelian patriarchal philosophy also undergirds Western democratic society and legal-political philosophy. Although the patriarchal family has been modified in the course of history, the split between the private and public spheres has been intensified through industrialization. Capitalism has not replaced patriarchy but modified and reinforced it.[7] In short, misogynist sexism, racist classism, and expansionist colonialism are ideologies that legitimate and perpetrate patriarchal inequalities and oppressions grounded in different human natures.

Moreover, the patriarchal separation between the public male sphere and the private female domain generates a separate system of economics for women[8] in Western societies. The women's society of economics is based on the assumption that every family consists of the ideal father earning the living for the family. It is justified by the assumption that all women are either temporary workers or work for pin-money because they will get married and become pregnant. Lower wages and lower level positions for women are justified because women's wages are presumed to be supplementary. Since it is believed that housework and child care are women's "natural" vocation they need not be remunerated or counted in the gross-national product. The result of this separate system of economics for women is the increasing feminization of poverty and the destitution of female headed households.

Finally, this separate economic system for women sustains female "sexual slavery"[9] that cuts across all lines of race, class, and culture. Whereas patriarchal racism defines certain people as sub-human in order to exploit their labor, patriarchal sexism seeks to control women's procreative powers and labor. Violence against women and children is increasing at a time when women claim the full human rights and dignity accorded to male citizens. The political Right's attack on feminism,[10] its battle for the re-criminalization of women and their doctors, and its rhetoric for the "protection of the Christian family" seek to reinforce women's economic dependency, to strengthen the patriarchal controls of women's procreative powers, and to maintain the patriarchal family as the mainstay of the patriarchal State. Sexual violence against women and children in and outside the home sustains the patriarchal order of the male dominance.

> Anonymous verbal and bodily assault: rape — rape in general, racial rape, marital rape, wartime rape, gang rape, wife and women bat-

tering; abortion and birth control laws; involuntary sterilizations; unnecessary hysterectomies; clitoridectomies and genital mutilations; prostitution and female slavery; sexual harassment in employment; aggressive pornography.[11]

All these and more are forms of sanctioned violence against women. While sociobiologists view rape as a natural, biological tendency in males, as a *biological* imperative, feminist studies have documented that rape and other forms of institutionalized violence against women are a *social* imperative necessary to uphold patriarchy through force.

The basic contradiction between the claim to full equality of all citizens and their subordinate position in patriarchal structures that defines Athenian and modern Western democracy also characterizes Christianity. Such a contradiction between the call to the discipline of equals and patriarchal ecclesial structures was introduced towards the end of the first century in the process of ecclesial adaptation of Greco-Roman society and culture. The so-called household code texts of the later New Testament writings that require the subordination of women, slaves, and all Christians to the patriarchal Greco-Roman order have codified the Aristotelian political ethos of submission and domination as Holy Scripture.[12]

Theologians such as Augustine and Thomas Aquinas have incorporated the Aristotelian construct of the inferior human "natures" of slaves and freeborn women into the basic fabric of Christian theology. This Aristotelian Christian theology has provided religious legitimizations of racism, colonialism, classism and hetero/sexism in society and Church. It interacts with androcentric linguistic and ideological systems of legitimization that sustain and contribute to the double invisibility and multifaceted exploitation of third world women oppressed by patriarchal racism, poverty, colonialism and hetero/sexism.

Insofar as in the long run the patriarchal organization and ethos of the Roman empire has also defined the self-understanding and structures of the Christian community, the Church has often become more Roman than Christian in its institutional structures and policies. Within this patriarchal model of Church we find two distinct hierarchical sub-systems, that of men and that of women. The patriarchal male system rests on the clerical obedience and subordination as well as clerical celibacy, i.e., a life without women. The female system is built on economic dependency and male control of women in marriage or canonical communities. In this model of Church the reality of the Church is coextensive with that of the male hierarchy. It is patriarchal in its structures because one ordained male — usually older — stands on top of the pyramid and has jurisdiction, i.e., ruling power over younger male clergy as well as over the laity.

This model of Church sustains communal life by control from the top to the bottom. Obedience to the pope, the bishop, the pastor, the superior, or the husband are the required responses from those who are the "subordinates."

The Church understood as clerical-patriarchal hierarchy is not only exclusive of women in leadership but also establishes its boundaries through sexual control. It does not center Church around the strength and needs of its members or of humanity as a whole but around institutional patriarchal interests.[13] Religious obedience, economic dependence, and sexual control are the sustaining forces of ecclesiastical patriarchy. The Protestant Reformation has not changed this patriarchal-clerical model of Church but only modified it insofar as it replaced celibacy through the clerical patriarchal family. If we have understood the interaction of societal and religious patriarchy in Western societies we will see that the struggle against it is at the heart of all liberation struggles against racism, colonialism, militarism, poverty and vice-versa.

Feminist theology does not just reflect on this struggle against patriarchy but it is an integral element in it. As we have seen, androcentric legitimizations of patriarchal domination and victimization become more pronounced and forceful whenever claims to equality and self-determination gain public recognition and broad acceptance. Feminist thought is labelled extremist, subversive, irrational, or abnormal because it seeks to put forward an alternative to patriarchy as the basis of Euro-American society or Church. It demystifies and rejects cultural or religious values of male domination and subordination which are the very standard of reasonableness, veracity, and knowledge. Therefore, liberal theologians and churchmen who are "for" the ordination of women are often opposed to "feminist theology" that places women's liberation at the center of its thought. They label "feminist theology" as "so-called theology" which is at best trivial and incompetent and at worst man-hating propaganda and unfeminine revolt. Instead they advocate a "theology of woman" or of "femininity." Therefore they are quick to play out the token woman theologian — the "good woman" who respects male scholarship and expertise against the female theologian — the "bad woman" who radically questions them. If women are admitted to the clergy they are ordained as long as they promise to shore up the patriarchal structures of the Church and to perpetuate its androcentric theology and symbol system. Liberal churches and theologians are willing to allow women to become visible in the Church and to let us preach and teach as long as we are prepared to represent the patriarchal Church and its androcentric theology and liturgy.

Because we have learned from the experienced ordained women in other Christian churches and from our own experience in theology and ministry the Roman Catholic Women's Ordination movement in the USA has always insisted that the incorporation of some token woman into the patriarchal hierarchy does not suffice. Roman Catholic women daily experience anger and pain because our Church is deformed by the structural and personal sin of patriarchal sexism. Yet the ordination of some women to the lower ranks of the patriarchal hierarchy would not eliminate the evil of patriarchal sexism but just conceal its destructive powers. We have come to understand that the "woman question" facing the Church is not just a question of ordination but that it requires *an intellectual paradigm shift from an androcentric world-view and theology to a feminist conceptualization of the world, human life, and Christian religion.*

Feminist Theory and Androcentric Ideology

If societal and ecclesiastical patriarchy generate misogynist legitimization and androcentric knowledge of reality then political struggle for women's rights and not feminist theory seems to be called for. Therefore the women's movement of the early seventies in this country often eschewed theory and scholarship as a male "headtrip" that co-opts women for its patriarchal ends. Many women found academic scholarship, argumentative reasoning, and abstract thought very much removed from their daily experience. Especially women students experienced that intellectual education alienated them from their own questions and institutions.

This has been true also for women in religion and in theology. Since most of us still cannot study with feminist professors, rarely find feminist works on the required reading lists for courses, and often have our questions declared as "non questions," women in theological schools have been rightly suspicious of academic education and theological systems. Yet such a healthy suspicion of androcentric scholarship easily can turn into anti-intellectualism that unwittingly serves the patriarchal interests in excluding women from defining the issues. I remember at one of the earliest conferences of women ministers and scholars in religion in 1972 it was seen as elitism when I called myself a theologian since we all were doing theology. However, no one had any problem with the title "minister" or "reverend" that introduced clerical distinctions among us. While access to the ordained ministry was considered a feminist achievement, access to theology seemed a male-defined aberration.

In the meanwhile we have recognized that knowledge *is* power and that androcentric language and patriarchal ideology produce meaning for the sake of domination. Therefore, the alternative *either* societal-ecclesial struggle against patriarchy *or* critical analysis and change of androcentric language and scholarship is a false alternative. Women's invisibility in the intellectual interpretations of the world and our forced silence in academy and Church are in the interest of patriarchy. That we are excluded from defining the world and the meaning of human life and society is an integral part of our oppression. To break the silence and to reclaim the "power of the naming that was stolen from us" (Mary Daly) must therefore become an integral element in our struggle for liberation from patriarchal structures.

Feminist scholarship unveils the patriarchal functions of the intellectual and scientific frameworks generated and perpetrated by male-centered scholarship that makes women invisible or peripheral in what we know about the world, human life, and cultural or religious history. Placing women's experience and subjectivity at the center of intellectual inquiry has challenged the theoretical frameworks of all academic disciplines. In all areas of scholarship feminist studies are in the process of inaugurating a scientific revolution or paradigm-shift from an androcentric — male-centered — world-view and intellectual framework of discourse to a feminist comprehension of the world, human culture, and history.[14]

While androcentric scholarship defines woman as the "other" of man or of male God and reduces us to "objects" of male scholarship, feminist studies insist on the reconceptualization of our language as well as of our intellectual frameworks in such a way that women as well as men can become the *subjects* of human culture and scholarly discourse. A feminist critical analysis of the ideological function of androcentric language and scientific knowledge not only challenges the claims of male scholarship to universality but also highlights its patriarchal bias. Far from being objective and descriptive, androcentric texts and knowledge maintain the silence and invisibility of women engendered by a patriarchal society and Church. Women's invisibility in androcentric culture and our concealed oppression in Western language, religious symbol systems, historical records, and scientific theories has therefore been the core problem and focal point of feminist studies.

The basic liberating insight of feminism has been that the personal *is* political, that our personal questions are not just our private problems. Simone de Beauvoir's insight that "women are made not born" has stimulated much feminist research on the social construction of sex and gender as well as on the socialization of children into acceptance of their cultural masculine and feminine roles. When my daughter Chris was in the so-called questioning stage, she would ask constantly: Why can only men be presidents; why are all the priests men; why do women earn less than men; why does God have only sons and not daughters; why are women against equal rights for women; why can't boys wear dresses; why were all the great figures in history men; why does the teacher always say "boys and girls" and not "girls and boys"; why is God he; why don't women keep their own names when they get married; why does Jessica's mother do all the housework; why do not all children have enough to eat; why do women wear makeup and not men; why, why???

These questions express women's basic experience of inferiority and "otherness" in a patriarchal society and religion. It is the experience that the "world" does not make sense. It is the experience that we are "out of place," that we do not matter and that we have no power to define and change the world in such a way that it corresponds to our experience of self-worth and to our image of how the world should be. This basic experience of women in patriarchal society and Church, however, is silenced through socialization and education into patriarchal language and value systems. Therefore, girls internalize that their experience of alienation and anger is just our personal problem, that something must be wrong with *us* and that we have to accept and adapt to things *as they are.*

Crucial for such an internalization of "secondary status" is what Casey Miller and Kate Swift have called "semantic roadblocks"[15] and Pierre Bourdieu has termed "symbolic violence."[16] Since language not only reflects the world but also shapes our self-understanding and our understanding of the world the very process of learning to speak socializes us into a world in which male and masculine is the standard of being human. "Those of us who have grown up with a language that tells them they are at the same time men and not men are faced with ambivalence — not about their sex but about their status as human beings."[17] Feminist studies have documented over and over again how much androcentric world-construction in and through language inculcates both the self-affirmation of men and the self-alienation of women.

Insofar as boys and girls learn to express themselves and define the world in grammatically masculine "generic" language that subsumes women under "men" and "he," they learn to understand themselves in terms of patriarchal superordination and subordination, of being in the center or being on the margin. That is why women's oppression is so "common sense" in Western society and culture. Therefore it is so difficult for both women and men to recognize the oppressive character of grammatically masculine language that renders women invisible and marginal. Moreover, such androcentric language makes poor women, women of color, or colonialized women doubly invisible. Insofar as we speak of those who suffer from patriarchal oppression and are disadvantaged in our society as the poor, Blacks, Native Americans, Africans, or Asians and *women* androcentric language makes poor, Black, Native American, African, or Asian women doubly invisible.

Sacred language legitimizes and intensifies women's alienation in an androcentric language structure.[18] For centuries women have had to "listen in" on the theological talks and sermons addressed to men. We have had to think twice in order to know whether we were meant or not with the address "brother," "faith of our fathers," "brotherhood of man," or "sons of God." Take for instance the following statement: "God who has fatherly concern for everyone has willed that all men should constitute one family and treat one another in a spirit of brotherhood. For having been created in the image of God who from one man has created the whole human race...all men are called to one and the same goal, namely to God, Himself."[19] Do women belong to the "family of men" and do we share in the "spirit of brotherhood?" Not only are men or humans "he" but so is also God himself in whose image we are made. Women do not figure in the language about divine reality and in the theological articulation of the "world."

Not only in and through language socialization but also through education and acquisition of knowledge women and men learn to respect men but not women, to internalize the patriarchal values of domination and submission, to adopt the patriarchal interpretation of the world and human life. However, we must not overlook that educated *men* have produced such androcentric interpretation and knowledge, they have defined the world and human life.

> We had believed, I guess, that women and men participate equally in a noble republic of the spirit and that both sexes are equal inheritors of a "thousand years of Western culture." Rereading literature by both women *and men,* however, we learned that, though the pressures and oppressions of gender may be as invisible as air, they are also as inescapable as air, and, like the weight of air, they imperceptibly shape the forms and motions of our lives.... The treasures of Western culture, it began to seem, were the patrimony of male writers, or put in another way, Western culture itself was a grand ancestral property that educated men had inherited from their intellectual forefathers, while their female relatives, like characters in a Jane Austen novel, were regulated to modest dower houses on the edge of the estate.[20]

It is still true what Virginia Woolf observed almost sixty years ago: almost all the books on the shelves of our libraries are written by men, even those on women. In the service of patriarchy educated men — consciously or not — have not allocated to women all the qualities they do not value in themselves. We all know the stereotypes: men are intellectual, assertive, logical, active, strong, born leaders, competent, have authority, etc., while women are emotional, intuitive, receptive, passive, beautiful, compassionate, religious, gossipy, submissive, self-sacrificing, silly, frivolous, etc. While some have feared women as whore, sinner, temptress, snare, devouring mother, others have praised the "eternal feminine" as the only salvation of men.

Women's subordination and powerlessness we are told is either the result of our inferior nature or explained with equal but different feminine qualities which enable us to fulfil our special role in life. Traditional catechesis and theology would answer that sin came into the world through a woman, that patriarchy is willed by God, our Father, and that his Son ordained only men to become his successors and leaders of the Church. In any case women learn early that we are the "secondary sex" and we internalize our own inferiority and invisibility. Self-worth and power can only be derived from men and/or a male God. The masculinity of theological and liturgical God-language is therefore not a cultural or linguistic accident but is an act of domination in and through proclamation and prayer. While androcentric language and intellectual frameworks make patriarchal domination "common sense," masculine God-language in liturgy and theology proclaims it as "ordained by God."

Although women have questioned these explanations and internalizations throughout the centuries, we remain ignorant of our own intellectual traditions and foremothers.[21] All "great" philosophers, scientists, theologians, poets, politicians, artists, and religious leaders seem to have been men who have for centuries been writing and talking to each other in order to define God, the world, human community and existence as "they saw it." However that does not mean that women have not been "great" thinkers and leaders. Yet their thoughts and works have not been transmitted and become classics of our culture and religion because patriarchy requires that in any conceptualization of the world men and their power have to be central. This is why women's thought, culture, history, and religion have so effectively disappeared or have been marginalized and trivialized. Women's words are censured, misrepresented, ridiculed, and eliminated in a male dominated society and then we are blamed because no "great" thinkers, scientists, artists, or theologians have emerged among us.

If we have understood the ideological function of androcentric texts, theological scholarship and ecclesiastical authority in the maintenance of societal and religious patriarchy we must develop a "hermeneutics of suspicion" in order to perceive what is said and what is not said about women's reality under patriarchy and our historical struggles against patriarchal oppression. Although women are neglected in the writing of history and theology, the effects of our lives, thoughts, and struggles are a part of our historical reality and theological meaning that is concealed from us. Just as other feminist scholars so also feminist theologians seek to break the silences, inconsistencies, incoherencies, and ideological mechanisms of androcentric records and scholarship in order to reappropriate the patriarchal past of women.[22] Women have suffered not only the pain and dehumanization of patriarchal oppression but also participated in its social transformation and prophetic critique as well as provided a vision of the Church as an alternative to patriarchy. Making visible our foresisters' struggles and religious experiences of liberation empowers us to affirm the validity of our own religious consciousness, spiritual experience, and historical struggles.[23]

In every generation women have to challenge anew the patriarchal definition of reality, we have so to speak "to re-invent the wheel" over and over again because patriarchy cannot tolerate the conscientization of the oppressed. Feminist theology has shown that our societal oppression and ecclesial exclusion is not women's "fault," it is not the result of Eve's sin nor is it the will of God or the intention of Jesus Christ. Rather it is engendered by societal and ecclesiastical patriarchy and legitimized by androcentric world-construction in language and symbol systems. Insofar as religious language and symbol system function to legitimate the societal oppression and cultural marginality of women, the struggle against ecclesiastical silencing and ecclesial invisibility is at the heart of women's struggle for justice, liberation, and wholeness.

Feminist theology not only reflects on this struggle but also seeks to explore whether religion and Church can provide resources and visions in this struggle in order to account for the hope that lives in and among us.[24] It seeks to make explicit that divine presence and revelation are found among the people of God who are women. Women are Church, and always have been Church, called and elected by God. Throughout the centuries and still today patriarchal Church and androcentric theology have silenced, marginalized, made women invisible, and kept us within theological or ecclesiastical powers because we are women. Nevertheless, women have always heard God's call, mediated God's grace and presence, and have lived Church as the discipleship community of equals.

Therefore, a critical feminist theology of liberation seeks to interrupt the patriarchal silencing of women and to make women visible as God's agents of grace and liberation. It shows that the need to silence women and to make us invisible in male linguistic systems and theological frameworks will no longer exist when the Church transforms its patriarchal structures of superordination that are exclusive of women or can admit us only in marginal and subordinate positions. The full participation of women not only requires the conversion and transformation of the patriarchal Church and its ministry into a discipleship community of equals but also the articulation of a new theology. Since a feminist liberation theology is committed to the struggle of all women against patriarchal oppression in Church and society, it seeks to transform androcentric, i.e., male-defined clerical theology that legitimizes patriarchal oppressions into a theology that promotes and enhances the liberation of the people of God, the majority of whom are women. Matilda Joslyn Gage has aptly articulated this task of feminist theology almost a hundred years ago: "The most important struggle in the history of the Church is that of women for liberty and thought and the right to give that thought to the world."[25]

NOTES

1. See the reflections of Ch. Schaumberger, "Die 'Frauenseite': Heiligkeit statt Hausarbeit," in *Theologisch politische Protokolle*, ed. T. R. Peters, Munich, 1981. On theological education see The Mud Flower Collective, *God's Fierce Whimsy: Christian Feminism and Theological Education*, New York, 1985.

2. "Vatican Declaration: Women in the Ministerial Priesthood," *Origins* 6 (1977), p. 522.

3. For the first articulation of such a theology see my article "Feminist Theology as a Critical Theology of Liberation," in W. Burkhardt, SJ, *Women, New Dimensions*, New York, 1977, pp. 29–50. For a review of the present discussion see Carter I. Heyward, "An Unfinished Symphony of Liberation: The Radicalisation of Christian Feminism among White US Women," *Journal of Feminist Studies in Religion* I (1985), pp. 99–118.

4. L. Lange, "Woman Is Not a Rational Animal: On Aristotle's Biology of Reproduction," in *Discovering Reality: Feminist Perspectives on Epistemology, Metaphysics, Methodology, and Philosophy of Science*, ed. Harding and Hintikka, Boston, 1983, pp. 1–15.

5. M. B. Arthur, "Liberated Women: The Classical Era," in Bridenthal and Koonz, *Becoming Visible: Women in European History*, Boston, 1977, pp. 60–89.

6. S. Moller Okin, *Women in Western Political Thought*, Princeton, 1977; J. Hicks Stiem, "The Unit of Political Analysis: Our Aristotelian Hangover," in *Discovering Reality*, pp. 31–43; H. Schrödder, "Feministische Gesellschaftstheorie," in *Feminismus, Inspektion der Herrenkultur*, ed. L. F. Pusch, Frankfurt, 1983, pp. 449–76; id. "Das Recht der Väter," pp. 477–506.

7. Z. L. Eisenstein, *The Radical Future of Liberal Feminism*, New York, 1981; H. Hartmann, "Capitalism, Patriarchy, and Job Segregation by Sex," in *The Sign's Reader: Women, Gender and Scholarship*, ed. Abel, Chicago, 1983, pp. 193–225.

8. See A. Schwarzer, *Lohn: Liebe*, Frankfurt, 1973; H. Scott, *Working Your Way to the Bottom: The Feminisation of Poverty*, Boston, 1984; E. Hochwald, "Studying Technological Discrimination: Some Feminist Questions," *Feminist Issues* 5 (1985), pp. 55–64 and the special issue on "The Political Economy of Women," *Review of Radical Political Economics* 16 (1984).

9. For this expression see K. Barry, *Female Sexual Slavery*, New York, 1979. The literature on sexual violence against women is too extensive to be listed here. For a review see Brines and Gordon, "The New Scholarship on Family Violence," *Signs* 8 (1983), pp. 490–531.

10. See, e.g., S. Rogers Radl, *The Invisible Women: Target of the Religious New Right*, New York, 1983. For a comparison of the rhetorics of the Political Right in America with the propaganda of Nazi Germany, see Conway and Siegelman, *Holy Terror: The Fundamentalist War on America's Freedoms in Religion, Politics and Private Lives*, New York, 1982.

11. Bleier, *Science and Gender: A Critique of Biology and the Theories on Women*, New York, 1984, p. 184.

12. For a discussion and theological evaluation of this development see my book *Bread Not Stone: The Challenge of Feminist Biblical Interpretation*, Boston, 1984, pp. 65–94.

13. For the analysis of such interests from a liberation theological perspective, see L. Boff, *Church, Charism, and Power*, New York, 1984.

14. The literature is too extensive to be listed here. For a comprehensive discussion see A. M. Jagger, *Feminist Politics and Human Nature*, Sussex, 1983. However, the Black feminist bell hooks argues that much feminist theory lacks a broad and inclusive analysis because it has emerged from privileged women. See her book *Feminist Theory: From Margin to Centre*, Boston, 1984.

15. Miller and Swift, *Words and Women*, New York, 1977. See also Dale Spender, *Man Made Language*, Boston, 1980; *Gewalt durch Sprache*, ed. S. Trömel-Plötz, Frankfurt, 1984; L. Pusch, *Das Deutsch als Männersprache*, Frankfurt, 1984.

16. P. Bourdieu, *Ce que parler veut dire: l'économie des échanges linguistiques*, Paris, 1981 and the critical discussion of his work by J. B. Thompson, *Studies in the Theory of Ideology*, Berkeley, 1984, pp. 42–72.

17. Miller and Swift, *Words and Women*, pp. 34ff.

18. See especially the collected essays of N. Morton, *The Journey Is Home*, Boston, 1985.

19. *Gaudium et Spes* II, 24. See for the English translation W. M. Abbott, *The Documents of Vatican II*, America Press, 1966.

20. S. M. Gilbert, "What Do Feminist Critics Want?" in *The New Feminist Criticism*, ed. E. Showalter, New York, 1985, p. 33.

21. See especially D. Spender, *Women of Ideas (and What Men Have Done to Them)*, Boston, 1983.

22. See the new series and first volume edited by Elisabeth Gössmann, *Das wohlgelahrte Frauenzimmer*, Archiv für philosophie-und theologiegeschichtliche Frauenforschung I; Munich, 1984.

23. See my book *In Memory of Her: A Feminist Theological Reconstruction of Christian Origins*, New York, 1983.

24. See the books by E. Moltmann-Wendel, *Das Land wo Milch und Honig fliesst. Perspectiven einer feministischen Theologie*, Gütersloh, 1985, and E. Sorge, *Religion und Frau. Weilbliche Spiritualität im Christentum*, Stuttgart, 1985.

25. M. Joslyn Gage, *Woman, Church & State*, first publ. 1893; Watertown, 1980, p. 237.

18

Images of Women in the Lectionary

MARJORIE PROCTER-SMITH

Theology presupposes liturgy. Theological reflection begins from the religious experience witnessed to in the Church's liturgical celebration and moves on to reflection. When Christians gather for worship, their identity as Christians is established or reinforced; the common heritage is recalled and celebrated; their heroes, founders, and holy people are commemorated; and the work of God in human history and in the life of the community is recognized. Therefore feminist theology must examine carefully and critically what the liturgy says and does in reference to women: how women are spoken of or ignored; which women are remembered and which are forgotten; in what ways women are included or excluded from actions of the liturgy.

For many women, the liturgical celebration is an event filled with ambiguity. Women have been and continue to be strengthened and empowered by the glimpse of Gospel freedom and equality embodied in the liturgy, and by the hope of triumph of life over death it proclaims. At the same time, women know that the Church in its liturgy has usually promised more than it has delivered. While affirming the baptismal unity and equality of all Christians, the liturgy has often recognized only the leadership gifts of men. While pointing to a vision of human wholeness, often in abstract terms, the Church's worship has failed to take seriously the daily struggles of women for survival, for dignity, for the right to control our own bodies, our own sexuality, and our own future. In the face of the psychological, physical, and sexual abuse inflicted on millions of women — much of it in our own homes — the liturgy has valued obedience, humility, and selflessness. In spite of pews filled mostly with women, the language of liturgy has assumed that the male is the norm, the fully human; the female, the exception, the sub-human. It has proclaimed that God too is male, and more: King, Lord, Father, and Master.

The issue of the language of liturgy — at least that of the Scripture

175

lessons read each Sunday — has been confronted head-on by the publication of *An Inclusive-Language Lectionary,* produced experimentally
by the Division of Education and Ministry of the National Council of
Churches of Christ in the USA.[1] The product of a committee of Biblical scholars, theologians, and Church leaders, the lectionary "recasts"
the language of the Revised Standard Version of the Bible to "reflect the
full humanity of women and men in the light of the gospel."[2] By avoiding excessive use of male pronouns and gratuitous male generic terms,
and by adding "sisters" to "brothers," "Mother" to "Father," the committee
has challenged the American churches to take seriously their generalized
claims to speak to "all sorts and conditions" of people.

However, as important a step as this project is for helping the liturgy to do as well as it says, it is hampered by its adherence to the
lectionary itself.[3] Because a lectionary is selective — it chooses to include some texts and to exclude others — it operates on a hermeneutical
principle. A church's lectionary implies that the texts it reads on Sundays are more important, more significant than those texts which are
not read. This might be called the first level of interpretation: this story,
or pericope, or text should be read. The second level of interpretation is
concerned with defining the limits of the text, that is, where the reading
is to begin and end. Thus certain material may be interpreted as part of
a story or peripheral to it. The third level is the relationship between the
three readings and, in particular, the selection of Hebrew scripture for
proclamation in a Christian context. The very fact that the Hebrew scriptures are read in Christian worship is already an interpretive statement
of considerable import; but the more particularized choices for seasons
and feasts, and their relationship to Epistle and Gospel, have yet further
hermeneutical implications.[4]

A critical feminist analysis of the interpretive principles guiding the
choices of the lectionary must consider, fundamentally, the biblical texts
about women which are included and those which are excluded, where
in the Church year they are found, and what the convergence of the three
texts seems to imply. Such an analysis must also recognize, however, that
the presence of women is often obscured by the use of androcentric language, either in the original or in translation. Direct references to women
in biblical texts are frequently there because women are perceived as a
problem or an exception. Therefore, while a simple enumeration of actual
references to women is helpful basic data, texts must be examined further
in order to identify the hermeneutical principles at work and to clarify
the impact of such principles on the Christian congregations. Finally,
the concept of "feminist hermeneutics of proclamation,"[5] as elucidated by
Elisabeth Schüssler Fiorenza, in which texts which empower and affirm
women can only be proclaimed as "Word of God," and texts which pro-

claim patriarchal patterns of dominance and submission must not be, may be compared with the hermeneutics guiding the lectionary.

The Common Lectionary

For the purposes of this study, we will focus on the *Common Lectionary* proposed by the (North American) Consultation on Common Texts. Also sometimes called the "consensus lectionary." This lectionary is the result of five years' work by a committee made up of pastors and scholars representing the Roman Catholic, Episcopal, Presbyterian, Lutheran, and United Methodist churches in the United States and Canada.[6] The *Ordo Lectionum Missae* was promulgated by Vatican II in 1969, and Protestant churches in North America moved swiftly to adapt it to their particular calendars and canons. Ecumenical use of the three-year cycle of the *Ordo* was encouraged by the publication of numerous commentaries and preaching aids following the lectionary cycle. Dissatisfaction with the lectionary was also expressed, however, especially with the use of the Hebrew Bible. The new consensus lectionary above all reconstructs the Hebrew scripture readings in response to several areas of concern, including the paucity of Hebrew narrative material and in particular the lack of texts from Hebrew scripture "illustrating the role of women in sacred history."[7]

The resulting lectionary, then, alters the Epistle and Gospel lessons minimally from the Roman lectionary. More drastic are the changes in the readings from the Hebrew Bible, where the typological or "prophecy-fulfillment" principle of earlier lectionaries has been largely abandoned for a broader system of correlation, chiefly in the Sundays after Pentecost (or Sundays of the year).[8] Consequently, far more Hebrew Bible material is covered over three years than in the Roman *Ordo* or other lectionaries following it. As far as scriptural material on women, then, we might expect the *Common Lectionary* to be an improvement on other versions of the lectionary, at least in terms of an increase in texts which mention women.

Finding the Women in the Text

Finding and evaluating the image of women in a set of texts may be done on two levels. The first level is that of frequency: How often are women mentioned? The second level considers the significance and value of the reference: are the women peripheral to the text or are they a central and significant concern of texts? And do the references value women, portraying them in a positive light, or do they denigrate or misrepresent women? Feminist critique has also pointed out the dearth of female images and symbols, especially for God. Such references are harder to identify than actual references to women, since they may be obscured by the translation. Some, however, are very clear, such as references to the city of Jerusalem as female, especially as a bride, and must also be evaluated both as to frequency and significance.

In an effort to acquire some kind of objective data, every text used in the lectionary was listed, combed for female references, evaluated for significance of references, and tallied. Because the lectionary must allow for the moveable date of Easter, there are more texts than Sundays of the year. Moreover, the *Common Lectionary* provides, in addition to texts for Sundays, readings for January 1 (as Holy Name of Jesus/Solemnity of Mary and as New Year's Day); Epiphany; Ash Wednesday; Holy Week; the Easter Vigil; Easter Evening; Ascension; Annunciation; Visitation; Presentation; Holy Cross; All Saints; Thanksgiving Day; and three propers for Christmas Day. Since one would find considerable variation among North American churches as to how many of these days would be celebrated, this study will simply consider *all* of the texts provided for the lectionary, while recognizing that many churches, especially Protestant ones, might not ever use some of them. This does have some bearing on our study, since most North American Protestant churches — especially Presbyterian and United Methodist — do not usually celebrate the Solemnity of Mary or the Visitation, or the Annunciation, their percentage of significant texts about women will be lower than that reflected for the lectionary as a whole. There will be other variables in practice as well, including whether all three lessons are read, whether first readings or alternate readings are used, whether the psalm is used, and, of course (even more imponderable), what Scriptural translation will be used.

In order to control some of these variables this study considers all texts provided for by the *Common Lectionary;* it presumes the Revised Standard Version of the Bible, as being the most commonly used translation in North American churches; and it tallies all clearly female references. No effort has been made in the statistical portion of this study to evaluate whether a given reference is to be regarded as a positive or negative image of women, although a distinction was made between "significant" and "peripheral" female references. Although such judgments were not always self-evident, the majority were. For example: some texts judged "significant" were Gen. 2:18–24, the creation of woman from the rib of man; Mark 5:21–43, the healing of the woman with the flow of blood and the raising of Jairus' daughter; and Ephesians 5:21–33, in which wives are admonished to be subject to their husbands. Some texts judged "peripheral" were: Exodus 20:1–17, which includes the commandment to "honor your father and mother"; Matthew 18:21–35, the parable of the wicked servant in which the servant's wife was to be sold into slavery to pay his debts; Romans 4:16–25, which makes passing reference to "the barrenness of Sarah's womb."

It should be clear from these examples that "significant" is not to be equated at all with "positive," nor will "peripheral" necessarily imply a neutral reference. An excellent example of a text with only a brief and passing reference to women but carrying enormous negative weight is one which is still found among the texts for the Easter Vigil in the United Methodist resource for the Christian Year:[9] "The Word of the Lord came to me: 'Son of Man, when the house of Israel dwelt in their own land, they defiled it by their ways and their doings; their conduct before me was like the uncleanness of a woman in her impurity'" (Ezek. 36:16–17).[10]

Likewise, a text may say a great deal about women, but it may not necessarily be good. In the case of the Ephesians household code, and of the creation of the woman from the man's rib, the history of the use of such texts to oppress and demean women is so long and the weight of that use so heavy that recent attempts to "reinterpret" them as helpful for women can hardly be generally successful. Other texts, such as the story of Mary and Martha in Luke, are more ambiguous. While this story has been used to keep women obediently "sitting at the feet" of male clerical authority ("contemplative" versus "active" religious life), it has also functioned as a resource for an affirmation of women's spiritual and intellectual life apart from household tasks. Thus the distinction between "significant" texts about women and "peripheral" texts is intended only to give some sense of the prominence or centrality of the reference to women in the context of the pericope. The evaluation of the reference is far more complex than simple enumeration can indicate. Each text, indeed, must be evaluated on its own merits in the context and in light of the present context in which it is being used. Although such a text-by-text evaluation is beyond the scope of this article, some indications and possible directions will be considered.

What can be said without ambiguity is that the majority of texts make no mention of women at all, either significantly or peripherally. The chart below indicates both the actual numbers of references to women and the percentages in all of the texts provided by the *Common Lectionary*.

	Hebrew Scriptures	%	*Epistles*	%	*Acts*	%	*Gospels*	%	*Total*	%
total pericopes[11]	249		232		33		258		772	
"significant"	56	22.4	11	4.7	1	3	47	18.2	114	14.7
"peripheral"	29	11.6	4	1.7	2	6	13	5	48	6.2
total references	85	34	15	6.4	3	9	60	23.2	162	20.9

The Use of the Hebrew Scriptures

A glance at the figures above suggests that the increased spectrum of readings from the Hebrew Scriptures does result in an overall increase in number of references to women. Not all of those references are to women as such, however. About 40 percent of them refer to what might be called "metaphorical women": that is, the use of female images or terms to refer to something not human, i.e., a city, or the people Israel. Seven of them (8.2 percent) refer to the Wisdom of God as female.

The readings from the Hebrew Bible refer to Eve; Sarah (God's blessings of her in Gen. 17:15–19); Rebekah (her pregnancy and delivery of Esau and Jacob); the mother and sister of Moses; Pharaoh's daughter; Ruth and Naomi (three sections from the book); Hannah the mother of Samuel; Bathsheba; the widow who feeds Elijah; the Shunnamite woman who provides for Elisha; and an assortment of general references to widows, "daughters of Jerusalem," and other generalities. Absent from the lectionary are, on the other hand, Rachel and Leah; Miriam in her role as leader of the people of Israel (there is a passing reference to her only in the text for 4th Sunday after Epiphany, Micah 6:18: "I sent before you Moses, Aaron, and Miriam."); Deborah (there are no readings from the book of Judges);[12] Judith (also not read); and Esther.

It is evident, moreover, that the texts about women which were included are there because of their place in the story of a male hero or actor, and not out of any interest in the women of the text. Thus, for example, the mother and sister of Moses and Pharaoh's daughter are included in the lectionary not because God may be seen here using women as agents of deliverance, but because they are part of the Moses-cycle which is emphasized in Year A. By the same token, the story of Rebekah at the well and her willingness to leave behind her family and go into a strange land among strange people are not told, but only the story of her delivery of Jacob and Esau, because it is important to the telling of the story of Jacob.

Thus one guiding principle of inclusion, at least for the Hebrew narrative material, seems to have been to regard certain male characters — Abraham, Isaac, Jacob, Moses, Elijah, and Elisha — as central actors in the drama of salvation-history. Women are included as they relate to these male characters, but are not regarded as actors in their own right.

A different principle seems to have been at work in the use of the creation stories from Genesis. The first creation story, Gen. 1:1–2:2, is assigned to the Easter Vigil, where it is one of the Old Testament readings. The second account, from Genesis 2, is divided up over three largely unrelated Sundays. The account of the creation of the man (but not the woman), the placing of him in the garden, and the temptation of the pair by the serpent and the subsequent Fall, is assigned to the first Sunday of Lent, Year A (Gen. 2:4b–9, 15–17, 25–3:7). The other readings emphasize sin and temptation: Romans 5:12–19, the sin of the man Adam, the righteousness of the man Jesus; and Matthew 4:1–11, the temptation of Jesus in the wilderness. The creation of the woman, while excised from this text, is placed in Proper 22 of Year B (Gen. 2:18–24) together with Mark 10:2–16, the saying about divorce and the blessing of children. According to the compilers' commentary, the Genesis passage is interpreted as depicting "the creation of woman and the institution of marriage."[13] Thus the principle of inclusion at work here seems to be not only an emphasis on male actors, but an identification of women with marriage and family. While the creation of woman is for protection. The Psalm for the day is Psalm 128: "Your wife will be like a fruitful vine within your house...."

The Use of the New Testament

References to women in Acts and the Epistles are few. There is a tendency in the lectionary's use of Acts to focus on the speeches of Peter and Paul, so that Tabitha, Lydia, Priscilla, and the four daughters of Philip are not included in the selections. The epistles, which in fact contain the names of numerous women who were apparently active as missionaries, leaders of house-churches, and ministers, in the lectionary include very few names of or references to women. Those included by name from the epistles are Chloe (1 Cor. 1:11, 3rd Sunday after Epiphany, Year A), Euodia and Syntyche (Phil. 4:2–3, Proper 23, Year A), Lois and Eunice (2 Tim. 1:5, Proper 22, Year C), and Apphia (Philem. 2, Proper 18, Year C). Once again, the assumption that male actors — in this case Peter and Paul — are most important has governed the choice of texts.

The two readings which contain the most sustained references to women in the Epistles are concerned with marriage. The reading for 3rd Sunday after Epiphany, Year B, is 1 Corinthians 7:29–35: "An unmarried woman or girl is anxious about the affairs of the Lord, how to be holy in body and spirit; but the married woman is anxious about worldly affairs, how to please her husband." These verses are printed in parentheses in the lectionary, however, indicating that they are optional and may be omitted. Verses 29–31 simply urge detachment from "the world," as it is passing away. The verses are clearly addressed to men, however, since "having wives" is among the activities to be given up in view of the coming time.

The second sustained text, for Proper 16, Year B, is Ephesians 5:21–33: "Wives, be subjected to your husbands, as to the Lord...." Careful scholarship has identified the form of this text as a "household code," common in Greco-Roman writings as a series of prescriptions for household behavior of husbands and wives, parents and children, masters and slaves.[14] The Ephesians code continues in Chapter 6 to give advice to children and fathers (but not mothers) (vv. 1–4) and to slaves and masters (vv. 5–9). These sections, however, are not included in the lectionary, implying that the text advising subjection of wives to husbands and identifying the husband with Christ is still valid in a way that the similar advice to other groups — children, slaves — is not.[15] The oppressive nature of this text has already been discussed.

The material from the gospels is perhaps best considered by examining first the significant texts which are omitted, and then by looking at how the women disciples fare in the lectionary. The parable of the leaven, in which the work of the Kingdom is compared to the bread-making of a woman, Matthew 13:33 and Luke 13:20–21, is omitted, even though the parable preceding it in Matthew, the wheat and the tares, is included, together with its explanation. Since the explanation of the wheat and the tares follows the parable of the leaven, the parable is in fact "skipped over" for the reading for Proper 11, Year A.

Also absent from the Gospel lectionary is the healing of the woman "bent double" who stood up straight and praised God in the synagogue, in defiance of the religious authorities.

Since even the Gospel texts themselves reflect the active presence of the faithful women disciples in particular during the events leading up to Jesus' death, the lectionary's treatment of them is of special interest. They appear in some of the readings for Passion Sunday, Monday of Holy Week, Good Friday, Easter Vigil, and Easter Day, but the inconsistency with which texts referring to the faithful women are used reveals that the compilers tended to regard them as peripheral rather than central to the action. For example: it is clear that in both Mark and Matthew the anointing of Jesus' head by the unnamed woman in whose memory the action is to be retold (Matt. 26:6–13; Mark 14:3–9) is the beginning of the passion narrative.[16] Similarly, the women — named this time — mark the end of the passion narrative, as witnesses: they "saw where he [Jesus] was laid" (Mark 15:47; see Luke 23:55, Matt. 27:61). Yet the lectionary includes the anointing story only in the longer reading for Passion Sunday of Year B, when Mark's account is read; it does not include it at all in Year A, when Matthew is read, and even in Mark's account it may be omitted when the shorter reading is used. The women's witness at the entombment may also be omitted in Years A and B if the shorter reading is to be used. In Year C, the women's witness to the entombment is also omitted in the shorter reading, but the women's witnesses to the crucifixion is retained. It is interesting to note that although all three synoptic Gospels mention the women as witness to the crucifixion (as well as the entombment), only Luke places the women in the larger company of all of Jesus' acquaintances, and only Luke's text is included in the shorter passion readings. The Matthean and Markan accounts, which single out the women, are cut off, for the short reading, at the preceding verse.[17] Evidently the women's role was not regarded by the compilers as essential to the proclamation of the passion and death of Jesus.

Implications of the Lectionary

It is evident that the lectionary's hermeneutical principles fail to take women seriously as active, significant agents in salvation history. They are regarded as adjuncts to male actors, they are important in relation to marriage; otherwise they are expendable. For example: the confession of Peter is read once in all three years, in its synoptic parallels.[18] On the other hand, the Messianic anointing by a woman at the beginning of the Passion, found in parallels in Matthew and Mark, is read (at best) only once in three years, even though it could just as appropriately be called a confession of Jesus as the Christ. One also notes the lectionary's tendency, when a reading seems too long, to omit the material about women, even if that material lies in the middle of the passage. If women are not as invisible in the new lectionary as in those which precede it, we are still only dimly perceived. It could be argued, of course, that women are not terribly visible or active in the Bible itself, and perhaps the lectionary simply accurately reflects that regrettable fact. But it is the function of a lectionary precisely to be selective rather than representative. Material which is regarded in the present Christian context as irrelevant or inappropriate is excluded. The overwhelming majority of the Old Testament laws, for example, are omitted, as are the more violent psalms, the majority of Ecclesiastes, all of the Song of Solomon, and the major parts of Daniel and Revelation. The same rubric should apply, it would seem, to texts about women: the inappropriate and irrelevant excluded, the significant emphasized.

Toward a Feminist Lectionary

The choice of texts for a lectionary is not governed so much by the findings of historical-critical Biblical research as by the shape of the Christian Year and the needs of the people of God to hear the Word of God proclaimed to them. Biblical texts read in church on Sundays are not presented as the object of critical study or of discussion in which varying opinions and interpretations may be heard and considered. Rather they are proclaimed, both explicitly by formulas of announcement and implicitly by gestures and postures of deference and honor, to be "the Word of God." Disagreement or debate is neither expected nor allowed for. Instead they are intended as the Scriptural witness to the central proclamation of all Christian worship, namely, the death and resurrection of Jesus Christ.

A lectionary which takes seriously the continuing struggle of women to survive and to live in dignity would not be able to include in it texts such as Ephesians 5–6 or any other text which demands the submission of the weak to the powerful, including Romans 13 (Proper 18, Year A). Texts which reduce women to wombs, to chattel, or to sexual objects must be excluded on the principle that such denigration is itself a violation of the promise of life and hope given in the resurrection (see Rom. 4:19, Matt. 18:25, and 1 Cor. 6:15).

Such a lectionary must instead proclaim the resurrection victory of life over death in texts which are not bound by sexist language or degrading images of women. Such texts if they genuinely transcend their patriarchal origins, need not mention women at all in order to be emancipatory (i.e., Rom. 8:31–39; Gal. 5:1; Eph. 6:10–20; etc.). At the same time, we need to recall and celebrate through whom God has worked: the stories of Sarah, Rebekah, Rachel and Leah; of Miriam and Deborah and Jael and Judith; of the wise woman of Tekoa and Huldah the prophet; of the women missionaries and disciples and leaders of the New Testament. Such stories, reclaimed as a central part of our own story, give legitimacy to the ongoing recognition of the courage and leadership of women in our more recent past and in the present.

We also need, however, in such a lectionary, to recall and retell what Phyllis Trible has called "texts of terror": stories of violence, suffering, and struggle of the women in our heritage.[19] We need such stories for two reasons. First, stories of the betrayal, rape, abuse, and murder of women are certainly part of the stories of women today. In any congregation, a significant percentage of the women present will know first-hand about such violence. The rest of us will at least know what it is to fear it. To tell such stories is necessary, not only in order to mourn the women in the stories and those like them who have been victims, but also to insure that such victimization does not continue. But there is also a second reason for reclaiming these tales. It is because at the very heart of the Christian proclamation is also a tale of betrayal, and abuse, and murder, and the apparent silence of God. To identify the sufferings of women with the sufferings of Christ is not to subsume or to legitimate the sufferings of women but to recognize that the abuse is blasphemy and an offense against God. It is to claim, simply, that women are daughters of God.

NOTES

1. *An Inclusive-Language Lectionary* (published for The Cooperative Publication Association by John Knox Press, Atlanta; The Pilgrim Press, New York; The Westminster Press, Philadelphia; Year A: 1983; Year B: 1984). The first volume, for Year A of the three-year cycle, followed the readings of the ecumenical lectionary in use before the common lectionary. With the publication of the volume for Year B, the readings follow the newer common lectionary.

2. *An Inclusive-Language Lectionary* I, "Introduction."

3. This problem was addressed in the second volume, for Year B, in which the committee included alternate readings about women and altered some lessons to eliminate negative references to women.

4. See Gerard S. Sloyan, "The Lectionary as a Context for Interpretation," *Interpretation* 31, no. 2 (April 1977), pp. 131–38.

5. See especially "Women-Church: The Hermeneutical Center of Feminist Biblical Interpretation," in *Bread Not Stone: The Challenge of Feminist Biblical Interpretation*, Boston, 1984, pp. 15–19.

6. *Common Lectionary: The Lectionary Proposed by the Consultation on Common Texts*, New York, 1983. See the Introduction, pp. 7–23, for a discussion of the process and those involved in the work.

7. Lewis A. Briner, "A Look at New Proposals for the Lectionary," *Reformed Liturgy and Music* 17 (Summer 1983), pp. 126–29.

8. Year A: Pentateuch and Mosaic narrative; Matthew; 1 Corinthians, Romans, 1 Thessalonians, Philippians. Year B: Davidic narrative and Wisdom literature; Mark/John; 1/2 Corinthians, Ephesians, James, Hebrews. Year C: Elijah/Elisha narrative; Luke; 1 Corinthians, Galatians, Colossians, Hebrews, 1/2 Timothy, 2 Thessalonians.

9. *Seasons of the Gospel: Resources for the Christian Year,* Supplemental Worship Resources 6, Nashville, 1979, p. 80.

10. The text suggested in *Seasons of the Gospel*, Ezek. 36:16–28, has been shortened in the *Common Lectionary* to exclude the verse in question.

11. The totals are for the three-year cycle, so that texts which would be used more than once in three years were counted as separate pericopes.

12. Judg. 4:4–9 is an alternative text for Lent 4, Year B in *An Inclusive-Language Lectionary*, p. 248.

13. *Common Lectionary*, p. 90.

14. There is a large body of literature on this subject. See for example: David L. Balch, *Let Wives Be Submissive: The Domestic Code in 1 Peter,* SBL Monograph Series 26, Chico, Calif., 1981; J. E. Crouch, *The Origin and Intention of the Colossian Haustafel*, Forschungen zur Religion und Literatur des Alten und Neuen Testaments 109, Göttingen, 1972; and Elisabeth Schüssler Fiorenza, *In Memory of Her: A Feminist Theological Reconstruction of Christian Origins*, New York, 1983, Chapter 7.

15. The *Common Lectionary* comments that this reading "is a self-contained theological piece." If by this the compilers have in mind the references to the mystery of Christ and the Church, one might note that the instructions to slaves also have Christological implications, as stated in the text. The *Inclusive-Language Lectionary* proposes to substitute the instructions to children and

fathers (they have rendered it "parents") in Eph. 6:1–4. Nevertheless, the principle of dominance and submission is still an irreducible element of the text, with the obedience being required of the weaker party. How could such a text be proclaimed as the Word of God to a child who is abused by her parent or parents?

16. See Elisabeth Schüssler Fiorenza, *In Memory of Her,* New York, 1983, pp. xii–xiv and notes.

17. Year A: Matt. 27:11–54; Year B: Mark 15:1–39.

18. Year A: Matt. 16:13–20: Proper 16; Year B: Mark 8:27–38: Proper 19; Year C: Luke 9:18–24: Proper 7.

19. Phyllis Trible, *Texts of Terror: Literary-Feminist Readings of Biblical Narratives,* Philadelphia, 1984.

19

Education to Femininity
or Education to Feminism?

MARY JOHN MANANZAN

There is a poster which proclaims, "Educate a woman and you educate a community." One can ask "Educate her to what?" If this slogan is true, it is indeed puzzling why, after slavery has been declared immoral and revolutions have been fought over class issues, the exploitation and subordination of women still prevails in almost all societies. It is even more appalling to think that women perpetuate their own oppression and that of their daughters and granddaughters. It is in this context that this article will discuss the socialization of women through education.

Main Forms of Socialization

The most important agents of the ideological apparatus of any society are the family, the educational system, religion and the mass media. They are the most significant means of forming the consciousness of peoples. And though they are distinct systems, they are actually all educational in function, the educational system being institutional and formal while the other three are more informal. These forms of socialization will not receive the same amount of coverage, as this article will concentrate on the more formal form of education.

Socialization in the Family

When a baby is born, and when she is put into a pink crib and he is put in a blue crib, the matter is more than an issue of color. This sets a whole life direction for the new-born baby. Caroline Bird writes:

A small girl learns by the time she is two or three that she is a girl. The nursery books that mother reads her tell what girls are like and what they do. Girls are mommies. Girls are nurses. Mommies care for children. Nurses are helpers. They help men, and doctors are men. The books do not show girl scientists. They do not show sisters leading brothers. They don't show girls making discoveries, creating inventions, making important decisions that others of both sexes follow. Experts tell us children live up to the unspoken expectations of parents. Girls are encouraged to be clean, neat, tender little charmers, while boys are expected to be physically active, exploratory, rebellious and noisy. Boys must be physically competent. They don't have to be talkers.[1]

From the attitude of the adult members of the family and of family friends, the girl somehow absorbs the value that what is important for a girl is to be pretty. Sibling rivalry is seldom caused by envy of the greater intelligence, but by envy of the greater attractiveness of the sibling envied. Girls and women are socialized into spending most of their time, energy and money in making themselves physically attractive. The multi-million-dollar beauty industry that depletes the world's natural resources which could otherwise be used for better purposes is based on their brainwashing of women that the most important thing is to be beautiful. This is somehow connected with the idea that a girl has to attract a boy so she can fulfill the highest dreams of girls, which is to get married and be wives and mothers. Boys seem to have more self-development ambitions in life, like becoming a pilot, a chief surgeon, etc. The formation of a girl, whether it be in deportment, manner of dressing, speaking, attitude, skills, training, etc., is entirely geared to making her valuable in the marriage-market.

Mothers are forever chiding daughters for being boisterous. Girls are enjoined to be quiet, sweet, pliable, soft, coy, unobtrusive and "ladylike" — in a word, "feminine." They are given dolls, miniature teacups, etc., systematically gearing them up to their domestic role. In a Filipino family, sisters are expected to cook for and wash the laundry of their brothers even if these are quite capable of doing this themselves and actually have more time to do such chores. The chores are considered "women's tasks." Daughters are usually given home chores while boys may roam about with the excuse that anyway "boys have no virginity to lose," whereas girls have to be kept busy at home so they are not put into the danger of "losing their virtue."

Socialization in the School

The seed of sex-role stereotyping planted at home is relentlessly pursued in the school. Sue Sharpe aptly describes what happens:

> School reinforces what children have learned about sex roles in the family, through the media and everyday experience outside the home. Children find for instance that boys and girls are treated differently, boys' activities have higher status than girls' and that boisterous aggressive behavior is less tolerated for girls. Inside the school these sorts of sex inequalities and differences are perpetuated, together with those of class and race.[2]

Most primary-school teachers are women, and most of them have internalized norms of femininity. They demand obedience, silence, conformity, passivity, all of which are considered characteristics of female behavior. Girls exhibiting such behavior gain approval, reinforcing the values learned at home. These are held up as a mark of their greater maturity and responsibility, but as Sue Sharpe laments, "It is ironic that these same attributes are later used to demonstrate inferiority!" (p. 147).

During this stage, girls are given fairy tales to read. It is alarming how this seemingly wholesome literature inculcates values and attitudes that adversely affect women (the wicked stepmother and stepsisters, the witch, etc.) and the messiah is the Prince Charming, who, when he kisses the heroine, saves her from whatever troubles her, marries her and "they live happily ever after."

As the girls go on to high school, the divergence between boys' subjects and girls' subjects becomes wider. Home economics is taught to girls and gardening to boys. Girls somehow get the idea that they are poor in mathematics and good in literature. In fact school timetables are based on the false assumption of what subjects are for boys and what subject, are for girls, without giving them any choice.

It is true that in high school the students no longer read fairy tales, but they go on to Mills and Boon romances which are actually just modern fairy tales with much the same plot and the same values. And because the girls have reached the adolescent stage where sex and romance become a priority, their heads are filled with romantic illusions which they seem never to abandon and which later on they bring to their marriage, thus heading for disillusionment and false expectations. Likewise, the belief that girls find their greatest fulfillment in a husband and children becomes the excuse for the opting out of higher academic pursuits.

When young women get into college their "feminine values" are fairly entrenched. They find nothing wrong with reading history books written as if no woman ever contributed to history. They are uncritical about literature that portrays women as passive and ineffectual and is written in sexist language. They don't question why there seem to be no great women scientists, artists, musicians. They take courses and major subjects that are expected of women. And they are afraid to complain when they are victims of sexual harassment by male professors. Their domestication is complete — ready to take their role in society as good wives and mothers: the sole responsible partners in making a marriage work or in making a home happy.

The Special Influence of Religious Education

It is amazing how the values of the most secular person who claims to have no religion are actually religious values that have become a part of one's culture and of the collective consciousness of people. Thus many of the sex-role stereotypes that have been discussed have actually come from religious beliefs and principles. Nevertheless, women who have undergone religious education are doubly socialized into the role.

Among the religious teachings that are detrimental to women are the insistence on her subordination as wife, the identification of her value with virginity if she is unmarried, and the shift of valuation to her reproductive function once she is married. A moral theology based on the dichotomy of body and soul has identified women with sex and sin and has implanted so much guilt in women that they feel guilty when they are raped; they feel guilty when they are beaten up; they feel guilty when their marriage breaks up; they feel guilty when their children do wrong. The Blessed Virgin who is presented as a model for the woman is often portrayed as a passive and submissive plaster saint instead of the valiant woman in the Bible who sang the strong verses of the Magnificat and stood courageously at the foot of the cross.

The teachings on marriage emphasize woman's secondary and passive role in the family, giving her very little decision regarding her reproductive functions but on the other hand burdening her with almost total responsibility for the good working or the breakdown of the family.

The socialization effected by education and religion is a result of a thousand and one "little" things which when taken individually may sound petty, but the cumulative effect of which is the successful perpetuation of a patriarchal society.

The Patriarchal Paradigm of Education to Femininity

The above description of the educational process which most women undergo shows very clearly the patriarchal paradigm of mainstream education in most parts of the world, in theory and in practice. Dale Spender analyzes the characteristics of this paradigm.[3]

In terms of organization, education is male-defined and controlled, with the result that "women — and their particular experience of the world — are excluded" (Spender, p. 144). Even if there are more women teachers, still men are the policy-makers in the educational system. It is the men who set the standards and who determine what is significant and relevant, and female experience that does not conform to the yardstick would be considered deviant. Men also predominantly control associations and agencies and periodicals that set the directions of the different educational disciplines. They also have a say in what does and does not get funded as research. The result: "At every level . . . men are able to exclude women from the construction of knowledge: they can exclude them as subjects when they set up research which is problematic to men, they can exclude them as researchers and theorists by not allocating funding to projects which are perceived as problematic to women and by dis-allowing women's unfunded research . . . " (Spender, p. 147).

The school as an institution is governed by a particular gender regime which may be defined as "the pattern of practices that constructs various kinds of masculinity and femininity among staff and students, orders them in terms of prestige and power, and constructs a sexual division of labor within the institution."[4]

Mainstream education, then, is actually *men's studies.* It is deeply entrenched. However, when power is exerted and exerted forcefully, it arouses resistance. In the last ten years, the patriarchal assumptions of the educational system have been questioned and challenged from the feminist movement. Counter-sexist programs have been started in schools. There is an astounding growth of women's studies courses in many countries. What are the characteristics of this developing feminist model of education? This will be discussed in the next half of this article, both in its general components as well as in the particular experience of a third world school.

Education to Feminism

It is difficult to give a finished concept of the feminist model of education, first of all because it is still evolving and because "it has not been confined to narrow, institutionalized parameters" (Spender, p. 149), but is being developed in varying venues from women's organizations' conscientization seminars to postgraduate courses in universities. However, there are definite trends that are manifested in these various forms.

Trends in the Feminist Model of Education

In the late 1960s, the emerging modern women's liberation movement started to ask questions about the condition of women. Then, there were no feminist books, no feminist experts, not even adequate data about the situation of women. So there was a need for women to produce this knowledge about themselves. Dale Spender recalls:

> Women found themselves meeting with other women and talking about their personal experience (and validating it in the process); they were constructing a new reality without necessarily being about to state explicitly what it was they were doing. . . . None of us (I recollect) had much more than our personal experience to go on. None of us was an expert who could rely on "book learning." We were all equals in the sense that we all felt that we had been "misled" and we all wanted to come to understand how it happened (and to make sure it didn't happen again).

This already brings out one trend: the lack of hierarchy in these endeavors and the necessity of co-operative and collaborative methods. Shared knowledge became collective insights which gave rise to new knowledge. And since the starting point of the process was women's experiences, this knowledge had a direct relation to life and not to abstract theories. The shared experiences also erased the boundaries between teaching and learning. Education became a dialogical process.

There is also an emphasis on the role of the personal which is opposed to patriarchal education. Because of this validation of personal experience, women feel good about themselves after taking women's studies. But women's studies are also political. They aim at empowerment of women, individually and as a group. They question structures: educational and social. They call for structural changes in the educational system, both in theory and in practice, and envision an alternative egalitarian society.

There is also the trend of interdisciplinarity. A. Fitzgerald explains:

> Women's Studies . . . is necessarily interdisciplinary. . . . In acknowledging the male-centeredness of the traditional curriculum, it points out the biases inherent in all disciplines and thus the political nature of education itself. . . . Questioning the underlying assumptions about the truth and supposedly objective knowledge of academic fields is to recognize that the very chopping up and categorizing of knowledge in the academy is itself a political act.[5]

Another feature is creativity in methodology and flexibility. Reacting to the purely rational methodology of mainstream education, feminist education makes use of the arts, performing and visual, in its teaching-learning process. Women perform their reports and do not just read them. In many women's awareness seminars, chairs and tables are pushed aside and learning happens in very relaxed postures, even some very "unladylike" ones.

As to the context of feminist education, it includes the analysis of the woman question, gathering data on the issues of women of all sectors, classes, ethnicity, religion, etc. It seeks to find an explanation of the origins of patriarchy and to describe all its manifestations in society. It exposes and neutralizes the forms of socialization that perpetuate the woman question and it outlines an agenda of societal transformation.

Women's Studies, Philippine Experience

It is perhaps interesting to trace the evolution of education to femininity to education to feminism by citing a particular case study.

St. Scholastica's College is a college for women run by Benedictine Sisters in Manila, Philippines. It was founded in 1906, and although it was first established for the poor, it soon became a school for women of the elite class. As such it aimed at educating women for the traditional roles society had assigned to them. In fact, whatever major subjects the students chose, all had to have Home Arts as their minor.

In 1975, in response to the situation of economic and political injustice in the country, the school was reoriented towards social justice. Its objectives, its curricula, its methodologies and its extra-curricular activities were all geared to create social awareness and to awaken social responsibility and commitment in the academic community.

In the late 1970s and the early 1980s, the feminist movement started in the Philippines, and by 1984 a coalition of women's organizations, *Gabriela,* was formed, embracing 105 women's organizations and about 45,000 individual members. Aside from *Gabriela* there were other women's federations. In other words, by then the women's movement was well on its way. But as usual, academe lagged behind.

In 1985, Sr. Mary John Mananzan, OSB, who was and still is the Dean of St. Scholastica's College, was elected national chairperson of *Gabriela.* Seeing how much the women's movement had advanced, it seemed to her appropriate that a women's college like St. Scholastica's College should spearhead the establishment of a women's studies program.

a. The introductory course to women's studies. In 1985 there were no women with a women's studies degree in the Philippines. This was a great blessing in disguise, because the women active in women's organizations were the ones who were recruited to conceptualize the first women's studies course and to teach it. Thus the gap between women's studies programs and the programs of activist women in women's organizations was avoided. Eighteen women committed themselves to pioneer in this new course. In the second semester of 1985, a pilot class was selected, composed of sixteen psychology majors. In the eighteen sessions of the course there were sixteen students and eighteen teachers!

The course included the following topics: Nature vs. Nurture, Physiology of Women, Psychology of Women, Relationships, Images of Women in the Arts and Media, Family and Marriage, Current Issues of Women in the Philippines, Women in Philippine History, Women and Religion, Patriarchy and Agenda for Renewal.

Because of the enthusiastic response of both students and the teachers and the very positive evaluation at the end of the semester, the introductory course was made a part of the general education program of the college, and therefore a requirement for graduation. In the following year, the Department of Education, Culture and Sports granted the permit for the Cognate on Women's Studies, which consists of twelve units of core studies and six units of electives.

After five years of offering the introductory course, an evaluation of the course was made, using a questionnaire given to all those who were taking the course during the school year 1989–90. The students once more gave an overwhelming positive evaluation, and to the question whether they would recommend the course, most of the students not only said "yes" but "most certainly yes," or "definitely," or "yes and also to the men," etc.

b. The establishment of the Institute of Women's Studies. The women's studies program soon developed other projects besides the curricular one. It was therefore considered advisable to found an Institute of Women's Studies, which received its Securities and Exchange Commission permit to operate in April 1988. Its brochure states the objectives of the Institute:

> to awaken consciousness and provide understanding of the woman question through a formal institutional education strategy; to conduct research studies pertaining to gender issues; to initiate and administer projects promoting the cause of women; to offer outreach programs for women outside the formal educational institution.

To concretize these objectives, it now offers the following programs:

The Research and Publication Program

In the assessment of the introductory course on women's studies, one difficulty that surfaced was the lack of local resource materials. The text used was a compilation of readings from the feminist classics written in the United States and Europe. Although these were very helpful, there was still a need to produce materials which took into account the particular culture and history of the students. This need gave birth to the research and publication program. The first book written was entitled *Essays on Women*, which was the compilation of the first articles written on women's issues and the women's movement in the Philippines. This is now in a second revised edition. The publication of three more books followed: *Women and Religion, Women in Arts and Media*, and a book on women in Philippine history written in Filipino.

A new development in this program is the establishment by seventeen women writers of a women's publishing collective. The women commit themselves to write, translate, illustrate and publish literary books. They have published three books of poems and essays to date. They dream of one day being a women's publication company.

Local Outreach

The question arose of extending the course to women who were not enrolled at the college. To answer this perceived need, a module was developed for a three-day awareness-awakening seminar for grass-roots women. Every year, four to six such seminars are given to peasant women, women factory workers, women workers in service industries, and urban poor women.

Another local outreach project focuses on teachers. One insight that has been gained through the years is the need not only to offer a women's studies course but also to develop a women's perspective in all the other disciplines and towards education as a whole. So in collaboration with the Women's Studies Consortium which St. Scholastica's College has formed with four other colleges and universities, a module called "Towards a Gender-Fair Education" was prepared, and seminars and consultations have been undertaken with teachers from the elementary, secondary and tertiary levels as participants. This module consists in analyzing the school system and determining sexism in the structure, in the attitudes and in the practices of the schools and the educational materials they use. It then discusses the values of feminist education and provides skill and methods to inculcate these values.

Resource Development Program

This program started with the collection of books and audio-visual materials. After some time a considerable amount of material for a vertical file was accumulated. It became clear that there should be a physical center to house these materials and to open the resource center to the public.

In 1988, a house and lot beside the school campus was bought for the future center of the Institute of Women's Studies. The old house was demolished, and in January 1990, the ground-breaking for the new building was held. On 16 December 1990 the three-story building was finished. It now houses the print and the non-print resources center, the offices of the staff, and dormitory and seminar facilities.

The Intercultural Course on Women and Society

Requests for training received from women from some countries in Asia and the Pacific prompted the initiation of a three-month course on "Women and Society" primarily for women of Asia and the Pacific. Its general objective is "to enable women within the Asia-Pacific region to share, learn and make solidarity linkages with each other in an alternative academic setting."[6] To date, two such courses have been offered, and the participants have evaluated the course very positively.

Conclusion

Feminist education is in its infancy when compared to the entrenched mainstream education, which for women means education to femininity. Helping to perpetuate the ideas and attitudes inculcated by schools is the powerful influence of the media, which are likewise still very sexist and dominated by patriarchal values. Feminist educators are therefore faced with formidable obstacles to their goal of awareness-awakening, empowerment of women and eventually structural changes in institutions and in society.

However, nobody can deny that the feminist movement has made real headway. Many young women today take for granted the freedom they enjoy in different spheres of life, which the feminists of the 1960s fought for. New life-styles and forms of relationships between men and women have emerged. Attitudes have also changed. For example, a study in the United States states: "While in 1957, 80% felt that an unmarried woman was sick, neurotic, or immoral, two decades later only 25% held that opinion. More than half the populace believes that husbands as well as wives should care for small children; as recently as 1970, just one third thought so."[7]

And even in feminist education, we read the following optimistic interim assessment (Spender, p. 143):

> It can be established that feminism has made great gains within the field of education: the astounding growth of women's studies courses in many countries, the development of alternative and successful models of teaching and learning, the systematic and convincing critiques of the way in which knowledge is constructed and disseminated, and the establishment of diverse and far-reaching research programs, are all testimony to the feminist achievement within the education field.

The future is bright!

NOTES

1. C. Bird, *Born Females*, Canada, 1971, pp. 40–41.

2. S. Sharpe, *Just Like a Girl*, Harmondsworth, 1981, p. 141.

3. D. Spender, "Education: The Patriarchal Paradigm and the Response to Feminism," in Madeleine Arnot and Gaby Weiner, eds., *Gender and the Politics of School*, London, pp. 143–53.

4. S. Kessler, et al., "Gender Relations in Secondary Schooling," in Arnot and Weiner, eds., *Gender and the Politics of School* (n. 3), p. 232.

5. A. Fitzgerald, "Teaching Interdisciplinary Women's Studies," in *Great Lakes College Association's Faculty Newsletter*, Great Lakes, 1978, p. 3.

6. IWS, *Final Report of the Second Intercultural Course on Women and Society*, 1990, p. 1.

7. D. Yankelovich, *New Rules*, New York, 1981, pp. 58, 93, 94.

20

The Construction of Women's Difference

ELISABETH GÖSSMANN

The construction of gender difference in the Christian tradition is connected with the reception of the philosophical systems of Platonism, Neoplatonism and Aristotelianism, which were read into the Bible. Though these interpretative syntheses made up of the Bible and Greek philosophy may have exercised different kinds of influence in particular instances, they were in agreement over the claim that the man was the principal and that the humanity of the woman was derived. To claim that the man was the principal meant that he was the beginning and had a vocation to rule. This presupposition was not questioned either by the church fathers or by most of the representatives of medieval Scholasticism. The construct "woman" was essentially explained as a negation or a reduction of the construct "man." Although there are counter-traditions which deviate from this andronormative picture of human beings, right down to modern times (and in both confessions) the main tradition of official theology has proved to be the dominant influence in history because time and again it has been endorsed by the church. The counter-traditions, whether grounded in the plurality of theological schools or conveyed by female mystics or poets, have been put to one side.

Because the same biblical text has continually been interpreted down the centuries, the andronormativeness of the picture of human beings has transcended the bounds of particular periods. Here, apart from some glances back to the patristic period, I shall confine myself to the Middle Ages, with an occasional look forward to the early modern period.

Adam, First to Be Created, the Perfect Image of God, and the Defects of Woman — Counter-Tradition: Eve, God's Masterpiece

Hannah Arendt remarks that action is the only activity of the active life which takes place directly between human beings without the mediation of matter, material and things. The basic condition for action is plurality, "the fact that not one human being but many human beings live on earth." According to her, this basic condition becomes clear in the human beings of Genesis 1, created male and female, in the plural. She criticizes the account of the creation in Genesis 2 as follows: "Here the plural is not original to human beings, but human multiplicity is explained from multiplication. Any idea of human beings, of whatever form, understands human plurality as the result of an infinitely variable reproduction of a primal model."[1] This applies particularly to the Christian tradition.

The Christian tradition, neglecting the first chapter of Genesis, the significance of which as an independent source (P) it did not yet recognize, concentrated on Genesis 2 (J): all human beings, including women, derive from Adam as the primal model. True, the fact that in Genesis 1 both sexes are in the image of God is not completely suppressed, but in the case of the female sex there are considerable qualifications. According to William of Auxerre (at the beginning of the high scholastic period): (1) the man is directly created in the image of God, but the woman is created only indirectly, through the man (*mediante viro*); (2) The man has a clearer intellect and the woman must be subject to him in accordance with the natural order; (3) all human beings, including women, are to be derived from the one human being, just as all that is created comes from the one God.[2] This results in the following defect, as far as woman is concerned: she is not the image of God directly, but only through the man — here there was a concern to do justice to 1 Corinthians 11:7. She is subordinate to the male "by nature," which makes her dissimilar to God and puts her on the side of creation, since she cannot portray God as Creator in his creativity. So what remains of her *imago Dei?* Scholasticism says that she is not inferior to man in portraying the Trinity through the triad of spiritual powers which Augustine identified (e.g., memory, insight, will). This is not significant, since faith and grace begin here and the equality of woman is grounded in redemption. But the consequence of the woman's defect is that she is not called to rule, though this is contrary to Genesis 1:26–28, the charge over creation given to both sexes. Where that is felt to be a contradiction, it is said that the woman forfeited this calling through her role as a seducer in Genesis 3.[3]

The counter-tradition of women, which can be traced continuously at least from the twelfth to the seventeenth centuries,[4] discovers "Eve," the first to be created, as the most perfect creature, the radiant image

of God and the trace of the divine wisdom. Hildegard of Bingen confirms the male's privilege of physical strength because of his creation
from the soil, but accords the woman the privilege of greater skillfulness,
subtlety and agility because she is created from human corporeality.[5]
Eve's bodily pre-eminence is used apologetically in the women's tradition against the scholastic argument that while the soul is sexless, it
can develop its powers better in a male body than in a female body.
Women leave aside in eloquent silence the scholastic restrictions on the
image of God in women, and stress the image of God in human beings
in an egalitarian way, seeking to oppose its distortions. An objection to
the denial of similarity to Christ to women is expressed in the saying of
Christ that Gertrude the Great receives in a vision: "As I am the image
of God the Father in the Godhead, so you will be the image of my being
for humankind."[6] What the women's tradition reclaimed was the image
of God in women, not just as human beings (which was the restriction
which Scheeben was still putting on it), but as women. In Marie de Jars
de Gournay this is even associated with a disguised demand for ministry
in the church;[7] there is also a sign here of the degree to which the concept of the image of God functioned as a forerunner to that of human
rights and this social significance was known to both women and men.

Sinful Eve — Counter-Tradition: Eve, Deceived or Indeed Innocent

Because (for Catholics at any rate) the interpretation of Genesis 2
which is hostile to women already begins within the Bible, in Sirach
25:24, and is continued in 1 Timothy 2:13f.,[8] it was almost inevitable
for the Christian tradition to project sin and death on to women, a process that also happens in other religions. Granted, church fathers and
scholastic theologians attempted to maintain a formal equality of original sin in man and woman by putting more of the burden of original sin
on the man in some instances and on the woman in others; however, as
the history of the idea demonstrates, it was far more significant that the
woman was made primarily responsible for the sin of wanting to be like
God. Augustine dismissed the sin of Adam *de facto* as a trivial failing,
seeing Adam as having indeed been sinful in disobedience, but making
him an accomplice of Eve, who had already incurred guilt, out of sym-
pathy with her, so that she would not be the only one to be lost. In the
twelfth century Peter Lombard, on whom all would-be theologians had to
comment, speaks of the (cancerous) sore of arrogance in Eve's breast.[9] In
the scholastic view the woman's sin was also made serious in that she
sinned not only against God and against herself, as the man did, but in
addition also against her neighbor, by leading him astray into sin.[10]

The identification of the female sex down the centuries with "Eve, the seductress" provoked a particularly sensitive defense. Whereas Hildegard of Bingen portrayed the first woman as being more deceived by the serpent than sinning and refers to the tumor of pride in the male breast,[11] and Mechthild of Magdeburg stresses the equality of sin of man and woman, Christine de Pizan begins to acquit Eve. We also sometimes find such an approach among males, but usually in an ambivalent way, as in Henricus Cornelius Agrippa von Nettesheim, in whose work the "bad Eve" and the "good Eve" are simply put side by side. However, with women the defense of their own sex in the world in which they live is the motive for the acquittal of Eve, in order to tackle the evil of discrimination at the roots:

> Finally, I must look at the most frivolous arguments of some men. For the most part they argue that Eve was the cause of Adam's sin and consequently of our fall and our misery. My reply is that Eve in no way led Adam to sin, but I believe that she rather simply suggested that he should eat of the forbidden fruit.... But she did not know that to eat of it was sin, any more than she knew that the serpent ... was the devil (Lucretia Marinella, 1600).[12]

On the basis of the particular character of Renaissance Platonism, Marinella even succeeded in incorporating the physical and psychological advantages of her own sex into the step-by-step ascent above the beautiful to the divine One, and thus in assigning to the woman the function of being the man's mediator. So this was the opposite of seduction to a "descent."

The Active Man and the Passive Woman — Counter-Tradition: the Co-operation of the Sexes

The claim in Augustine and in Scholasticism that the male intellect has greater charity is based on biological views from antiquity, derived from natural philosophy and historically obsolete, above all the theory of elements and humors. In the twelfth-century school of Chartres, which was influenced by Platonism, we read that in creating woman God did not mix the elements as well as he did when creating man.[13] The superior elements of the cosmos (fire and air) are identified as "masculine" and the inferior elements (water and earth) as "feminine." From this there results the heat and dryness of the man, which effects a mixture of temperaments more favorable to intellectual development (hence his clearer intellect); the moistness and coldness of the women is the cause of the less favorable mixture of temperaments and consequently of her intellectual weakness. But the activity of the man and the passivity of the woman are also explained in this way: this is a doctrine which becomes increasingly influential, the more Aristotle is accepted without reservations. As a result, with few exceptions, for the theologians in the tradition too there is a philosophical explanation for the "biblical" hierarchy of the sexes, male and female. The harmony of "Bible" and "philosophy" proved attractive, and there was no recognition that this was a circular argument.

However, it was not accepted without objections. So already in the twelfth century Hildegard of Bingen developed a cosmic anthropology which broke up the hierarchy of the sexes by pointing to the prominence of the median elements, air and water, in the body of woman, and of the extreme elements, fire and earth, in the body of the man.[14] Consequently the characteristics of the sexes develop in a polar way; their activities complement each other and each comes to the help of the other. There is an addition to Paul's saying that Eve was created for Adam: as he was created for her.[15] Even if this was long opposed by a legal order determined by androcentrism, here already there are indications of a more or less hidden infiltration of sexual hierarchy.

Strictly speaking, the Franciscan school also took this course, though a first inspection may prove deceptive. Aristotle, who did not understand anything of *sacra scriptura* (=the Bible and salvation history), was not an authority for the Franciscans in this sphere. We notice this at the latest in studying Franciscan Mariology, though at the same time Bonaventure's doctrine of creation also shows a certain proclivity towards a polar image of human beings.[16] The man receives benefits from the woman as she does from him, though the latter is rated higher in the context of the sexual hierarchy of male and female. As the Franciscans did not allow Aristotle, but Hippocrates and Galen, in their biology and psychology of the sexes,[17] they assumed that there was an effective female seed;[18] here they come considerably nearer than the Aristotelian line to the discovery of the female ovum in the 1820s. Actively and passively there is a reciprocity between the sexes, even if the activities of the male predominates. So the Franciscans were also interested in a conception of Mary that was free from original sin: like any woman, she too is active in her motherhood, and despite her virginal conception, which prevents the transference of original sin to her child, can nevertheless bequeath her Son a human nature which has been violated and weakened by the consequences of sin, which would disqualify him as redeemer.

This also explains the lack of interest of Thomas Aquinas and his school in the immaculate conception of Mary. There is no questioning of her handing on any of the consequences of original sin to her son because of the passivity of the woman, to which she is no exception. By contrast, with this objection to the sheer passivity of the woman, the Franciscan tradition overcomes a defect in the female sex.

Woman Disadvantaged by the Natural Order, Natural Law, and Divine Law — Counter-Tradition: Male Usurpation

One question often raised in the tradition is whether monogamy is called for by natural law, since the fathers of the faith in the Old Testament evidently did not live in that way. In order to exonerate the Old Testament patriarchs, the answer was that, depending on the requirements of individual periods of history, natural law required at one time that a man should increase his offspring with several wives, or could limit himself to the children of one wife. The latter was regarded as an irreversible rule of the time of the gospel. However, a wife's polyandry was from the beginning and always declared to be an offense against the order or the law of nature: as the Franciscan *Summa Halensis* put it, covering many schools and periods, this was because a woman could not be pregnant by several men at the same time, but several women could bear the children of one man at the same time (*quia una non protest fecundari a pluribus, sed unus bene potest fecundare plures*).[19]

It is illuminating that in the fiction of a woman's polyandry the hierarchy of the sexes is not reserved; the second reason given as to why such a state is contrary to nature is that for many men to be ruled by one woman would not further peace in the family.

Hugo Grotius still thinks just like the Scholastics on this point. Some authors identify authority grounded in natural law with that of an absolute ruler. However, Pufendorf limits the polygyny of the man which is possible by natural law by stressing that the marked increase in the number of the population throughout the world has really made it superfluous.

In 1669, Gisbert Voetius of the Reformed Academy at Utrecht held in his *Politica Ecclesiastica* that the greater dignity of man than that of woman was inscribed in the heart of all human beings by the natural law which destines man to rule and women obey. For him, too, the authority of the father of the house is by divine and natural law. Thomas Aquinas had once, in a Neoplatonic-sounding sentence, described man in his character of ultimate principle within the world and the image of the creator God as origin and goal of woman;[20] Voetius does the same thing, without citing him. The total withdrawal of the woman behind the man can hardly be expressed more clearly.[21] Of course there was also resistance to this during the transition to the early modern period, when natural-law thinking moved from the sphere of moral theology to that of law. Here we should think not so much of the party with a positive attitude in the struggle for gynaecocracy, since it required women who succeeded to the throne in hereditary monarchies because of the lack of male offspring to give up the feminine ethic of obedient subjection and adopt the male ethic, i.e., as it were, undergo a mental change of sex.[22] It is more important to remember the attempt of highborn wives like Marguérite of Navarre, who like many other women, especially in France, wrote an apologia for her own sex. In it she cites the privileged creation of Eve as God's masterpiece as the reason for the political skill of women and roundly declares that the whole of male rule is usurpation.[23] For her the subordination of the woman is the consequence of a male transgression of the law which was noted only by God (Gen. 3:16).

Women Are to Become Male — Counter-Tradition: We Shall Encounter Christ in the Completeness of Our Sex (Hildegard of Bingen)

There is a well-known passage in the apocryphal Gospel of Thomas in which Peter seeks to send Mary Magdalene away from the group of disciples on the grounds that women are not worthy of life. The Jesus of this text replies that he will guide her so that she makes herself masculine, so that she becomes a living spirit and thus can enter the kingdom of heaven.[24] It is also well known that church fathers like Ambrose and Jerome make similar statements: the wife who still serves her husband and children and has not yet arrived at full knowledge of faith is called "woman," but the one who abstains from procreation or is advanced in the faith is called "man."[25] Women are enjoined to give up the fleshly and to become spiritual, this being understood as a symbolic (or real?) change of sex, or the possibility is held open for them; here Christianity is by no means alone, but precisely at this point shows parallels with Buddhism (mediated through Gnosticism?).[26]

From the male side, the perfection of a feminine being can be thought of only as "elevation" and assimilation to the male sex, as a reduction to the one, authentic humanity with a male stamp. So the offer of equality,[27] gladly accepted by those women of Christian antiquity who with male hair styles and clothing lived as eunuchs in the wilderness or as virgins with their families, was "Become like us!" In the situation of the time no hostility to women was intended, but the invitation allowed two quite different interpretations: first, the sublation of the female (as the imperfect) into the masculine-perfect (as the first and the last); and second, the abolition of sexuality altogether, including male sexuality, as a liberation conceived of in Neoplatonic terms. Scotus Eriugena is to be understood in this sense.[28] But the eschatological character of the ascetical movement of late antiquity points to a utopia of sexless human beings.

This is the point at which Augustine tried to direct thought in another direction. Although in his work in particular the positive-negative symbolism of the male and female is presented very strongly where it affects earthly life, Augustine guards against giving up the otherness of the woman as something which could not be worth preserving for the world to come. He resolutely rejects a resurrection of all women as males. As transfigured corporeality has left behind it *libido and vitium*, i.e., its weakness conditioned by sin, no conflicts can arise any longer through the female form of humanity, so that Augustine can recognize it in its creaturely beauty: "To be a woman is no vice, but is natural."[29] This had to be said at all because of the mood of the culture of late antiquity into which Christianity was born, and to which it had assimilated itself in its interpretation of the Bible.

With his doctrine of the preservation of womanhood in the eschaton, Augustine gave the Middle Ages a good dowry. This gift also proved useful in the fight against dualistic sects which still spoke of women (eschatologically) becoming men. Medieval women who write and who stress their womanhood as *virgines* — though also showing signs of solidarity with the *matres* — leave the symbol of becoming male behind them and combine their theme of feminine modesty, with which they introduce their works, with a strong consciousness of election.

I hope that it has become clear from this abbreviated account that despite the tenacity of the androcentric, patriarchal tradition, some modifications were possible to its construct "woman." For want of relevant research we cannot determine clearly to what extent counter-traditions were the occasion for this. However, the fact that the counter-traditions had to struggle for centuries in attempts to refute the same prejudices against the female sex indicates their lack of success.

If the impression has arisen that the doctrines of the counter-traditions were mere reversals, i.e., over-valuations of feminine humanity which had previously been undervalued, the answer must be that this is not the case. For the counter-traditions are concerned with a "negation of negation."[30] The construct of a femininity which has not attained complete humanity, defined in andronormative terms, is rejected: the starting point is that of the originality of woman's being and an attempt to describe this not as derived, but as independent humanity. Meditating on texts like this can help present-day women and men to get past thinking in terms of a single principle and develop that dual (not dualistic nor even just polar) model of humankind which we still lack.

Translated by John Bowden

NOTES

1. Hannah Arendt, *Vita activa oder vom tätigen Leben*, Stuttgart, 1960, pp. 15f.

2. William of Auxerre, *Summa Aurea*, ed. Pigouchet, Paris, 1500, Frankfurt am Main, 1964, fol. 58v.

3. Ian Maclean, *The Renaissance Notion of Women*, Cambridge, 1980.

4. Cf. my article "Eva, Gottebenbildlichkeit und Spiritualität," in *Wörterbuch der Feministischen Theologie*, Gütersloh, 1991.

5. Elisabeth Gössmann, "*'Ipsa enim quasi domus sapientiae.'* Zur frauenbezogenen Spiritualität Hildegard von Bingen," in Margot Schmidt and Dieter R. Bauer, eds., *"Eine Höhe über die nichts geht." Spezielle Glaubenserfahrung in der Frauenmystik?*, Stuttgart and Bad Cannstadt, 1986, pp. 1–18, esp. pp. 9–11.

6. Gertrude the Great, *Legatus divinae pietatis*, translated by Johanna Lanczkowski, Heidelberg, 1989, p. 25.

7. There is an introduction to Marie de Jars de Gournay in Elisabeth Gössmann, ed., *Archiv für philosophie — und theologiegeschichtliche Frauenforschung*, vol. 1, Munich, 1984, ch. 1, cf. esp. pp. 28f.

8. Cf. Helen Schüngel-Straumann, *Die Frau am Anfang: Eva und die Folgen*, Freiburg, 1989.

9. For Augustine and Peter Lombard, see the relevant chapters in Monika Leisch-Kiesl, "Eva in Kunst und Theologie des Frühchristentums und Mittelalters: Zur Bedeutung 'Evas' für die Anthropologie der Frau," theological dissertation, Salzburg, 1990.

10. For this theme see also the chapter, "Der Mensch als Mann und Frau," in my Habilitation thesis, "Metaphysik und Heilsgeschichte: Eine theologische Untersuchung de Summa Halensis," Munich, 1964, pp. 215–29, and my "Anthropologie und soziale Stellung der Frau nach Summen und Sentenzenkommentaren des 13. Jahrhunderts," *Miscellanea Mediaevalia* (Berlin) 12, no. 1 (1979), pp. 281–97.

11. Cf. Barbara J. Newman, "O feminea forma: God and Woman in the Works of St. Hildegard," Ph.D. dissertation, Yale University, 1981.

12. There is an introduction to Lucretia Marinella in Elisabeth Gössmann, ed., *Archiv für Philosophie — und theologiegeschichtliche Frauenforschung* 2, Munich, 1985, Chapter 1; the quotation is on p. 41. For Henricus Cornelius Agrippa von Nettesheim, cf. vol. 5 of the same archive, Munich, 1988, introductions and text.

13. Cf. Hans Liebeschütz, *Kosmologische Motive in der Frühscholastik: Vorträge der Bibliothek Warburg 1923–24*, ed. F. Saxl, Leipzig and Berlin, 1926, esp. p. 128.

14. Cf. Prudence Allen, *The Concept of Woman: The Aristotelian Revolution*, Montreal and London, 1985; id., "Two Medieval Views on Woman's Identity: Hildegard of Bingen and Thomas Aquinas," *Studies in Religion: A Canadian Journal* 16, 1987, pp. 21–36.

15. *Scivias* I.2, Migne, PL 197, 393; CCM 43, 21.

16. Cf. my attempt to investigate the connection between system and the

image of woman among the Franciscans in Theodor Schneider, ed., *Mann und Frau — Grundproblem theologischer Anthropologie*, Freiburg, 1989, pp. 44–52.

17. Cf. Emma Therese Healy, *Woman according to St. Bonaventure*, Erie, Pa., 1965, pp. 11f. Albertus Magus also assumed that the seed in woman was inactive. Cf. Paul Hossfeld, "Albertus Magnus über die Frau," *Trierer Theologische Zeitschrift* 91, 1982, pp. 221–40.

18. Cf. Elisabeth Gössmann and Dieter R. Bauer, eds., *Maria für alle Frauen oder über allen Frauen?* Freiburg, 1989, pp. 63–85.

19. *Summa Fratris Alexandri*, Tom. IV, L. III, Quaracchi, 1948, nos. 253–55.

20. Thomas Aquinas, *Summa Theologia* I q. 93 a. 4 ad 1; *"Nam vir est principium mulieris et finis, sicut Deus est principium et finis totius creaturae."*

21. *Politicae Ecclesiasticae Pars II*, Amsterdam, 1669, Liber I Tr. 4, *De mulieribus*, p. 186: *"Vir est origo et principium ex quo mulier, et est finis propter quem producta est mulier."*

22. Cf. Maclean, *Renaissance Notion* (n. 3), pp. 62f.

23. For Marguérite of Navarre, cf. *Archiv* (n. 7), pp. 13f.

24. For the Gospel of Thomas and its cultural environment see Peter Brown, *The Body and Society: Men, Women and Sexual Renunciation in Early Christianity*, New York and London, 1988, esp. p. 113, with further literature.

25. A long time ago attention was already drawn to these texts and connections by Haye van der Meer, *Priestertum der Frau? Eine theologiegeschichtliche Untersuchung*, Freiburg, 1969. For Jerome and Ambrose see pp. 97f.

26. Cf. Elisabeth Gössmann, "Haruko Okano, Himmel ohne Frauen? Zur Eschatologie des weiblichen Menschseins in östlicher und westlicher Religion," in *Das Gold im Wachs, Festschrift für Thomas Immoos*, ed. E. Gössmann and G. Zobel, Munich, 1988, pp. 397–426.

27. Cf. Ruth Albrecht, *Das Leben des hl. Makrina auf dem Hintergrund der Thekla-Traditionen*, Göttingen, 1986; Kari Vogt, "Becoming Male: One Aspect of an Early Christian Anthropology," *Concilium* 182, 1985, pp. 72–83.

28. For Scotus Eriugena cf. the works by Werner Beierwaltes, esp. *Denken des Einen: Studien zur neuplatonischen Philosophie und ihrer Wirkungsgeschichte*, Frankfurt am Main, 1985.

29. *"Non est autem vitium sexus femineus, sed natura,"* *De civitate Dei* 22.17, 18.

30. The formula comes from Katharina Fietze, "Spiegel der Vernunft: Theorien zum Menschsein der Frau in der Anthropologie des 15. Jahrhunderts," Munich philosophical dissertation 1990 (planned publication Paderborn, 1991).

21

Women's Difference and Equal Rights in the Church

ROSEMARY RADFORD RUETHER

The full incorporation of women into the ministry of the Christian Churches has become the critical issue for Christianity today. How churches handle the issue may well determine whether they survive as viable religious options for humanity in the future. Christianity inherits from its historical past a fundamental contradiction in its views and treatment of one half of humanity, women. On the one hand Christianity, from its beginnings, has committed itself to a universalist soteriological egalitarianism. All human beings, regardless of gender, class, or ethnicity, are created by God and saved by Christ. Salvation knows no distinction between human beings.

On the other hand, Christian understanding of the nature of being, both of God and Christ and of normative humanity, has been cast in male generic terms. This male generic understanding of being has been used to subordinate women, both as members of humanity and as persons capable of exercising authority and representing God and Christ. The exclusion of women from ordained ministry, and indeed from all public leadership in past Christian societies, has been rooted in this male generic understanding of human and divine being.

Only in the present century have women gained access to political rights in society and to higher education and so have been, for the first time, in a position to challenge these exclusions from Christian leadership in the churches. By and large, liberal societies have been ahead of the churches in recognizing women's rights as full human persons, although there are still many issues that remain unresolved in the social arena. This fact has been used by some conservatives to claim that the whole issue of human rights in the church is inappropriate. They claim that feminism is the importation into the churches of a purely "secular" issue.[1]

However, this separation of religion and secular society in regard to sexism is misleading. The male dominant patterns in Christianity originate from a time when the church and patriarchal society were integrally related, when the church borrowed patterns of organization from patriarchal society and buttressed those patterns with theological symbolism and argumentation. The issue of women's subordination is both social and religious. It is a part of the heritage of secular and theological ideologies. The churches must deal with this issue both in terms of ecclesiastical organization and in terms of theology.

Liberal Protestant churches, over the last 130 years and particularly the last 30 years, have changed their practices and begun to ordain women. But most of them were not prepared to recognize that this change demanded a rethinking of theological symbolism and ecclesiastical organization. Consequently, women have been integrated into ministry in token numbers and in low-paid, marginal positions in a system that still symbolizes human and especially divine being as male. This of course, is not unlike the treatment of women in secular culture and society.[2]

In Catholicism the celibate clerical system of ministry is in crisis. Laywomen, especially nuns, are doing an increasing proportion of the actual ministry of the church, but without official recognition as ordained ministers. The Vatican has mobilized itself against any liberalization in the areas of reproductive rights and the ordination of women.

The American Catholic bishops are caught in the middle between rising women's consciousness in the church and this Vatican intransigence. This is true of many other national episcopacies as well. On the one hand, the bishops recognize that they cannot do without women. Women are both the majority of the active churchgoers and the majority of the volunteer workers in the church. An increasing share of the professional, that is, paid, ministry is done by women.

The bishops are tied to the Vatican by a system of universal jurisdiction and appointment of bishops that was created by nineteenth-century ultramontanism. This means that bishops lack the independence to challenge the Vatican on any critical matters of doctrinal or moral teaching in such areas as reproductive rights and ordination. Even the question of artificial birth control, which was actually settled, as far of the consensus of moral theologians and of laity goes, twenty years ago, remains unchanged in official teaching.[3]

The drafts of the American bishops' pastoral letter on women reveal these contradictions all too painfully.[4] On the one hand, the episcopal authors of the letter attempted to give full rhetorical affirmation to the legitimacy of women's concerns for full equality in society and in the church. They condemned in no uncertain terms the "sins of sexism that violate the basic tenets of our faith." But their ability to follow up these words with practical changes in areas such as reproductive rights, support for the Equal Rights Amendment, or ordination of women, is totally lacking. The structures that tie women to subordinate positions in society and in the church remain largely in place.

The bishops took as their theological starting point the scriptural text, Genesis 1:27, which says that "man" is created in the image of God, male and female. They take for granted that this term means, and has always meant, the equality of men and women. This ignores the fact that for most of the history of Christian tradition this text was interpreted asymmetrically. That is, it was understood to mean that the male possesses the image of God normatively, and women are included in the image of God only under the male as their head.[5]

More recent Catholic anthropology moved from arguments about women's natural inferiority to arguments for women's difference and complementary relations to males. In the first draft the bishops disregarded the anthropologies of subordination and of complementarity. They adopted an anthropology of equals between men and women in the family, in society, and in the church. However, they seem to have been caught up short by the Vatican and more conservative American Catholic bishops. As was evident from the Pope's statement on the "Dignity and Vocation of Women" (August 1988), he favors an anthropology of complementarity that divides females and males into two opposite psycho-symbolic ontologies.[6]

The inability of the American bishops to affirm any real peer relations of men and women becomes explicit when we turn to the question of the participation of men and women in the ministry of the church. In their pastoral letter, all the bishops were able to offer was an increased participation of women in the ministry of the laity. The ordained clergy remains an all-male preserve. They endorse the position of the 1976 Vatican Declaration (reaffirmed by John Paul II in his letter) against the ordination of women which declared that women are ontologically incapable of being ordained because they cannot image Christ.[7] Both the Pope and bishop seem oblivious to the contradiction between this statement and their own theological starting point of equality of men and women in the image of God.

The inability of the American Catholic bishops to carry through their theological starting point of women's equality in creation ends in a contradiction of this theological starting point. Women are said to be fully equal to men in the image of God and yet incapable of imaging Christ. What is the root of this contradiction? How can it be that bishops, who presume to be the primary theological teachers of the church, do not recognize such blatant contradiction between their theological anthropology and their christology?

The roots of this contradiction lie in the 1976 Vatican Declaration itself, which attempted to create just such a schism between anthropology and christology. This declaration attempted to separate the issue of women's civil equality in society from ordination. It asserted that the Catholic Church (the *magisterium*) had always supported women's civil equality, but the question of women's ordination is not a question of civil rights or equality in the natural order, but belongs to a separate and higher plane of sacramental relations between the church and God. In effect, what this does is to separate the created or natural order and the sacramental order or order of grace into two different spheres unrelated to each other. Women are said to be equal in the natural order of creation, but this has no implications for the ecclesial or sacramental order of salvation.

Interestingly, this dualism partly reverses the classical view taken by the church fathers, in which women were presumed to be unequal and fundamentally inferior in nature, but equal in order of grace. The church fathers thought of women as lacking equality in the image of God and as being under the headship of the male in the created order. But in Christ this inequality has been annulled. In the language of Galatians 3:28, in Christ there is neither male or female.

Classical Christianity suffered from a contradiction between its creational anthropology and its christology, but in the opposite direction. Women were presumed to be unequal in nature. This inequality dictated the temporal structure of the church as patriarchal. But on the plane of salvation, which anticipated heaven, this patriarchal hierarchy of man over women has been annulled. How do we seem to have developed to a reversed view in modern Catholic teaching, in which women become equal in nature or creation (secular society), but unequal in grace (in Christ and in the Church)?

Basically, this has come about because civil societies in the West have moved to grant women civil equality. Contrary to the Vatican Declaration, this reform was not supported by the Pope or the bishops when it was happening. In fact, both opposed women's suffrage when this struggle was going on in the first part of the twentieth century.[8] But this history is conveniently forgotten. The Catholic *magisterium* (more or less) concedes to women this new arena of civil equality. This means that it also changes its previous teachings that women are unequal in nature to men. It declares itself to have "always taught" that women are equal to men in nature. This means that, in order to defend the tradition of excluding women from ordination, it must invent a new distinction between the natural and the sacramental planes.

This hierarchical ordering of nature and grace echoes the scholastic or Thomistic tradition, but it contradicts Thomas's own understanding.

In the teaching of Thomas Aquinas, women were fundamentally unequal in nature. He borrowed the false biology of Aristotle to declare that
women were defective or "misbegotten" humans who lacked full normative human nature. For this reason they cannot represent human nature
in any leadership in society. Only the male could represent the full or
normative human nature.[9]

Thomas's christology and theology of priesthood followed this patriarchal anthropology. Since only men possessed full, normative human
nature, it followed that Christ had to be male to possess the fullness
of humanness. Only men in turn could represent Christ in the priesthood. Thomas's patriarchal construction of anthropology, christology
and priesthood was coherent. Only on the soteriological level did Thomas
diverge from this patriarchal construction. In keeping with ancient Christian tradition he assumes that this inequality of women is overcome
by the grace of salvation won by Christ. Thus women are included in
salvation, despite their incapacity for full humanness.

This Thomistic tradition is the root of the startling statement in the
1976 Vatican Declaration which claimed that women cannot be ordained because they do not image Christ. But the Vatican Declaration
attempts to eliminate the anthropological roots of this theological viewpoint. Women's ability to image Christ now hangs in the air as a matter
of sacramental symbolism alone, no longer based on natural inferiority.

One can only wonder, then, whether the other pole of the relationship
is now in jeopardy. If the maleness of Christ now becomes a limitation
of grace rather than nature, does this mean that women, in fact, are not
equally included in grace? If women's inability to image Christ lies in the
realm of grace, rather than nature, does this mean that the grace won
by Christ no longer equally includes women? If women cannot represent
Christ, how does Christ represent women? Or, to put it another way, if
women cannot be ordained, they cannot be baptized, either.

What all this means is that the church is challenged in a new way
today to make coherent sense out of its theology, to bring together its
anthropology, its christology and its soteriology. If women are understood to be equal both in nature and in grace, there is no longer any
basis for declaring that they cannot represent Christ sacramentally. The
flight back to an anthropology of complementarity, and the abandonment
of the anthropology of equivalence in the second draft of the American
bishop's pastoral, seeks to evade this issue. The result is a reactionary
document that makes no positive contributions to the issues and should
be rejected altogether.[10]

As Roman Catholic patriarchalism loses its social basis in patriarchal feudal society, and faces instead societies which are, in theory if
not in practice, democratic and egalitarian, there has been an increas-

ing temptation to support its traditional social patterns inherited from the past by self-enclosed dogmatism. The church's social pattern no longer has the larger society as its reference and so can no longer argue that these patterns derive from the "natural order," as Thomas Aquinas might have in the thirteenth century. In order to maintain these patterns, the church now sacramentalizes an archaic patriarchal and monarchical social system, making it appear to be a special expression of divine ordering of the church, apart from and unconnected with society. This self-enclosed authoritarianism was expressed in the dogma of infallibility, which was promulgated in 1870 at precisely the moment when the Catholic Church was losing its relation to feudal Catholic society and facing new democratic societies.

The Second Vatican Council appeared to promise a change in this self-enclosed dogmatism. But the present papacy is making a major and total assault on these developments and attempting to reassert a system of power rooted in self-enclosed monarchical infallibilism. This system of power no longer acknowledges any need to base itself on consultation with the rest of the church at any level, from bishops to priests to lay people. If there is to be any future for the Catholic church or ecumenical relations between Catholics and Protestants, this entrenchment of papal absolutism must be resisted. No church teaching can stand which does not possess an authentic consensus of the people.

Thus, the question of women's ordination, or indeed the discussion of any development in church teaching, opens up the deeper question of authority in the church. Catholicism stands today at the crossroads between two directions. It can either take the direction of Vatican II and progress toward a more authentic participatory community, in which all members are given a voice, or it can retreat in the direction of Vatican I and seek to restore papal absolute monarchy. This latter direction can only create a dwindling Roman sect, not a Catholic church. Women and men who are self-respecting of their own humanity will increasingly desert such a church.

The question of how Catholic feminists seek to find ways of participating in local churches, parishes and religious congregations is of critical importance. What sort of a thing can we and should we try to do in the light of the ambiguous and increasingly limited efforts of the American Catholic bishops to widen the space for women's ministries?

Women should move in and occupy any space for ministry that is opened to them and seek to make it liveable space. This means insisting on decent working conditions, legally and humanly. That is to say, reasonable contracts and remuneration and shared decision-making. But we should do this with our eyes wide open to the spiritual dangers of patriarchal working conditions. These conditions are dangerous to our spiritual health. So one should not put one's whole life and soul into such communities, but also create alternative free communities of spiritual nurture and support.[11] Both of these options need to exist side by side, if we are to survive spiritually and help the institutional church to reform.

We need to find creative ways to bring institutional and free communities into interaction so that they can enliven each other, rather than assuming that they are mutually exclusive options. Institutional churches typically offer two alternatives, either to conform to their limits or to leave as isolated individuals. We need to refuse both options. Instead, we need to establish new ground on the outside edge of historical communities, while retaining a base on the inside edge of these communities. In this way one has the freedom for new creativity, while taking over and using institutional resources to develop and communicate these projects. Christian feminists need to find the creative ways to make use of this dialectical strategy of transformation of culture and social structures, refusing to be either isolated or co-opted.

Oppressive power relations will not disappear in any institution completely. Moreover, the capacity for such oppressive power relations is in ourselves, as much as in our opponents. We are all in the process of continual conversion. What we need to work for here and now is not perfection, but good working and living space for ourselves and for one another. Wherever we can do something concretely to extend such good living space for ourselves and for some others, that is worth doing. Whatever we can do to shape communities where love and prophetic witness are at least glimpsed, that is worth doing. That is fundamentally what ministry and what being the church of Christ is all about.

NOTES

1. William Oddie, *What Will Happen to God: Feminism and the Reconstruction of Christian Belief*, London, 1984.

2. Jackson W. Carroll, Barbara Hargrove, Adair T. Lummiss, *Women of the Cloth: A New Opportunity for the Churches*, San Francisco, 1981.

3. Robert Blair Kaiser, *The Politics of Sex and Religion*, Kansas City, 1985.

4. The first draft, released in March 1988, was titled "Partners in the Mystery of Redemption." The second draft, released on 5 April 1990, was titled "One in Christ Jesus: A Pastoral Response to the Concerns of Women for Church and Society."

5. The ambiguities of the inclusion and exclusion of women from the image of God in traditional Christian theology is explored in *Image of God and Gender Models*, ed. Kari Borresen, Oslo, 1991.

6. John Paul II, "The Dignity and Vocation of Women," 15 August 1988.

7. Congregation for the Doctrine of the Faith, "Declaration on the Question of the Admission of Women to the Ministerial Priesthood," 15 October 1976.

8. See Rosemary Radford Ruether, *Contemporary Roman Catholicism: Crises and Challenges*, Kansas City, 1987, pp. 36–37, 79 n. 22.

9. Thomas Aquinas, *Summa Theologica*, I, 92.

10. There has been a general condemnation of the second draft of the pastoral by progressive American Catholic women's groups. Even Bishop Rembert Weakland of Milwaukee, Wisconsin, called for the pastoral to be dropped as counter-productive. See Rosemary Ruether, "Dear Bishops, You Insult Our Intelligence," *National Catholic Reporter,* 18 May 1990, p. 16.

11. Rosemary Radford Ruether, *Women-Church: Theology and Practice of Feminist Liturgical Communities*, San Francisco, 1986.

22

Ecclesiastical Violence

Witches and Heretics

E. ANN MATTER

In the Middle Ages and the early modern period, Christian women faced a dilemma of self-knowledge and self-definition. On the one hand, women had been identified since early Christian times as the origin of sin in the world and, consequently, a source of heretical ideas. On the other hand, an idealization of the female, especially evident in the growth of the cult of the Virgin Mary, ascribed to the abstract category "woman" a variety of spiritual powers much at odds with the idea of women as the source of evil. Ecclesiastical violence against women was born in this deadly ambivalence.[1] Since Christian doctrine teaches that the incarnation of God was made possible through the body of a woman, the ambivalence manifested itself in increasing control of women's minds and bodies, and resulted in punitive strictures on both psychic and physical levels.

The history of women's monasticism in Western Christianity is a good venue for an analysis of this double-barreled approach to women by the ecclesiastical hierarchy. As early as the turn of the fourth century, women in religious life were urged by their male religious mentors to think of themselves as "brides of Christ." Jerome's famous letter to Eustochium *(Epistle 22)* describes female ascetic chastity as a sacred marriage, invoking the love-language of the Song of Songs over twenty times.[2] As women's monasticism became an established medieval institution, a concern for strict enclosure of nuns was articulated with increasing clarity. To some extent, cloistering of nuns was thought necessary to protect women (and especially the "brides of Christ") in a world in which women had no means to protect themselves. But it is also clear, as early as the sixth-century monastic rule for women written by Caesarius, Bishop of Arles, that there was a connection between the assumption that women are responsible for sin in the world and the strict control of religious women by the ecclesiastical hierarchy.[3] This pattern is repeated in the sixteenth century, when the rulings of the last session of the Council of Trent decreed that all women's religious communities must be kept under strict enclosure.[4]

Women's minds were not, however, enclosed as easily as their bodies. One irony of the history of women's monasticism is the fact that some women found the cloister a rich ground for creative expression. Although it cannot be denied that some women entered religious life unwillingly, as political pawns of their families, many others chose the cloister to take advantage of the opportunity for autonomy and intellectual life available to women nowhere else. In a very real sense medieval women were, as Penelope Johnson puts it, "equal in monastic profession" to medieval men.[5] Women's daily activities in the cloister may have been strictly controlled by the ecclesiastical hierarchy, but their spiritual and intellectual creativity enjoyed a free range which may be surprising and even shocking to modern sensibilities. We know, for example, that from the tenth century to the seventeenth women wrote and presented plays behind cloister walls.[6] There seems to have been as lively a tradition of musical composition and performance by nuns in the early modern period.[7]

But it was in the realm of spiritual creativity that medieval and early modern nuns became best known, where they were seen as at once more powerful and more dangerous. Medieval and early modern religious women were famous in their own day for their visionary and mystical writings, spiritual counsel and religious autobiographies. This body of Christian literature, neglected by scholars for centuries, has recently been made available to a wide reading public, and has become an important part of a revaluation of the master plot of Christian history.[8] Whereas women once were seen as peripheral to the story, at least until the emergence of the "witch phenomenon" in the later Middle Ages, it is now understood that many powerful women were held up as recipients of a special type of grace of the divine presence which was granted far less frequently to men. The complex relationship between these visionary women and the male hierarchy who both controlled and venerated them established the pattern for ecclesiastical violence against women.

Two documents from the late fifteenth and the very early sixteenth centuries will illustrate this claim. The first text, the famous *Malleus maleficarum,* published by Heinrich Krämer and Jacob Sprenger, two inquisitors of the Dominican order, vilifies women as the cause of all men's woes.[9] The title of this book, literally "The Hammer of (Female) Evil-Doers," is often translated as "The Hammer of Witches," indeed, the pursuit, capture and destruction of witches (by definition, female

witches) is its obsessive theme. Many of the most extravagant, outra-
geous claims of the *Malleus* have been quoted by feminist authors who
argue that ecclesiastical violence against women derives from an assumption of female inferiority linked to an assessment of women as
naturally carnal.[10]

Certainly, the authors of the *Malleus* show a puerile obsession with
women's sexual powers, elaborated in the chapters devoted to lascivi-
ous descriptions of intercourse between witches and the devil, and in
the truly amazing accounts of witches who, through intercourse, deprive
men of their sexual organs.[11] As the most quoted phrase of the *Malleus*
puts it: "all witchcraft comes from carnal lust, which is in women insatiable."[12] Yet an overly-literal interpretation of this type of material, such
as Rosemary Ruether's suggestion that "the very word *fe-minus* was constructed as meaning 'lacking in faith,'"[13] misjudges the chilling depth of
this accusation against women. Even the *Malleus* makes it clear that
the power of women for evil is inherently possible because of women's
greater power for good. Musing on the question "Why Superstition is
chiefly found in Women," the *Malleus* explains:

> For some learned men propound this reason: that there are three
> things in nature, the Tongue, an Ecclesiastic, and a Woman, which
> knows no moderation in goodness or vice; and when they exceed
> the bounds of their condition they reach the greatest heights and
> the lowest depths of goodness and vice. When they are governed by
> a good spirit, they are most excellent in virtue; but when they are
> governed by an evil spirit, they indulge the worst possible vices.[14]

Given the zeal with which the *Malleus maleficarum* elaborates on the
theme of female vice, it is understandably easy to ignore the claims of
this passage for women's goodness and virtue. Yet it is striking that
women and ecclesiastics are lumped together here, for even this is an
acquiescence to a special type of spiritual power available categorically
to women, but only to spiritually advanced men. In fact, the idea that
women are the recipients of special spiritual powers is found in other
writings of the age, outside the prurient context of this inquisitorial
document.

A striking example is the testimony of Ercole d'Este ("Ercole il Mag-
nifico"), Duke of Ferrara, about the political visionary Lucia Brocadelli da
Narni. Lucia, a Dominican tertiary in Viterbo famous for her reception of
mystical visions and of the stigmata, was brought to Ferrara by Ercole
in 1499, a prize possession he had sought for several years and obtained
only by trickery.[15] Lucia was set up as the head of a new house of Dominican tertiaries in Ferrara, but her most important job was to advise

Ercole on matters of state; she was one of the many "pious counsellers of princes" of early modern Italy.[16] Ercole's satisfaction with her advice is reflected in two letters he wrote about Lucia which were printed together, in Latin and German versions, in 1501, where he argues that all Christian princes should have female spiritual counsellors to guide them. In the case of Lucia, Ercole professes special faith in her guidance because of the fact that she bore the stigmata, explaining that "these things are shown by the Supreme Craftsman in the bodies of His (female) servants to confirm and strengthen our Faith, and to remove the incredulity of impious men and hard of heart."[17]

But, even though Lucia Brocadelli is an example of the real spiritual power exercised by religious women, her story also shows the limits of this power. Upon the death of Ercole, Lucia's status changed dramatically. The new Duke, Alfonso I, immediately banished her from court and revoked the privileges that had been granted to her house. At the tender age of twenty-eight, Lucia was a spiritual and political has-been; for the next four decades of her life, until her death in 1544, she was virtually a prisoner in her monastery. Lucia Brocadelli's life thus illustrates both a belief that women are invested with power, and the deep ambivalence of the male hierarchy towards this power.

Similar stories abound in Christian history. One of the most obvious (indeed, infamous) confirming examples is the career of Joan of Arc. The Maid of Orleans was obviously taken seriously and granted spiritual and political authority when it suited the rulers of church and state; and just as obviously abandoned, slandered and tortured when her usefulness was less apparent. As has been noted by recent scholarship, Joan's sudden rise to fame was possible because her actions were interpreted in the context of female religious prophecy.[18] Compared to the fate of Joan of Arc, who was burned at the stake as a heretic in 1431, the ecclesiastical violence suffered by Lucia Brocadelli was slight. Nevertheless, both women were victims of a culture of deep ambivalence wherein, to paraphrase Adrienne Rich, their wounds came from the same source as their power.[19]

The subtlety with which medieval and early modern Christian women recognized this ambivalence and used it for their own empowerment is one of the more complicated aspects of the history of ecclesiastical violence. Hildegard of Bingen, the twelfth-century visionary and polymath known as "The Sibyl of the Rhine," was particularly articulate about what Barbara Newman has called "the divine power made perfect in weakness," that gave women a type of authority out of their very limitations.[20] As Hildegard wrote to the monks of Eberbach:

> But I — a poor woman, weak and frail from my infancy — have been compelled in a true and mysterious vision to write this letter. And

lying in bed with a serious illness, I have written it by the command and assistance of God to present it to the prelates and masters who are sealed for God's service, that in it they might see who and what they are....And I heard a voice from heaven saying: Let no one despise them, the vengeance of God fall upon him.[21]

Three themes vie for prominence in this passage: the assumption of women's weakness, the certainty of God's revelation, and the warning to those who might doubt Hildegard's specific powers. The coexistence of these strands make possible the weaving of a strategy of survival in a climate of repression. Hildegard's claim for direct knowledge of God's will, couched in a protestation of weakness, is paralleled by the experience of other religious women of the Middle Ages and early modern period: Elisabeth of Schönau, for example, became a source and conduit of divine revelation for her brother Ekbert.[22] More complex is the relationship of Catherine of Siena and her confessor/amanuensis Raymond of Capua; in this case, Raymond not only reflected the inspiration of the woman in his spiritual care, but actually stressed the aspects of her experience that resonated most closely with his own, to a large extent creating the Catherine passed on to posterity.[23]

Lucia Brocadelli da Narni, Joan of Arc, Hildegard of Bingen, Elisabeth of Schönau, Catherine of Siena, were all exceptional women, famous in their own day, and vindicated by posterity. Joan, who suffered most from the violence of the church towards women, was canonized in the twentieth century; Lucia Brocadelli was officially beatified in the eighteenth century; Hildegard, Elisabeth and Catherine are finally being taken seriously by historians of Christianity. It is harder for us to reconstruct the ecclesiastical violence endured by women who did not become enshrined in the historical record of official Christianity. Na Prous Boneta is only one the many Cathars (male and female) destroyed by the Inquisition of the fourteenth century; like Joan of Arc, Na Prous's voice survives only in inquisitorial records.[24] But who were the "begghini combusti," the burned Beguines, to whom she compares herself? How many women were killed in the fervor of witchcraft persecutions between the fourteenth and the eighteenth centuries? Even this question has been politicized; "only 100,000," say those who wish to protect Christianity from its own worst characteristics; "nine million," answer those who find satisfaction in comparative genocide studies.[25] The search for statistics, like the study of the exceptions, only shows us to what extent the violence of ambivalence has afflicted women in the Christian tradition.

The final irony of this ambivalence is its historical pervasiveness. Although ecclesiastical authors no longer assume, as did the medieval scholars and canon lawyers, that women are not in the image of God,[26]

most statements by twentieth-century hierarchies of Roman Catholicism that deign to mention women theologians and spiritual authors do
so only to condemn and dismiss "radical feminism." But the history of
Christianity has shown us that women's spiritual insights have been far
more influential than the hierarchy wants to admit. In 1310, the Inquisition burned a Beguine named Marguerite Porete, author of a book called
The Mirror of Simple Souls. The book, nevertheless, circulated widely, for
centuries, in Old French, Latin, Italian, and Middle English; it was at-
tributed to other, orthodox mystics, or presented as anonymous. Only in
1965 did Romana Guarini publish a critical edition of the Old French
text along with the proof that the author of this celebrated text was
Marguerite, the woman condemned and executed for heresy.[27] Christian women's spiritual insights have, in spite of everything, sometimes,
somehow, managed to survive ecclesiastical violence.

NOTES

1. For general discussions of this ambivalence, see Frances Gies and
Joseph Gies, "Eve and Mary," in *Women in the Middle Ages*, New York, 1980,
pp. 37–59; Mary Daly, "The Pedestal Pushers," in *The Church and the Second
Sex*, Boston, 1968, 1975, 1985, pp. 147–65.

2. Elizabeth A. Clark, "Uses of the Song of Songs: Origen and the Later
Latin Fathers," in *Ascetic Piety and Women's Faith: Essays on Late Antique
Christianity*, Lewiston/Queenston, 1986, pp. 403–6, text ed. J. Hillberger, Cor-
pus Scriptorum Ecclesiasticorum Latinorum 54, 1, 1910, pp. 143–211. See
also Jo Ann McNamara, "Muffled Voices: The Lives of Consecrated Women
in the Fourth Century," in *Medieval Religious Women*, vol. 1 *Distant Echoes*,
ed. John A. Nichols and Lillian Thomas Shank, Kalamazoo, Mich., 1984,
pp. 11–29.

3. Jane Tibbets Schulenberg, "Strict Active Enclosure and Its Effects on
the Female Monastic Experience (500–1000)," in Nichols and Shanks, *Distant
Echoes* (n. 2), pp. 51–86.

4. Raymond Creytens, "La riforma dei monasteri femminili," in *Il concilo
di Trento e la riforma tridentina*, Rome, 1963, 1:45–83; Katherine Gill, "Open
Monasteries for Women in Late Medieval and Early Modern Italy: Two Roman
Examples," *The Crannied Wall: Women, Religion and the Arts in Early Modern
Europe*, ed. Craig Monson, Ann Arbor, Mich., 1992, pp. 15–47.

5. Penelope D. Johnson, *Equal in Monastic Profession: Religious Women in
Medieval France*, Chicago, 1991.

6. For Hrosvit, a German author of the tenth century, see *The Plays of
Hrotsvit of Gandersheim*, translated by Katharina Wilson, New York, 1989,
and Elizabeth Avilda Petroff, *Medieval Women's Visionary Literature*, New York,
1986, pp. 114–35; for Tuscan convent drama in the sixteenth and seventeenth
centuries, see Beatrice del Sera, *Amor di Virtu, Commedia in cinque atti 1548*,
ed. Elissa Weaver, Ravenna, 1990; Elissa Weaver, "Convent Comedy and the

World: The Farces of Suor Annalena Odaldl (1572–1638)," *Annali d'Italianistica* 7, 1989, pp. 182–92; and Elissa Weaver, "The Convent Wall in Tuscan Convent Drama," in Monson, ed., *The Crannied Wall*, 1992, pp. 73–86.

7. Robert Kendrick, "The Traditions of Milanese Convent Music and the Sacred Dialogues of Chiara Margarita Cozzolani," in Monson, ed., *The Crannied Wall*, 1992, pp. 211–33; Craig Monson, "Disembodied Voices: Music in the Nunneries of Bologna in the midst of the Counter-Reformation," in Monson, ed., *The Crannied Wall*, 1992, pp. 191–209.

8. In English alone, collections of writings by medieval religious women include Peter Dronke, *Women Writers of the Middle Ages*, Cambridge, 1984; Petroff, *Medieval Women's Visionary Literature*; Katharina M. Wilson, *Medieval Women Writers*, Athens, Ga., 1984; Emilie Zum Brunn and Georgette Epiney-Burgard, *Women Mystics in Medieval Europe*, New York, 1989.

9. Heinrich Krämer and Jacob Sprenger, *Malleus maleficarum*, translated with introductions, bibliography and notes by Montague Summers, New York, 1971.

10. Rosemary Radford Ruether, *New Woman New Earth: Sexist Ideologies and Human Liberation*, New York, 1975, pp. 19, 72, 97–98, 101–2; Rosemary Radford Ruether, *Sexism and God-Talk: Toward a Feminist Theology*, Boston, 1983, p. 170.

11. *Malleus maleficarum*, Part II, Question 1, Chapter IV, ed. Summers, pp. 109–14; Part II, Question 1, Chapter VII, ed. Summers, pp. 118–22, including the famous account of the woman who kept a collection of stolen penises (the biggest one of which belonged to the village priest) in a nest in a tree, ed. Summers, p. 122.

12. *Malleus maleficarum*, Part I, Question 6, ed. Summers, p. 47.

13. Ruether, *New Woman New Earth*, quoting an unpublished paper by Barbara Yoshoika, 34, n. 21.

14. *Malleus maleficarum*, Part I, Question 6, ed. Summers, p. 42.

15. For the story of the smuggling of Lucia out of Viterbo in a laundry basket, see Serafino Razzi, *Vite dei santi e beati, cosi huomini come donne del sacro ordine de' frati predicatori*, Florence, 1577, pp. 151–7; P. F. G. Marcianese, *Vita della b. Lucia da Narni*, Viterbo, 1663; the entry under Lucia Brocadelli's name in *Dizionario biografico degli Italiani*, Rome, 1972; and Edmund G. Gardner, *Dukes and Poets in Ferrara: A Study in the Poetry, Religion and Politics of the Fifteenth and Early Sixteenth Centuries*, New York, 1968, reprinted from the 1904 edition, pp. 379–88.

16. Gabriella Zarri, "Pietà e profezia alle corti Padane: le pie consigliere dei principi," in *Le sante vive: Cultura e religiosità femminile nella prima età moderna*, Turin, 1990, pp. 51–86; "Le sante vive," in *Le sante vive*, pp. 87–163.

17. Ercole's two letters about Lucia, dated 4 March 1500 and 23 January 1501, are printed in *Spirituallum personarum feminel sexus facta admiratione digna*, Nürnberg, 1501, six unpaginated folia. This text is discussed by Gardner, p. 367.

18. Andre Vauchez, "Jeanne d'Arc et le prophétisme feminin des xive et xve siècles," in *Jeanne d'Arc: une époque, un rayonnement*, Colloque d'histoire médiévale, Orléans, 1979, pp. 159–68; Francis Rapp, "Jeanne d'Arc, témoin de la vie religieuse en France au xve siècle," in *Jeanne d'Arc*, pp. 169–79; Debo-

rah Fraioli, "The Literary Image of Joan of Arc: Prior Influences," *Speculum* 56, 1981, pp. 811–29.

19. "Her wounds came from the same source as her power," Adrienne Rich, "Power," in *The Dream of a Common Language: Poems 1974–1977*, New York, 1978, p. 3.

20. Barbara Newman, "Divine Power Made Perfect in Weakness: St. Hildegard on the Frail Sex," in *Medieval Religious Women*, vol. 2: *Peaceweavers*, ed. Lillian Thomas Shank and John A. Nichols, Kalamazoo, Mich., 1987, pp. 103–22; Barbara Newman, "The Woman and the Serpent," and "The Daughters of Eve," in *Sister of Wisdom: St. Hildegard's Theology of the Feminine*, Berkeley, Calif., 1987, pp. 42–120.

21. Hildegard, Epistle 51, PL 197:268C, translated by Newman, "Divine Power," p. 103.

22. Anne L. Clark, "Conclusion: The Prophetic Voice of a Twelfth-Century Woman," *Elisabeth of Schönau: A Twelfth-Century Visionary*, Philadelphia, 1992, pp. 129–35.

23. Caroline Walker Bynum, *Holy Feast, Holy Fast: The Religious Significance of Food to Medieval Women*, Berkeley, Calif., 1987, pp. 166–80; Karen Scott, "Saint Catherine of Siena, 'Apostola,'" *Church History* 61, 1992, pp. 34–46.

24. Petroff, *Women Visionaries*, pp. 276–77, 284–90.

25. Ruether, *New Woman New Earth*, III n. 1.

26. E. Ann Matter, "Innocent III and the Keys to the Kingdom of Heaven," in *Women Priests: A Catholic Commentary on the Vatican Declaration*, ed. Leonard Swidler and Arlene Swidler, New York, 1977, pp. 145–51.

27. Romana Guarini, "Il Movimento del Libero Spirito," *Archivio italiano per la storia della pietà* 4, 1965, pp. 351–708; Petroff, pp. 280–82, 294–98.

23

Maria Goretti

Rape and the Politics of Sainthood

EILEEN J. STENZEL

Introduction

For years I taught an undergraduate course on Catholicism. The canonization of Maria Goretti in 1950 was included in an overview of Catholic attitudes and practices regarding women. Inevitably, students would end up in a heated debate. Some would claim that the rationale for Maria's canonization was understandable given the social climate of the 1950s. Others were outraged that the Roman Catholic Church would ever have said that a woman is better dead than raped.

A feminist pastoral theology concerned with violence and the politics of sainthood addresses the problem these students shaped in their debate. On the one hand, it recognizes that ecclesial thought and practice must be understood within its many contexts. On the other hand, it offers criteria for evaluating these traditions.

The canonization of Maria Goretti (1890–1902) is compelling to feminist theologians because it is a pastoral-theological response to violence against women. Women, like men, are victims of random violence. However, there are forms of violence which are directed against women-as-women. Rape, battering and sexual harassment are examples of gender-based violence. They represent the epitome of all that is wrong about sexism and all efforts to portray it as normal. It is an awareness of women's increased vulnerability to violent attack within patriarchal systems that fuels the efforts of feminist scholars to assess critically how these systems find justification within our respective disciplines. Feminist theologians share this commitment to identify how patriarchal ecclesial consciousness and praxis function to legitimate violence against women by supporting the conditions which cause it.

A feminist pastoral theology concerned with violence and the politics of sainthood must do four things: (1) identify a working understanding of women's experience of violence; (2) show how patriarchal norms have been incorporated into ecclesial pastoral traditions; (3) propose non-sexist alternatives to ecclesial self-understanding and praxis; and (4) submit those proposals to critical assessment.

Feminist Consensus on Violence against Women

Prior to the development of feminist perspectives on rape in the late 1960s, societal definitions of rape excluded the victim's experience of rape and insisted that rape was a form of sexual deviance often precipitated by its victims.[1] Additionally, these definitions of rape presumed a woman's need for protection and limited that right of protection to those women who adhered to traditional female roles and behaviors.

Feminist scholars have viewed rape in the context of patriarchal culture and defined it in terms of victims' accounts of their experience of rape. Feminists have argued that the dominant-subordinate model of male-female relatedness is an inherently violent structure of relatedness. Patriarchal culture fosters a spectrum of behaviors including at its most violent end rape, battering and sexual harassment. In this context, women's experience of violence becomes a paradigm because it conveys basic assumptions about the reality of sexism.

While differences in interpretation of paradigm continue, there is a growing consensus among feminist scholars about the cause and function of violence against women as women.[2] There is general agreement that violence against women rises from a systemic cultural acceptance of power and control as a means of affecting and defining human relationships.[3] Our very definitions of formal relationships carry the connotation of power-as-control: leaders and followers, adults and children, religious and lay, employers and workers, men and women, young and old, white and black, rich and poor.

The structure of power-as-dominance involves myths which function to legitimize the controlling behavior of the dominant group. Structures of male dominance are supported by mythical stereotypes about women. Among these are: (1) the identification of women only in terms of sexuality and reproduction; (2) the assertion that women have a distinct nature that best suits them to bear the greater burden of responsibility for sexual morality, nurturance and service; and (3) the assumption that aggression is the natural mode of male behavior and submissiveness the natural mode of female behavior, thereby defining female submission as consent.

Mythical assumptions about the relationship between men and women have been incorporated into legal, social, political and religious thought and practice. Prosecution of rape has required proof of excessive use of force because it has been assumed that some degree of force is normal in male-female sexual relatedness. In many countries women are unable to charge a man to whom they are legally married with rape because of assumptions about the conjugal rights of married men.

This model of male-female relatedness denies personal, social and moral autonomy to women. Denial of the right to self-determination and equal partnership with men are the conditions of subordination which increase the likelihood that a woman will be abused in her home, in her job, by a stranger and even in her church by those designated to wield power over her.

There is also general agreement about the function of gender-based violence. Studies of rapists and men acknowledged to be batterers suggest that the purpose of the violent behavior was to assert dominance and/or to punish inappropriate female behavior.[4] While interventions with offenders vary, there is general consensus on the goals of treatment. These are: (1) changing the offender's attitude towards women; (2) changing controlling behavior; and (3) learning to deal with anger.

The Context

To read the lives of the saints literally is to misunderstand the polemics and politics of sainthood. Ecclesial polemics about saints are shaped with a purpose in mind: to promote as moral one set of values and behaviors and to condemn others as immoral. Canonization is, by its nature, political. What is at issue is the nature of the politics at work in the thought and practice of the canonizing church.

We know very little about Maria Goretti. The story says that she was the daughter of a poor peasant farmer whose family shared a house with Giovanni Serenelli and his son Alessandro. Maria is said to have rejected the repeated advances of the sixteen-year-old Alessandro who made threats against her each time she refused him. Finally, fearful and enraged by her rejection, Alessandro stabbed her repeatedly. She lingered for days. Before her death, it is reported that she forgave Alessandro.

During his thirty years in prison, Alessandro reported dreams in which Maria appeared to him and forgave him. Upon his release he is said to have sought out Maria's mother, begged her forgiveness and lived out his life in seclusion. Maria was canonized on 24 June 1950. The cause of her canonization was her willingness to die rather than be "defiled" and her role in the conversion of her assailant.

The canonization of Maria Goretti needs to be read in the context of nineteenth- and early twentieth-century papacies. The rationale for her sainthood developed in the tradition of these popes.

Two anti-patriarchal movements developed in the nineteenth century: political liberalism and feminism. Both redefined social problems in political and economic terms rather than in terms of personal morality. Feminism applied the principles of individual liberty to women.

Nineteenth-century feminists rejected the Common Law tradition that viewed society as a composite of free families in which the rights of individual men were protected from intervention by the state. Since women's roles were defined almost entirely in terms of family roles, the Common Law tradition placed the relationship between men and women outside the protection of law. Feminists insisted that the political and social empowerment of women would, of necessity, always involve issues of marriage, family life, sexuality and reproductive freedom.[5]

The papal response of the Roman Catholic Church to both of these movements was condemnation. Pius IX (1864–78) reasserted the primacy of the church and the papacy in society (cf. *The Syllabus of Errors*). Leo XIII (1878–1903) rejected the definition of social problems in political and economic terms, insisting on the primacy of spiritual and religious values in the social order (cf. *Rerum Novarum* and *On Christian Marriage*). Pius X (1903–1914) insisted that the mission of the church was to maintain an unchanging order in both church and society (cf. *Lamentabili*). Benedict XV (1914–1922) reasserted the primacy of the church in the social order and blamed social unrest on the anti-authoritarianism of social movements (cf. *Ad Beatissima*). Pius XI (1922–1939) denounced the movement for women's emancipation as criminal and heretical (cf. *Casti Connubi*).

The canonization of Maria Goretti in 1950 was a culminating moment in this anti-modernist, anti-feminist papal tradition. Pius XII (1939–58) insisted that the subordination of women to men was a dictum of the natural law and, therefore, divinely intended. He espoused the identification of women with sexuality by insisting that women were created to fulfil sexual and reproductive roles (cf. *Papal Directives for the Woman of Today*).

The social control which the church sought, in the name of natural (divine) law, could not, by 1950, be established by recreating medieval theocracy. It could be exercised through the control of its members, who would be expected to conduct their personal and political lives in submission to the church. This authority had to extend to reproduction and the family, especially women, since the primary obligation of Catholic couples was to produce and raise new members for the church. Consistent with this view, Alessandro Serenelli's sin was not his attack on

Maria Goretti. It was his attempt to engage in illicit sexual behavior. Had
Maria submitted in an attempt to save her life, she, too, would have been
condemned.

Feminist Reinterpretations of the Sainthood of Maria Goretti

The papal tradition outlined above confronts contemporary Catholicism with a fundamental option. Will the church continue to see itself
as the depository of correct thinking and behavior? Or, will the church
understand itself to need new perspectives, knowledge and skills as
a participant in the struggle to realize greater freedom and justice in
the world?

The Second Vatican Council reflects movement towards the latter.
However, post-Vatican II Catholicism remains entrenched in patriarchal
theocracy. Paul VI reduced priesthood to maleness and reiterated the
teaching that women must be subject to male rule (cf. *The Declaration on
The Ordination of Women, The Role of Women in Evangelization, Humanae
Vitae* and *The Declaration on Sexual Ethics*). These positions continue to
be offered as the true liberation of women. Feminist objections continue
to meet condemnation. A church which excludes the victims of oppression from efforts to overcome that oppression and persists in defining
the ability to mediate God's presence on the basis of genetic chance and
hormonal differences cannot possibly be participating fully in the liberating and saving work of God. A feminist reinterpretation of Maria's
sainthood must critique the incompatibility of patriarchal theocracy and
feminist commitment and establish the link between gospel values and
anti-patriarchal feminist values.

For those persuaded by orthodoxy, the stories of the saints contain
authoritative papal teaching which cannot be ignored. A feminist reinterpretation from this perspective would focus on the redemptive imagery
used to convey the story of Maria's fidelity. Sin and evil are located in
the disobedience of a world that has turned from its obligation to live in
accord with God's intent as conveyed in church teaching. Grace and redemption (Alessandro's conversion) came into that world through Maria's
act of obedience even unto death. The use of the biblical/ecclesial image
of Jesus' own redemptive act, applied to Maria, portrays her as Jesus'
representative in the ongoing work of redemption. An orthodox feminist
reinterpretation can offer this representation of Jesus by Maria Goretti
as a challenge to the current position of Rome that women cannot be ordained because women cannot represent Christ on earth. Maria Goretti
is pastoral testimony to the priesthood of women.

A second feminist reinterpretation of the sainthood of Maria Goretti sees the key pastoral moment as the affirmative act of rejecting the anti-feminist pastoral intent of her canonization. A true canonization of Maria Goretti by the faithful could rise from a refusal to accept her as anything other than a martyr to violence nurtured by a church which was willing to sacrifice the powerless in the name of its own patriarchal interests.

A feminist interpretation of the sainthood of Maria Goretti must offer a new image of the church, one which has within itself the capability of engaging competently and humbly with those who struggle against the forces of political and economic oppression. A new ecclesiology can de-velop out of the ministry of the faithful who voice the experiences of all victims of all forms of power-as-dominance.

A feminist reinterpretation of the sainthood of Maria Goretti that takes seriously the accounts of victims of gender-violence can imagine its way past the polemical portrayal of Maria Goretti to what her experience as a victim of attempted rape and murder might have been.

Maria's voice has long been lost to us. We can, however, try to imag-ine her anguish. Imagine the fear of a twelve-year-old child resisting unwanted advances and threatened death by someone with whom she lived. Imagine the struggle that enabled her to survive for however long. Imagine Maria screaming, begging and fighting against the force of her assailant. Imagine the possibility that for Maria, life was worth saving but what she feared more than death was the certain rejection and peril she faced in society that defined rape as a crime one man committed against another and in which rape could be used to force marriage. Imagine a so-ciety that renders a child too frightened by social consequences to seek the protection of adults from threatened rape and death. Imagine a child too frightened by possible condemnation by her priest to seek his refuge. The world in which Maria struggled to survive promoted the belief that a woman was better dead than raped, and the church agreed.

Alessandro killed her because she refused to submit to him. The Ro-man Catholic Church canonized her because she submitted to the higher authority of the church. Neither her attacker nor the church recognized Maria's right to decide her own fate. But perhaps Maria did.

Maria's sainthood rests in part on her forgiveness of her attacker. Maria did not urge him to seek out a priest for forgiveness. She forgave him. God did not send angels to a sleeping prisoner; Maria appeared to him and forgave him. Maria's acts of forgiveness reflect her own sense of oneness with God.

The 1950 canonization of Maria Goretti arose from the perspective and practice of a patriarchal, theocratic church. A feminist reinterpretation of the sainthood of Maria Goretti arises out of our individual and col-lective efforts to overcome the dehumanizing affects of patriarchy. That experience gives rise to a new vision of the church and to its redemptive mission. The voice we give to this martyred child is our own. The church we envision cannot understand the problems of violence and oppression or work to overcome them without the participation of its victims.

The stories about the saints function to hold up an ideal to which we can aspire. A feminist reinterpretation of the sainthood of Maria Goretti is an act of faithful imagination that rejects anti-feminist ecclesial practice as the norm for Christian self-understanding and, instead, identifies the gospel with an anti-patriarchal commitment. It functions not only as a critique of patriarchal theocracy but also as an affirmation of the new church now living in our midst. The ideal function of sainthood allows us to imagine what could have happened had this church been Maria's church.

Had the church lived in more solidarity with the poor and oppressed it could have condemned the attempted rape of Maria and her murder as further evidence of the violence to which women were repeatedly subjected. A church that rejected the abuse of power and aligned itself more consciously with the poor and oppressed could have condemned the poverty and special vulnerability of women in poverty that gave rise to such violence, then as now. A church confident in the presence of God could have re-examined its own views of sexuality, which associated force and sex. Instead, a theocratic church reasserted a patriarchal view of both women and its own power-as-dominance which is, simply, another word for violence.[6]

Conclusion

Maria Goretti was a child murdered by another child. The reality of powerlessness and the cycle of violence it breeds is devastating. Every aspect of the future for which we bear full responsibility is challenged. The sacramental ministry of Roman Catholicism celebrates life at all stages; promotes the hope born in reconciliation, healing and change; and affirms Christian vocation as a life-long commitment to justice, peace and love as gospel values. That Catholic-Christian vision to embrace the world with hope and skill is not contradicted by challenging patriarchal theocracy. That vision is affirmed as an ultimate act of faith and love.

NOTES

1. M. Amir, *Patterns in Forcible Rape*, Chicago, 1971.

2. P. L. N. Donat and J. D'Emilio, "A Feminist Redefinition of Rape and Sexual Assault: Historical Foundations and Change," *Journal of Social Issues* 48,

no. 1 (1992), pp. 9–22; D. Herman, "The Rape Culture," in *Women: A Feminist Perspective,* ed. J. Freeman, 2d ed., Mountain view, Calif., 1975.

3. J. D'Emilio and E. B. Freedman, *Intimate Matters: A History of Sexuality in America,* New York, 1988; G. Lerner, ed., *Black Women in White America,* New York, 1973; K. Millet, *Sexual Politics,* New York, 1970.

4. A. N. Groth and A. W. Burgess, "Rape: A Sexual Deviation," *American Journal of Orthopsychiatry* 47 (July 1977), pp. 400–406; A. N. Groth, *Men Who Rape: The Psychology of the Offender,* New York, 1979.

5. S. B. Anthony, "Social Purity" (1875), in *Up from the Pedestal,* ed. A. S. D. Kraditor, New York, 1975, pp. 159–66; M. Wollstonecraft, *A Vindication of the Rights of Woman,* ed. M. Brody Krannick, Harmondsworth, 1975, pp. 24ff.

6. V. L. Erickson, "Back to the Basics: Feminist Social Theory, Durkheim and Religion," *Journal of Feminist Studies in Religion* 8, no. 1 (Spring 1992), pp. 35–46.

24

Daughters of the Church

The Four Theresas

MARY COLLINS

In her recent biography *Teresa: A Woman*, Victoria Lincoln confirms that the dying Teresa of Avila recited over and over "Cor contritum et humilem, Deus, non despices" — "a contrite and humble heart you will not despise, O God." Then, after she had received viaticum she whispered as *apólogia:* "After all (or: in the end) Lord, I am a daughter of the Church."[1] Many who have revered Teresa of Avila since her death in 1582 have resonated with the rich significance of that deathbed phrase. In the 1940s a French Carmelite wrote a semi-popular compendium of Carmelite spirituality and entitled his second volume *Je suis fille de l'Eglise.* The work was translated into English and was a staple on shelves of convent, seminary, and rectory libraries in the U.S., along with translations of Teresa's own writings. The phrase "daughter of the church," in French or English, even without historical context, had a clarity and simplicity which seemed to say what finally mattered in any Roman Catholic woman's vocation.

This essay — in a volume concerned with women's invisibility in the Church and the Church's work of theological reflections — takes as its starting point the phenomenon of the striking visibility of four women named Theresa, all recognizable daughters in the contemporary Church. They are uncommon in that regard. For while the Church has millions of daughters, most of them are invisible, unknown, women — anonymous wives and mothers, nameless "good sisters" and "pious nuns," and "selfless" single women. Other essays in this volume attend to the structures and social dynamics which guarantee most churchwomen's invisibility. What is of interest in the case of the four Theresas — Teresa of Avila, Thérèse of Lisieux, Mother Teresa of Calcutta, and Theresa Kane of the

United States — is the paradox of their public visibility in a Church which characteristically conceals its female members.

Paradox is the issue. It will be argued that these women's heightened visibility in the Church requires the concealment of their actual identities and the manipulation of personas. When the real Theresas whose rich lives have symbolic depth are reduced to types of churchwomen, the historical Theresas and with them all other real women are silenced. Yet it is also true that symbols have their own dynamism and resist control through reduction to types. Sooner or later something of life will reveal more of the latent power concealed within them than what official typologists may intend.

As Victoria Lincoln says of the selective presentation of the truth of Teresa of Avila during the past four centuries: "I should like to believe that God wanted her to be remembered and used the world as it then was in the hope that what was so saved of her reality would be better understood in an age that could respect her life, and, yes, her sanctity, for what it is."[2]

It will be important in understanding the paradox in the case of the four Theresas to look first at the selective popular presentations of each woman and the effect of such selectivity. Then it will be possible to ask some questions about that process.

The Four Theresas

By coincidence the four churchwomen who have enjoyed international celebrity or notoriety in the recent past and so become available for this study are each named Theresa. The widespread interest in the four Theresas can be readily established through a check of periodical literature from 1970 through 1984. Focal events served to intensify interest in each of them at certain times during this past fifteen years. Teresa of Avila was proclaimed Doctor of the Church in 1970 by Pope Paul VI; then in 1982 the Carmelite Order led the Church in celebrating the fourth centenary of her death. These two pivots kept the Spanish Carmelite in view in both popular and scholarly religious periodicals.[3]

The centenary of Thérèse of Lisieux's birth in 1973 became the occasion for an upsurge of interest in Thérèse Martin, "the Little Flower," and gave rise to new popular presentations and scholarly studies of this nineteenth century French Carmelite woman and her spirituality of the little way. Her persistent popularity, already well-established at the time of her canonization in 1925, guaranteed that this already well-known churchwoman would come to new prominence in a centenary period.[4]

Mother Teresa of Calcutta's visibility and popularity spanned the period. In 1970 Pope Paul VI had conferred the John XXIII Peace Prize on her; in 1979 she also received the Nobel Peace Prize. Throughout the era, the public apparently could not hear enough about the living saint of India, the Albanian Agnes Gonxha Bojaxhiu, for twenty years an Irish Sister of Loretto who then left her community to begin a new work among the poor and to become Mother Teresa. In 1984, the importance of this seventy-year-old holy woman for popular religious culture in the English-speaking world was signalled by the presentation of her life in comic book form, a genre designed to reach the masses of the young.[5]

In 1979, Theresa Kane, then administrator general of the U.S. Sisters of Mercy of the Roman Union, was also elected president of the Leadership Conference of Women Religious, the official conference of women religious superiors in the United States. In that capacity she greeted Pope John Paul II during his pastoral visit to the U.S. in the fall of 1979. Her address was no more than 600 words. What made it memorable, and what made it overshadow the fuller context of her own life as a churchwoman, the works of mercy pursued by her sisters for more than a century, the dedicated lives of a hundred thousand women religious in the U.S., and the pledge of fidelity to the Church which she conveyed to John Paul was the single sentence: "I urge you, Your Holiness, to be open to and to respond to the voices of women coming from this country whose desire is for serving in and through the Church as fully participating members."[6] The next year, Theresa Kane received an award as Outstanding U.S. Catholic, an honor conferred by the editors of the popular religious monthly called *U.S. Catholic.*

The coincidence of names and the circumstance of public prominence in the contemporary Church are not the only elements of convergence which invite comment. Significantly, all four of them have lived their adult lives as vowed members of established ecclesiastical communities for women. None are married or single. Further, their personal histories point to recurrent motifs and to repeated confrontations with ecclesiastical givens on the part of independent women.

Two of them, not only Theresa Kane but also Thérèse of Lisieux, presumed to speak directly to popes to accomplish their purposes when these were at odds with the norms of ecclesiastical life. Two of them, not only Theresa Kane but also Teresa of Avila, met with strong public disapproval from churchmen who worked alternately to discredit them and to control them. Two of them, Theresa Kane and Thérèse of Lisieux, openly entertained the unthinkable possibility that women might be called by God to the Church's priestly ministry. Two of them, Teresa of Calcutta and Teresa of Avila, left the habits and communities of their original religious profession in order to follow their true vocations.

All of them or any one of the Theresas might have been the subject of a recent scholarly judgment made about Thérèse of Lisieux. Commenting on the illusory perception that Thérèse Martin fit the traditional model of femininity, that of the woman who is "sweet, pliable, childlike, living only to please others," Joann Wolski Conn says: " . . . a closer look at the evidence can reveal quite the contrary model. Thérèse is a strong, creative, mature young woman who thought independently and originally, and who could thus give a genuine self in a free loving relationship to God."[7]

The two models that Conn identifies suggest two ways of being "daughters of the Church." The biographies of all four women have been interpreted for the public more or less consistently according to the preferred traditional model. For those for whom the living-only-to-please model is essential to a churchwoman's reality, Theresa Kane's public raising of a difficult question for churchmen was a source of embarrassment, confusion, and anger. In her brief appearance she presented herself as an independent woman able to risk original thought. Many of the embarrassed, confused, or angered viewers of the international telecast were thus moved to the judgment that her loyalty was suspect, that she was dangerous to the faith and the well-being of the Church, indeed that she was evil.

This latter summary evaluation and interpretation of the case of Theresa Kane is not offered gratuitously, but as the result of weeks of careful research on LCWR archival materials made available to me in 1980. The secretariat invited me to collaborate with them in a study of the 5,000 letters which reached that office after their president had greeted the pope on behalf of women religious in the U.S.

If priesthood was not named in the key sentence cited above, nevertheless the officially unimaginable, unthinkable, and unspoken had resounded across the country and across the globe. The letters which poured into the LCWR secretariat were largely appreciative. The vitriolic were fewer but their emotional content was more electrifying. Interestingly, the rhetorical thread which joined both groups of letters was the "daughters of the Church" motif.

Circumstances contributed to the wide-spread appropriation of Teresa of Avila's deathbed *apologia* to deal with the Theresa Kane–John Paul II meeting. The meeting took place on 7 October 1979. Many letters were dated in mid-October, between the feasts of the two Carmelite Theresas on 3 and 15 October. The liturgical calendar may have stimulated both the letter writing and the comparison and contrast of Theresas. Was it earlier spiritual reading, remembered retreat conferences, or a long-forgotten book title that made the phrase "daughter of the Church" so readily available to writers? No matter the reason; the rhetorical tool was at hand.

That recurring rhetorical link provided me with a research method and a working hypothesis for the 1980 study. A content analysis of the letters generated profiles of what the writers perceived to be the characteristic attitudes and behaviors of an authentic "daughter of the Church." The detailed results of that research do not bear immediately on this consideration of the controlled visibility of women in the Church except insofar as it identified clearly the importance of the projected *persona* as a way of relating to visible Church women. The correspondence taken cumulatively revealed more about the dynamics of symbolic appropriation of the real than about five minutes in the life of Theresa Kane.

It will not come as a surprise to those who have followed feminist scholarship for a decade or more that what was regularly configured typologically by those who wrote to express disapproval of what they had seen or heard was a profile of the good woman or the wicked one. In these cases, the criteria for determining goodness and wickedness came from the traditional understanding of a faithful churchwoman as one "living only to please" churchmen. Where that model was honored as touchstone for interpreting the event, any woman who was evidently interested in "growth beyond conventional roles" or who was "striving for an autonomous, adult personality" was inevitably suspect. By such standard criteria, Theresa Kane was no authentic daughter of the Church. Interestingly, those who pronounced such judgments regularly offered her the example of one or more of the visible Theresas — Calcutta, Avila, or Lisieux — as typical daughter.

Neither will it be surprising that those other letter writers who acclaimed Theresa Kane as an authentic daughter of the Church had feminist inspiration for their own normative configuration of the good woman. She was courageous, forthright, capable of originality, a faithful seeker of truth. Yet once again writers linked Theresas, citing or alluding to instances of risk-taking in the biographies of the other women, instances of their readiness to go beyond conventional thinking and acting out of love for God and the Church.

In fact, all four Theresas have had minds of their own and have shown them in matters of the papacy, priesthood, and conformity to established ways. In the late nineteenth century a young Thérèse Martin had disrupted papal protocol to speak directly to a pope. In a public audience she broke rank to ask Pope Leo XIII about a matter that concerned herself, namely her desire to enter Carmel to serve God. At the end of her brief life in Carmel, Thérèse Martin's desire for service to God had expanded beyond the thinkable and the reasonable role of a Carmelite woman. Only a short time before her death she wrote to a sister: "I feel within me the vocation of the PRIEST" (emphasis in the original). In context she noted that she no doubt ought to be satisfied that her true vocation lay with being Jesus' Spouse, a Carmelite, and a Mother of Souls. But she was not.

Death spared her the anguish of confronting the late nineteenth-century Church or another pope with this vocational question. Her impending death did not cause her to repress the question. She left it recorded in manuscript for the twentieth-century Church to reflect upon.[8] Despite her actual willingness to entertain the forbidden, the "Little Flower" set out for popular emulation within the Church shows neither originality nor boldness. She is stereotypically cast as selfless and submissive. Why? What purpose does this serve? And whose?

Teresa of Avila's vocation to a life of prayer did not lead her to a comparable sense of priestly vocation. But neither did she repress her own distinctive sensibilities and aspirations when these came into conflict with those of the ordained churchmen of her day. Her critical biographer Lincoln notes that "Teresa was bound with the greatest of fidelities to her inner 'voice,' the signs from her meditation." Yet she observes the complexity of the woman, who "tied [herself] to several theologians, confessors, and superiors at the same time," creating a situation which allowed her to follow her own voice since there would always be one "to command as the 'voice' wished."[9] She came up against and eluded the control of ecclesiastical superiors and the Spanish Inquisition. In such confrontations she was tenacious, confident that what she knew from inner experience no theologian or ecclesiastical authority could successfully dispute. The Church which canonized her and which named her doctor nevertheless represses the memory of the conflictive process by which an independent Church woman set out her teaching and prevailed. Why? For what purpose? And whose?

Mother Teresa of Calcutta, too, prevailed in her own vocation because she refused to be deterred by established institutions and approved behaviors. So it is highly ironic that the independent Albanian churchwoman Agnes Gonxha Bojaxhiu, who readily set aside her original commitment in the 1940s in order to accomplish her own purposes for God has subsequently become, as Mother Teresa, a symbol for womanly conformity to ecclesiastical institutions. Her persona, confirmed by churchmen from pope to local pastor to priest journalist, belies her biography. The puzzle is how the story of an independent, autonomous, assertive woman has been so successfully retold as a tale of compliant daughter of the Church.

Typology and Its Uses

Persona, type, and *symbol* have all been used as interpretative categories in the discussion of the visibility of the four Theresas. The concepts need not be distinguished in order to advance this study of the occasional visibility of some churchwomen in an institution which prefers to conceal women's presence.

C. J. Jung borrowed the Latin *persona*, designating an actor's mask, to identify the 'face to the world' which individuals adopt in response to society's demands. One's persona, in Jung's accounting for personality dynamics, enables the individual to arrive at a compromise between deep inner promptings, on the one hand, and the collective situation which communicates expectations about appropriate roles, behaviors, and attitudes.[10] In the ecclesiastical milieu, the conventional 'daughter of the Church' role carries with it not the rich complexity of the woman from whose biography the phrase arose but the time-honored configuration of behaviors and attitudes discussed throughout this issue of *Concilium*. The letter writers in 1979 witnessed clearly to that narrowing. Women who have membership in established communities have been systematically socialized to appropriate and to sustain what psychologists identify as the "public mask."

One does not have to be a systematic Jungian to recognize in the biographies of Teresa of Avila, Thérèse of Lisieux, and Mother Teresa of Calcutta what a Jungian might identify as successful adaptation to role expectations through the internalization of a suitable persona. Each of them achieved a workable balance in her own identity as a woman in the Church by taking on aspects of the authorized role while successfully avoiding overidentification with her persona so that she could also risk giving expression to her own inner promptings.

Each of these women's skillful negotiation of both surface and depth demands in her life provides a biographer or a hagiographer with ample data for selective presentation of her life and her work as a conventional "daughter of the Church." These selective presentations can easily be directed toward institutional ends, and that matter will be considered shortly. First, it is necessary to look at the "breach" of the traditional daughter of the Church role experienced in the 1979 public appearance of Theresa Kane with Pope John Paul, a breach which generated such emotion within the institution.

Is it possible to propose that the "fault" in the event must be found simply in a prior breakdown of traditional societal expectations about appropriate roles, behaviors, and attitudes for women? The traditional womanly "face to the world" internalized by all women living in traditional religious cultures has come under heavy critical scrutiny by feminist thinkers who have recognized and exposed the androcentric and patriarchal foundations of the traditional female persona. The rejection of the traditional womanly persona does not eliminate the need for workable social roles to guide human behavior. In fact, Conn's article on Thérèse of Lisieux, cited earlier, suggests that new attitudes and behavioral expectations for Church women are emerging. But this time, they are coming under the guiding influence of feminist reflection of women's own experiences.

Interestingly, those new behavioral expectations reflect the behaviors of traditional women like Teresa of Avila, Thérèse of Lisieux, and Mother Teresa precisely in those moments when they risked moving beyond a persona to be attentive to the deeper inner promptings of their spirits. The "deviance" of the feminist woman is to be found in her open acknowledgment of aspects of women's truth that have heretofore been operative but concealed within adaptive conformity to the socially acceptable womanly role. The notion that there are both traditional and emerging feminist daughter-of-the-Church personas may serve to shed light on the distinctive balance of deviance from and compliance with ecclesiastical expectations which is part of the biography of each Theresa.

But we must also account for the institutional dynamic by which the Church accords such women as these visibility and promotes them either as models to emulate or as *persona non grata.* Institutions are maintained in their being and their well-being by public rituals celebrating and confirming social relations.[11]

The cult of the saints is a ritual expression of a belief in a communion of saints transcending culture and history. The cult is served by a limited number of normative constructs or types of holy men and women. For example, the revised Roman liturgy continues to offer only two generic models for women's holiness: virgin and holy woman not a virgin.[12] The nomenclature suggests that there is a preferred status even within this narrow classification; it marginalizes married Christian women, who are numerically the most sizeable adult population within the total Church membership.

Each of these holy womanly types promotes a persona; the most highly developed in ecclesiastical literature is that of the virgin, the woman whose role is defined precisely through her relationships to institutions directly under the authority of official churchmen. Thus the daughters of "mother Church" who are members of religious communities figure more directly in the work of the institution and its maintenance and so come under greater scrutiny and supervision by those churchmen who stand *in persona ecclesiae.* Ecclesiastical promotion of the cults of Teresa of Avila, Thérèse of Lisieux, and Mother Teresa, with selective emphasis on the feminine persona rather than the more complex historical personalities promotes public internalization of the values, attitudes, and behaviors expressed in the persona of the ideal churchwoman. Among these are loyalty to the Church and submission to the wisdom of its male leaders; humble, hidden service of God; and a disengaged, timeless ministry to the world's weak and suffering.

Theresa Kane's guileless approach to the pope with a new question about women and the Church set her up as a classical *persona non grata,* one who breached role expectations. A woman presenting herself with directness and clarity, asking the hard question, may be a normative feminist persona; it is not a persona pleasing to churchmen. Subsequently Theresa Kane and many women religious like her in the United States have been treated as non-persons, refused ordinary human courtesies by churchmen in the Vatican and at home. They themselves are no longer willing to maintain the approved but dysfunctional persona. Ecclesiastical authorities have as yet no other available construct for dealing with Carmelites and Sisters of Mercy. They quite literally cannot imagine dealing with women simply as persons. Hence, the current impasse and the attempts at the repression of feminist women religious in the Church.

Meanwhile, feminist scholars have begun to provide revisionist accounts of the lives of the French and Spanish Theresas which break through their personas and uncover powerfully symbolic women whose lives are marked with the rich ambiguity of their female humanity. A critical feminist study of the story of Mother Teresa of Calcutta is in order. Churchmen's sustained promotion of three Theresas as models for women may yet yield the unintended results of exposing the deficiency of the traditional feminine persona and promoting original theological reflection on the emergence of new daughters of the Church.

NOTES

1. V. Lincoln, *Teresa: A Woman,* Albany, 1984, pp. 420–21.

2. Ibid., p. 425.

3. The bibliography is vast, with most studies in Spanish and French and significantly fewer in English.

4. Feminist and psychoanalytic studies provide the most original contributions to a new understanding of Thérèse of Lisieux.

5. *Mother Teresa of Calcutta* was published by the Marvel Comics Group of New York. The Franciscan Communications Office of New York provided the text; Paulist Press, a major U.S. Catholic publisher, has distribution rights. It follows upon earlier successful attempts by others like Malcolm Muggeridge of Great Britain at mass communication of the story of Mother Teresa.

6. *Origins* 9, no. 18 (18 October 1979), pp. 284–85.

7. J. W. Conn, "Thérèse of Lisieux from a Feminist Perspective," *Spiritual Life* 28, no. 4 (Winter 1982), p. 239.

8. *Story of a Soul,* newly translated by John Clarke, OCD, Washington, D.C.: Institute of Carmelite Studies Publications, 1975. See Manuscript B, pp. 185ff.

9. Lincoln, the work cited in note 1, p. xiii.

10. For a brief treatment, see "Jung, Carl," in *The Encyclopedia Dictionary of Psychology,* ed. Rom Harré, Cambridge, Mass., 1983, pp. 322ff.

11. V. W. Turner, *Dramas, Fields, and Metaphors: Symbolic Acts in Human Society,* Ithaca, N.Y., 1974. See especially "Social Dramas and Ritual Metaphor," pp. 23–59.

12. See the organization of Commons in the current Roman Missal.

25

Europe as a Sexist Myth

MARY GREY

Introduction

The story is told that Caractacus, the British chieftain taken to Rome as captive in the reign of the Emperor Claudius (c.e. 51), on seeing the might and grandeur of ancient Roman places, exclaimed, "You have all this, yet you covet our poor huts!"[1] For me this story functions as a parable for the European "syndrome," since those who were once captive went on to be conquerors and exploiters of the dwellers of "the poor huts" in lands outside Europe. More tragically, ever since the Emperor Constantine's famous vision of the cross in the skies and the prophecy, "By this sign you will conquer,"[2] a militarist ethic has been imposed on the world at large by Europeans in the name of Christianity itself.

This so-called "seamless garment" of European culture which extends from the Caspian Sea to the South of Spain is in fact a sexist myth, built as it is on the invisibility and exclusion of women from its structures and foundational thinking. The earliest example of a European woman who found a prophetic voice but was condemned by the god (Apollo) as mad was Cassandra, princess of Troy at the time of the Trojan War. It is significant that her madness consisted in prophesying the imminent destruction of the nation through war: she was listened to as little as are the prophetic voices from peace movements today.[3]

"Europe" is a sexist myth, even if we take "myth" in both the two current, common usages of the word. A myth is a narrative, a foundational symbolic story or set of stories through which a nation or cultural group within it understands and remembers its origins and envisions its "endtimes" in order to live life meaningfully in the present. But "myth" is also currently used in the sense of "half-truth," the false consciousness, or "bad faith" induced by commercial advertising, ill-grounded popular opinions and a lazy acceptance of fictitious ideas. In both these senses, the cultural construction which is Europe can be regarded as a sexist myth. In the foundational stories of Europe — the philosophical, psychological and scientific building blocks which underpin the formation of the European liberal democracy — women are either invisible, or defined in relation to men with certain severely restricted roles within the patriarchal household. Speaking about the lack of gender-awareness of fifth-century Europe, Peter Brown remarked that "it is a comfortable and dangerous illusion to assume that, in much of the evidence, the presence of women is even *sensed.*"[4] Yet Virginia Woolf called attention to the fact that women appeared numerous times in the catalogue of the British Library, men not at all.[5] In other words, women's presence consists in being written about, defined and controlled. Small wonder that the same writer cried "As a woman I have no country!"[6]

It is one thing to be written out of the founding myths; it is another thing to be present as part of "false consciousness," present as "guilty Eve," as "the Angel in the House," as witch, temptress and fertility goddess. The terrifying thought arises, given the prevalence of such false consciousness, that without such stereotypical female roles the whole cultural seamless garment would collapse like Alice in Wonderland's pack of cards! What has to be asked is, first, what part has Christian theology played in the construction of this sexist myth? And, second, can anything be salvaged from Europe's past as ingredient for a new myth? What creative remembrance will offer liberating possibilities for the way men and women relate — within Europe, and far beyond its boundaries?

Europe's Monocultural Myth

If we examine the philosophical and cultural movements and periods of European development, the so-called great landmarks of cultural progress, the dilemma becomes sharper. It is true that Plato allowed a few intelligent women within his Republic — because the philosophers needed to procreate. But Aristotle — as is well known — clearly excluded women from public life as "a-political" and as "misbegotten males." What is not so often perceived is how movements such as the Renaissance and the Enlightenment are understood as focusing exclusively on Renaissance "man" and male subjectivity. The French Revolution began by enthroning the Goddess of Reason in the Cathedral of Notre Dame, while at the same time excluding women from its aims of "liberté, egalité and fraternité." The Romanticism of Goethe and Rousseau idealized and sentimentalized "women," ignoring the suffering of real women. Such idealization of feminine identity then made it easier to achieve the nineteenth-century split between the private and public worlds: the "feminine" virtues of docility and nurturing tenderness were "appropriately" exercised in the home, leaving competition, military struggle and striving for success to be regarded as masculine activities whose proper scenario was the public sphere.

The great achievement of the European myth is usually held to be liberal democracy, which has been exported to various parts of the world. This in turn is underpinned by the post-Enlightenment rationalist concept of the human subject. But Liberal democracies until this century excluded women from voting. When Simone de Beauvoir wrote, in 1943, the classic *La Deuxième Sexe,* which would provide such stimulus for the second wave of the feminist movement, she was still the "a-political" woman envisaged by Aristotle, unable to vote.[7] Yet it is rash to unload the blame for the extremes of the rational individualism of post-Enlightenment subjectivity on to one person or cause.[8] This has a far more complex development. One cannot simply blame Cartesian or Lockean disengaged rationalism, or Platonic idealism, the industrial revolution or capitalist economics, the dualistic split between inner and outer self, between body and mind, or spirit. All have played their part. But the one feature common to all of these is that the experience and resources of women as articulated by women themselves have never been incorporated into the narrative. The European hero has been a wanderer — from the days of the Greek hero Odysseus, to the fifteenth-century capitalist conquistador "discovering" Latin America, to the contemporary director of a large multi-national firm. The price of his wanderings is the sedentary, subservient Penelope who keeps the hearth, with a kind of passive waiting which prohibits her own self-awareness and the growth of her own subjectivity.

Christian theology has played its own part in suppressing the full subjectivity of women, in limiting the participation of women in the social contract to that of motherhood, and of making it almost impossible for women to recover from its damaging views on female sexuality. To the objection that I am identifying Christianity with the European myth, whereas in fact Christianity is a world-wide faith, I would reply that this is precisely the damaging consequence of this myth, that it has managed to dominate and impose its interpretation of the liberating gospel message on to the whole world, and in so doing obscure the crucial contributions to early Christianity both of non-European cultural and ethnic groups.

Thus the *civitas Christiana* established by Constantine and Charlemagne demanded the sacrifice of female subjectivity for the sake of the propagation of the species.[9] Become anonymous in order to gain a place in the socio-symbolic contract, in time and history, guaranteed by paternal authority, with God the Father as ultimate guarantor. What was originally a social need then acquired theological justification through a theology of the indissolubility of monogamous marriage.[10] This in its turn is supported by a mystique of suffering service, a spirituality of meditated subjectivity, in which women acquire identity "in relation to" (husband, child, father), and holiness through the quality of their care and self-denial. That this is still the case is witnessed to by the Pastoral Letter *Mulieris Dignitatem:*

> Motherhood implies from the beginning a special openness to the new person: and this is precisely the women's "part": in this openness, in conceiving and giving birth to a child, the woman "discovers herself through a sincere gift of self"... Scientific analysis confirms that the very physical constitution of women is naturally disposed to mother-hood.... At the same time this also corresponds to the psycho-physical structure of women.... Motherhood *is linked to the personal structure of the woman and to the personal dimension of the gift* (italics in original).[11]

It is far from the case that a feminist analysis wishes to underrate the experience of motherhood: what is criticized is, first, the restriction of women's identity to motherhood; second, the idealization of motherhood as the pre-eminent way to holiness; third, the linking of motherhood with an essentialist view of female identity; and fourth, the use of motherhood as social institution to control and dominate the lives of women.

Christian theology has locked a distorted view of female sexuality deep into its symbol system. This is most clearly seen in the discourse of Mary, virgin and mother: although the symbolism of Mary has not *always* functioned in an oppressive way for women — for example, in medieval times she was a vibrant reminder of the humanity of Jesus, and she clearly has a liberating function in Latin American liberation theology,[12] yet because she is extolled even to the level of "the feminine dimension of God,"[13] and this because of the unique combination of virginal motherhood, she is an icon impossible for ordinary women to follow: moreover, given the popularity of the doctrine of the virgin birth, it is difficult for ordinary married women to come to any healthy view of sexual pleasure, of female "jouissance." Although Christianity has constantly condemned the pornographic exploitation of women in its many forms, yet its symbols preserve the dualistic split between the holiness of the Spirit and the unearthly, and the corruptibility and degradation of the body, symbolized by the pornographic female body. It has refused to make the connection between the structures of patriarchal control over women through monogamous marriage and the family, and the encouragement of domestic violence and abuse within it.

Finally, Europe has shown its contempt for the female body preeminently through the Great European witch-craze of the late fifteenth century. It could be said that this is the most overwhelming expression of "Europe as a sexist myth." Estimates very as to how many women were burned, from 300,000 to several million. The point which needs stressing is that those most victimized were the women who deviated from the sacrificial symbolism of the social contract — motherhood, biological or spiritual — by being unmarried or widowed. As a scholar as recently as 1972 put it:

> ...we can concede that the small trials may indeed have served a function, delineating the social thresholds of eccentricity tolerable to society, and registering fear of a socially indigestible group, unmarried women.... Until single women found a more comfortable place in the concepts and communities of Western men, one could argue that they were a socially disruptive element, at least when they lived without family and patriarchal control. In this restricted sense the small witch trial may have even been *therapeutic....* [14]

But what can we salvage from Europe's past? Must women be content with being written out of history?

Reclaiming Our Story

I will now look at the European "seamless garment" with a hermeneutic of suspicion which has five elements. First, Europeans are not the elite of Christianity: the blossoming of faith is certainly coming from other parts of the world today, and feminist theology has committed itself to solidarity with the most oppressed of the world, specifically to the eradication of the interlocking oppressions of sexism, racism and the structures of poverty. The sexism of the European myth has prevented white European women from discovering their own racism and collusion in oppressing women from other parts of the world. In fact the current debate on the future of a strengthened Europe presents the real danger that Europe re-forms around exactly the same center, enacting a new form of the older, sexist myth. The experience of many East European women in the wake of many "liberation" movements is witness to this: many feel they are still wandering the desert of poverty, of lost ideals, and with no outlook on a Promised Land.

Second, there never has been a European "seamless garment" — rather, a variegated "coat of many colors." It is another "myth" that European culture is represented solely by the art of Michelangelo and

Rembrandt, the music of Mozart, the architecture of the Gothic cathedral and the plays of Shakespeare. There has been a profusion of
multi-cultural richness in Europe's midst: even before the Roman army
brought North Africans to Britain, the Celtic cultures — whose origins
were Mongolian — were enshrining their creative gifts in stone and story
in many parts of Europe. There have always been women trying to express themselves in art and poetry. I imagine, too, that there were many
Héloises, trying to acquire a theological education in the shadow of the
great masters.

Yet the domination of the Christian story and ethic has obscured other
faith communities and cultures within Europe's midst, crushing Jew
and "infidel" alike with fire and sword. The ultimate tragic intolerance
of another faith story is, of course, the Holocaust.

The third element of a hermeneutic of suspicion with regard to the
sexist myth of Europe springs from the damage and exploitation inflicted
on many parts of the earth to fill the treasuries of Europe, and to ensure the continuance of a consumer life-style. This relates directly to the
exclusion of women from the formative ethic. For European patriarchal
monotheism flourished at the expense of the suppression of the older
goddess religions of Greece, Rome and the Celtic deities. With these vanished a sense of respect and reverence for the presence of the divine in
the rhythms of the earth, as a *central* value for Christianity (although this
has survived in folk religion, in devotions to Mary queen of creation, and
in certain mystical writings). The present crisis demands a willingness
to listen to the goddess movements, to learn what they teach us about
non-exploitative life-styles and sustainable levels of consumption.

And so, fourth, the only way to uncover another story to live by is
to track the roots of the sexist myth to its source: *tracking the roots of
the sexist myth to its source is an act of feminist liberation.* It is also a
theological activity, rooted in faith in a divinity in love with all creation,
particularly with those who are the most oppressed.

"Till we have faces" expresses hope in the justice of the kingdom of
God,[15] hope that women will acquire visibility as full human subjects,
and not serve merely to be mirrors for the post-Enlightenment super-
individual. It recalls one of Europe's foundational stories — the myth of
Eros and Psyche. Psyche was not allowed to look on the face of Eros,
her husband. Because she yielded to temptation she was condemned to
wandering grief-stricken in search of Eros, compelled to fulfill the most
dreadful tasks. They were only allowed to behold each other in full mutuality when each had accomplished a journey to maturity. For Christian
theology this means that "psyche" ("soul"), in traditional Augustinian
theology more accurately represented by men (and imagined as totally
a-physical and a-sexual), must discover a new integrating relationship

with Eros. Christian agapé must embrace mutuality. Just as Psyche was joyously re-united with Eros, the Christian psyche-soul can re-discover a sense of God-given embodiment, of being "earthed" in an elemental energy which is the grace of creation. If Psyche and Eros are re-envisioned, then perhaps there is hope that Europe will discover a new "logos" other than the "logos" of the founding European myth. If "logos" is again to be the divine living Word of communication in mutuality, then it will not be defined in opposition to affectivity and emotion, or limited to an over-rational, objective analysis. It would become a "listening" logos, which understood its very roots to spring from listening, and from "hearing into speech."[16] Only then could Europe discover an alternative logic to that of retaliation, control and dominance.

And so, finally, the task is to re-claim other memories, re-claiming myth in its truest sense as a foundational story. But this time tradition is being challenged and re-membered by those without face or voice in the dominant strand of history, who seek sustaining memories beneath and beyond the dominant sexist myth; who seek to keep faith in a vision of Christian freedom far more radical than the liberalism of the democracies which are the hollow triumph of the sexist myth of Europe.

NOTES

1. Tacitus, *The Annals of Imperial Rome*, London, 1956, p. 258.

2. Eusebius, *Vita Constantini* (F. Winkelmann, Eusebius' Werke 1.1, 2d ed., G.C.2, 1975, 1.27ff.

3. For a re-telling of the Cassandra story, see Christa Wolf, *Cassandra*, London, 1984.

4. Peter Brown, *The Body and Society: Men, Women and Sexual Renunciation*, New York and London, 1988, pp. xvi–xvii.

5. Virginia Woolf, *A Room of One's Own*, London, 1977, pp. 28–36.

6. Virginia Woolf, *Three Guineas*, New York, 1938, p. 109.

7. Simone de Beauvoir, *The Second Sex*, Paris, 1943; London, 1972.

8. For a careful, reflective analysis of all the influences contributing to the modern sense of self, see Charles Taylor, *Sources of the Self*, Cambridge, 1989.

9. For the theme of female sacrificed subjectivity, see Julia Kristeva, *Women's Time*, in *The Kristeva Reader*, ed. Toril Moi, Oxford, 1986, pp. 187–213; also *About Chinese Women*, in ibid., pp. 138–59.

10. The problems of monogamy in Christian theology are well discussed by Susan Dowell, *They Two Shall Be One: Monogamy in History and Religion*, London, 1990.

11. *Mulieris Dignitatem*, Apostolic Letter of Pope John Paul II, London, Catholic Truth Society, 1988, pp. 68–69.

12. See Ivone Gebara and Maria Clara Bingemer, *Mary, Mother of God: Mother of the Poor*, Maryknoll, N.Y., 1989.

13. See Leonardo Boff, *The Maternal Face of God: The Feminine and Its Religious Expressions,* London, 1989.

14. H. C. Erik Midelfort, *Witchhunting in South Western Germany, 1562–1684: The Social and Intellectual Foundations,* Stanford, 1972, p. 3.

15. *Till We Have Faces: A Myth Retold,* is actually the title of C. S. Lewis's retelling of the Psyche-Eros story, London, 1956.

16. For an attempt to discover another interpretation of logos within European history, see Andrea Nye, *Words of Power: A Feminist Reading of the History of Logic,* New York and London, 1990; Gemma Corradi Fiumara, *The Other Side of Language: A Philosophy of Listening,* New York and London, 1990.

26

The Image of the "White Lady"

Gender and Race in Christian Mission

KWOK PUI-LAN

The nineteenth century has been called by church historians the "great century of Christian mission." Christianity was brought to many parts of the world simultaneously with the rapid expansion of the West and colonization of third world countries. The missionary movement has been interpreted in conflicting ways according to different perspectives. Some emphasize the benevolent role of missionaries in introducing the gospel, Christian reform, and Western civilization to non-Western societies. Others criticize the missionary enterprise as culturally imperialistic, supporting the political and economic interests of Western colonial powers.

In the past debate of Christian mission, the role played by women in the missionary movement has not been sufficiently explored. In fact, Christian mission expanded during the latter half of the nineteenth century with the proliferation of women's mission and reform societies on both sides of the Atlantic. A significant part of mission funding came from donations by women in the church. Through sending women missionaries to work among the "heathen," Western women established important links with women in other parts of the world. In the mission field, the missionary ladies preached not only the gospel but also the Western ideal of womanhood. In their home base, they helped to shape Western women's ideas about third world women through their letters, reports and the bulk of missionary literature.

This essay examines the myth and reality behind the image of the "white lady" in Christian mission and Western colonialism. Exploring the interaction of gender and race constructions in the encounter between the West and other cultures, it raises important questions of identity and difference among women in cross-cultural perspective.

Women Missionaries and Christian Mission

Before examining the image of the "white lady" in detail, it is important to discuss the social and cultural reasons for sending women as missionaries. In the beginning, only men were sent as missionaries to foreign lands. If they were accompanied by their wives, the ladies were expected to take care of responsibilities at home and the children. Sometimes these missionary wives would also assist mission work by visiting women at their homes and running small mission schools. It was considered too dangerous to send women to travel and work alone in a strange and unfamiliar land.

The need to send women missionaries arose because in some countries, such as China and India, the two sexes were segregated in society. Social propriety made it improper for male missionaries to approach women. Anti-Christian propaganda often portrayed male missionaries as having a craving sexual appetite and using charms and medicine pills to gain access to women.[1] Therefore, women missionaries had to be sent to work among women, who were reported as much more receptive to mission work than men. It was hoped that these women, once converted to Christianity, would influence their families and bring up their children in the Christian way. In addition, white female missionaries were considered to be less threatening than the white men. In places where antipathy towards Christian mission was exceptionally strong, white women were sent as pioneers to open the mission field.

The demand for female missionaries received a favorable response from the women's mission boards, newly formed in Europe and America. The upsurge of interest in missionary activities was fuelled by religious fervor brought about by the evangelical revival movement. At the same time, white women also deemed it their duty to save their "heathen" sisters from their degraded and lowly position. In 1869, when the Congregationalist women in the United States organized the women's board, an appeal was issued to Christian women which said: "Can there be anything more appropriate than for woman, elevated by the gospel to the high position she holds in Christian lands, to extend the helping hand to woman 'sitting in the region and shadow of death' — ignorant, degraded, and perishing for lack of vision?[2] Similar rhetoric was frequently found in missionary literature to solicit support and funds for mission.

At first, there was some hesitation about sending single women to the mission field for fear that they could not take care of themselves in foreign lands without the protection of their families. But the single ladies showed that they could share living quarters and form a supportive network of their own. Without family burdens, they could devote more time and energy to mission work and travel around as itinerants. The female missionaries were chiefly responsible for "woman's work" in Christian mission, consisting of evangelism, female education and medical service. Mission work was divided distinctly along the gender line because of the segregation of the sexes.

The number of single women sent as missionaries by the women's boards continued to increase in the latter half of the nineteenth century. Together with the missionary wives, the total number of women in a particular mission field might even outnumber that of men. The feminization of the mission force was clearly evident, for example, in China. Although sent and supported by the women's boards, the female missionaries were supervised by the male missionaries in charge of a particular mission. In some denominations, missionary women could not perform leadership roles similar to those of men. Tension existed in some missions, where missionary women were not content with their subordinate position and demanded more control of their work. They also criticized the male missionaries for overlooking the importance of the distinct component of "woman's work" in Christian mission.

The "White Lady" in Mission: Myth and Reality

The white missionary women who traveled long distances to save their "heathen" sisters were portrayed almost as saints in missionary literature and their "hagiographic" biographies. It was true that many of these women were prompted by a strong religious conviction to join the Christian mission, but the mission field also provided opportunities not readily available at home. A study of the social background of American women missionaries at the turn of the century indicates that a high percentage of them came from middle-class families in small towns in the Midwest.[3] The newly opened female colleges in America also provided a growing number of graduates who might not find an appropriate job easily on the home front. A missionary career in a foreign land offered new challenges and freedom denied to them in their own societies.

Motivated by their religious zeal and enchanted by the possibilities abroad, young white women dedicated themselves to be missionaries in the name of self-denial and sacrifice. Yet, the mission field offered them unexpected authority and power, contrary to their own beliefs of feminine subordination. They could lead an independent life, pursuing a career as teacher, doctor or missionary. In a colonial or semi-colonial situation they enjoyed privileges and commanded respect as members of the white race. The historian Jane Hunter, who has studied American women missionaries in China, describes how these white ladies adjusted themselves to this new environment:

> At first they were troubled by the discrepancy between their expected demeanor of modesty and self-effacement, and their experience of authority. Gradually, however, the experience of authority transformed self-expectations, and missionary women came to discover inner certainties to match their circumstances. Gradually, they developed colonial temperaments to accord with their colonial status.[4]

Living in a foreign place, some of these women missionaries learned the language and tried to adjust themselves to local customs. But a greater number would stick to the Western habit of life rather than living like the local people. Many continued to wear Western dresses, although they were not suitable for the hot climate and inconvenient for travel. They lived in the mission compounds and decorated their homes as they did their homes in the West, with pieces of furniture and sometimes even an organ shipped across the ocean. These women missionaries tried to maintain their identity not only because they were homesick and wished to live in the traditional way, but also because of the privileges associated with it. The fact that they lived differently from the common people increased their appeal. For example, many village women were curious to have a look at a foreign woman, and they would touch her clothes, or visit her to see how she lived.

The female missionaries often assumed a self-styled mothering role in their relationship with native Christians. In their letters and writings, they referred to those under their instruction and supervision as "children," even though these people were adults. They often established close emotional bonding with women and girls under their tutelage and sought to influence them through personal ties. But just like any mother, missionary women sometimes found that their "daughters" could act in ways beyond their expectation and control. When in 1872 Mary Porter, a missionary in China, demanded that girls in her school unbind their feet, she could not have expected what this would lead to: "The best result of the unbinding of feet in the Peking school was not foreseen by the missionaries. The girls, by submitting to this break with established custom . . . learned to think and act for themselves."[5] Later, other missionary women were also surprised to see their students participate in mass demonstrations and nationalistic activities against foreign domination and colonialism.

As white women enjoying power and privilege, they related to men of a different race in an ambiguous way. On the one hand, their independence and status allowed them to break from certain gender stereotypes prescribed in their home countries. On the other hand, they found Asian or African men smaller in size and less masculine than Western men. Although sensitivity, gentleness and moderation were virtues valued by the Christian tradition, white women considered men of color who displayed such qualities as unmanly or timid according to their Western gender expectations. White women sometimes called their male students "lads," and their servants "boys," just like the blacks at home.[6] They harbored ambivalent feelings on seeing these young "lads" being ordained one day, preaching from the pulpit, and exercising ecclesiastical duties which they, as women, were barred from performing.

The encounter with a different social and cultural ethos made missionaries more aware of how women were treated in various contexts. They emphasized that Christianity had contributed to the uplift of women in the West, whereas heathenism and superstition were causes of the degradation of women in other parts of their world. In a book called *Women of All Lands,* an American missionary Young J. Allen remarked that the best single test of the civilization of any people is the degree to which their women are free and educated.[7] The prevalence of footbinding, concubinage, seclusion of women and female illiteracy was taken as a sign and symptom of the inferiority of other cultures. Within an unshakable belief in their own cultural superiority, Allen and other missionaries stressed that other countries should take heed of the benefits of Christian civilization to transform their culture and society.

Female missionaries believed that Christianity accorded them a higher status in society and that they had the responsibility for imparting the "Christian ideal of womanhood" through Christian schools and the example of missionary households. As products of their own time, these women missionaries perceived the "Christian ideal of womanhood" as being not much different from their own Victorian values of domesticity and subordination. For example, they prescribed that women should have "refined and womanly qualities," keeping their homes comfortable and clean. Wives should win respect from their husbands through their intelligence and learning, and they should handle relations with in-laws to the satisfaction of all. As enlightened mothers, they should treat their children conscientiously, judiciously and with self-control. Displaying less tolerance towards the indigenous ideals of womanhood, female missionaries wished to transmit their own life-style, social manners and cultural value to their "heathen" sisters.

The original purpose of their missionary career was to save feminine souls. Judging from their own standards, however, missionary women found that their sisters could not possibly be "saved" without adopting some of their customs and values, such as monogamy, the nuclear family and female education.[8] At the turn of the century, mission ideology shifted from converting individual souls to regenerating "heathen" culture through the transmission of Western civilization and institutions. Female missionaries played their part by introducing female education, Christian reform, the temperance movement, the YWCA and Western medicine to other cultures.

Compared with other radical women who were fighting for women's rights back home, women missionaries were generally considered more conservative in their political outlook. It seems ironic that they should have taken upon themselves the responsibility of advocating women's emancipation in the mission field. The historian Alison R. Drucker has tried to provide a plausible explanation: "It was less disturbing to criticize another culture for injustice to women than to castigate one's own; religious women frequently avowed that introducing Christianity to the heathen would raise the status of women abroad."[9] In order to justify their work, missionary reports focused invariably on the pitiful condition of women of other lands and their immense needs. This missionary literature, widely read by church women in the nineteenth century, tended to reinforce the belief of uncritical readers in their own cultural superiority.

Gender, Race and Christian Mission

The study of Christian mission reveals the complex juxtaposition of gender, cultural superiority and religious identity. Mission ideology emphasized the essential difference between white women and women of color: the former as liberated because of their Christian religion; the latter as ignorant and degraded in their heathenism. Other cultures were understood to be diametrically opposite and hierarchically inferior to Western culture, and the subordination of women was taken as one sign of manifestation of this inferiority. Such beliefs could be used to justify the ecclesial interest of Christian mission, and also the ethnocentrism of the West.

To maintain such a mission ideology, the "white lady" had to be mystified, so that she could be put on top of a pedestal. The struggle of Western women against the male power structure of the church in the first wave of feminism in the nineteenth century could not be told. The limitation and oppression of the Victorian conception of true womanhood has not been examined in missionary literature. On the other hand, the life and reality of women of color was misrepresented in this social construction of gender identity. Recent feminist analyses by third world women have cautioned us against the biases and falsehood of such misrepresentations. For instance, Barbara Omolade has pointed out that African women could participate as human beings with firmly entrenched rights and status in their tribal communities. This position contrasted sharply with their situation under chattel slavery.[10] Similarly, Mary John Mananzan of the Philippines asserts that Philippine women enjoyed a higher status in society before the introduction of Catholicism into their land.[11]

The myths and partial truths of the "white lady" were maintained as part of an ideology for the domination of the West over other peoples. Western colonialism rested on the assumption of essential differences between the rulers and the ruled. Colonized or subjugated peoples were not treated as equals or subjects, but as "the other," according to the Korean feminist theologian Chung Hyun Kyung:

> Western colonizers portrayed the Asian as "the other," not fully "advanced" like people in the West. Western colonizers did not want to encounter Asians as people by whom they could be challenged, influenced and transformed. Westerners objectified Asians without any willingness to meet and learn from them.[12]

When colonized people were treated as "the other," their cultural identity and their way of life were not respected or regarded as valuable. White colonizers assumed the supremacy of their own culture, and mission ideology unconsciously provided the religious sanction. Indigenous cultures needed to be transformed to meet the standard of Christian civilization, which was equated simply with white culture. In the name of uplifting their sisters, missionary women played no small part in this cultural transformation. It is often difficult to draw a fine distinction between genuine cultural transmission and ethnocentrism, the more so if the parties involved hold unequal power. On the one hand, white missionary women introduced new conceptions of gender through their work and role model. On the other hand, they were easily tempted to define their own terms.

Living under multiple oppression, third world women saw feminism very differently from the view espoused by evangelical Christianity with its implicit Victorian ideal of womanhood. Many students at mission girls' schools participated in the revolutionary struggles and people's movement at the turn of the century, to the surprise of their missionary teachers. To them, the liberation of women could not be separated from the total liberation from colonialism, economic control and militarism. The rising consciousness of women provided the critical context for them to challenge the patriarchal practices of the church, and the ecclesiologies inherited from the West.[13] Third world women increasingly found the kind of feminism advocated by the "white ladies" inadequate, because it overlooked the unequal power relations between women.

From the above discussion, it can be seen that the image of the "white lady" is a social construction which functions to create artificial polarization among women. According to the feminist theorist Trinh T. Minh-ha, identity under conditions of hegemonistic rule is structured so as to keep apart members of different groups by reifying into cultural and social institutions superimposed, mutually irreconcilable essences. At the same time, the uniqueness of other people and the differences shaped by historical and cultural forces are not acknowledged. As a result, the diversity is flattened with no respect for the inviolability of the other's boundaries that delineate our separate identities. According to Trinh:

> Hegemony works at levelling our differences and at standardizing contexts and expectations in the smallest details of our lives. Uncovering this levelling of differences is, therefore, resisting that very notion of difference which, defined in the master's terms, often resorts to the simplicity of essences. Divide and conquer has for centuries been his creed, his formula of success.[14]

The separation of women into different categories prevents them from forming female bonding among themselves. The levelling of differences masks the unarticulated white privileges and power in a colonial situation. Both of these techniques function to serve the political, economic and ecclesial interests of white male supremacy. In order to struggle in solidarity with each other, women must resist the false categorization which places some women on top of others. We have to begin to see our struggles as deeply intertwined and interrelated. Furthermore, we must learn to respect our differences with a recognition that we are each rooted in a separate culture. There is possibility for real dialogue and creative response to this separateness in our co-existence in a multi-cultural and multi-ethnic world.

NOTES

1. E. C. Carlson, *The Foochow Missionaries, 1847–1880*, Cambridge, Mass., 1974, pp. 28–29.

2. Mrs. A. Bowker and Mrs. J. A. Copp, "To Christian Women, in Behalf of Their Sex in Heathen Lands," *The Missionary Herald* 64, 1868, p. 139.

3. J. Hunter, *The Gospel of Gentility: American Women Missionaries in Turn-of-the-Century China*, New Haven, 1984, pp. 28–29.

4. Ibid., p. 265.

5. A. H. Tuttle, *Mary Porter Gamewell and Her Story in the Siege of Peking*, New York, 1907, p. 69.

6. Hunter, *Gospel* (n. 3), pp. 204–6.

7. Y. J. Allen, *Quandi wu dazhou nüsu tongkao* (Women of all lands), Shanghai, 1903, Preface.

8. See P. R. Hill, *The World Their Household: The American Woman's Foreign Movement and Cultural Transformation: 1870–1920*, Ann Arbor, 1985.

9. A. R. Drucker, "The Role of the YWCA in the Development of the Chinese Women's Movement, 1890–1927," *Social Service Review* 53, 1979, p. 425.

10. B. Omolade, "Black Women and Feminism," in *The Future of Difference*, ed. H. Eisenstein and A. Jardine, New Brunswick and London, 1986, pp. 247–57.

11. M. J. Mananzan, "The Filipino Women: Before and After the Spanish Conquest of the Philippines," in *Essays on Women*, Manila, 1987, pp. 7–36.

12. H. K. Chung, *Struggle to Be the Sun Again: Introducing Asian Women's Theology*, Maryknoll, N.Y., and London, 1991, p. 33.

13. P. L. Kwok, "The Emergence of Asian Feminist Consciousness of Culture and Theology," in *We Dare to Dream*, ed. V. Fabella and S. A. Lee, Maryknoll, N.Y., 1990, pp. 92–100.

14. T. M. H. Trinh, "Not You/Like You: Post-Colonial Women and the Interlocking Questions of Identity and Difference," *Inscriptions* 3, no. 4 (1988), p. 72.

27

Our Name Is Church

Catholic-Christian Feminist Liturgies

DIANN NEU

Women celebrating feminist liturgies in the Roman Catholic tradition are making a decisive contribution to the life of the Church of the Eighties. My thesis is that such feminist liturgies celebrate and nurture feminist Christians on our long faith journey to liberation. We women are searching together for the language, symbols, stories, liturgies, and justice-based spirituality which express the faith experiences of women. Our search is challenging the traditional systems of the Church's hierarchical-patriarchal culture because it is empowering women to proclaim ourselves Church.

Three typical feminist liturgies are presented and commented on here to shed light on the spiralling movement that describes the process of feminist liberation. By feminist liberation I mean identifying the historical and contemporary oppression of women as well as articulating a strategy for changing the interstructured reality of oppression, particularly classism, racism, terrorism, and heterosexism as different expressions of patriarchal sexism.[1] This is not to be confused with the stereotypic notion of feminism which sees women as wanting to imitate male privilege without seeking to make changes in the socio-economic and political structures. The first phase of women's liberation demands the telling of our untold stories to link our personal experiences. It is celebrated liturgically in a Litany of naming. The second phase calls for bonding for struggle to name our spirituality. This bonding is celebrated in a liturgy of the Laying on of Hands. The third phase of the continuous movement is the claiming of our power to give birth to a new vision of Church and community. We celebrate this power in a Eucharistic Meal.

The liturgies together embody the experiences of a people moving from a patriarchal past towards a feminist future.[2]

Telling Our Stories: The Litany of Naming

The process of liberation begins as women "hear one another into speech."[3] The listening and speaking that happens in a community of women is a profound revolutionary act of love which has power to break open truth. With the revelation that occurs, the lies of patriarchal sexism lose control and women strengthen one another to change attitudes and structures according to feminist criteria. As noted above, the new vision which comes with the experience also sensitizes us to voices of other oppressed peoples. Liturgically, we have celebrated this telling of our stories through a Litany of Naming. The litany presented here is a composite of various such litanies that have been celebrated in local ecclesias of women and at the beginning of events such as the 1978 Women's Ordination Conference in Baltimore; a regional conference in Berkeley, California, in 1980; the Network 10th Annual Legislative Seminar and a national conference entitled "Women Moving Church," both in Washington, D.C., in 1981. Both women and men participated in these liturgies.

The Litany of Naming

Narrator: Let us begin by remembering the stories of our foremothers and praying that their courage to name, claim, and move with their visions may be shared by women and men of our time and spark us to be women moving church. We come here as daughters and sons of the women in our own families who have gone before us and given us life. Let us share the names of these women now as we name ourselves as their descendants.

Self-naming is done around circular tables: e.g., "I am Diann Lynn, daughter of Mary Kathryn, daughter of Catherine Anna, daughter of Anna...."

Then names are called to our memory by thirteen people speaking in different languages:

In English: Mothers in our families, you have named us and have given us life.

Our Mothers, move here with us: strengthen us as Church! (A comparable invocation is repeated after each subsequent naming.)

All sing: We are people telling stories,
And we are singing, singing for our lives. . . . [4]

In English: Eve and Lilith, Mothers of life, you claimed your own power by reaching for knowledge and you found that it was good.

In Hebrew: Ruth and Naomi, your devoted love for one another renewed your faith in the working of the divine.

In Greek: Mary, you listened, pondered, and knew that you had been chosen to give birth to Jesus, one who is Truth and Life.

All sing: We are the people naming issues,
And we are singing, singing for our lives. . . .

In German: Mary Magdalene, you were the apostle to the apostles, sharing with them the first news of the resurrection.

In Latin: Catherine of Siena, you reconciled warring factions of state and Church and we name you Doctor of our Church.

In French: Simone Weil, your sensitivity to the inclusive values of both Judaism and Christianity demanded that you refuse membership in a Church that did not include everyone and that you protest war and murder by your own death.

All sing: We are people bonding for struggle
And we are singing, singing for our lives. . . .

In Swahili: Women artists, you symbolize political messages about life in your country through your art work and crafts.

In Spanish: Mothers of the Plaza De Mayo, you gather weekly at the plaza in Buenos Aires to uphold human rights by demanding the reappearance of your 'disappeared' family members, friends, and citizens of your country.

In English: Matilda Joslyn Gage, you lost your rightful place in history, even in women's stories, because you too clearly named and focused the central women's issues: women's oppression by the Church, State, capitalism, and rigid family structure.

All sing: We are people claiming power,
And we are singing, singing for our lives. . . .

In Japanese: Working Women, you toil in factories, fields, and families to steward the people of the earth.

In Spanish: Ita Ford, Maura Clarke, Dorothy Kazel, Jean Donovan, you risked your lives providing for the basic needs of the poor of El Salvador in their struggle for human rights.

All languages: Babies born in the 1980s, to you is given the challenge of a world bursting with possibilities for justice. In you we place dreams for peace and harmony, visions of equality and transformation. Be. Move with us here, strengthen us as Church!

All sing: We are women moving Church,
　　　　And we are singing, singing for our lives. . . .

Theological Reflection on the Litany of Naming

While this litany expresses personal experiences of the liberation of women, it also contains elements typical of feminist liturgy. First, the word spoken through the stories of women's lives proclaims the truth of a people silenced and misinterpreted by a patriarchal sexist church. Breaking the silence of centuries, the stories reveal a raised consciousness among women. Second, by reclaiming a traditional prayer form of litany which calls to memory the saints of the Roman Catholic Church, the ecclesia of women expresses faith in the universal call to holiness. Like the early Christian community, we acclaim that each person, woman or man, must follow his/her vocation from God even at the cost of loyal disobedience to existing structures.[5] Women's stories highlight the power of women's visions and actions and invite us to remember that the Christian identity of women and men alike, the imaging of Christ, is derived from our baptismal call to discipleship and to sainthood which transcends biology and gender.

Further, bonding as the ecclesia of women[6] is a contemporary expression of the Catholic Church's tradition of recognizing communities of women. Religious communities of women and secular institutes as we have known them for centuries are the only canonical models of women's communities. The ecclesia of women offers another mode. It seeks to transcend the patriarchal dualism which divides women according to sexually based criteria: religious women and secular women, married women and single women, heterosexuals and lesbians; home-makers and career women, mothers and non-mothers. In feminist liturgies all women are called to liturgical celebration as the ecclesia of women. We gather to tell our stories, heal one another, and celebrate the womanspirit rising within a world-wide movement.

Finally, the language of this liturgy embodies feminist values. Feminists know the deep oppression that results from exclusion; therefore, we treasure and include "the other." Hence, we use inclusive and non-sexist language to tell women's stories from many cultures and life-styles, to speak in a variety of languages, and to search for universal symbols that bond women. We recognize always that the universals are based on the collective experiences of women and that agreeing on universals is a long, slow, complicated process. As the subsequent liturgies will show, the symbols and actions of feminist liturgy reveal the vitality of feminist values by mediating the transcendent with concrete, sensuous, life-centered meaning. Symbols of water, oil, bread, wine, light, fire, and blood, reclaimed through women's experience, increase sensory awareness and joy in celebration. The circle and the spiral are inclusive symbols which capture feminist values. Furthermore, touching, listening, dancing, and movement flow throughout feminist liturgy to celebrate the body and to remind the community that the power of Spirit-Wisdom moves with, within, and among us.

Thus, the feminist values celebrated in such a Litany of Naming are a prelude to the new church that is emerging as women bond together. The stories, language, symbols, and spirituality of such liturgies express the transforming values of feminism: community, mutuality, empowerment, wholeness, equality, participation, transformation. These values negate false myths about human interaction, namely privatism, hierarchical decision-making, domination and submission, dualism, passivity, and co-optation. With feminism we find the possibility to relate in a fully human way.

Bonding for Struggle: The Laying on of Hands

Feminist-Christian spirituality proclaims the life-giving power of Spirit-Wisdom for the process of liberation. When women experience this creative power, we are free to risk journeying along uncharted courses. Once awakening to our own authentic experiences, we recognize the injustices and life-destroying powers of structural sin. We scream in rage at the dehumanizing consequences of patriarchy for women, men, and children. We dare to dream of and begin creating a new community of Church and world. The feminist liturgy of the Laying on of Hands condensed for presentation here was developed for and celebrated at the 1981 conference "Women Moving Church." Its four movements — Waiting, Awakening, Rage, Empowerment — culminate in a mutual laying on of hands. At the completion of each movement, participants have time to speak of their own experiments.

The Laying on of Hands

A central dancer and two readers present the texts. Four additional dancers emerge from the community at various moments. The refrain of an opening song is repeated throughout the liturgy:

Lean on me, I am your sister;
Believe in me, I am your friend.[7]

WAITING (proclaimed and danced simultaneously)

Voice 1: I am a child born of the union of tradition and crisis. . . . I am a daughter, not a son: My name is waiting . . . I have waited in the deserts of Syria, in the streets of Egypt, in the land of Babylon. . . . I have waited in houses — washing, cooking, cleaning . . . I have sheltered the orphan, welcomed the stranger, embraced the lonely. . . . I have known the coming of despair. . . . I have given birth. My throat has grown parched thirsting for truth and justice. . . . I have known blood and want and pain and joy. . . . I have been to the mountain top. I am a daughter of the church. My name is waiting.[8]

Voice 2: Bring her out/to know you. . . . Sing her rhythms. . . . Sing her song of life . . . she's been dead too long. She's half-notes scattered without rhythm/no tune. . . . Sing the song to her possibilities. . . . Let her be born![9]

The dance ends and the participants talk briefly about their experiences of waiting as women of the Church. Then they sing:

Lean on me, I am your sister. . . .

AWAKENING (proclaimed and danced simultaneously)

Voice 1: The mountain moving day is coming. . . .
Only a while the mountain sleeps . . .
in the past all mountains moved in fire.
All sleeping women now awake and move. . . . [10]

Voice 2: The voice of those who hunger and thirst for justice has aroused me. It has awakened me from somnolent silence . . . from lethargic legalism . . . from hierarchy-induced hypnosis. . . . [11] I have been aroused. I am awake. I stand. I ache. I move. I feel. Move with me. All sleeping women now awake and move. Stand up. Stand with me.

When the dance ends, participants talk about experiences of awakening. Then they sing, while the dancers move among them.

Lean on me, I am your sister. . . .

RAGE (proclaimed and danced simultaneously)

Voice 1: Can you hear the river? . . . if you listen you can hear it . . . grinding stones into sand. Yet you may not hear it. O man, this alone hear. All silent women scream in rage. . . . [12]

Voice 2: I am angry. I was roused from comfortable sleep . . . only to find it still oppressive. I stood up. Doors with great crosses carved in them closed in my face. I moved and barren men in white collars turned away from me. I named myself woman: But my beloved Church sang of me with such reluctance. I have come out of my safe places. And I have been raped. I am angry. . . . Will anyone stay awake with me? Just one more hour? I need to be angry. But I can't be angry alone. [13]

Participants tell stories of their rage when the dance ends, and then sing: Lean on me, I am your sister. . . .

EMPOWERMENT (proclaimed and danced simultaneously)

Voice 1: Here I am as I am. A woman birthed in your creation. A woman birthed in dignity. Flesh and blood. Spirit and life. Redeemed.

Voice 2: O God my Mother, You know me better than I know myself. You love me better than I love myself. Your love is my gift. It sustains me.

Voice 1: Lose faith? I shall not. Lose heart? I cannot. Lose hope? I will not. You have made it known that I am loved. . . . You will touch us with your hands. I will touch us with my hands. And we will birth your vision once again.

At the dance's end, the women share stories of empowerment. Then the dancers receive a blessing and pass a blessing on: a laying on of hands. Meanwhile, all sing: lean on me, I am your sister. . . .

Theological Reflection on the Laying on of Hands

The laying on of hands bonds the ecclesia of women as it has strengthened Christians throughout our historical struggle for liberation. Women walk the road at various paces in a journey that spirals from the emptiness of waiting to the arousal of awakening, to the passion of rage, to the healing creativity of empowerment. Through feminist liturgies, we celebrate and nurture our Christian feminist spirituality. Laying hands on one another liberates the energy of the Spirit who is rekindling her fire among women.

Many women are still waiting. Feminists listening to the Spirit-Wisdom are awakening to the obvious oppressions that the hierarchical-patriarchal Church has sanctioned, perpetuated, and propagated for centuries: languages and symbols that make males normative and exclude femaleness; head-oriented and body-less theology; hierarchical-patriarchal decision-making and leadership; stale traditions and lifeless laws. The scandalous sins of the beloved Church dedicated to love and justice nullify the message of Jesus, beg for forgiveness, and demand transformation.

As a result of this awakening, women who experience the intensity of this injustice scream in rage. The dark night of patriarchy, the spiritual colonization of women by men, has produced the most insidious of all heresies: God is male and the male is God.[14] This deception of the Fathers has perpetuated the systematic marginalization of women; it has programmed women to internalize life-destroying and victimizing roles of submission, dependence, and exclusion.

Feminists are recognizing the violence inherent in the hierarchical-patriarchal Church structure. This violence takes two forms: violence the Church wreaks upon women through systematic exclusion; violence women wreak upon one another because they have internalized patriarchal structures. Feminists who see that these forms of violence feed on each other become Pentecostal fires calling the Church to conversion. Women are uniting in the anger of the Spirit to resist oppression and to risk the creation of an alternative vision of love and justice. Laying hands upon one another, we release our collective power-filled energy of rightful rage. Our anger calls patriarchal sexism by name and challenges its violent structures and actions. Thus, Christian feminist spirituality calls women together as the ecclesia of women bonded for struggle.

Claiming Our Power

The Eucharistic Meal

The ecclesia of women, enlivened by the power and gifts of Spirit-Wisdom, celebrates and nurtures the quality of life of the community. In eucharistic celebration, we remember the living presence of God/

Goddess in our brokenness and our liberation. We give thanks for the divine call to turn from oppression to freedom expressed in Jesus' life, passion and resurrection and in women's attempt to follow faithfully in his path. The particular eucharistic meal described here was prepared for "Women Moving Church" by members of Sisters Against Sexism (SAS), an ecclesia of women in Washington, D.C.

The liturgy began with a gathering in the Church and a series of extended questions to the community:

> *Voice 1:* Sisters and Brothers, when you see racism . . . (classism . . . sexism . . . heterosexism . . . militarism . . . imperialism . . .), why do you stay in the struggle?

Members of the group offered spontaneous personal answers. Then the final question was posed:

> *Voice 7:* Sisters and Brothers, when you realize your heritage as a Church community is part of the patriarchal structure which crushes the spirit of liberation, mutuality, and cooperation inherited from our brother Jesus, why do you stay in the Church?

"Because we are Church" was repeated rapidly by all as we joined hands and processed in song out of the church into the dining room. The singing continued until all had gathered around circular tables. A single lighted candle and dishes and tableware for nine place settings were on each table. The liturgy proceeded with an invitation to those assembled to affirm themselves as Church, first, by sitting down at table, and then by gathering the bonds of oppression and transforming them into life-giving elements.

> *Voice 1:* The bonds of racism that keep us apart we transform into unity. . . . Whereas color once determined the servant and the served, now that is no more. . . . We call forth a server from the small tables. Come forward and circle our serving table. . . .
>
> *All sing:* We will unite all together/Sisters, Brothers, All.[15]
>
> *Voice 2:* Bonds of imperialism maintain economic and political domination over the lives of so many of our sisters and brothers. . . . We transform them into freedom and self-determination. . . . Set your tables, determining your own space yet realizing you are linked in community.
>
> *All sing:* We will determine who we are/Sisters, Brothers, All.

Voice 3: Classism keeps workers apart, separated from the creation of one's own labors. We choose to work and build together. Bread symbolizes the creative act of laborers. We invite our server to bring this bread to our tables.

All sing: We will work and build our union/Sisters, Brothers, All.

Voice 4: Bonds of militarism demand that death be purchased rather than life. . . . We choose to spend our money wisely. As a sign of choices that steward our resources and provide nourishment and life, we ask one from your table to come to the serving table and receive a main dish. . . .

All sing: We will spend our money wisely/Sisters, Brothers, All.

Voice 5: Women are lovers, lovers of life, of beauty, of persons. Heterosexism creates an arrogance that prevents and condemns the love that one woman shares with another, and one man with another. . . . We transform that oppression into a gentle touch that will affirm whatever and whoever we encounter as being beautiful. Take the flower to your table to symbolize that beauty.

All sing: All we touch is turned to beauty. . . .

Voice 6: Through bonds of sexism women have found their identity in relation to husband, boss, child. Women's reason for being is systematically blurred by male society's expectations. . . . We transform those bonds. Wine symbolizes the purpose of our lives. Blood-red speaks to the life-giving blood of menstruation, of birth. . . . Receive this wine and bring it to your table.

All sing: We have purpose in our lives. . . .

Voice 7: The patriarchal structures of the Church recognize a few and overlook the fullness of the gifts of the community. We transform these bonds into round table sharing, where equality is the norm and sharing is key. Join hands and bless those who share your table.

All sing: We believe in tablesharing/Sisters, Brothers, All.

Voice 8: Now in a spirit of prayer let us bless our food and our table. Let the person who brought the bread to your table begin the blessing and sharing of bread.

Voice 9: Let the person who brought the wine to your table begin the pouring and sharing of the wine.

Voice 10: Now that we have shared the bread and wine, let us continue our celebration and ask one person to receive our main dish at the serving table.

After the bread, wine, and food were shared, the community again sang:

We will unite all together/Sisters, Brothers, All.
We believe in tablesharing/Sisters, Brothers, All.

Following the sharing of food, the gospel was read. The text was Luke 24, the disciples' meeting with the Risen Christ Jesus on the road to Emmaus and the recognition of him in the breaking of bread. After the reading, the meal ended in mutual blessing at the tables, silent prayer, and a circle dance.

Theological Reflections on the Eucharistic Meal

Women listening to Spirit-Wisdom calling through the community are celebrating Eucharist. The Spirit empowers us to recognize the fullness of our baptismal call to discipleship and our giftedness in the Spirit. Responsible for what we have seen and heard, we know we must act in loyal disobedience to a Church built on the structural sin of sexism. We must act in faithful obedience to Spirit-Wisdom who is rekindling gospel tablesharing based on faith and love. Our vision-in-action challenges institutional, clerical structures of Church by bonding us together to remember and celebrate our Church heritage.

As women awaken not only to the violence done to women by the hierarchical-patriarchal Church's sexist structures, but also to our own spirit-filled identity, we are freed to act without male permission and with the vision of Spirit-Wisdom. Denied recognition of our baptismal birthright of imaging Christ, ignored in our priestly and episcopal vocations, raped of our heritage as Church, many of us have been compelled to absent ourselves from Eucharist and to move out of male Church structures. More creatively, this Spirit-energy is inflaming women to celebrate the creation of a new model of Church.

The world-wide ecclesia of women, quiet but persistent, is emerging everywhere and expressing itself eucharistically. The occasions for celebrating are many: women in traditional religious communities gathering at motherhouses or in local communities; women coming together at national and international meetings; women of various backgrounds and traditions gathering in each other's homes; women gathering for shared retreats, women and men gathering to break the bread of friendship. Universally, this ecclesia of women (and some men) claims Jesus and the early Christian movement as our heritage, our life source and our beginning.

Feminist Eucharists break through the established structures of the sinful Church. They redeem and reclaim the gospel message of table-sharing: women eat food, break bread, share wine, tell stories, give thanks, claim power, and actualize visions in the memory of Jesus. In community tablesharing, the Spirit of God breaks forth and renews the face of the earth. Those who walk this spirit-journey choose to actualize this vision over and against the oppressive structures of this world, especially ecclesial patriarchy. As for all Christians, the faith of feminists must be expressed and celebrated in community if it is to survive and flourish.

The Eucharist celebrated by the ecclesia of women is not simply bread and wine. The whole life of the ecclesia becomes Eucharist.[16] Women are the Body of Christ in the world. The sharing of our lives becomes the eucharistic symbol. Women celebrate Eucharist when we tell stories of our foremothers' journey from oppression to liberation, when we bond for struggle as an ecclesia of women laying hands upon one another, and when we gather to share the Spirit-Wisdom among us. The liturgical celebration of these and all the events of our lives expresses the process of our liberation as Catholic-Christian women. This movement, as we have seen, spirals from personal experience told through stories to communal bonding for struggle to claiming our power for the birthing of a new community and Church.

Conclusion

In conclusion, we now ask: Can we always celebrate Eucharist? According to the hierarchical-patriarchal Church's articulation of eucharistic celebration, the ecclesia of women can never celebrate Eucharist. According to the ecclesia of women, women would never want to celebrate Eucharist in the present hierarchical-patriarchal Church guilty of the sin of sexism. Yet, according to sound eucharistic theology, Eucharist must flow from and express the spirituality of the whole life of the community.[17] Therefore, women can and must celebrate Eucharist.

Accordingly, the ecclesia of women poses these questions: Can the institutional Church change enough to welcome this new energy of women which invites the Church to conversion?

Can women move from the fringe into the mainstream of a Church which is life for all of us together?

Can women continue to be both Roman Catholic and feminist?

When will women and men immersed in the hierarchical-patriarchal

Church realize their personal and communal deprivation in rejecting and ignoring women's eucharistic celebrations?

Can the dualities of the hierarchical-patriarchal Church and the ecclesia of women co-exist? How are they transformed?

How long must we wait? How long should we wait? How long will "they" wait? The ecclesia of women is listening to the call of Spirit-Wisdom for liberation, a call that is resounding world-wide. Bonded together for our long journey towards freedom, we celebrate the Eucharist as Church.

NOTES

1. This concept of interstructuring is found in the works of R. R. Ruether, *New Woman, New Earth*, New York, 1957, and M. E. Hunt, "Feminist Liberation Theology: The Development of Method in Construction," dissertation, 1980, Berkeley, Calif.). For the concept of patriarchal sexism, see Elisabeth Schüssler Fiorenza, "To Comfort or to Challenge," *New Woman, New Church, New Priestly Ministry*, ed. M. Dwyer, Rochester, N.Y., 1980, p. 45.

2. M. E. Hunt elaborates on this concept in "Roman Catholic Ministry: Patriarchal Past, Feminist Future," *New Woman, New Church, New Priestly Ministry*, ed. M. Dwyer, Rochester, N.Y., 1980, p. 31.

3. N. Morton, "Beloved Image," *The Challenge of Feminism to Theology*, ed. M. E. Hunt and R. Gibellini, February 1982.

4. H. Near, "Singing for Our Lives" (Hereford Music; Redwood Records 1979). Used with permission. Text had been adapted for the celebration.

5. E. Schüssler Fiorenza, "Feminist Spirituality, Christian Identity, and Catholic Vision," in *Womanspirit Rising*, ed. C. P. Christ and J. Plaskow, San Francisco, 1979, p. 140.

6. E. Schüssler Fiorenza, "Gather Together in My Name.... Toward a Christian Feminist Spirituality," unpublished paper for the conference Women Moving Church, Washington, D.C., 1981: "In the Greek Old Testament *ecclesia* means 'the assembly of the people of Israel before God.' In the New Testament *ecclesia* comes through the agency of the Spirit to visible, tangible expression in and through the gathering of God's people around the table...."

7. C. Williamson, "Sister," *The Changer and the Changed*, Olivia Records, 1976.

8. S. Copeland, "Your Daughter Shall Prophesy," *New Woman, New Church, New Priestly Ministry*, ed. M. Dwyer, New York, 1980, p. 155.

9. N. Shange, *For Colored Girls Who Have Considered Suicide/When the Rainbow Is Enuf*, New York, 1977, pp. 4–5.

10. A. Akiko and N. Weisstein, "Mountain Moving Day," in *Mountain Moving Day*, ed. E. Gill, New York, 1973.

11. R. Nudd, unpublished reflection paper, "Women Moving Church," Washington, D.C., 1981.

12. Akiko and Weisstein, *Mountain Moving Day*, ed. E. Gill.

13. R. Lucey, unpublished reflection paper, "Women Moving Church."

14. M. Daly, *Beyond God the Father*, Boston, 1973, and *Gyn/Ecology: The Metaethics of Radical Feminism*, Boston, 1978.

15. Black Spiritual, "Jacob's Ladder," paraphrased.

16. *Lumen Gentium* 9, Rome, 1966.

17. J. Powers, "Eucharist, Mystery of Faith and Love," in *The Sacraments*, ed. M. J. Taylor, New York, 1981, p. 120.

PART IV

CHANGING THEOLOGICAL DISCOURSES

28

Opium or the Seed for Revolution?

Women-Centered Religiosity in Korea

CHUNG HYUN KYUNG

Shamanism (Musok) is the "women-centered" popular religiosity that is widely practiced among poor people in Korea. Is it a revolutionary seed that empowers both Christians and non-Christians to fight for their liberation or is it a sedative which makes them accept their situation of oppression?

For many years, many educated people in Korea despised Shamanism as "opium of the poor." They referred to it as a superstitious religious practice which provided "ignorant people" (especially "emotional women") with an escape from the *real world*. It could not, therefore, provide any revolutionary impetus for socio-political changes in Korean society.

Recently, however, another interpretation of Shamanism has emerged in Korea. Korean young workers, farmers and students in the liberation movements have begun to use Shamanistic ritual (*Kut*) as one of the most important tools for their movement. They perform the *Kut* in the midst of their demonstrations against the dictatorial government, U.S. imperialism, and multi-national corporations. As Christians invite the Holy Spirit to be present with them in worship and in times of distress, farmers, young workers and students offer a similar invitation to the *Han*-ridden ghosts at the beginning of the *Kut*.[1] These ghosts are the spirit of the people who died from sickness or were killed unjustly in the liberation movement without seeing the "New World" they dreamed of in Korean history. The demonstrators offer food, dance, song and prayer to the *Han*-ridden ghosts so that the latter will empower the former in their struggle against the forces of oppression. According to the demonstrators, *Kut* is the most nationalistic Minjung ritual which is not from the colonialists' religion such as Christianity.[2]

275

Some Korean theologians also have begun to appropriate Shamanistic resources in their attempt to develop a theology out of everyday life experiences of the oppressed Minjung. They contend that the world of the Minjung can be taken seriously only to the degree that the religion of the Minjung (Shamanism) is *appropriated as the main source* for their theology.

Not surprisingly, many Korean women — especially participants in women's liberation movements or in women's studies — also turn to Shamanism as a source of power. They contend that Shamanism is the only religious context where women's power and leadership has been sustained throughout Korean history, providing women-centered space within a patriarchal society.

It seems that a new Shamanistic Renaissance has emerged among justice concerned people in Korea. As a Korean woman who feels compelled to do theology in the context of the Korean people's movement, I have naturally nurtured my interest in Korean Shamanism. This natural interest has become a passionate obsession. It began a few years ago after I heard the news that my high school friend, Jiheh, had become an initiated Shaman (*Mudang*), largely influenced by her participation in the student movement.[3] I sometimes feel almost possessed by her being. But then I realize that she is not an *object* for my observation. Rather, she is a *person,* a *comrade* who, like me, is deeply concerned about the liberation of our homeland.

My theological journey as a third world woman prepared me for my recent encounter with Jiheh as a Shaman. As Aloysius Pieris has said, "the irruption of the Third World is also the irruption of the non-Christian world."[4] This is particularly true for Asia. If we, as third world theologians, expect to create a theology that is faithful to the liberation struggle of the poor, then we must listen to and learn from the religion of the non-Christian poor, which is also *the religion from the underside of religion.* In doing this, we should also remember that women are the majority of the poor who actively participate in creating and nurturing popular religiosity.

Shamanism in Korea was considered *devil worship* by western missionaries. It was regarded as animistic, primitive and thus an inferior religion because it focused on women's mundane life and *the earth.* Shamanism was often considered as an a-historical, a-moral cosmic religion which had to be *corrected,* that is, *domesticated* by the higher, male-centered, meta-cosmic religions.

To learn about Shamanism, therefore, is to encounter a typical woman-centered religion from the underside of the dominant world religions. Third world theologians' study of Shamanism should not be out of mere curiosity. It is a necessity for all who have genuine interest in the people who are the most hurt and oppressed and who are determined to be liberated from their bondage.

Theological Presuppositions

Before searching for the liberating impetus of Shamanism, it is necessary to make my theological presuppositions explicit.

First, my interpretation is "gender specific" — that is, defined by women's experience. *Third world women suffer because they are poor.* While their suffering includes material poverty, it is more than that. Third world women are poor because they are not treated as equal partners in the human community. That was why Mercy Oduyoye named women's reality as an "irruption within the irruption,"[5] a reality that EATWOT men found difficult to understand and to incorporate into their theology. Women also resonate with the feeling of "the anthropological poverty" that Engelbert Mveng expressed as an African at the Fifth Assembly of EATWOT in New Delhi.[6] Many male theologians often talk about the poor. But as third world women, we frequently feel that they are talking about poor *men* and not necessarily poor *women.* Therefore, in order to make the voices of women heard, we must emphasize the "female gender specificity" in our definition of the meaning of suffering and liberation.

Second, my interpretation of Korean Shamanism is also defined by the contemporary People's Movement for liberation in Korea. This means that my interpretation of the "liberating" and "oppressive" dimensions of Shamanism is made through the eyes of the people who are participating in the third world liberation struggle. In other words, I intentionally limit my examination of Shamanism to those aspects which liberation activists find useful and will not, in this essay, be concerned with characteristics which the observers of the struggle define as negative. I believe that the "liberating" and "alienating" aspects of Shamanism can only be judged by those who are actively seeking to establish justice in society. They may be nationalistic students, farmers, workers, religious persons (especially women), or *anybody who is at the front line of the movement for liberation and self-determination of our people.*

Third, my interpretation of Shamanism is shaped by my commitment to the Christian gospel. By birth I *became* a Christian, and by choice I decided to *remain* a Christian, but not without a difference. My perspective on the Christian Gospel is not defined by the particular missionary brand that initially introduced me to Jesus Christ. Rather it has been carved out of my solidarity with the struggle of Koreans and other third world people for liberation. This liberation struggle is not separate from the movement of freedom that has also inspired a new liberation impetus in Shamanism. Therefore, liberation-centered Christianity and liberation-centered Shamanism are not totally separate realities. In some sense they are *one* reality that empowers the poor to fight for justice and freedom.

Because Christianity and Shamanism are linked together in the democratic struggle in Korea, I have chosen to speak of a kind of "liberation-centered syncretism." In their struggle for justice, poor people come to many different religious sources for sustenance and empowerment. What matters for the people are not Christian doctrines in contrast with Shamanist beliefs. What matters is *liberation of the people from bondage!* What matters is not Jesus or Buddha or General Choi Young[7] or Samshin Grandmother,[8] but rather *the spirit of liberation* which empowers the people to claim self-determination for themselves.

Fourth, Shamans and Shamanistic believers (the majority of whom are women), must be encountered as *subjects* and not as *objects for observation.* In male-centered traditions, women have been observed as merely objects and in relation to the interests of men. In academic discourse and general public definitions of religion and culture, male hegemony presupposes that a woman is defined by her *relationship to men* — father, brother, husband, or son. However, I agree with other third world women who say that *our reality must be defined by ourselves.* As Sun-Ai Park has said, "neither Third World men nor First World women can determine the Third World women's agenda."[9] *We are the subjects of our own history.*

In order to meet the Shamans and Shamanist believers *as subjects,* it is important to encounter a "socio-biography"[10] of a young Shaman in the movement: my honorable high school friend, Jiheh.

Jiheh's Socio-biography: A Prototype of a New Generation of Shaman in the Liberation Movement

When I first heard about Jiheh's story six years ago I was shocked. I could not believe what happened to her. *She had become a Shaman!* I thought it could not be true because the majority of Shamans in Korea were considered to be ignorant, superstitious women. Jiheh did not fit that image. During our high school years, she was a brilliant and talented student. Writer, painter and ballet dancer, Jiheh excelled in many things and was greatly admired by many people.

As most people who knew her expected, Jiheh entered one of the most élite art colleges in Korea. During our college years, we lost contact. She became an active participant in the student movement. It soon became clear to her that the western art, which she studied in school, could not serve as an effective tool for the liberation of the Korean people. She dropped out of college and started to collect Korean Minjung art forms — especially songs and dances from the grass-roots people.

While Jiheh was collecting art forms, she became sick. The reason for her illness was unclear. One day she went to a Shaman's place to learn Korean Shaman dance. The Shaman, however, recognized that Jiheh was suffering with possession sickness (*Sinbyong*), a common occurrence in persons before they become an initiated Shaman. Initially, Jiheh strongly resisted her "calling" as a Shaman. Her western training hindered her appreciation of Shamanism. However, eventually she decided to become a Shaman, and her illness disappeared.

After becoming an initiated Shaman, Jiheh gave an interview for a women's magazine in which she revealed her family background. Jiheh's mother conceived her with a man who deceived her. He told Jiheh's mother that he was a bachelor, and he persuaded her to develop a serious relationship with him. However, when Jiheh was born and had to be registered as *his* child (according to patrilineal Korean social law), he refused to acknowledge her publicly as his daughter. Jiheh's mother found out that he was a married man with a family of his own. Therefore, Jiheh had to take her mother's last name, which was very scandalous in terms of Korean culture. Because she was conceived in deception, rejected by her father, and raised with the name of her mother, Jiheh embodied Korean women's *Han*.

Jiheh's activities as a Shaman have been very *socially* oriented. The day that a Korean women's liberation organization (Yeo Sung Pyung Wo Hoe) was founded, she performed the *Kut* to bless the group. She celebrated women's power by dancing on a sharp sword while holding her infant daughter. She also performed *Kut* in front of a factory while women workers demonstrated against multi-national corporations. According to some people's testimony, she exorcised capitalism, multi-national corporations and military dictatorships. They contend that her guiding spirit is the spirit of the *Baek-Du* mountain, located on the boundary of North Korea and China. Some people believe that the *Baek-Du* mountain spirit will guide Jiheh in her work toward the unification of Korea by casting out the evil ghost of imperialism.

Shaman as a Priestess of "Han"

Jiheh's initiation into Shamanhood can be interpreted as the symbolic embodiment of young liberationists' historical consciousness. Most persons who accept this interpretation are young people whom I call "second generation liberationists." "First generation liberationists" experienced *Japanese colonialism, the division of the nation,* and *the Korean War.* They worked hard to save our country from these tragedies. Their main concern was "nation building" — emphasizing the need for education, development, and modernization. The first generation liberationists were critical of the behavior and culture of the Minjung, since the latter's "ignorance" seemed to hinder the advancement of Korean society into the modern world.

The "second generation liberationists" were born *after independence* from Japan and have become disillusioned by the first generationists' promises of freedom which education and modernization were intended to achieve for Korean people. The people who received most of the benefits of the western-style education and modernization were a few power élites who had direct connections with neo-colonial power. The majority of *Minjung* — the poor people of Korea — remained in poverty.

As second generation liberationists realized the great limitations of modernization, they began to ask, "where do we turn for the power of liberation?" It seemed clear to them that the people responsible for creating the great gap between the rich and poor in Korea simply would not provide the tools to effect radical changes in the society. The place to turn then was to the wisdom of the people at the bottom — the *Minjung.* Our generation has come to know that *Minjung* are the real subject of the history of liberation and not a small élite. This understanding encouraged many educated young people to learn their history, culture and religion — humbly — from the *Minjung.* Now we see many young people learning maal dances, farmer's dances, orally inherited songs and learning how to play traditional Korean instruments.

Buddhist, Confucianism and Christianity are *imported religions* in Korea. They have been used by the ruling élite to maintain the *status quo.* Shamanism, however, was not imported but was created out of the people's lives. Some young people define Shamanistic ritual, *Kut,* as both the community organization of the *Minjung* and a celebration of the hope derived from their refusal to bow down to the forces of oppression.[11] Through historical research, direct connections have been discovered between Shamanism and many *Minjung* revolutionary movements in Korea. By becoming a Shaman, it could be said that Jiheh embodied the consciousness of these young liberationists.

Who are the Shamans? What are their functions and roles in the Minjung community? Most Shamans have been the victims of hard life situations. With no public channels to express their *Han,* they internalize it — and their bodies revolt. They fall sick without an identifiable medical reason. This is called *sinbyong.* The *sinbyong* (possession sickness) disappears *only when they accept the Shaman's role.* Many people believe that if possessed persons do not accept their role as a Shaman, they will die. *Sinbyong* is the unmistakable sign that one has been destined to become a Shaman.

In Korea, more than seventy percent of Shamans are women. This statistic shows that *women are the primary transmitters and embodiment of Han* in Korean history. More specifically, poor women are the chief carriers of *Han*. They are at the bottom of the bottom in Korean society and thus may be said to embody the *Han* of the *Han*. Their possession sickness, *Sinbyong*, does not fall from the sky. Rather it comes from their everyday concrete experience of suffering. Their *Han* is caused by extreme poverty and maltreatment in a patriarchal society. When they suffer *Sinbyong*, they have:

> feelings of listlessness and later complain of many or all of the following conditions: anorexia, circulatory distresses such as extreme coldness and/or numbness of hands and feet, diarrhea, faintness, insomnia, nausea, palpitations of the heart, respiratory congestion experienced as "heaviness of the heart" or "tightness of the chest," acutely painful ringing in the ear, sudden fevers, and weight loss.[12]

All of this is usually accompanied by what some would call mental disorder like "auditory and/or visual hallucinations and strange dreams."[13]

A Korean woman anthropologist, Young Sook Kim Harvey, named the following as the most personal characteristics among Korean women Shamans:

a. a high level of intelligence,

b. above average capacity for creative improvisation (they were imaginative and capable of improvising verbally, behaviorally, and in the use of available resources).

c. above average verbal fluency and persuasiveness,

d. strong goal orientation (they tended to be willful, self-centered, self-reliant and self-directed),

e. keen sensitivity to intuitive cues of others,

f. calculating and manipulative inter-personal skills which enabled them to manage social situations strategically,

g. a sharp sense of justice in terms of their own standards,

h. an above-average repertoire of aptitudinal and/or achieved dramatic and artistic attributes, such as singing and dancing. In addition, all but one were exceptionally attractive in appearance.[14]

Shamans are strong women, "organic intellectuals," wounded healers, exorcists, household therapists, singers, dancers, comedians, actresses — beautiful, attractive and sensual women. They are best known, however, as *priestesses* who become *mediators between the living and the dead.* In the communities of Shamanistic *Minjung,* they have no church buildings or hierarchical, clerical structures among themselves. Shamans treat people in their home or their client's home. There are no strict, orthodox texts in Shamanism.

Han-ridden ghosts are people who died in the world unjustly. Shamans call upon them during the Shamanistic ritual, *Kut,* to speak about the unjust treatment they received in this world. Then Shamans console the ghosts, negotiate with them, argue with them and play with them. Shamans make people cry, laugh, dance and sing through *Kut.* Shamans urge the whole community to do something for these *Han*-ridden ghosts in order to let them release their *Han* and leave this world completely with peaceful hearts. A Shaman is the spiritual center of the community.

However, in Korean society the woman Shaman has not been treated honorably like Buddhist monks, Confucianist scholars or Christian priests and ministers. People have asked for her supernatural power to solve their problems, but they have feared her power. At the same time, they have ostracized her and her family as *the other.* Her children could not marry into so-called "respectable" families. Traditionally, people believed that the woman Shaman exhibited a very loose sexual life. It was also believed that any man who married a Shaman would lose his masculine power and become a "woman-like man." A Shaman has lived an ambivalent existence. Publicly she had been powerless; but privately she is very strong.[15]

NOTES

1. According to a Korean theologian, Suh Nam-dong, "*Han* is the suppressed, amassed, and condensed experience of oppression caused by mischief or misfortune so that it forms a kind of 'lump' in one's spirit." See his article "Towards a Theology of Han," in *Minjung Theology,* ed. The Commission on Theological Concerns of the Christian Conference of Asia, London, New York, and Singapore, 1981, p. 68.

2. *Minjung* means people, specifically oppressed people.

3. "Jiheh" is not my friend's real name. I use a pseudonym to protect her privacy.

4. Aloysius Pieris, "The Place of Non-Christian Religions and Cultures in the Evolution of Third World Theology," in *Irruption of the Third World: Challenge to Theology,* ed. Virginia Fabella and Sergio Torres, New York, 1983, p. 113.

5. Mercy Amba Oduyoye, "Reflections from a Third World Women's Perspective: Women's Experience and Liberation Theologies," in *Irruption of the Third World: Challenge to Theology,* p. 247.

6. Engelbert Mveng, "Third World Theology — What Theology? What Third World? Evaluation by an African Delegate," ibid., p. 220.

7. General Choi Young was a real historical figure who was killed unjustly in Korean history. People have venerated him as a guardian spirit in some branches of Korean Shamanism.

8. Samshin Grandmother is a kind of goddess who is in charge of fertility in Korean Shamanism.

9. Virginia Fabella and Sergio Torres, eds., *Doing Theology in a Divided World*, New York, 1985, p. xv.

10. The term "socio-biography" of Minjung is proposed by Korean Minjung theologian Kim Yong-Bok. According to Kim, the reality of Minjung can be known best not by a scientific or philosophical definition of them, but by their own life stories. For more information on "socio-biography" of Minjung, see Kim Yong-Bok, "Messiah and Minjung: Discerning Messianic Politics over against Political Messianism," in *Minjung Theology*, pp. 183–94.

11. From the preface of *Minjokwa Kut* (Nation and *Kut*), ed. Minjokkuthoe, Seoul, 1987, p. ii.

12. Young Sook Kim Harvey, "Possession Sickness and Women Shamans in Korea," in *Unspoken Worlds: Women's Religious Lives in Non-Christian Cultures*, ed. Nancy Falk and Rita Gross, San Francisco, 1980, p. 44.

13. Ibid.

14. Young Sook Kim Harvey, *Six Korean Women: The Socialization of Shamans*, New York, 1979, pp. 235–36.

15. Laurel Kendall, *Shamans, Housewives, and Other Restless Spirits*, Honolulu, 1985, p. 164.

29

Ecclesiastical and Feminist Blessing

JANET WALTON

Throughout liturgical history women have received blessings — virgins, mothers, daughters, wives, and abbesses — but they have not had the authority to impart blessings or to propose appropriate texts for them. Feminists are raising significant questions about this situation. They are addressing the form, content, and meaning of blessings for women in current liturgical use. They are also suggesting alternative expressions of blessing for and by women. This article is an occasion to probe these questions and to establish principles which may evoke further discussion.

The material is organized in three sections: (1) an examination of two rites of blessing for women (an abbess and a mother) seen in relationship to similar blessings for men (an abbot and a father); (2) an exposition of four principles to provide a basis for an alternative, feminist rite of blessing; (3) a description, by way of example, to illustrate new possibilities of blessing which women may give and receive.

The Blessing of an Abbess[1] and of a Mother[2]

The blessings designed for these two classifications of persons, from very different lifestyles, are examples of a number of blessings in current liturgical use that demonstrate a monolithic and disturbing perception of women. The demeaning nature of this perception becomes clearer when compared with similar blessings for their male counterparts. In the rite of blessing, the abbess, like the abbot, is first of all instructed. She is reminded to be obedient to the Church and the Pope, to teach her sisters by constant dedication to the monastic life and by her good example. However, unlike the abbot, she is not asked to stand in the place of Christ, to guide others in the way of the Spirit, to teach by sound doctrine, to be concerned for the spiritual good of those entrusted to her care, to be a faithful steward of goods, a good shepherd, or to pray without ceasing for God's people.

One need not wonder why a woman with very similar responsibilities to her male counterpart is not recognized fully and openly for her contributions. Clearly, female persons cannot transmit nor witness the most cherished aspects of the Christian tradition. Not only are they limited by the institutional arguments against the ordination of women and therefore cannot "stand in the place of Christ," but, in addition, they are not acknowledged as spiritual directors, nor as teachers of the Church's doctrine. They are not identified as responsible leaders of their respective communities nor as astute collaborators in caring for the earth's resources. They are not perceived as those whose life of prayer contributes to the "shepherding" and care of God's people. In contrast to abbots, who are given authority equal to that of a bishop, abbesses are granted minimal power.

The differences do not end here. In the final prayer of blessing in each rite, there are some significant variances in the texts. The Church petitions God to "strengthen" the new abbot, but, to "sustain" the new abbess. It recognizes the abbot's duties as "demanding" and "heavy." It does not characterize the duties of the abbess. In the prayer for the abbot, God is asked to give him "a heart full of compassion, wisdom, and zeal so that he may not lose even one of the flock entrusted to his charge." There is no similar section in the blessing of an abbess.

The definitions of "strengthen" and "sustain" offer a clue to some conclusions. To strengthen is to make powerful or strong. To sustain is to keep in existence, to maintain, prolong, provide for, or support. The respective descriptions and mandates for leadership of an abbot and abbess are based on stereotypical sex role differences rather than upon one's faithfulness in responding to God's gifts. Abbots need strength to empower, whereas abbesses need sustenance to endure. Imparting power is signified as a singular manner of participating in the work of God, "demanding and heavy," and therefore calls for a specially endowed person. Supporting or maintaining is viewed as secondary. It does not warrant the same gifts of God.

This exposition of texts leads to a variety of conclusions:

a. Whereas abbots and abbesses at one time were recognized as equally significant leaders in the life of a monastic community these texts show the erosion of their similar identities.

b. Whereas God created all of humankind in God's own image, female and male (Gen. 1:27), the power to reveal God and to impart the divine tradition falls only to the male, or at least, is his in far greater proportion.

c. Whereas both women and men are recognized by the Church as leaders of a community, the potential of that leadership is determined by gender. The potential of women is strictly limited.

These conclusions are alarming and distressing. They demand the attention of the whole Church. Should one argue that the blessing of an abbot or abbess is rarely experienced by most people, the very fact that such a rite has been published in an edition of the *Rites of the Catholic Church* as revised by the Second Vatican Council and as recently as 1980 should be a source of concern for all the Church's members. As an authorized statement, it represents the Church's perspective, one that identifies how God is known and experienced. And this statement both restricts and undermines the contributions of women.

An examination of the brief blessing for a mother and a father raises similar concerns:

Holy God, you compare your own love for your people to the love of a mother for her children. Look with kindness on these mothers, give them comfort in moments of sorrow, and joy in their work for their families. Listen to their prayers, and bless them in all they do for you. Let them share with Jesus your Son and Mary our mother in the everlasting happiness of Heaven. Father, we ask this grace through Christ our Lord. Amen.

Lord Jesus our brother we praise you for saving us. Teach us to love you and your Father by keeping your commandments. Bless these fathers, and deepen their love for their wives and families. By their work and example and prayer, may they lead their children to follow you. Lord Jesus, hear our prayer as we offer you glory for ever and ever. Amen.

The image of a mother conveyed in this blessing straddles being like God on the one hand — a person who is aware, active, and faithful — and, on the other, being helpless and weak, one whose primary responsibilities are so vague they can only be described as "work for their families." The representation is clearer again in contrast. The image of father is carefully defined. He is reminded that love is not ambiguous but is located in one's response to the commandments. He is acknowledged as responsible for the love among members of his family. He is commissioned to lead his children through work, example, and prayer. In both the opening and closing phrases he is recognized for his ability to offer praise and glory to God.

Both the words and the quality of the blessing offer points for our consideration. In the text for the mother the first sentence leads quite naturally to a description of God's love for her/his children which the mother actualizes. "You compare your own love ... to the love of a mother. ... " Instead, the quality changes, spelling out the mother's need for comfort and joy rather than enumerating her gifts or responsibilities. She is blessed simply "for *all* she does," with no mention of anything in particular.

On the other hand, the blessing of the father is specific. Once again, like the abbot, the male person is entrusted with teaching, and an example of love, work, action, and prayer. The father is the model of the Christian tradition and is responsible for imparting it. The stereotypes perdure. The female assumes a passive role, the male an active one. The female, an inferior one, the male a superior one. The female is invisible, supportive to the male.

The very rite of blessing raises a number of questions:

1. Do we as a Church continue to believe that men can image God more specifically than women because of the form and functions of their bodies?

2. Are we as a church *afraid* to accept women's experiences as interpretations of the Christian life?

3. Are we as a Church perpetuating an identity of men that is based on an invisible or inferior position of women and then blessing that identity?

A Feminist Perspective

The rites for an abbess and for a mother illustrate an image of woman that is affirmed throughout the liturgical practice of the Roman Catholic Church. From within this Church, women and men are calling for repentance and change. Their call, rooted in a feminist perspective, can be expressed in concrete principles. Four of these convictions are appropriate to this topic: (a) Authority is a gift, the power to impart and to receive freedom. (b) "Power is experienced as power of presence to ourselves and to each other."[3] (c) Power is shared not bestowed. (d) "Power is where power is perceived."[4]

Authority Is a Gift, the Power to Convey and to Receive Freedom

To participate in the act of giving or receiving a blessing is to share in the authority of God. It is to join the flow of power that moves between

God and humankind in mysterious and unpredictable ways. It is to experience moments of freedom for oneself and others. It is to enter into a sacred arena where choice is available to everyone. It is to acknowledge what is good, beautiful, and just.

Feminists perceive blessing very differently from the traditional ideas conveyed by current ecclesiastical formulas and practice. To bless is to identify the unique dignity of every human person. To bless is to proclaim publicly that a person is released from her/his own bondage and the enslavement of society. To bless is to open new doors for self-determination.

To receive a blessing means to acknowledge the possibility of transformation for one's self and for society. To receive a blessing means to respond positively to untested experience. To receive a blessing means to give up what is known for what is yet unexplored. Rather than a static reinforcement of stereotypical images, blessing, from a feminine perspective, is an act of freeing and of being freed.

"Power Is Experienced as a Power of Presence to Ourselves and to Each Other"

The long struggle of women to free themselves from imprisoning dominance, stereotypical imaging and patriarchal structures has provided a fresh understanding of power. They acknowledge power in themselves, rather than solely and primarily beyond themselves. They connect this awareness with a similar awakening in others. Personal and political power are interactive. Such a recognition affects the experience and meaning of blessing. Blessing is perceived as a form in which human beings link with the divine reality. Power from within touches the power of God and this experience is extended to another. Alice Koller describes such an encounter, "When she blessed me, I understood that she was giving me something of what constituted the core of her being."[5] Such a blessing is not mechanical and impersonal. It is rooted in a recognition of the locus of power. The exchange testifies to the responsibility of each individual to identify her/his power and to spread its benefits.

Power Is Shared, Not Bestowed

The most persuasive intrusion into the integrity of women has been accomplished through domination. Such superiority sets male against female as well as rich against poor, white against other races. Within a liturgical structure domination is constantly being expressed in the division of clergy and laity as well as in the exclusive use of male language for God and humankind. Females and female characteristics are rarely regarded with respect. Feminists have unmasked the evil of this situation and have identified the possession of power as a primary target. Since the rite of blessing is expression of power, it too must undergo radical changes.

Seen from a feminist perspective, blessing is a collaborative experience. Blessing is given and received simultaneously. Human beings share blessings. They give shape to that which is invisible. Such an understanding changes the content and meaning of blessing, and it affects the form in which it is given. No longer is a situation tolerable in which some persons stand above, while others kneel or stand below with bowed heads. Blessing does not flow from high to low. It loses its authenticity when the leader uses a second person pronoun (you) instead of an inclusive one (May God bless *us*) — as though that person had no need of the grace she/he is invoking — or when one assumes a subservient position to receive a blessing. Blessings are symbols of *common* need, each for each other, as well as the divine and human. Words and gestures reinforce this concept.

"Power Is Where Power Is Perceived"

The overload of the tradition of centuries locates power in those individuals who are most articulate, well-educated, persuasive and authorized. The time is fast fading when a woman who walks into the parish house is satisfied to brush past a priest in the hall and to receive a requested blessing for an object or for herself. In the past she acknowledged that power, and in her view, it was transmitted.

Feminists offer an alternative view. The power to bless and be blessed is released at birth, and for Christians it is reinforced in baptism. Feminists believe what Abraham Heschel says so well, just to be is holy. All human beings can be subjects as well as receivers of blessing. Such a recognition changes one's perception of oneself as well as of others. The power to bless and receive blessing is not restricted to a few but rather abundantly available to all who are willing to accept such a privilege and responsibility.

A New Model of Blessing

Since the form, content, and meaning of blessing for and by women will be affected by the principles mentioned above, the action must be participatory both in word and gesture. Its content must emphasize women's strength, courage, and faithfulness. Its meaning must convey an image of woman whose love embraces and extends a vision of freedom.

The following example shows how such a new form of blessing might be imparted and written.

The women gather in a circle. The shape of the space emphasizes the collaborative power of blessing and is quite unlike the familiar hierarchical arrangement where one person faces all the others. The women connect with each other by touching through the palms of their hands. Since our hands enable us to love, play, and work, the gesture not only calls to mind the importance of this part of our body but also the interdependence of these aspects of our lives. It also makes one more aware of the warmth, power, and uniqueness of the persons whom one touches. One *feels* the energy that links them. There is a moment of silence when each person can experience the power of this gesture. The words of the blessing punctuate the silence. Five women, spaced throughout the circle, read the invocation to which all respond.

> *Leader:* Let us affirm the goodness in each other, the integrity and beauty of our bodies, the insights of our minds.
>
> *All:* We stand together.
>
> *Leader:* Let us acknowledge the pain in each other, the strain of struggle, the sorrow of defeat and death.
>
> *All:* We stand together.
>
> *Leader:* Let us uphold the daring in each other: the boldness of spirit, the resoluteness of action.
>
> *All:* We stand together.
>
> *Leader:* Let us esteem laughter and joy in each other; the irony of circumstances, the delight of relationships.
>
> *All:* We stand together.
>
> *Leader:* Let us go forth empowered from this space and time knowing that as we bless each other so we are blessed in God and with God and by God.
>
> *All:* We stand together.

We, the Church, shape our liturgical history. We learn from the past in order to change the present and the future. The rite of blessing for women in present liturgical books and actions in parishes reinforces a submissive and demeaning vision of women. We, the Church, have the duty to acknowledge this misinterpretation and to initiate change. We, the Church, call each other to create a community where the rite of blessing is a symbol of our transformation.

Then women and men will feel and share more fully the unremitting love that connects them to a divine reality and to each other. Then women and men will surrender restricted stereotypes that limit choice and freedom.

Then women and men will identify their own power and acknowledge its interdependent nature.

This invitation is the gift of women to the Church.

NOTES

1. *The Rites of the Catholic Church*, vol. 2, Pueblo, 1980, pp. 117–21, 127–29.

2. Canadian Conference of Catholic Bishops, *A Book of Blessings*, Ottawa, 1981, pp. 51–52.

3. Mary Daly, "The Qualitative Leap Beyond Patriarchal Religion," *Quest* 1, no. 1, p. 21.

4. A concept credited to Delyte Frost found in Barbara Starrett, "The Metaphors of Power," in *The Politics of Women's Spirituality*, ed. Charlene Spretnak, New York, 1982, p. 191.

5. Alice Koller, *An Unknown Woman*, New York, 1983, p. 220.

30

Motherhood or Friendship

ELISABETH MOLTMANN-WENDEL

Two Biblical Traditions about Women

The attentive reader of the Bible will be continually struck by the firm way in which the Church's tradition has put Mary, the mother of Jesus, in the foreground while pushing Mary Magdalene, the first proclaimer of the resurrection message, to the back of the stage. The tradition about Mary, the mother of Jesus, is fed largely by Luke's gospel. But we find the tradition about Mary Magdalene in all four gospels; and it is the tradition about the women which is best attested, and from the most unified standpoint.

Mary Magdalene, the First Witness of the Resurrection

Mary Magdalene is witness to the very beginning of the resurrection message. The gospels differ only about the circumstances. In Mark, Mary Magdalene is accompanied by Mary, the mother of James, and Salome. In Matthew, her companion is "the other Mary." In Luke, too, we are told about another Mary, as well as Joanna and other women. In John and in the late closing passage of Mark she is alone. The character of the charge she is given varies too. In Luke and in the late final passage of Mark she tells the disciples only what she has experienced, while in Mark and Matthew she and the other women are charged by the angel to proclaim to the disciples what they have heard. In John she is given this charge by the risen Jesus himself.

These are not chance variations. They are different emphases by the individual evangelists to the story about the women. Luke tells of no special charge, and there the group of disciples is already viewed as an élite, celibate community which the group of women serves,[1] and in which Mary Magdalene's function is restricted, too. Her presence at the cross

292

is not explicitly mentioned either, though this is reported by the three other gospels. Nor is there any mention of her presence at the tomb, to which Mark and Matthew refer. Luke puts the story of her call, as the healing of a demonic sickness, in the same context as the call to other women, thereby neutralizing its unique character.

In spite of these differences, the picture of Mary Magdalene remains the self-contained portrait of a particular woman. As we have it, it is in striking contrast to the clashes and conflicts of the picture which the four evangelists give us in their varying picture of the mother of Jesus, who was favored by the Church's tradition.

The Mother of Jesus as Antitype

Mark brings out all the sharpness of the conflict between mother and son, which was probably based on historical fact. Matthew tempers this by leaving out the family's suspicion that Jesus was mad (Mark 3:20, 21).[2] Luke softens Jesus' hard saying that only the person who does the will of God belongs to the eschatological family, mitigating it by presenting Mary, in the nativity and childhood stories he includes in his gospel, as the obedient handmaid who fulfills these demands (1:38).

But the gospel of John does not carry through this picture of the believing, obedient Mary. It is true that John puts her at the foot of the cross (unlike the other traditions, which only know about the group of women associated with Mary Magdalene). He does so in order to make her the mother of the beloved disciple, who represents the ideal picture of the believing Christian. But "because of her imperfect faith in Cana" she cannot be compared with the Lucan Mary.

So we can see that the picture of Mary in the New Testament is a conflicting one; and the two main themes of later Mariology — the virgin birth and the presence under the cross — are clearly later in origin. Yet these two themes penetrated deep into devotional practice with the help of pietàs and nativity scenes. All the same, the "uprating" of Mary in Luke and John was not able to push out Mary Magdalene entirely. For she is associated with the very center of Christian faith: the resurrection.

The Repression of the Friendship Tradition

Nonetheless, we can already see in Luke that there was a tendency to minimize Mary Magdalene's uniqueness in favor of the group of women. The original tradition has come down to us in Mark particularly. This tells us that, unlike the disciples, who were in love with success, the women were the real followers of Jesus: it is they who perceive the mes-

sianic secret, and it is they who serve Jesus as he himself came to
serve, and to give his life. This tradition is now joined by another, which
stresses feminine obedience and motherliness, but still favors the group
of male disciples.

Our ideas have been molded by the theology of the mainstream
churches, and we are too little informed about heretical theologies, especially their conceptions about women. This means that we have lost
our eye for the two different traditions about women which can already
be found in the New Testament. I should like to call these *the tradition
of friendship and the tradition of motherhood.* The first of these traditions
made itself felt particularly in the Christian traditions of protest. The second has been mainly cultivated in the mainstream Church. Even though
the term "Jesus' friend" is seldom applied to a woman — although the
middle ages and the nineteenth century were two periods which were
especially creative in their view of friendship: the friends of God and romantic friendship[3] — yet the fact itself has remained clear throughout the
centuries: Jesus was on terms of intimate friendship with women. The
two differing relationships put their stamp both on notions about women
and on the picture of Jesus himself.

Distortions

In the first centuries of the Church's life, both traditions were able to
go on existing side by side, unhindered and with equal validity. Mary
was one saint among others. But when, at the Council of Ephesus, the
Church decided in favor of Mary as *theotókos,* thereby picking up an
image of popular piety, it pressed all ideas about women into the same
mold. Consequently the friendship traditions were increasingly pushed
aside. Jesus' women friends found no entry into the creed. Mary Magdalene remained illegitimate. Like the "three Marys," the women lost
themselves in local cults; or they forfeited their biblical background and
fell into line among the growing army of martyrs and saints. But above
all we can see the original figures changing into the images required by
the anxieties and needs of a male society.

Mary Magdalene is the most fatal and typical example, and it is one
which has affected the Christian idea of women down to the present
day. Her story (Luke 8) was fused with the story of the woman "who
was a sinner" (Luke 7). Her flask of ointment also led her be identified with Mary of Bethany, who anointed Jesus (John 12). So in the
churches of the West, three independent women turned into a monster
and model of sin and grace. As Karl Künstel points out, this development
goes back to Augustine especially: "Because she (Mary Magdalene) had

once been bound by fetters of sensuality" and had been a consolation to him.[4]

The figure of Martha underwent a parallel development. According to the gospel of John, she is the person strong in faith (Bultmann). She prompted the raising of Lazarus and her confession of Christ must for some Christian communities have had a meaning like the confession of Peter. She was turned into the active but less valuable housewife. She was then even typified, with her sister Mary (Magdalene): Martha became the *vita activa*, Mary the *vita passiva;* Martha the Jewish Church, Mary the gentile Church; and so on. The figures of the women were robbed of their originality and distorted; and it was in this form that they put their impress on the history of art and culture. The Mary-Martha antithesis is "the undisputed possession of medieval spiritual writings."[5] We already find it in Origen, later in Augustine, Gregory the Great, Cassian, the monastic Fathers Norbert of Xanten and Bernard of Clairvaux, and elsewhere.

During the flowering of medieval theology the biblical women lost their original significance. They were touched up, distorted or typified. We can compare this with the way goddesses were partriarchalized: research into matriarchy today detects this process in the prolonged transition from matriarchy to patriarchy: female figures lost their original independence, one aspect was isolated, and they forfeited their universality.[6] Artemis ceases to be the triple pre-Olympian goddess and becomes the virgin; Aphrodite becomes a whore, and Hera Zeus's matronly housewife. In the same way the biblical women were also drawn into the age-old patriarchal pattern of male fantasies. Their real historical role in Jesus' history was smothered under the feminine stereotype into which they were forced. Even the mother of Jesus did not escape, although in her case other ways emerged of integrating undercurrents of popular piety.

Even when the Reformation turned back to the gospels, this brought no change. Luther did not follow the enlightened Faber Stapulensis, who again separated the three different people, Mary Magdalene, Mary of Bethany and the woman who was a sinner, pointing to the fatal error that had crept in. For Luther, Mary Magdalene remained the sinner; and in accordance with Calvin's notions of morality, the women who followed Jesus were "of ill repute." Martha was the person whose works were to be made "as nothing." The women were models for a new theology of justification. They were images of sin and grace; while their history, their relationship to Jesus, and their function at the resurrection remained undiscovered. The alteration in the Roman breviary of 1970 did at least put an official end to the fatal Magdalene tradition.[7]

Friendship

We are used to thinking and working in the concepts and ideas of the literature belonging to the mainstream churches; and we have also, without knowing it, internalized many patriarchal notions about women. As a result, the tradition of friendship, of a spontaneous, free human relationship, tied to no fixed conceptions about a particular order, has been suppressed, falsified and forgotten. But in spite of everything it runs like a scarlet thread through the whole of Christian history, the history of the sects, the history of new social and religious awakenings, the history of women. It became an infection whenever women broke out of the usual order of things, or had to break out of it, and where new social possibilities opened up for them.

The Magdalene Tradition

In the rest of the present essay I shall confine myself to the Magdalene tradition, although the unknown Martha sub-culture especially, in its different way, throws a classic light on the undersurface of history.[8]

In the early Christian congregations, where women held office in many places, Mary Magdalene was reverenced more than Mary, the mother of Jesus, as Jesus' intimate friend and the one he loved more than all the disciples. Unencumbered by betrayal like Peter, she represented an immediate relationship to Jesus and his message which was unequalled. She was the vehicle of revelation and could even (in the gospel of Philip) become Wisdom, "the woman who knows the universe."

We see the same thing in the Cathar movement in twelfth-century France: Mary Magdalene becomes the model of steadfastness, whereas Jesus' mother recedes noticeably into the background. As Gottfried Koch remarks, "The veneration of Mary has little to do with recognition of the woman's equal role in the Church."[9] In the women's movement which was part of the Cathar movement, Mary Magdalene as she is found in the New Testament came to life once more. In the medieval *Golden Legend* of Jacobus de Voragine, we are told that Jesus "enflamed her entirely with love of him," and that people were enchanted by "the sweetness of her discourse and the beauty of her countenance." In succeeding centuries this picture of Mary Magdalene lived on in art. She is the beautiful preacher who is to be seen on medieval pulpits; in a stained-glass window in Chalons-sur-Marne she even baptizes; and on an altar triptych in Lübeck she makes her brother Lazarus a bishop.[10] We know from isolated statements made by the Fathers that, in spite of all the patriarchal changes to which her image was subjected, she was still called "the apostle of apostles." But the breadth of this sub-culture only becomes clear when we look at the rich visual material which has not hitherto been taken seriously theologically.

Modern Traces of the Magdalene Tradition

The Reformers, and consequently the major Protestant churches, showed no interest in this tradition. The female models that accorded with their ideals were the matrons and mothers of the Bible, like Sarah and Rebecca. But the Magdalene tradition revived again in the Protestant movements of succeeding centuries. When women became more self-sufficient, Mary Magdalene became the model which an independent reading of the Bible made available to them; whereas it was only in isolated cases that increased reverence was paid to Mary, the mother of Jesus.

Katharina Zell, the wife of the Strassburg Reformer, spoke a public valediction over her husband on his death, excusing herself for this "scandal" on the grounds that she was acting like Mary Magdalene, though adding that "she had no thought of being an apostle" — a rider significant of her theological tradition.[11] But in the following century (1676) the Quaker Margaret Fell already based her claim that women had a right to speak in the Church on the forgotten figures, "the three Marys," Joanna and Mary Magdalene: They passed on the message, she said . . . how else should the disciples have known it since they were not there?[12] The black Methodist Jarena Lee deduced the right of women to preach from this central resurrection message of the Christian faith which was entrusted to a woman.[13]

In the changing churches and societies of the nineteenth century, the women who endured to the end with Jesus became paradigms for women's own social struggle. Taking the pattern of the women surrounding Mary Magdalene, women overcame their feminine role-fixation and discovered anew the first Christian charge given to the women: the task to witness to the resurrection and a changed world. In all social revolutions women found an identification here and preserved this special tradition.

But even the male theologians of the Protestant churches supported the change in the role of women which was beginning to make itself felt in the free churches. The Quaker John Rogers, for example, called Mary Magdalene "the first preacher of the resurrection." As a defense against Catholic Mariology and in support of a new Protestant typology, George Fox even altered the symbolic pattern which had been generally accepted ever since Irenaeus, changing the Eve-Mary typology to an Eve-Magdalene one: "So when Christ was risen, the woman that was first in the transgression, the woman went first to declare the Resurrection out of death, out of the grave."[14] Luther had already placed Mary Magdalene above the mother of Jesus as the prototype of greater sin and hence of greater grace. But now attempts were made to get away fundamentally from the concept of Mother Church and its images.

The Topical Force of the Magdalene Figure

Yet the apostle Mary Magdalene played no official part in the ordination debate carried on in major Protestant churches in the twentieth century. Only outsiders like Elisabeth Malo have drawn on her.[15] In the 1975 Vatican declaration her role was again played down: the women were merely supposed to prepare the apostles to become the official witnesses of the resurrection. Up to now the friendship tradition has had no theological legitimation.

Catholic women theologians have meanwhile recognized that the mother tradition is unduly one-dimensional. Elisabeth Gössmann sees that it was Mary Magdalene's task "to witness to the faith in Christ which transforms time." For Elisabeth Schüssler Fiorenza, her significance is that she helps women to find "the meaning of their discipleship and the whole discipleship of the church."[16] Rosemary Ruether, finally, believes that the symbol of Mother Mary has overshadowed the friend and disciple who was the first to accept the faith in the resurrection on which the Church rests.[17]

Apart from the claim it makes to the apostolate of women, the friendship tradition has theological and ethical claims too. It broke with — and will always break with — the idea of Jesus as an aloof master. Instead it stresses the mutuality and partnership of God and man. We find this in the gnostic fantasies about a marriage between Mary Magdalene and Jesus, and in the "groupie" idea of the rock opera *Jesus Christ Superstar;* and it is repeated in Heinrich Böll's demand that the Church acquire Mary Magdalene's tenderness. Today these are desires of vital importance, which can no longer be satisfied by the domesticated sexuality of the mother cult of a Church which has been afraid of sexuality for almost 2,000 years. Friendship as Hegel understood it, friendship as "the concrete concept of freedom,"[18] embodies the hope for new human relationships of the kind we find illustrated in the forgotten New Testament tradition about Jesus' friendship with women, and its subsequent suppressed sub-culture.

Friendship was the constitutive mark of the eschatological community of the disciples. As the imminent expectation of the eschatological End-time retreated, archaic myths of origin were taken up. This was the source of the Church's Mariology. Early on, Mary, the ancient Mother Earth, met religious needs — later the needs of the Church — today the needs of depth psychology. But she cannot provide what continually breaks through in the person of Mary Magdalene, in the New Testament and in traditions of protest: that the promise of life was given to a woman friend of Jesus, and that this divine friendship is the model for faith and for a messianic community of women and men.

Translated by Margaret Kohl

NOTES

1. Elisabeth Schüssler Fiorenza, *The Twelve: Women Priests,* New York, 1977, p. 119.

2. See here and for the following *Maria im Neuen Testament: Eine ökumenische Untersuchung,* Stuttgart, 1981.

3. E.g., Jacobus de Voragine, "...he took her to be his special friend," *Die legenda aurea,* Heidelberg, 1979, p. 472; Meister Eckehart, "...the dear Martha and with her all God's friends...," *Deutsche Predigten und Traktate,* Munich, 1977, p. 285.

4. Karl Künstel, *Ikonografie der christlichen Kunst,* Freiburg, 1926, p. 427; Hans Hansel, *Die Maria-Magdalena-Legende,* Bottrop, 1937.

5. Matthias Bernards, *Speculum virginum,* Cologne, 1955, pp. 194f.

6. Heide Göttner-Abendroth, *Die Göttin und ihr Heros,* Munich, 1980, p. 32.

7. Elisabeth Moltmann, *The Women around Jesus,* Eng. trans., London, 1982.

8. Ibid.

9. Gottfried Koch, *Frauenfrage und Ketzertum im Mittelalter,* Berlin, 1962, p. 100.

10. E. and J. Moltmann, *Humanity in God,* New York, 1983.

11. *Religion and Sexism,* ed. Rosemary Radford Ruether, San Francisco, 1981, p. 214.

12. Joyce L. Irwin, *Womanhood in Radical Protestantism 1525–1675,* New York, 1979, pp. 179ff.

13. *Women and Religion in America,* ed. Rosemary Radford Ruether, San Francisco, 1981, p. 214.

14. *Early Quaker Writings 1650–1700,* ed. H. Barbour, Grand Rapids, 1973, p. 505.

15. *Frau und Religion: Gotteserfahrungen im Patriarchat,* ed. Elisabeth Moltmann, Frankfurt, 1983, pp. 87ff.

16. Elisabeth Schüssler, *Der vergessene Partner,* Düsseldorf, 1964, pp. 126f.

17. Rosemary Radford Ruether, *Mary: The Feminine Face of the Church,* London, 1979, pp. 73–74.

18. Jürgen Moltmann, *The Church in the Power of the Spirit,* London, 1977, pp. 115f.

31

Transforming Moral Theology

MARY HUNT

Nowhere is the invisibility and exclusion of women in the doing of theology and the articulation of meaning and value more apparent than in
the field of moral theology or ethics. Here the patriarchal nature of the
Christian tradition makes the clearest and most decisive difference in
people's daily lives. Moral theology as presently conceived seems, para-
doxically, immoral. It lacks the minimum criterion for adequacy, namely,
a careful consideration of human experience in the light of traditional
teachings, cultural contexts and deeply held convictions of the Christian
faith: love, justice, equality and mutuality. The fact that it systematically
excludes half of the very people whose lives it pretends to reflect, and the
extent to which it often pronounces and rarely listens render its claims
to morality tenuous at best.

A radical revision of the discipline cannot be accomplished in a
short article. But I hope to point the way toward a more adequate and
meaningful method for theo-ethical reflection. I will do so not by filling
women's experience into the cracks of patriarchal ethical theory, nor by
insisting that what has been traditionally taken as "the good" ought to be
left aside simply because its roots are suspect. Rather, I will explore the
pressing need I see for a new method which involves foundational and
not cosmetic changes.

This shift in ethical method is from an essentially static moral vision
carved out of pre-conceived categories to a dynamic methodology which
takes *experience*, especially of the most deeply affected persons, *as central*. It embraces experience *on its own terms*, assumes that the myth
of objectivity has been disproved, and moves on. This feminist liberation approach has its starting point in the struggles of people who find
themselves constrained by oppressive systems and who opt for liberation. Women have been subject to the constraints of patriarchy. Thus our
life experience is a natural starting point for such reflection, as are the

life experiences of many other oppressed groups. As we become moral agents the discipline has to change.[1]

Several salient features of contemporary moral theology illuminate the impoverishment of the discipline. They form the backdrop for my ethical presuppositions. First, most ethical work still takes maleness as normative. It reads female experience in that light, and considers what is human that which is commensurate with what is male. While this was challenged twenty-five years ago by Valerie Saving Goldstein, it remains a general assumption in the literature.[2] Contemporary studies and statements, including for example those by U.S. Catholic bishops on nuclear weapons and the economy, belie a certain generic "human" long after feminist writers have made vigorous cases for the now obvious, simply that women and men have different life experiences in patriarchy. Small sections on women's lives are no substitute for a thorough-going feminist liberation approach. My presupposition is that women's experiences of oppression affect our way of being in the world so deeply that ethical questions must be asked by and of us on our own terms in order to draw any, however tentative, conclusions. This is equally the case for women of color and white women, for old as well as young women, i.e., the particularity of each must be respected.

Second, the prevailing patriarchal moral theology not only passes over women's unique experience, but also serves to negate it. Misogyny is well documented in the works on domestic violence, rape and incest which in many instances reflect women as victims if not also as seductresses wishing to be violated. More subtle but equally devastating dynamics of oppressions are found in the literature on so-called artificial birth control, abortion and voluntary sterilization, all prohibited by the Roman Catholic Church. What becomes clear is that women's silenced voices in the formulation of such policies correlate directly with the anti-female character of the field of ethics. My second presupposition therefore, is that women must be a part of any group's agenda setting and question asking in order to guarantee that women's experience will be reflected in the outcome.

A third aspect of patriarchal moral theology is that it tends to result in male control. Since women's experiences are passed over, and since the fundamental posture is anti-woman, the result tends to be male control over women's bodies, hearts and spirits. This is apparent in the seemingly extreme cases of clitoridectomy and infibulation, but it is equally the case in all instances where women's experiences are not deemed suitable input for moral theology.[3] Rather, women are only the recipients of the *magisterium's* dubious wisdom, our experiences not sought in the formulation of policy. Recent Vatican clarification on abortion, made in retaliation for the *New York Times* advertisement on pluralism and diversity among committed Catholics in the United States (7 October 1984) made this clear. The dispute emerges not so much over abortion as over control or power. Nowhere in the Vatican response are any fundamental moral issues addressed with any need for dialogue acknowledged.

The focus is always on the re-exertion of the *magisterium's* authority to pronounce once and for all. My presupposition is that empowerment, and not control, is the hallmark of any feminist liberation ethic. Empowerment of women and men, not control of women by men, will be possible only when women's voices are heard in ethical debates. Women may well articulate a different vision, but cannot have our moral agency denied in the effort to exert it.

These presuppositions hint at a two-part problem on which I base my critique of and hope to overhaul the ethical methods used currently. First, the scope of the problems in moral theology about which women are considered to have any input, however limited, is usually confined to the so-called women's issues of sexuality and reproduction. Here women's voices are not heard on our own terms. If they were, I suspect that we would say that sexuality is a natural part of relationships of mutuality; we would probably affirm that reproductive responsibility must be seen in a socio-economic and political context of women's needs to ground decisions in our consciences formed in communities of accountability. This claim, that those who are the most involved must be heard on their own terms, is the challenge of feminist liberation ethics.

Second, my proposal for another look at the discipline rests on the fact that the ethical problems which women do address are far broader than the specifically sexual ones. These include the economic structures, wars and weaponry, health care and other concerns which feminists have recognized as the interstructured web of oppression rooted in a hierarchal/dualistic manner of thinking. But the fact that even white, middle class, educated women have no access to moral/ethical systems makes it clear that the poor, women of color, third world people, etc., have no fair share in the issues which have an impact on their lives. This impact is usually greater on them than on those who pretend to speak for them. It causes economic, psychological and spiritual harm that casts serious doubt on the integrity of ethics as a field of truth-seeking. If we are to live in anything like "right relation," then some transformation is in order.[4]

As a first step I suggest that we look at some of the sexuality issues and see how women's moral agency will make a difference. This is not to presume that solving difficult matters of sexuality will free the discipline from its limits. And I am hesitant to begin my reformulation with sexual ethics for fear of misleading the reader by reinforcing the notion that women's moral realm begins and ends in sexuality. For most women sexuality is not a problem on its own terms. It is made into one by those who deny women's moral agency thus preventing us from exercising our responsibility. But if we begin to transform the discipline in one area, recognizing that all of the ethical questions are connected, we can hope for a spill over effect in other areas as well. If women's experiences challenge ethical decision making such that many new voices have to be listened to, perhaps we will see progress for other marginalized groups as well.

This is not an effort to turn the tables and to make women's voices predominant to the exclusion of men's. It is not an attempt to replace men with women in a hierarchical/dualistic decision making structure. Such would be antithetical to the transformation I intend, one which takes the ethical process as a shared responsibility in a community of faith.

Actually, I consider the moral realm to have relatively little to do with sexuality. It has to do with the economic, political and social structures in which all sexuality is set. These structures can be changed to enhance human life especially for the most marginalized. Yet my focus on sexuality is rooted in a commitment that the *personal is political* and that a healthy integrated view of person must replace contemporary anthropology. Until we begin with that starting point I question whether work done on any ethical issue can really reflect values of mutuality and accountability which are the goal of a liberation ethic.

The paucity of feminist liberation ethical thinking makes me agree with Beverly Harrison when she wrote that "One need not be sophisticated in moral theory to make conscientious life choices, but moral theory can provide a check on our ethical reasoning."[5] Such moral theory can be poisonous. Rather, I would claim with her that much of what has passed as moral theory has been the very stuff of the oppression of women and other marginalized persons. Thus the imperative to transform the discipline in which our oppression is sanctioned is part of a feminist liberation agenda.

I propose that we probe the most invisible of women's experiences, namely, *lesbianism or same sex love as a way to begin to transform the discipline.* Little has been said of it in the ethical literature which really reflects it on its own terms and not as a hybrid of male experience. Its uniqueness lies both in its hidden potential to shed light on another aspect of human experience, and in its uniquely female character. Why not explore birth control or abortion instead, some may wonder, since those too seem like uniquely female issues. But both have been probed deeply with "valiant" efforts to define them outside of women's control whether through resorting to the intricacies of technology or to the censure of excommunication. But lesbianism has had no such history, its taboo nature so strong, perhaps, that not even the boldest of men have tried to circumscribe it or claim it for their own.

It can only be understood through women's experience. In short, like it or not on this one we have to hear women on our own terms. Lesbianism has its analogue in male homosexuality, but it is a thoroughly female phenomenon. To understand it is to understand women on our terms, a rare instance in patriarchy, perhaps part of patriarchy's transformation in ways deeper than most imagine. Efforts to collapse it into a generic "homosexual" simply will not work. The cultural, economic and sociopolitical factors of patriarchy make female homosexuality qualitatively different. Women begin with the oppression as women which is common in patriarchy, and then have the experience of lesbian women as yet another layer, not different in kind but in degree from the oppression of all women.

Patriarchy spawns heterosexism, the normative claim of heterosexuality to the exclusion of the moral possibility of healthy same-sex (especially among women) relationships. My effort to reflect on lesbian experience is meant to give it visibility on its own terms. By so doing I try to make a dent in the ethical tradition which seeks to silence so many others on their own terms, thus to *maintain control instead of encouraging empowerment.*

My definition of lesbian reveals how I approach the task of ethical reformulation. I begin in real experience, not in pre-determined, male centered definitions. For many women the experience of what I call lesbianism or the lesbian insight on our terms emerges from a pro-woman stance in a patriarchal, heterosexist culture. This means taking women radically seriously in a world which would have us do otherwise. It means being able to value, love and empower women without sanction and with celebration. This includes, but in no way demands nor is circumscribed by, the possibility of sexual expression with women. Its emphasis lies on the fundamental self-definition of all women in a feminist liberation context, a definition which is of a *Self-identified woman understood relationally in community.* I am indebted to Elisabeth Schüssler Fiorenza for her clarification of the Self-identified woman, and to Carter Heyward for her insights on relationality.[6]

My stress in this definition lies on the community dimension. It is an effort to reflect faithfully on what for many women is an essential part of a lesbian self-understanding, namely, rootedness in a community of women in which we can be fully ourselves, working, playing, worshiping, and relaxing. The stress on community is purposeful since it serves as a deliberate corrective against those tendencies of patriarchy to define lesbianism as genital activity between women. As such it rejects the male image of lesbians on the one hand, and on the other reinforces the fact that where genital activity is appropriate in committed, responsible relationships between women, even sexual expression is rooted in and accountable to a larger community.

Women who find our emotional, political and spiritual longings fulfilled in a patriarchal, heterosexist context among women in communities of accountability of all sorts (not to be confused with religious
communities, most of which had their origins in patriarchy) do not make
distinctions between/among us on the basis of sexual preference. Rather
we aspire for this self and other to a sense of community for all women in
a cultural context in which we can empower one another and our menfolk as whole human persons. We are creating such safe spaces, where
we can look anew at what we call lesbian experience and see it on its
own terms.

A new look at lesbian experience will be useful for understanding what
it may have been over the years. Women are persecuted by their families
and churches, purged from their religious communities, and alienated
ever so deeply from themselves as lesbians in a world which rejected
their choices. Perhaps there was no conscious identity with what I am
calling lesbian insight. But by the very revisioning of the word lesbian,
and by rethinking the experience in our day I hope to shed light on our
foresisters as well as on ourselves. Thus through this generation there
might be a new understanding, respect and acceptance of all women on
the terms that we choose for ourselves.

This begins to approach what women really want. It is not power over
others, but the opportunity to see and evaluate ourselves in terms that
are faithful to our experiences, and of course the chance to empower
others to do the same. Then we can engage in the weighing and balancing
of ethical discourse, emerging afresh from the best of the human spirit
set free. Then we can know something about the fierce tenderness of loving whom we will and not whom we must if we wish to love at all. We
can know something about the passion of women (and men, as I think
there is much here which opens up the nature of male experience as
well) for life and creativity, not simply for motherhood. We can appreciate something new about brokenness, emptiness and even sin which is
revealed when separation, death or mistreatment end relationships. This
is perhaps more painful than what heterosexist patriarchy has ever seen
because in a feminist liberation context it happens in relationships of
freer choice. This is to expose a depth of pain and suffering which is devastating yet part of our ongoing understanding of the human condition.
This is the ethical heart of the matter, what deserves attention.

The price of the invisibility of lesbian experience in moral theology has
been clear. No male-defined logic nor pretension to understand lesbian
women as other will suffice. What has been lost has been immeasur-
able. Even having a new understanding for our generation is not enough.
Simply to add lesbian experience to a list and use categories of ethical
analysis laid out without taking its uniqueness into consideration is in-

sufficient. Rather, we need the necessary luxury of truth-telling to have the data on which to reflect. We need to hear all women's life experiences without sanction.

The challenge of feminist liberation ethics begins in this work. It is critiqued by the competing claims of the main marginalized groups whose experiences have also been left aside, lest it become a new form of oppression. One by one they need to be heard on their own terms — people of color, the poor, persons from third world countries, etc. Only then can the circles of ethical reflection be expanded to include such persons in the formulation of ethical questions, not simply in being footnotes in the answers.

The result will be the empowerment of many people who have hitherto been controlled. Resistance to such a challenge is all too predictable. Hence I will pass over any, however judicious, suggestion that a moratorium be placed on ethical work until this critical phase is completed. I will not urge "creative listening" on the part of the ethical establishment for fear of being labelled a reverse oppressor when no analysis of power accompanies such liberal statements. Instead, let the record show that it is from a feminist liberation perspective that the challenge has been sounded to transform the discipline. Then we can all strive for a participatory ethical method which helps us to listen to people on their own terms, encourage them to ask their own questions, and thus empower them. This will give new meaning and content to the moral life well lived.

NOTES

1. Beverly Harrison, in *Our Right to Choose: Toward a New Ethic of Abortion,* Boston, 1983, makes a strong case for women's moral agency.

2. Valerie Saving Goldstein wrote "Human Experience: A Feminine Viewpoint" in the early 1960s. See the reprint in *Womanspirit Rising,* ed. Carol P. Christ and Judith Plaskow, San Francisco, 1979.

3. See Mary Daly, *Gyn/Ecology,* Boston, 1978, for information on atrocities against women.

4. Carter Heyward, *The Redemption of God: A Theology of Mutual Relation,* Washington, 1982.

5. Beverly Harrison, in the reference cited in note 1, p. 12.

6. See Elisabeth Schüssler Fiorenza, *In Memory of Her: A Feminist Theological Reconstruction of Christian Origins,* New York, 1983. See Carter Heyward, the work cited in note 4.

32

The Maleness of Christ

ELIZABETH A. JOHNSON

The story of Jesus of Nazareth, crucified and risen, confessed as the Christ, is at the center of Christian faith in God. In the gracious power of Sophia-Spirit unleashed through his history and destiny, the community of disciples continuously retells and enacts that story as the story of God with us to heal, redeem and liberate all people and the cosmos itself. Good news indeed. But that good news is stifled when Jesus' maleness, which belongs to his historical identity, is interpreted as being essential to his redeeming christic function and identity. Then the Christ functions as a religious tool for marginalizing and excluding women. Let us be very clear: the fact that Jesus of Nazareth was a male human being is not in question. His sex was a constitutive element of his historical person along with other particularities such as his Jewish racial identity, his location in the world of first-century Galilee, and so on, and as such is to be respected. The difficulty arises, rather, from the way Jesus' maleness is construed in official androcentric theology and ecclesial praxis.

The Effective History of Jesus' Maleness

Feminist theological analysis lays bare at least three ways in which such distorted interpretation occurs.

1. Since the man Jesus is confessed to be the revelation of God, the Christ symbol points to maleness as an essential characteristic of divine being itself. This is exacerbated by exclusive use of father and son metaphors to interpret Jesus' relationship to God, and by use of the *logos*, connected in Greek philosophy with the male principle, to articulate his personal reality as God with us. "Who has seen me has seen the Father" (John 14:9). This is taken literally to mean that the man Jesus is the incarnation of the male Logos and revealer of a male Father-God,

despite the evidence in scripture and tradition that the mystery of God transcends all naming and creates female reality in the divine image and likeness.

2. The belief that the Word became flesh and dwelt among us as a male indicates that thanks to their natural bodily resemblance, men enjoy a closer identification with Christ than do women. Men are not only theomorphic but, by virtue of their sex, also christomorphic in a way that goes beyond what is possible for women. Thus men alone among human beings are able to represent Christ fully. While women may be recipients of divine grace, they are unsuited to carry out christic actions publicly because of their sexual difference from his maleness. For this mentality, the idea that the Word might have become female flesh is not even seriously imaginable, so incapable of christic identity are women thought to be; and this, despite the doctrine of creation and the church's praxis and theology of baptism.

3. Given the dualism which essentially divorces male from female humanity, the maleness of Christ puts the salvation of women in jeopardy. The Christian story of salvation involves not only God's compassionate will to save but also the method by which that will is effective, namely, by plunging into sinful human history and transforming it from within. The early Christian aphorism, "What is not assumed is not healed," sums up the insight that God's saving solidarity with humanity is what is crucial for the birth of the new creation. As the Nicene Creed confesses, *"et homo factus est"* ("and was made man"). But if in fact what is meant is *et vir factus est,* if maleness is essential for the christic role, then women are cut out of the loop of salvation, for female sexuality was not assumed by the Word made flesh. Thus, to Rosemary Radford Ruether's searching question, "Can a male saviour save women?" interpretation of the maleness of Christ as essential can only answer "No," despite Christian belief in the universality of God's saving intent.[1]

The effective history of the Christ symbol presents striking evidence of how an unbalanced focus on maleness distorts theology of God, Christian anthropology and the good news of salvation. To reconstruct christology it is imperative to rethink both the foundational anthropology which has led to such a fixation on maleness, and the theological meaning of the Christ symbol.

Anthropology: From a Dominance of Maleness to a Celebration of Difference

The social location of this problematic usage is an ecclesial community where official voice, vote and visibility belong by law only to men.

Rising into intellectual expressions which of necessity support the *status quo*, this patriarchy is the bedrock for the androcentric construction of gender differences shaping the misuse of the maleness of Christ. Envisioning a different kind of community laced by relationships of mutuality and reciprocity allows feminist thought to design anthropology in an egalitarian gestalt, to practical and critical effect. Then the maleness of Christ is open to interpretation at once less important and more liberating.

In the beginning of this effort it was clear what model of anthropology feminist thought did not want, namely, the prevailing dualistic model which casts women and men as polar opposites, each bearing unique characteristics from which the other sex is excluded. Here male and female are related by the notion of complementarity, which rigidly predetermines the qualities each should cultivate and the roles each can play. Apart from naiveté about its own social conditioning, its reliance on stereotypes, and the denial of the wholeness of human experience which it mandates, this position functions as a smokescreen for the subordination of women since by its definition women are always relegated to the private, passive realm.[2]

In contrast to this dual anthropology, feminist thinkers at first developed a single-nature anthropology, which views sexual difference as biologically important for reproduction but not determinative of persons as such. Since the meaning of male and female is still historically emerging, each is free to develop the best of masculine or feminine characteristics in the search for wholeness, and may assume public and private roles according to their giftedness. Here the stress is on basic similarity rather than difference, to the point where differences become relatively inconsequential. Apart from its neglect of the importance of sexual embodiment, which affects far more than reproduction in the life of every person, this view also comes under criticism for tending to hold out a single human ideal, possibly androgynous, which can be destructive of genuine human variety.

On the one hand, feminist thought resists an unrelieved binary way of thinking, a sexual polarity view of human nature which inevitably leads to a dominant/subordinate pattern. On the other hand, reduction to an equality of sameness by ignoring sexual difference is also unacceptable. Two separate types of human nature, or unisex?

A way beyond the impasse is emerging beyond those options: one human nature celebrated in an interdependence of multiple differences.[3] Not a binary view of two male and female natures, predetermined forever, nor abbreviation to a single ideal, but a diversity of ways of being human: a multi-polar set of combinations of essential human elements, of which sexuality is but one. Human existence has a multi-dimensional character. If maleness and femaleness can be envisioned in a more holistic context, their relationship to each other can be more rightly conceived.

All persons are constituted by a number of anthropological constants, essential elements which are intrinsic to their identity. These include relation to one's body, and hence one's sexuality, as the medium of human consciousness; relation through the body to the whole ecological network of the earth; relation to significant other persons as the matrix in which individuality arises; relation to social, political and economic structures; conditioning by historical time and place; the play of theory in the praxis of one's culture as opposed to instinct alone; and orientation to hope and the pull of the future.[4] These constants mutually condition one another, and in their endless combinations are constitutive of the humanity of every person. Significantly change any one of them, and a different person results.

It is short-sighted to single out sexuality as always and everywhere more fundamental to concrete historical existence than any of the other constants. Take, for example, documented cases of cruelty to black slave women in the ante-bellum American south. On what basis would one tell such an abused woman that sex is more fundamental than race and the economic system of slavery in the design of her identity? Present-day African American womanist thinkers are highly critical of white feminism for overemphasizing sex discrimination to the exclusion of racial and class prejudice, from which black women also suffer. These biases are so intrinsically tied together in their experience that women of color cannot distinguish the suffering that comes from one rather than another.[5] Another example: in older years, when sexual attraction diminishes, the biological differences between women and men recede in importance compared to the question of the resources available for living out life's last years in dignity or destitution.

Focusing on sexuality to the exclusion of other equally constitutive elements is the equivalent of using a microscope on this one key factor of human life when what is needed is a telescope to take in the galaxies of rich human difference. Sexuality must be integrated into a holistic vision of human persons instead of being made the touchstone of personal identity and thus distorted. The anthropological model of one human nature instantiated in a multiplicity of differences moves beyond the contrasting models of either sex dualism or the sameness of abstract individuals towards the celebration of diversity as entirely normal. The goal is to reorder the two-term and one-term systems into a multiple-term schema, one which allows connection in difference rather than constantly guaranteeing identity through opposition or uniformity. Respect can thus be extended to all persons in their endless combinations of anthropological constants, boundlessly concrete. And difference itself, rather than being a regrettable obstacle to community, can function as a creative community-shaping force. As the poet Audre Lorde appreciates, "Difference is raw and powerful connection. . . . "[6]

A multi-polar anthropology allows christology to integrate the maleness of Christ using interdependence of difference as a primary category, rather than emphasizing sexuality in an ideological, distorted way.

Christ: From the Static Image of the Perfect Man to the Eschatological, Living Community

Feminist hermeneutics has blazed a trail showing how the gospel story of Jesus resists being used to justify patriarchal dominance in any form.[7] His preaching and life-style lived and breathed the opposite, creating a challenge which brought down on his head the wrath of religious and civil authority. They crucified him. In the light of this history Jesus' maleness can be seen to have a definite social significance. If a woman had preached compassionate love and enacted a style of authority that serves, she would have been greeted with a colossal shrug. Is this not what women are supposed to do by nature? But from a social position of male privilege Jesus preached and acted this way, and herein lies the summons. The cross, too, is a sturdy symbol of the "kenosis of patriarchy," the self-emptying of male dominating power in favor of the new humanity of compassionate service and mutual empowerment.[8] The Gospel story of Jesus makes it clear that the heart of the problem is not that Jesus was male, but that more males have not been like Jesus.

What then of Christ? Clues for feminist interpretation can be found in the resurrection, wisdom christology, and the biblical symbol of the body of Christ.

The resurrection is a mystery of faith enveloped in the mystery of God. It negates a simple literalism that imagines Jesus still existing as in the days of his earthly life, only now invisible. Jesus has truly died, with all that this implies of change: he is gone from the midst of history according to the flesh. Faith in the resurrection affirms that God has the last word for this executed victim of state injustice and that word, blessedly, is life. Jesus with all his historicity is raised into glory by the power of the Spirit. What this ringing affirmation precisely means is inconceivable. His life is now hidden in the holy mystery of God, while his presence is known only through the Spirit wherever two or three gather, bread is broken, the hungry fed. But this indicates a transformation of his humanity so profound that it escapes our imagination. The humility of the apophatic approach acknowledges that language about the maleness of Christ at this point proceeds under the negating sign of analogy, more dissimilar than similar to any maleness known in history.

New Testament wisdom christology construes Christ Jesus in terms of the powerful female figure of Sophia who is creator, redeemer and divine renewer of the people of Israel, and indeed of the whole earth (Wisdom 7:10). Speaking her words, doing her deeds, and encountering her rejection, Jesus is depicted as the child of Sophia, her prophet, and ultimately even her incarnation (Luke 11:49 and Matt. 23:34; John 1). It is this identification which links the crucified prophet to the very creation of the world, and sets the church's feet on the road to Nicaea. The christology of Jesus Sophia shatters the male dominance carried in exclusive language about Jesus as the eternal male Logos or Son of the Father, enabling articulation of even a high incarnational christology in strong and gracious female metaphors.[9]

From the beginning, Christians are marked by the confession that Jesus Sophia is the Christ, the anointed, the blessed one. But this confession also witnesses to the truth that the beloved community shares in this christhood, participates in the living and dying and rising of Christ to such an extent that it too has a christomorphic character. Challenging a naive physicalism which collapses the totality of the Christ into the human man Jesus, metaphors such as the Body of Christ (1 Cor. 12:12–27) and the branches abiding in the vine (John 15:1–11) expand the reality of Christ to include all of redeemed humanity, sisters and brothers, still on the way. Amid the suffering and conflicts of history, members of the community of disciples are *en christo* and their own lives assume a christic pattern. Biblical cosmic christology expands the notion of Christ still further (Col. 1:15–20), seeing that the universe itself is destined to be christomorphic in a reconciled new heaven and new earth.[10]

Women as "Imago Christi"

The fundamental egalitarianism of the baptism and martyrdom traditions bears out women's character as *imago Christi* in ways that are newly appreciated. One in Christ Jesus, baptized women precisely in their female bodily existence and not apart from it are clothed with Christ (Gal. 3:27–28). Paul makes the meaning of this identification highly precise, using the evocative idea of image/icon. Hope makes us act with great boldness, he writes, for we unveil our faces to gaze right at Christ. Then through the power of the Spirit "all of us are being transformed into that same image from one degree of glory to another" (2 Cor. 3:18). The inclusive "all of us" makes clear that the whole community, women as well as men, are gifted with the transformation "into the same image," in Greek the same *eikon*, that is, the image/icon of Christ. Another example: in God's design the community is called "to be conformed to the image" of Christ (Rom. 8:29). The Greek is instructive, for the members of the community are identified as *sym-morphos* to the *eikon*, that is, sharing the form of the likeness, or formed according to the image of Christ. No distinction on the basis of sex is made, or needed. Being christomorphic is not a sex-distinctive gift. The image of Christ does not lie in sexual similarity to the human man Jesus, but in coherence with the narrative shape of his compassionate, liberating life in the world, through the power of the Spirit. Theologically, the capacity of women and men to be *sym-morphos* to the *eikon* of Christ is identical.

A similar assessment of women in the image of Christ runs through discourse about those who suffer for the faith. In one stunning narrative Luke makes this christomorphism explicit:

> But Saul, still breathing threats and murder against the disciples of the Lord, went to the high priest and asked him for letters to the synagogues at Damascus, so that if he found any belonging to the Way, men or women, he might bring them bound to Jerusalem.

When the light from heaven flashes, when the voice asks "Why do you persecute *me?*" when Saul wonders "Who are you, Lord?" the momentous answer comes: "I am Jesus, whom you are persecuting" (Acts 9:1–5). Persecuted women are here explicitly identified with Jesus as are men, without distinction. Saul's murderous intent and tormenting actions against women disciples are actions against Christ, without qualification.

Writing on the martyrs centuries later, Vatican II continues this long-standing tradition of interpretation. Martyrdom transforms a disciple into an intense image of Christ, *imago Christi*, for the martyr "perfects that image even to the shedding of blood."[11] In this conciliar text no distinctions are made on the basis of the martyrs' sex, nor should there be. The four North American church women murdered in El Salvador in 1980 and the six university Jesuits with their housekeeper and her daughter killed a decade later all give a witness in the uniqueness of their own persons and circumstances that is theologically identical.

The baptismal liturgy to this very day enacts the reality that the fundamental capacity to be icons of Christ is a gift not restricted by sex; women are the Body of Christ. The martyrdom tradition recognizes that in the giving of their lives women are christomorphic in a most profound and graphic way. The practical and critical effect of this gospel truth breaks any intrinsic connection between maleness and Christ, and arrives as a challenge to patriarchal rule.

The Maleness of Jesus in the Whole Christ

Key elements of a feminist christology have been assembled, although not yet synthesized. In that synthesis the symbol of Christ the redeemer will take its place, but its symbolic nexus will change, expanding to include symbols drawn from female experience.[12] Without the blinders of dualistic anthropology, the Christ symbol itself will be interpreted inclusively and eschatologically. In the power of the Spirit the story of Jesus lets loose a history of discipleship equally among women and men, which goes forward in anticipatory fragments of healing and liberation. Amid a multiplicity of differences Jesus' maleness is appreciated as intrinsically important for his own personal historical identity and the historical challenge of his ministry, but not theologically determinative of his identity as the Christ nor normative for the identity of the Christian community. In the power of Sophia-Spirit women and men are christomorphic, as are black and white, old and young, Jew and Greek, and the cosmos itself, all on the way to the new heaven and the new earth. Ideally, if the equal human dignity of women is ever recognized in ecclesial theory and praxis, this discussion about the maleness of Christ will fade away. In a more just church it would never have become such an issue.

NOTES

1. R. Ruether, *Sexism and God-Talk: Toward a Feminist Theology*, Boston and London, 1983, pp. 116–38.

2. For this and the following model see A. Carr, *Transforming Grace: Women's Experience and Christian Tradition*, San Francisco, 1988, pp. 117–33; and M. A. O'Neill, "Toward a Renewed Anthropology," *Theological Studies* 36, 1975, pp. 725–36.

3. See M. Marx Ferree and B. Hess, eds., *Analyzing Gender: Perspectives from the Social Sciences*, Beverly Hills, Calif., 1987; J. Scott, "Deconstructing Equality-Versus-Difference," *Feminist Studies* 14, Spring 1988, pp. 33–50. Theological use of this model is clear in R. Chopp, *The Power to Speak: Feminism, Language, God*, New York, 1989.

4. E. Schillebeeckx, *Christ*, New York and London, 1980, pp. 731–43.

5. b. hooks, *Ain't I A Woman? Black Women and Feminism*, Boston 1981; and a response by S. Thistlethwaite, *Sex, Race and God: Christian Feminism in Black and White*, New York, 1989.

6. A. Lorde, *Sister Outsider*, Freedom, Calif., 1984, p. 112.

7. See E. Schüssler Fiorenza, *In Memory of Her: A Feminist Theological Reconstruction of Christian Origins*, New York and London, 1983; R. Nakashima Brock, *Journeys by Heart: A Christology of Erotic Power*, New York, 1988.

8. R. Ruether, *Sexism and God-Talk* (n. 1), p. 137.

9. E. Johnson, "Jesus, the Wisdom of God: A Biblical Basis for a Non-Androcentric Christology," *Ephemerides Theologicae Lovaniensis* 61, 1985, pp. 261–94.

10. Elisabeth Schüssler Fiorenza, "Wisdom Mythology and the Christological Hymns of the New Testament," in Robert Wilken, ed., *Aspects of Wisdom in Judaism and Early Christianity*, Notre Dame, Ind., 1975, pp. 17–41.

11. *Lumen Gentium* 42.

12. See retrieval by M. Grey, *Feminism, Redemption and the Christian Tradition*, Mystic, Conn., 1990.

33

Jewish Feminist Theological Discourses

ADELE REINHARTZ

Jewish feminist discourses range over many issues, some of which are common to the Jewish community as a whole, and others of which are specific to particular geographical, political and social contexts. This survey will focus on Jewish feminist attempts to "image" divinity. Two principal questions will be addressed. What are appropriate liturgical expressions for feminist God-images? What are the implications of these expressions for Jewish feminist theology and community? Although these questions are broadly relevant, the survey will center on the work of Jewish feminists who share certain cultural similarities (North American, white, Ashkenazi [of Eastern European origin], Jewish educated, middle-class), though not sexual orientation or denominational affiliation.

The starting point for Jewish feminist God-imaging is the recognition of the profound patriarchy of traditional Jewish God-language. Classical Jewish theology recognizes that God-language is metaphorical; God is neither male nor female. Nevertheless, masculine God-language is deeply and firmly embedded in traditional liturgy and theology; the occasional use of female imagery does not detract from this in any significant way. Inherent in this male imagery are the concepts of domination and hierarchy which mirror male social roles. These images function as "models of and models for," claiming to describe the divine nature, while in fact legitimating a human community that reserves power and authority for men.[1]

The task of Jewish feminist theology is therefore to transform the metaphors for God that have informed the Jewish imagination and shaped Jewish self-understanding and behavior.[2] Approaches to this task fall into two categories: reinterpretation of traditional imagery, and revisioning of God-language.

Feminist Reinterpretation

Though Jewish feminists dissent from the patriarchal emphasis of the traditional liturgy, they may nevertheless value the connection which that liturgy provides to the broader Jewish community in space and time. Feminist reinterpretation of patriarchal language allows for the retention of at least some of the traditional divine epithets while imbuing them with a content that is more consistent with a feminist theology.

Rabbi Lynn Gottleib has experimented at some length with this approach. Her reinterpretations of traditional God-images, based on a creative exploration of their Hebrew meanings and/or the Hebrew letters of which they are composed, infuses them with a vivid feminist spirituality. *Elohim* is not God but "all spirits"; *Adonai* is not Lord but the "I as the ground of experience," and "the door to the mystery of life"; *Shaddai* becomes "my breasts" and *Shekhinah,* "She who dwells within."[3]

Another candidate for feminist reinterpretation is the epithet *Ha-Makom* (literally "the place"). This spatial term may be used to express the sense of community as the space within which God's activity is made known and acknowledged.[4] Even the traditional male image of God as father might find its place in the context of a re-imaged feminist Judaism, not as a paternalistic image of hierarchy and domination, but simply as a paternal image.[5]

Feminist Revisioning

Most effort, however, has been directed towards the creative use of Jewish tradition and the Hebrew language to give theological and liturgical expression to Jewish feminist "God-wrestling."[6]

Feminine God-titles

One way of creating feminist God-language is to replace masculine personal pronouns and images with feminine ones, while retaining the traditional structure of blessings and other liturgical formulae. The ubiquitous title *ha-kadosh barukh hu* ("the Holy One, Blessed be He") is feminized by adding the feminine ending to Hebrew for "Holy One" and replacing the masculine pronoun with the feminine. Similarly, the familiar image of God as "King of the Universe" can become "Queen of the Universe" by adding the feminine ending to the Hebrew word for king. This simple solution, however, is often considered inadequate. Replacing the masculine images with feminine equivalents does not erase the images of domination, which are seen as inappropriate in a feminist liturgy.[7]

A second approach is to utilize the Hebrew words for goddess: *Elohut* (a feminine noun meaning divinity), and *Elah* (meaning Goddess).[8] Though goddess language may have polytheistic connotations for some,[9] others argue that reimaging the Goddess through the lens of Jewish monotheism may enrich the range of metaphors for addressing God.[10]

The most popular female God-image is *Shekhinah,* frequently incorporated into a feminized blessing formula, "Blessed be the *Shekhinah*."[11] Although the term appears in a variety of contexts in rabbinic literature, it is not until the thirteenth century Kabbalistic (mystical) text that it is used to represent the feminine element in God.[12] In the Zohar, the *Shekhinah* is identified with the tenth *Sefira* (divine emanation), which must be united with the Godhead in order for salvation to occur. This union is depicted in explicitly sexual terms; indeed, "every true marriage is a symbolical realization of the union of God and the Shekhinah."[13]

The attractiveness of this term lies in the explicitly feminine language in which it is described. Identified with the community of Israel, *Shekhinah* represents "the mystical idea of Israel in its bond with God and in its bliss, but also in its suffering and its exile. She is not only Queen, daughter and bride of God, but also the mother of every individual in Israel."[14] On the other hand, the concept of sexual union between the *Shekhinah* and the rest of the *Sefiroth* reinforces the image of God as masculine and limits the notion of the feminine to sexuality.[15] For this reason, some feminist theologians argue that *Shekhinah,* though a feminine term, can be useful only if at least partly wrenched free from its original context and radically reinterpreted.[16]

Images of Mutuality

The feminine God-titles maintain the classical covenantal notion of a hierarchal relationship between God and Israel. In sharp contrast are images of God as lover, friend, companion and co-creator which impute mutuality and partnership to this bond. In English these labels are not gender-specific and may denote either male or female, while in Hebrew they may be translated as either masculine or feminine. Such images emerge from traditional Jewish sources, though they may be found outside those sources as well.[17] The feminist understanding of God as lover, for example, is taken not from Hosea, which maintains the patriarchal relationship between God as male lover and Israel as errant but beloved woman, but from the Song of Songs, which presents male and female as pursuer and pursued.[18] The idea of God as friend is present in the Yom Kippur (Day of Atonement) liturgy, providing a symbol of mutuality in the covenantal relationship between God and Israel. The image of companion, while lacking the exclusiveness of friendship, implies a sense of equality and community, shared goals and shared work. Similarly, epithets prefixed with "co-," as in "co-creator," imply the notion of partnership between divinity and humanity in "the larger project of world-creation, "emphasize communal endeavors, and conjure up "a sense of personal empowerment and mutual responsibility."[19]

Because these images, while personal, are applicable to both male and female, they resist the restriction of particular attributes to either male or female aspects of God. The human community that exists in the image of such a God is a collective of women and men whose social roles and relationships are not dictated by their gender. In imputing mutuality to the God-human relationship, such images emphasize human responsibility. Erasing the notion of hierarchy, however, requires radical rethinking of foundational Jewish symbols such as the Exodus, which has traditionally been seen as the confirmation of God's caring action on behalf of Israel as God's people. Furthermore, images of mutuality do not give expression to the range of negative emotion and experience, including the feelings of powerlessness in the face of misfortune and tragedy, which often act as a stimulus for prayer.

Non-personal God-language

Non-personal God-language has been explored most extensively by Marcia Falk, in her reworking of traditional blessings. Falk does not simply substitute a different set of imagery for the masculine language of the formula, nor does she create a set formula of her own to introduce each blessing. Rather, she considers the spiritual significance of the blessing and then reformulates it in such a way as to reflect that meaning. For example, the traditional blessing to be recited on special occasions (such as wearing new clothes or eating a new type of fruit) is as follows: "Blessed are you, O Lord, King of the universe, who receives us, sustains us and brings us to this time." Falk's version reads: "Let us bless the flow of life [*ma'ayan hahayyim*] that revives us, sustains us, and brings us to this time."[20]

Falk has changed two important parts of the blessing. The initial change, which substitutes "Let us bless" for "Blessed are you," shifts one's attention from the one being blessed to the individuals/community invoking the blessing. Second, the divine epithet "flow of life" is both non-personal and non-hierarchal. Falk's rendering of the blessing evokes the passage of time as well as the special moments in time for which the blessing expresses thanks.

In her blessing for the sanctification of wine at Sabbath and festival

meals, Falk departs further from the traditional form while still maintaining its sense of rhythm and some of its vocabulary. The traditional
form reads: "Blessed are you, O Lord, King of the universe, creator of [or:
who creates] the fruit of the vine." Falk's version reads: "Let us bless the
source of life [*eyn hahayyim*] that nurtures fruit on the vine as we weave
the branches of our lives into the tradition."[21] The term "source of life,"
a non-personal feminine term in Hebrew, evokes the nurturing and sustaining of life rather than the creation of life from nothingness implied
in the traditional term "creator." Rather than simply expressing thanks
for the Sabbath wine, the blessing articulates the meaning of the act of
sanctification for the individuals and community invoking the tradition.

Falk's blessings counter the image of God as a personal power that
stands above, outside, or even alongside creation. Instead, the divine
is envisaged as the force within creation from which the world and its
inhabitants draw their sustenance and creative power. Human beings
are transformed from passive recipients of God's largesse to active participants in the creative process and in the divine-human relationship
itself. The epithets "source of life" and "flow of life" imply that human
beings created in the image of God are similarly participating in the creative cycle of nature as well as in the creation of community through
the distinctly Jewish practices which many of the blessings accompany.
Submerged in this approach to God-talk, however, is the notion of a
personal God, a Being to whom one might cry out, in gladness and
in pain, in gratitude and in anger. The shift from the personal to the
non-personal God similarly has implications for the conception of the
historical relationships among the individual, the community of Israel
and the divine.

Liturgy, Theology and Community

The above discussion demonstrates the diversity of Jewish feminist
theological discourses. None of these opinions is satisfying and complete
in itself, nor, in fact, is intended to be. Rather, feminist God-formulations
are not understood as mutually exclusive, but complementary; not de-
finitive, but simply directions "towards" a feminist theology.[22] Though
individual theologians may have their own preferences, diversity is valued as a source of strength, not feared as a threat to the whole.

In addition to the value of diversity, several other points emerge. First,
a primary concern of Jewish feminist theological discourse is not simply
to talk *about* God but to name and re-name the divinity. One reason for
this concern is the connection between God-talk and liturgy, to which
divine epithets are more suited than abstract theological discourse. The-

ology is therefore important not only for its own sake but also as a preparation for the transformation of liturgy and as an undergirding for the reformation of the praxis of communal prayer.

Second, Jewish feminist discourses exhibit the tension between universality and particularity that is inherent in Jewish sources and Jewish thought as a whole. Feminist discourse, however, has been more successful in depicting the universality of humanity than the particularity of the Jewish experience thereof. Although Jewish feminist God-names and the ritual contexts in which they are used are drawn from Jewish tradition, the divine-human bond which they imply is frequently grounded not in the particularity of Jewish experience but in universal human experience. Yet the creative tension can be maintained only if the particularity of Jewish experience is also given theological expression. The hierarchical language traditionally used for describing the Exodus, Sinai and the covenantal relationship between God and Israel needs to be reformulated in a way which gives expression to a feminist consciousness without submerging or erasing these pivotal experiences.

Equally important, and equally problematic, is the relationship between *halakhah* (Jewish law) and theology. *Halakhah* is traditionally seen as the expression of the divine will for the Jewish people. Yet *halakhah* not only contains specific laws which limit women's social and religious roles and activities but also embodies a view of women as fundamentally "Other." Can *halakhah* be transformed so as to allow for the retention of a distinctively Jewish identity while at the same time eliminating its patriarchal and androcentric world-view?

The problem of *halakhah* looms large in the arena of communal prayer. In Orthodox Judaism, women are not counted in the prayer quorum, nor are they allowed access to religious leadership roles.[23] The specific laws in which this exclusion is grounded have been the subject of considerable halakhic discourse on the part of both men and women.[24] But feminist theologians argue strongly that one cannot achieve full equality for women by isolating and "fixing" particular *halakhot*. Rather, the halakhic system as a whole, its theological basis and its liturgical expression must be subjected to feminist critique. Such critique fosters attempts to incorporate feminist God-language and women's experience into the content and structure of Jewish communal prayer.

Departing from the fixed liturgy in these respects, however, raises a new challenge: how can communal prayer, which presupposes at least a measure of uniformity in content and structure, give expression to the individuality of women's experience and the diversity of Jewish feminist God-naming? One community that has taken up this challenge is B'not Esh, a group of women that has been meeting annually since 1981 and has developed a model for building sustained community across considerable geographic distance.[25] Martha Ackelsberg, a charter member of B'not Esh, has detailed their efforts to develop a model for communal prayer that also respects individual experience. Because no one form could possibly satisfy everyone, these efforts "generated high levels of frustration and anger."[26] Nevertheless, the process of working through these expectations over time, and experimenting with different forms, resulted in the development of a liturgy which permitted group prayer.[27]

The creating of feminist liturgy and community is a never-ending process. Jewish feminist theological discourses will continue God-wrestling, not only by further development of feminist God-images but also by confronting a range of related questions, such as the nature of evil, the meaning of covenant, the impact of feminist micro-communities on the larger Jewish community, and education and access of feminists to leadership roles in Jewish communal and religious institutions. Such attempts will no doubt be characterized by continued creativity and a positive evaluation of human diversity within the context of strong commitment to Jewish feminist spirituality and transformation.

NOTES

1. Judith Plaskow, *Standing Again at Sinai: Judaism from a Feminist Perspective*, San Francisco, 1990, pp. 123, 127.

2. Ibid., p. 121.

3. Ellen Umansky, "Creating a Jewish Feminist Theology," in *Weaving the Visions: New Patterns in Feminist Spirituality*, ed. Judith Plaskow and Carol P. Christ, San Francisco, 1989, pp. 192–93.

4. Plaskow, *Standing Again* (n. 1), pp. 141–42.

5. Ibid., p. 166.

6. Ibid., p. 33.

7. Marcia Falk, "Notes on Composing New Blessings," in *Weaving the Visions* (n. 3), p. 129.

8. Neither is biblical, however. The former is found in rabbinic literature (e.g., Genesis Rabbah, ch. 46), while the latter is found in modern Hebrew dictionaries.

9. Umansky, "Theology," (n. 3), p. 192.

10. Plaskow, *Standing Again*, (n. 1), p. 152.

11. Annette Daum, "Language and Liturgy," in *Daughters of the King: Women and the Synagogue*, ed. Susan Grossman and Rivka Haut, Philadelphia, 1992, p. 187.

12. Gershom G. Scholem, *Major Trends in Jewish Mysticism*, New York, 1941, p. 229.

13. Ibid., p. 235.

14. Ibid., p. 230.

15. Daum, "Language," (n. 11), p. 187; cf. Falk, "Blessings," pp. 192–30.

16. Plaskow, *Standing Again*, (n. 1), pp. 139–40; cf. Daum, "Language," (n. 11), p. 200.

17. The images of God as friend and lover, for example, are developed by Sallie McFague, *Metaphorical Theology: Models of God in Religious Language*, Philadelphia, 1982, pp. 177–92.

18. Plaskow, *Standing Again*, (n. 1), p. 162.

19. Ibid., p. 163.

20. Ellen Umansky and Dale Ashton, eds., *Four Centuries of Jewish Women's Spirituality: A Source Book*, Boston, 1992, p. 242.

21. Ibid.

22. Judith Plaskow, "The Coming of Lilith: Toward a Feminist Theology," in *Womanspirit Rising: A Feminist Reader in Religion*, ed. Carol P. Christ and Judith Plaskow, San Francisco, 1979, pp. 198–209; Rita Gross, "Steps Toward Feminine Imagery of Deity in Jewish Theology," in *On Being a Jewish Feminist*, ed. Susannah Heschel, New York, 1983, pp. 234–47.

23. Non-Orthodox Jewish denominations as well as many nondenominational groups have addressed this problem to varying degrees. For the history of the process within Conservative Judaism see Neil Gillman, *Conservative Judaism: The New Century*, New Jersey, 1993, pp. 124–49.

24. Contrast, for example, the Orthodox views of Moshe Meiselman, *Jewish Women in Jewish Law*, New York, 1978, pp. 43–57, and the feminist perspective of Rachel Biale, *Women and Jewish Law*, New York, 1984, pp. 10–43.

25. Martha A. Ackelsberg, "Spirituality, Community and Politics: B'Not Esh and the Feminist Reconstruction of Judaism," *Journal of Feminist Studies in Religion* 2, 1986, p. 118.

26. Ibid.

27. Ibid., p. 113.

34

Mother God[1]

SALLIE McFAGUE

We can speak of God only indirectly, using our world and ourselves as metaphors for expressing our relationship with the divine. One of the oldest and most powerful metaphors has been the parental one; however, in the Christian tradition only one parent — the father — has been allowed to image God. To be sure, maternal language is very prevalent in other ways: for the Church, in relation to Mary, as the proper role for all women. But as a metaphor for relating to God, Christians have been wary.

One must ask why this is the case. Surely one reason is Christianity's Hebraic heritage in which Yahweh, the one, holy, transcendent deity defeats the fertility goddesses of early Mediterranean culture. This tradition does not easily accommodate the female (as it does not accommodate nature or the body either). The male sky God under whom all things are hierarchically and dualistically ordered became the pattern for subsequent theology, as it also became the pattern for much of Western culture. The hierarchical dualisms which are so prevalent in our ways of thinking owe much to the patriarchal understanding of the divine: God as the dominating head of the family of "man" became a form of social organization which supported other hierarchical dualisms such as male/female, spirit/flesh, human beings/nature, white people/people of color, rich/poor, straight/gay, Christian/non-Christian. Patriarchal language for God promotes an entire way of thinking, social constructions of race, class, and gender, for instance, that benefit males, especially white, affluent males.

In this essay, we will experiment with the metaphor or model of God as mother in order to decenter the patriarchal model and to provide an alternative to it. It will also serve to recontextualize the paternal model in a parental direction, in opposition to its traditional patriarchal direction (having been assimilated into the monarchical, triumphalistic language of God as king, master, and lord). As we begin this experiment, we must avoid several possible pitfalls. First, the intention is not to turn the tables and establish a new hierarchal dualism with a matriarchal model of God. Rather, it is to investigate a rich — and neglected, if not repressed and suppressed — source for expressing some aspects of the God/world relationship in our time, most specifically, the interdependence and mutuality of all life. In our contemporary world which is increasingly a global village and in which ecological deterioration and nuclear holocaust are definite possibilities, we need to underscore the interconnectedness of all living things. A model of God as mother of the earth and all its beings is a strong candidate for encouraging a sensibility that will support the realities of late twentieth century existence.

Second, we must not sentimentalize maternal imagery. We will not suppose that mothers are "naturally" loving, comforting, or self-sacrificing. Our society has a stake in making women think that they are biologically programmed to be these things, when, in fact, a good case can be made that the so-called qualities or stereotypes of mothers are social constructions — women are not born, but become, mothers through education and imitation.[2] Rather, we will focus on the most basic things that females (as mothers) do among most, if not all the species and which human mothers do as well: give birth, feed and protect the young, want the young to flourish.

Third, we need to recognize how dangerous and oppressive maternal language can be, both to women and to all human beings in relation to God. It poses problems for women because it suggests that women who are not mothers are not true or fulfilled women; it gives power to the one role that has probably oppressed women more than any other over the centuries; it can appear to be pro-life or anti-abortion at a time when population problems loom very large on the horizon. Therefore, we must be careful to see this model of God as only *one* model and by no means one that would eliminate speaking of God as sister, as midwife, or in other female terms. The model poses problems for all human beings in relation to God because if the parental model, mother or father, is used exclusively for God, it places us always in the role of children. At a time when we need desperately to be "adults," to take responsibility for our world and its well-being, we cannot support a model that suggests that the "great mother" or "great father" will take care of our crises of poverty, discrimination, damage to the ecosystem, and so forth.

Nevertheless, in spite of all these qualifications, the maternal metaphor is so powerful and so right for our time that we *should* use it. If the heart of Christian faith for an ecological, nuclear-threatened age must be a profound awareness of the preciousness and vulnerability of life as a gift we receive and pass on, with appreciation for its value and desire for its fulfillment, it is difficult to think of any metaphor more apt than the paternal one and especially the maternal one. God as the giver of life, as the power of being in all being, can be imaged through the metaphor of mother — and of father. Parental love is the most powerful and intimate experience we have of giving love whose return is not calculated (though a return is appreciated): it is the gift of *life as such* to others. Parental love wills life and when it comes, exclaims, "It is good that you exist!"[3] Moreover, in addition to being the gift of life, parental love nurtures what it has brought into existence, and wants it to grow and be fulfilled. These are the three basic features of the model which we will investigate.

The physical act of giving birth is the base from which this model derives its power, for here it joins the reservoir of the great symbols of life and of life's continuity: blood, water, breath, sex, and food. In the acts of conception, gestation, and birth all are involved, and it is therefore no surprise that these symbols became the center of most religions, including Christianity, for they have the power to express the renewal and transformation of life — the "second birth" — because they are the basis of our "first birth." And yet, at least in Christianity, our first birth has been strangely neglected; another way of saying this is that creation, the birth of the universe and all its beings, has not been permitted the imagery that this tradition uses so freely for redemption, the transformation and fulfillment of creation. Why is this the case?

One reason is surely that Christianity, alienated as it always has been for female sexuality, has been willing to image the second, "spiritual," renewal of existence in the birth metaphor, but not the first, "physical," coming into existence. In the Judaeo-Christian tradition, creation has been imaginatively pictured as an intellectual, aesthetic "act" of God, accomplished through God's word and wrought by God's "hands," much as a painting is created by an artist or a form by a sculptor. But the model of God as mother suggests a very different kind of creation, one which underscores the radical dependence of all things on God, but in an internal rather than an external fashion. Thus, if we wish to understand the world as in some fashion "in" God rather than God as "in" the world, it is clearly the parent *as mother* that is the stronger candidate for an understanding of creation as bodied forth from the divine being. For it is the imagery of gestation, giving birth, and lactation that creates an imaginative picture of creation that is profoundly dependent on and cared for by divine life.[4] There is simply no other imagery available to us that has this power for expressing the interdependence and inter-relatedness of all life with its ground. All of us, female and male, have the womb as our first home, all of us are born from the bodies of our mothers, most of us are fed by our mothers. What better imagery could there be for expressing the most basic reality of existence: that we — all of us in our planet and the entire rest of the universe — live and move and have our being in God.

Of equal importance to the birth aspect is the ability of the model to express the nurturing of life. Parents feed the young. This is, across the entire range of life, the most basic responsibility of parents, often of fathers as well as mothers. Among most animals, it is instinctual and often accomplished only at the cost of the health or life of the parent. It is not principally from altruistic motives that parents feed the young but from a base close to the one that brought new life into existence, the source that participates in passing life along. With human parents, the same love that says, "It is good that you exist!" desires that life to continue, and for many parents in much of the world that is a daily and often horrendous struggle. There is, perhaps, no picture more powerful to express "giving" love than that of parents wanting, but not having the food, to feed their children.

The Christian tradition has paid a lot of attention to food imagery, in fact, one could say it is central to it: from Jesus feeding the crows and eating with sinners to the eucharistic meal as the main sacrament of the Church. But, again, as with the birth imagery, it has spiritualized the imagery, and has not taken with utmost seriousness the physical necessity of food. One of the implications of adopting the maternal model would be the restoration of food as a necessity for all of God's children. A theology that sees God as the parent who feeds the young and by extension, the weak and the vulnerable, understands God as caring about the most basic needs of life in its struggle to continue. A justice ethic is the direct implication of the maternal model: *all* the children must be fed.

Finally, God as mother (parent) wants *all* to flourish.[5] God is the mother of all existence, all beings, as well as the ecosystem that supports them, and while human parents tend to focus on our own species and specific individuals within that species, God as mother is impartial and inclusive as we can never be. The fulfillment of the entire created order, its growth and well-being, is the wish of the mother who brought it into being and who nurtures it. Again we see the implications for how we view the world: our anthropocentric bias which understands all other creatures and things in the world as instruments for our use is undercut. If we take a "theocentric" point of view, we also must take a "cosmocentric" point of view, for the mother/creator of all that is loves *all*, not just human beings. We see here also the relationship of the mother and judge models: God the mother judges those who thwart the nurture and fulfillment of her beloved creation. God as mother is angry because some of her created beings desire everything for themselves, not recognizing the *intrinsic* worth of other beings. In this view, "sin" is not "against God," the pride and rebellion of an inferior against a superior, but "against the body," the refusal to be part of an ecological whole whose continued existence and success depends upon a recognition of the interdependence and interrelatedness of all species. The mother-God as creator, then, is also involved in "economics," the management of the household of the universe, to ensure the just distribution of goods to *all.*

What is also evident is that this model undercuts the hierarchical dualism of the tradition and of the Genesis creation story in which God, absolutely distinct from and external to the world, creates it, with a hierarchy of beings. An alternative imaginative picture emerges from the model of God as mother. The kind of creation that fits with this model is creation not as an intellectual or artistic act but as a physical event: the universe is bodied forth from God, it is expressive of God's very being: it could, therefore, be seen as God's "body."[6] It is not something alien to God but is from the "womb" of God, formed through "gestation," a process symbolizing the long evolutionary history of the universe. There are important implications of our picture, but first we must remind ourselves that it is a picture — but so is the artistic, intellectual model of creation. We are not claiming that God creates by giving birth to the universe as her body; what we are suggesting is that the birth metaphor is both closer to Christian faith and to a contemporary, evolutionary, ecological context than the alternative craftsman model.

A critical implication of our model is that it overturns the dualisms of mind and body, spirit and flesh, humanity and nature, male and female. God's body, that which supports all life, is not matter or spirit but the matrix out of which everything evolves. In this picture, God is not spirit over against a world of matter, with human beings dangling in between, chained to their bodies but eager to escape to the world of spirit. The universe, from God's being, is properly body (as well as spirit) because in some sense God is physical (as well as beyond the physical). This shocking idea — that God is physical — is one of the most important implications of the model of creation by God the mother. It is an explicit rejection of Christianity's long, oppressive, and dangerous alliance with spirit against body, an alliance that has oppressed women as well as nature and for the good of all needs to come to an end.

In closing this experiment with the model of God as mother, I would stress that it is an "experiment." It is an heuristic, imaginative enterprise. As a remythologization, such theology acknowledges that it is, as it were, painting a picture. For most people, the imaginative picture of the relationship between God and the world they hold influences their behavior more powerfully than concepts do. In a time when life on our planet is threatened in so many ways, an imaginative picture that underscores the radical and intimate interrelatedness and interdependence of all life; that insists that the basic necessities of life must be justly shared;

that insists that species other than human being have intrinsic worth; and that undercuts dualistic hierarchies of all sorts is the sort of picture needed. No imaginative picture of the God of Christianity — the God who is on the side of life and its fulfillment — can last forever, because what is understood as "fulfillment," as salvation, changes. We must try out new pictures that will bring the reality of God's love into the imaginations of the women and men of today just as others have done in Scripture and the tradition. God as mother is *one* powerful model appropriate for our time; it is by no means the only one.

NOTES

1. This essay is based in part on my book *Models of God: Theology for an Ecological, Nuclear Age*, Philadelphia, 1987.

2. See Nancy Chodorow, *The Reproduction of Mothering: Psychoanalysis and the Sociology of Gender*, Berkeley, 1978.

3. The phrase is from Josef Pieper, *About Love*, trans. Richard and Clara Winston, Chicago, 1974, p. 22.

4. Paul Tillich says that the symbolic dimension of the "ground of being" points to the mother-quality of "giving birth, carrying, and embracing" (*Systematic Theology*, Chicago, 1963, vol. 3, pp. 293–94). Arthur Peacocke sees maternal, creation imagery as a corrective to the traditional view: " . . . it is an analogy of God creating the world within herself . . . God creates a world that is, in principle and in origin, other than him/herself but creates it . . . within him/herself" (*Creation and the World of Science*, Oxford, 1979, p. 142).

5. This must not be interpreted as a pro-life or anti-abortion stance. If the various species are to thrive, not every individual in every species can be fulfilled. In a closed ecological system with limits on natural resources, difficult decisions must be made to ensure the continuation, growth, and fulfillment of the many forms of life (not just one form and not all of its individuals).

6. This image, radical as it may seem, is an old one with roots in Stoicism and elliptically in the Hebrew Scriptures. For a treatment of its Christian history and contemporary viability, as well as a critique of creation *ex nihilo*, see Grace Jantzen, *God's World, God's Body*, Philadelphia and London, 1984.

35

Spirituality of the Earth

JULIA ESQUIVEL VELÁSQUEZ

Introduction

From the Central American viewpoint, it seems impossible to stop the process of turning the isthmus into a desert. This is not caused by ignorance or lack of studies or programs, but by lack of responsibility, decision and political will. Mere rational conviction suffers from impotence because the earth's growing devastation is directly linked to the attacks, which still continue, on the indigenous and peasant populations, causing their increasing impoverishment and dependency. This perspective is also valid at planetary level and is particularly acute in rural areas all over the third world.

The biologist Mary Mersky told me that she was convinced that without a change, a deep conversion on the part of governments and all of us, it will be impossible to recover the power to respect the earth's life and cooperate in its recovery, or at least defend what is left to us of nature. We Christians learned and believed that "man is the king of creation." This error led us to feel we were above all creation. Arrogantly we believed that we were masters.

Men with economic and military power have conquered, sacked, abused, sold the earth and treated it and all it produces and contains as simply for their use. They have sacrificed its wealth and beauty to produce capital and goods manufactured in their factories, in order to satisfy their lust to possess and to dominate. This behavior demonstrates their spiritual emptiness, pride and vanity.

Ignorant of ecological laws, they have introduced chaos into the natural order. Where there were wonderful jungles, they have destroyed the vegetation to introduce enormous herds of livestock. They have deflected the course of rivers, burned forests and introduced species alien to the environment in places originally destined by nature for a different kind of fauna and flora.

And if this were not enough, in 1984 the arsenals of the great powers included nuclear warheads whose accumulated power represented approximately one million two hundred times the power of the bomb that destroyed Hiroshima. Sometimes this power is translated as corresponding to four tons of explosive for every human being on earth.[1] The economic and military system constructed by Western human beings feeds insatiably on the constant destruction of the peoples of the South and of nature. It displays symptoms of spiritual emptiness and a destructive fury.

Human Beings Are Creatures among Other Creatures

The indispensable condition for a true conversion is to put away pride, and honestly admit that we are mistaken. We are putting the earth and all life, including our own, in grave danger and we must humbly recognize that we are merely creatures on this earth.

In the Chouaqui version of the Bible, Adam in Genesis is called "Le Glébeux" ("man made of earth, dust"). As dust, we are part of nature, formed from and dependent on the same primary material from which all creation is made.

From Einstein to our own days, physics and the discoveries of the new biology and ecology confirm that: "The whole earth is a single cell, and we are all simply symbiotic particles, related to one another. There can be no 'us' and 'them.' The global politics that flows (should flow) from this vision is truly *a bios* and *a logos*."[2]

"Nature recycles its materials again and again without generating any kind of waste." Dieter Teufel, of the Heidelberg Umwelt und Prognose Institut, has calculated that "all the carbon there is in our bodies, our food, the carbon dioxide in the atmosphere and limestone rocks, has already formed part of other organisms six hundred times in the process of life production." In the body of each one of us, there are about half a billion carbon atoms, which were part of the organism of persons living two thousand years ago, for example Jesus Christ. Likewise, according to Teufel's models, all "the nitrogen there is on earth has already formed part of the organism of living beings and been eliminated from them approximately 800 times; the sulphur 300 times; the phosphorus 8000 times; the potassium 2000 times," etc. Thus nature is the cleanest, most efficient, astonishing and instructive factory imaginable, an example which humans must follow if we want to survive.[3]

The whole creation's source of life is one and the same. According to the new physicists, this source is intelligent and communicates in energy impulses throughout all created things. Without it, it would be impossible for photosynthesis to happen, for our hearts to beat, or for any of the biological phenomena of living beings that we can observe, or the invisible energy movements we find in the subatomic world, to happen.

The new science shows us that we are related very closely not only to other creatures, but also to all things. In her book *Gaia and God*, Rosemary Radford Ruether says: "If we tried to experience this relatedness and to keep it present in our awareness, an *intense spirituality* would flow from it."

"Dust thou art and to dust thou shalt return" is precisely true. It reminds us that the generation and sustaining of life is one single process. We are inter-connected creatures, who need one another.[4] Another witness calling us to this humility is the relationship with nature of the original peoples of Abya Yala (the continent of America today).

A letter dated 1854, from Chief Seattle of the Duamich League of North Western territories, afterwards called the state of Washington, addressed to Franklin Pierce in reply to the proposal to "sell their lands," is an example of this prophetic wisdom.

I can only quote briefly from it. The white man

> treats his mother the earth and his brother the sky as things to be bought and sold. His appetite will gobble up the earth and leave behind merely a desert . . . What is happening to the earth will happen to the earth's children. Man cannot control the web of life. He is only a thread to this tapestry. What he does to the tapestry he will do to himself. . . . The air is precious to the red-skinned people because all things share the same breath: animals, trees and humans. . . . The sap circulating in the trees carries the memory of the red-skinned people. . . . Our God is the same god. You may think now that he belongs to you, just as you wish to possess our land; but it is not possible. He is the God of all human beings, and his mercy is equal towards the red-skinned and the white. This earth is precious to him, and violating it is despising its Creator. . . . My words are fixed as the stars.

Western Christian creation doctrine set up an abyss between "the Christian" as a human being and all others. The Christian was above all others and even his own being was split into matter and spirit. Consequently during the Conquest Christians proceeded to baptize masses of Indians and then to kill them, with the justification that they were saving their souls. This same justification, of conquest in order to evangelize, betrays the contradiction that led to genocide.

Another example of this attitude which is in accord with the vision of the new science can be found in the Maya Tojolabal language. After his experience of living with the Tojolabales for twenty years, Carlos Lenkersdorf writes in his book *Lengua y Cosmovisión mayas en Chiapas* that in the grammatical construction of the Tojolabal language, the subject-object relationship does not exist, because it is not a language with an accusative character like the European languages. Existential and agent subjects exist in a dynamic, complementary and reciprocal relationship, which is impossible to translate into Spanish. The determining factor is the presence of "multiple and qualitatively different subjects," through which events occur. The name we might give to this peculiarity would be inter-subjectivity. This excludes objects and, as it were, raises all to the level of subjects. According to Lenkersdorf, this linguistic structure corresponds to the Tojolabal way of relating among human beings and between all things. For them there is no dead matter: all things have a heart. Like other pre-Columbian peoples, they live immersed in a cosmic community: "we all live and share life with everything in the cosmos."

The Tojolabal language is another window into the Mayan soul. Here again we find that humble and respectful attitude to creation peculiar to the original peoples, which agrees with the vision of the new physics and biology. They have a way of life expressing a spirituality unknown to Christians, which we must try to understand. We must recognize that we are going the wrong way, in a direction leading us to destruction, and that "there is no end to the chain of influences which are the consequence of my decision."[5]

At individual, family, national and global level, each decision sets in motion an endless chain of influences either for life, health and the balance of nature or for the lessening of life, unbalance and chaos, in other words, death. The death of 40,000 children every day from poverty is caused by decisions taken at supra-national level. These affect the weakest peoples and sectors, when they are converted into economic plans the aim of which is the production of capital, arms and unnecessary things.

The destruction of communities of aborigines and in the Amazon jungle in Brazil is caused by the creation of "artificial needs" by big companies, whose sole interest is in accumulating more capital in an endless cycle, which is like a whirlwind of death for human beings and nature.

A real conversion means changing our awareness, attitude, decisions and will, so that there is a real change in our way of life:

Therefore, brothers and sisters, I pray you by the mercies of God, to present your bodies as a living sacrifice, holy and acceptable to God, which is your spiritual worship. Do not be conformed to this world but be transformed by the renewal of your mind, that you may prove what is the will of God, what is good and acceptable and perfect (Rom. 12:1–2).

Changing: Experiencing Grace, Gratitude and Free Giving

Perhaps only we human beings have the power to become aware of ourselves. If we were to heal ourselves, we could open our eyes and see who we really are. This sight would make us realize the miracle of life and the infinite wealth surrounding us, and give us insight into the enormous possibilities of being and of the whole creation. We can only receive this revelation through grace and compassion. What we are and have received has all been freely given. In Chief Seattle's letter there is infinite gratitude and respect for all that exists and profound astonishment at the white man's craziness and insensitivity.

Jesus tells us: "Freely you have received, freely give." Here it is not a case of giving, because we are not owners; we are receivers and beneficiaries like all creatures. It means gratefully receiving what we have been given and gratefully sharing it. God, the source of life, has offered us the possibility of becoming a reflection of his own being (like him), without expecting anything more or anything less from us than love.

This pristine vision is muddied by the selfishness of human beings, who instead of gratefully receiving, take over, dominate, commercialize and convert God's gifts into the golden calf, capital. Believing they are the creator, they have set their hearts on their "possessions." Jesus says of these people: "It is easier for a camel to go through a needle's eye than for a rich man to enter the kingdom of heaven." The spirit of gratitude and free giving nurtures the conversion necessary to save ourselves as a species, avoid the destruction of the planet, and consciously contribute to our own renewal and that of all things.

With new eyes and heart, all things will be made new, as they really are each morning, fresh from God's hands. This was the prayer of Chief Seattle, the spirit of St. Francis of Assisi's *Canticle of the Creatures*, and is the key to Jesus' words: "Is not life more than food, and the body more than clothing?" (Matt. 6:26). This is our own heart's desire. Encountering moment by moment life's abounding grace, we become aware of the joy of heavens and earth singing God's glory. This change of mind restores the damaged sensitivity of our whole being, so that we grasp the messages of wisdom emitted from one day to the next, pierce night's stillness and decipher the mysteries transmitted night after night (Ps. 19:2–3).

Grace, gratitude and free giving are resonances of love, notes in a single tune, compassion. Grace rescues us from the most subtle baseness, that of clinging to things and getting stuck to them. It leads us to give freely, to share. A true conversion leads us away from selfishness towards communion; from competition to co-operation; from plundering to giving freely; from covetousness to respect in our relationship with all creatures great and small.

Changing: Healing and Growing in Order to Assume Our Responsibility

Only those who know they are loved are capable of loving themselves and others. Beginning to love means beginning to heal. In the process, every natural happening recovers a deeper sense: rain which refreshes the earth, the air which is the breath of life; the warm kiss of the sun and fire, its child, our friend.

Gratitude makes us members of a great fellowship in which we become consciously responsible for our own inner development and a revolution in our relations with the earth, all creatures, all things, nourished like us by our common mother.

Our lives which have so often been turned in upon an isolated and fearful ego have not known true communion even with ourselves, let alone with others, creation, or the Creator. Healing means spreading our tent-pegs infinitely wider, transcending our individual ego, our own little family, country, religious circle, outward to embrace the great family of the earth and the cosmos. True love is inclusive.

If human beings, particularly in the West, have not been able to have sane relations with their fellows and the planet, it is because they are sick. Nevertheless, our human potential can reach out for something better, because we are part of the intelligent miracle which creates and sustains life. Our deepest desire is to grow and share in our own process of evolution.

We Christians know that the Spirit which dwells in us wants us to grow. What we are now discovering with new awareness and new eyes is that all our seeking, the thirst in us for something greater, is the expression of that Spirit who constantly presses us on. From a wider viewpoint it is a call to co-operate and share in the growth and transformation of all created things.

Yet among the mature we do impart wisdom, although it is not a wisdom of this age or of the rulers of this age, who are doomed to pass away. But we impart a secret and hidden wisdom of God, which God decreed before the ages for our glorification. None of the rulers of this age understood this; for if they had, they would not have crucified the Lord of glory. But as it is written,

"What no eye has seen, nor ear heard,
nor heart of man conceived,
what God has prepared for those who love him,"

God has revealed to us through the Spirit. For the Spirit searches everything, even the depths of God. For what person knows a man's thoughts except the spirit of the man which is in him? So also no one comprehends the thoughts of God, except the Spirit of God. Now we have received not the Spirit of this world, but the Spirit which is from God, that we might understand the gifts bestowed on us by God (1 Cor. 2:6–12).

Therefore our groans are united with all creation's (Rom. 8:18–30), even though we have become deafened through conforming to this system, which has exchanged spiritual growth for the thirst to possess and cling on to things. But this growth, which means understanding and responding to the Spirit's purpose, enables us to see why the Tojolabales believe that all things have a heart. For it is essential both for them and us to live in harmony with things, rather than dominating them.

Dr. Derek Chopra says in his book *Cuerpo sin edad, mentes sin tiempo:* "Although we often identify love with grasping and possession, there is a profound truth here: losing the power of detachment means losing the power to love." Love is inclusive and expansive. It does not cease at the boundaries of our skin or our senses, or the walls of my house, or the frontiers of my country. If we cultivate love it expands infinitely.

People with many possessions lose their soul by clinging on to them. They are imprisoned or possessed by what they have accumulated. They are not free. They suffer an emptiness. They are ignorant and afraid of the meaning of fellowship, respect, gratitude and free giving. They have lost sight and hearing and heart. They are mortally sick.

In this context Einstein says: "Our task must be to free ourselves from this prison, broadening our circle of compassion to embrace every living creature and the whole of nature in all its beauty."[6] Love heals us, driving us out of a narrow sectarianism towards ever deeper and more inclusive communion, transcending frontiers in order to appreciate the wealth of diversity and glimpse a planetary home, in which each people and culture and religion, enthusiastic for the welfare of the world, asks itself: How can I contribute to humanity? What fruits can we bring to life's great banquet?[7]

Changing: Praising and Communing with All Creation

What scientists, original peoples and mystical traditions have been trying to tell us in a language we have not understood very well, is that all creation comes from one single source of life, wisdom and compassion (love that shares). God is giving himself to us in the grass that invites us to lie on it, in the dew that refreshes, in the wind, the cock crowing, crickets chirping, and in this miracle which is ourselves. The psalmist was right to cry: "For so many marvels I thank you; a wonder am I and all your works are wonders" (Ps. 139:14). God shares himself with us in what we are, and in this gift of love that surrounds us, even in what we have thought of as our very own, our self-awareness. So it makes sense to share fully in life's festival, the praise of all creation.

We are not alone or isolated, we never have been. Because we are in communion with everything that is. We are the fruit of Love, Wisdom, the Life Force. From the spiritual desert of the sick human heart that is isolated, afraid, possessive, comes all the negative power (sin) which erodes and destroys itself, others and the very earth. Likewise, from the fruitful love of the open and wholesome heart springs praise, abundant life, gratitude and rejoicing in all that exists. Being converted to love means beginning to share more and more in the praise, adoration and communion of all creatures. Life and its continuation on the planet is only possible because it is a dynamic process of sharing, communing with one another.

This is what we mean by ecological balance. Only now we are beginning to understand that there is no waste in nature. Even death itself means life for the whole. From microbes to human beings, we are all designed for the subsistence of all. We could say that life truly consists of living in communion.[8]

This is the spiritual meaning of the incarnation of the Logos. In creation God breathes life into us. In the incarnation the Logos itself shares in the same matter of which we are made. It envelops itself in the dust which we are, and thus, as it were, enters into that constant ecological communion which is the life of the earth and all its creatures. The incarnation unites heaven and earth (Phil. 2): the incomprehensible mystery of life and the actual life of human beings on earth, what we see and what we cannot see.

This was Jesus' whole life: sharing and sharing himself. Because he shared bread, the fruit of men and women's labor, the fruit of the earth, he could call himself the bread of life. Even in the face of death he maintained this attitude of self-giving and gave himself up to it without resisting. Even after he rose from the dead, the disciples on the road to

Emmaus sat down to table with him as a stranger, and recognized him when he broke bread and shared it.

The words of the cultural historian William Irving Thompson are illuminating here: "When Jesus takes the bread and wine and says: 'Take this in memory of me, because it is my body and blood,' he is not the masochistic psychopath imagined by Freud, but a poet with an ecological vision of life, which uses myth and symbol to express that all life eats and is eaten by one another. The Upanishads express this idea in a different poetic language when they say: 'The earth is food; the air lives on the earth; the earth is air; they are food for one another.'"

Therefore St. Paul's theological idea of Christ's mystical body is a vision of a planetary being, a single cell in which all of us are individual particles. If sharing food is the mainspring and source of our original humanity, then we really fulfill this humanity when we eat together.[9]

Wasn't this perhaps what Jesus was teaching us in the multiplication of the loaves and fishes? The first Christians understood that communion fundamentally meant sharing, being life for one another. This is not a matter of theology but of spirit. And it is a question of sharing not just the earth and its products but all the resources that a few people concentrate in their own hands, claiming they own them: information, knowledge, culture, points of view, methods, struggles, disasters and victories, worries and dreams: life.

Jesus is life sharing itself, resurrection and salvation. When people learn to share and share themselves, we will know what "ecology of awareness" means. The life of our mother the earth depends on this change. And "what happens to the earth will happen to earth's children."

NOTES

1. R. H. Stram and U. Oswald, *Por esto somos pobres*, Cuernavaca, Mexico, 1990, pp. 21, 23, 27, 35, 37.
2. W. I. Thompson, *GAIA: Implicaciones de la nueva biología*, Barcelona, pp. 117–21.
3. Id., *Biología: La naturaleza vuelve a la vida integral nueva concienza*, Barcelona, pp. 123f.
4. F. Capra, *The Tao of Physics*, London and New York, 1983, pp. 160, 167.
5. D. Zohar, *La conciencia cuántica*, Barcelona, pp. 86–88.
6. Quoted in P. Russell, *La tierra inteligente*, Madrid, 1992, p. 21.
7. A. Vittachi, ed., *Simposium sobre la tierra*, Barcelona, p. 116.
8. Thompson, *La naturaleza vuelve a la vida*, (n. 3), p. 103.
9. Ibid.

36

Justified by All Her Children

Struggle, Memory, and Vision

ELISABETH SCHÜSSLER FIORENZA

Often, when a Puerto Rican woman is asked how she is, how things are going, she will respond with "Pues, ahi, en la lucha" ("well, struggling" or "in the struggle"). This phrase, therefore, represents a statement about survival, a comment on economic and social circumstances, a comment on coping and perseverance, and contains seeds of a commitment to be engaged, to be in struggle.[1]

Feminist theology begins with a critical reflection on and systemic analysis of experience. It seeks to write theology out of our experiences and back into our experiences. Such experiences are particular and multivocal. Rather than to repeat throughout the article the "confessional" formula: "white, German, alien living in America, middle-aged, professional, married, theologian, Roman Catholic, feminist and so on" in order to particularize my own limited experience and heterogeneous identity, I have chosen epigrams to place my analysis into the context of other feminist struggles.[2] These "voices" seek to interrupt and at the same time to contextualize the universalizing tendencies of my own arguments: I begin with questioning the historical contextualization of our theological reflections here and by re-situating them in the context of "democratic" struggles around the globe. Then I move to a critical hermeneutical model of interpretation that can recover the Christian memory surfacing in a particular New Testament text. To understand Galatians 3:28 and its interpretations as a site of rhetorical argument and struggle allows us to reclaim it as "subversive memory" for today.

I

> ... if Miriam lies buried in sand
> why must we dig up those bones?
> Why must we remove her from sand
> and stone where she belongs?
>
> The one who knows not how to question
> she has no past,
> she can have no present,
> she can have no future,
> without knowing her mother,
> without knowing her angers
> without knowing her questions.[3]

At first, I welcomed the opportunity to discuss at [*Concilium*] the hermeneutical model for biblical interpretation which I have developed in the context of a critical feminist theology of liberation. Strategic elements in such a critical feminist hermeneutical model are conscientization and suspicion, historical reconstruction and remembrance, theological assessment and evaluation, creative imagination and ritualization.[4]

The historical sites of a critical interpretation for liberation[5] are the diverse struggles to overcome patriarchal[6] oppression structured by racism, class-exploitation, sexism, and colonialist militarism. Its aim is to recover biblical history as memory and heritage of the *ekklēsia*, of women-church. Therefore, it seeks to retrieve early Christian history not just as the memory of suffering and victimization. It also seeks to re-possess this heritage as the memory of those who have shaped Christian history as religious interlocutors, agents of change, and survivors[7] in the struggle against patriarchal domination.

To that end a critical feminist *hermeneutics of suspicion* interrogates the rhetorical strategies of biblical texts as to their oppressive dynamics or liberating visions in particular situations. For instance, the narratives of Christ's passion are deeply entwined with anti-Judaism. Their formulaic enunciation continues the patriarchal narrative of the divine Father sacrificing his Son. Or: the apocalyptic vision of a "new world" presupposes the destruction of this world. One cannot simply assume that androcentric biblical symbols and texts such as Exodus,[8] Galatians 3:28, or the Magnificat are liberating. Rather they must be contextualized and tested out in a critical process of reinterpretation. Such a process must be repeated again and again in particular contexts if it is to be a critical reflection, empowering heritage, and liberating vision for the struggle to overcome patriarchal relations within biblical religions and cultures.

At first glance then, the invitation to explore the "liberative potential and vision" of Christian history and theology which has been often "contradicted by the empirical history of the Christian churches," seems to have a perfect "fit" with my own hermeneutical interests. However, this "fit" is seriously in question when one looks at the overall theme of this Congress: "Church and World on the Threshold of the Third Millennium." This theme was chosen to celebrate the twenty-fifth anniversary of *Concilium* and what it stands for. It seeks to chart the theological direction and ecclesial influence of its work "on the threshold of the third millennium."

But why not reclaim our Jewish roots and posit our discourse on the threshold of the last quarter of the sixth millennium? To situate the discourses of *Concilium* in terms of Christian historical periods unwittingly contextualizes them within "the history of the winners." To place the world on the threshold of the third millennium asserts universalistic historical significance for Christian ethnocentrism and its structures of domination. It calls for a *hermeneutics of suspicion* rather than for a *hermeneutics of consent and remembrance*.

To interrupt the reality-constrictions of the "historical winners," feminist historians have argued, one must question the organizing categories of their histories. Hegemonic historiography utilizes schemes of dividing history into periods as a principal means of evaluative interpretation. For instance, Joan Kelly has argued that the Renaissance was not a Renaissance for European women.

> To take the emancipation of women as a vantage point is to discover that events that further the historical development of men, liberating them from natural, social, or ideological constraints, have quite different, even opposite effects upon women.[9]

Similarly, one could ask whether the Second Vatican Council was a historical watershed for women in Roman Catholicism. The celebration of twenty-five years of *Concilium* means something different for Catholic women from what it does for men, just as the 500th anniversary of the "discovery of the Americas" evokes memories for Native Americans, African Americans, or Asian Americans different from those for Euro-Americans. As Bishop Ricardo Ramirez reminded the U.S. hierarchy at their recent meeting:

> "500 years of evangelization in the Americas" is not something to be celebrated. Because what happened 500 years ago was the beginning of the plunder of the earth...the enslavement of many peoples, the genocide of millions, the elimination of indigenous

peoples on this continent. There was a terrible clash of cultures, and not all were winners.[10]

The classification schemes and organizing categories which we use to construct hegemonic history as memory and identify for the present are not disinterested and value-neutral. Rather they are rhetorical-political. That history is written by the winners has become a commonplace among liberation theorists and theologians, but it is hotly contested by objectivist historical scholarship. However, the recent events in China have graphically proven the truth of this dictum.

After the world had watched on satellite TV the peaceful mass demonstrations for greater democracy, human rights, and freedom of expression, we were stunned and horrified by the bloodbath in Tiananmen Square and elsewhere. The swift official denial of what had happened and its immediate re-interpretation on national and global television produced even more violence, bloodshed and repression. It painfully showed *how* history is written by the winners. Those Chinese who expressed outrage to Western reporters were publicly punished; those on the wanted list were denounced by relatives; workers and student leaders of the pro-democracy movement were executed as "thugs" and counter-revolutionaries; the bloodstains in Tiananmen Square have been painted over and the corpses burnt immediately so no one could accurately count the dead.

Public commentary in the U.S. media wrote history *differently* but still re-wrote it. When it became clear that condemnations by the Bush government would remain tepid in order not to jeopardize U.S. business and military interests, the media did not analyze this as the bankruptcy of democratic policy. Instead commentary on the worldwide failure of communism increased. No connections were made between the bloodshed in Central America and that in Tiananmen Square. As time went on, the Chinese government was seen as re-establishing "law and order." The leaders of the pro-democracy movement in turn were characterized as young, naive, and without a political program. In the process the Goddess of Freedom became the "Statue of Liberty" heralding venture capitalism. That a young woman, Chai Ling, had emerged as one of the movement's major moral leaders was barely registered at all.[11]

This contextualization of my reflections in recent political events should make it clear why a critical feminist theology of liberation cannot position itself "on the threshold of the third millennium." While Christendom moves toward this threshold, this is not the case for "the world." For many cultures and religions in the world, Jews, Chinese, Iranians or the aboriginal peoples of Australia — to mention just a few — the locution "third millennium" does not herald the inbreaking future. It has long become a part of the past to be remembered. Dividing history into periods "before and after Christ" posits the birth of Christ as a universal historical watershed keeping alive Christian imperialism and cultural prerogatives. At the same time it erases from our historical consciousness the fact that Christianity is only one moment in the cultural and religious history of the world.

II

The root of oppression is loss of memory. An odd thing occurs in the minds of Americans when Indian civilization is mentioned: little or nothing.... How odd then must my contention seem that the gynocratic tribes of the American continent provided the basis for all the dreams of liberation that characterize the modern world.... The vision that impels feminists to action was the vision of the Grandmothers' society, the society that was captured in the words of the sixteenth-century explorer Peter Martyr nearly five hundred years ago. It is the same vision repeated over and over by radical thinkers of Europe and America...That vision as Martyr told it, is of a country where there are "no soldiers, no gendarmes or police, no nobles, kings, regents, prefects, or judges, no prisons, no lawsuits.... All are equal and free" or so Friedrich Engels recounts Martyr's words.[12]

If what we see depends on where we stand, then we must locate our theological discourse at another historical watershed. *Concilium* must situate the reflection of the "liberating and burdening memories from the past of the Church and the world" *differently*. While Christendom stands on the threshold of the third millennium, the world stands at a different crossroads. Satellite dishes, telecommunications, fax machines, global ecological movements, the threat of nuclear and biological accidents and warfare, mass tourism, the displacement of whole populations because of war, hunger, poverty, and political or religious persecution have increased our awareness of global interdependence. They have made us neighbors in the "global village." Either this "global village" will realize the "Grandmothers' society" and become a global democratic confederation governed by the well-being of all its citizens. Or it will turn into a tightly controlled and manipulated patriarchal dictatorship that concentrates all economic and cultural resources in the hands of a few and assigns the majority to a permanent dehumanized underclass. Or the world will have no future at all.

Democratic movements around the globe struggle to reclaim the "power of the people" in the face of military dictatorship, terrorism, political trials, torture, and execution. In her 1989 Harvard commencement address Prime Minister Benazir Bhutto of Pakistan, herself a survivor of political repression, called for the creation of an Association of Democratic Nations to "forge a consensus around the most powerful political idea in the world today — the right of people to freely choose their government," and to "promote what is a universal value — democracy." Its members would cooperate in the protection of human rights, principles of justice, and due process. Such an Association could set up international channels for supervising elections and for giving economic assistance and moral force to fragile emerging democracies.

To situate the work of *Concilium* and those associated with it on the threshold of the global *polis,* is to call for a multi-voiced theological "forum" that can nurture a critical theological "rainbow theology."[13] Such a "rainbow coalition" (Jesse Jackson) could begin to articulate a multi-cultural, multi-ecclesial, and multi-religious catholic theology rooted in particular struggles for liberation and democracy around the globe. Affirming cultural and religious particularity and pluralism, such a "rainbow theology" must claim as its "common ground" the commitment to the struggles of all non-persons[14] for dignity, freedom, and well-being. It can do so because it has a common faith in a liberating God[15] who is "justified (*edikaiothe*) by all Her children" (Luke 7:35).

Acknowledging the example of Western democratic institutions, Benazir Bhutto nevertheless asserts that in her country the love of freedom and human rights "arises fundamentally from the strong egalitarian spirit that pervades Islamic traditions." She points to herself, a Muslim woman and Prime Minister of hundred millions of Muslims, as the living refutation of the argument that Pakistan cannot be a democratic country because it is Muslim. Bhutto does not defend the spirit of Islam as democratic over and against competing interpretations. She also affirms the role of religion in the liberation struggle. Islamic religion and its strong democratic ethos, she insists, have inspired and provided sustenance to our democratic struggle — "faith in the righteousness of our cause, faith in the Islamic teaching that 'tyranny cannot long endure.' The criterion for measuring whether a religion is democratic and liberating, consists in the practical test whether it allows for the full participation and leadership of women."

Listening to her words I asked myself whether I could speak with the same confidence of the democratic ethic and spirit of Roman Catholicism as Benazir Bhutto does of Islam. Not only did the Roman Church defend monarchy as the "divinely ordained" form of the state until very recently. Its leaders still insist today that the Church is not a democracy. I do not need to list the silencing of dissent, the exclusion of loyal critics, or the violations of basic civil rights and religious freedoms which we have seen in the past ten years or so. Obedience, submission of intellect and will, uncritical loyalty to the Pope, and especially silence are the patriarchal virtues required of the "faithful" theologian, nun, clergy, and laity. Although, unlike the Chinese gerontocracy, the ecclesiastical Fathers in the Vatican no longer have the power of internment and execution, they nevertheless still have the power to ruin the lives of their most faithful "sons and daughters," if they are economic, professional, or spiritual dependents.

Members of the *Concilium* have articulated different theological analyses and visions in this struggle to transform the patriarchal Church into the Church of the people of God. In this struggle for a participatory Church in service of the poor and disadvantaged some of us have been among the most prominent victims of ecclesiastical repression. However, this struggle for a more democratic and inclusive Church often appears to be waged as a power-struggle between "fathers and sons" in a man's Church rather than as a struggle for the freedom to "vision" and articulate a democratic-ecumenical "rainbow theology" and practice for the emerging global *polis.*

If one accepts Prime Minister Bhutto's practical criterion that one can judge whether a religion can sustain and nurture a democratic society by whether it allows for women to exercise leadership, then such a "rainbow theology" on the threshold of the "global village" must be created in a feminist/womanist key. How far away Catholic theology still is from doing so, can be judged by the exclusion of women not only from decision making and sacramental powers but also from the teaching "authority"[16] of theologians.

Since the control of public discourse is a central element of maintaining authority and power (Foucault), the absence of central feminist questions from public theological discourse is another form of our ecclesial exclusion. True, many theological institutions admit women as students and some as professors, but they do so only so long as we accept the androcentric norms of scholarship and respect the boundaries of patriarchal doctrine. Feminist theologies remain a women's issue and as such do not affect the central questions of theological discourse. Allow me to illustrate my point:

Contemplating the magnificent mosaics of Ravenna, I was struck by the absence of women in the iconography of the two baptistries: Their center is occupied by a decidedly male Christ surrounded by the twelve apostles (one of whom is Paul!) waiting to be baptized by John while the river-god Jordan is the witness. When I remarked that to anyone not familiar with Christian iconography the Orthodox as well as the Arian baptistry gives the impression of being a shrine of initiation for an all-male cult, this observation was considered to be "cute." Some moved away without comment, obviously embarrassed by my irreverence. Others pointed out that such a moralistic perspective does not do justice to the beauty of the artistic expression. Inspired by the sheep iconography of other mosaics one colleague sought to persuade me to develop a "theology of sheep" because of their traditional connection with the laity and in view of the ecological crisis. When told about my observation another colleague responded crisply: The past is past. One cannot change it!

It would not be worthwhile to recall this episode if it were not typical. Feminist scholars have observed again and again that feminist questions are met with silence, trivialization, displacement, co-optation, or historical positivism.[17] Postmodern feminist theory has explored how Western thought is articulated by elite white men who define rationality as masculine and therefore exclusive of women.[18] This is the structural reason why academic institutions cannot permit women to emerge as investigating subjects[19] and shapers of theory in our own right or allow feminist questions to become a central theoretical focus of academic disciplines. Our published work must remain marginal in the master-discourse of the university, if they mention it at all.

Whether and how in the face of the overwhelming androcentric and patriarchal character of Western tradition, culture, and religion Christian theology can articulate a "dangerous memory" (J. B. Metz) and liberating vision in "solidarity with the historical losers" and theological non-subjects who are women, remains to be seen. As long as this question continues to be just a "woman's question," androcentric theological scholarship will consider it a theological non-question. This fundamental question propelling feminist theoretical, historical, and theological work will continue to be a theological "non-question," as long as its structural and ideological underpinnings are not changed. While some feminist scholars contend that we should affirm our position on the margins of the academy, I have argued that a critical feminist/womanist[20] theology of liberation must move its work into the center of the struggles to transform patriarchal institutions.[21]

Insofar as theology as an intellectual and ecclesiastical discipline — be it conservative, liberal, political, or liberation theology — shares in the patriarchal paradigm of Church and academy, it constitutes an important site of struggle for feminist/womanist discourse. Biblical interpretations and canonical texts are a site of competing arguments and struggles[22] rather than the terrain of facts unearthed by historical scholarship, the quarry of prooftexts for systematic theologians, or the vendor of spiritual consumer goods. Rather than succumb to the historical positivism of fact or to the theological positivism of "given" revelation, biblical interpretation must become a critical interpretation for liberation. As such it must lay open the rhetorical character of competing theological arguments and ecclesial interests in biblical texts and their later interpretations to assess them in terms of the liberation struggle.

III

To write as a complete Caribbean woman, or man for that matter, demands of us retracing the African past of ourselves, reclaiming as our own, and our subject a history sunk under the sea, or scattered as potash in the canefields, or gone to bush, or trapped in a class system notable for its rigidity and absolute dependence on color stratification. On a past bleached from our minds. . . . It means realizing our knowledge will always be wanting. It means also, I think, mixing in the forms taught us by the oppressor, undermining his language and co-opting his style, and turning it to our purpose.[23]

Canvassing the exegetical literature on Galatians 3:28c[24] one discovers two seemingly different strategies of interpretation: one theological and the other critical-historical. However, a closer scrutiny shows that despite its historical-critical posture the second suffers from theological bias as much as the first.

Over and against those who claim Galatians 3:28 as a *magna carta* and authoritative prooftext for equality, emancipation, and liberation, traditional exegesis has insisted that the text must be understood in a religious but not in a social or ecclesial sense: Paul teaches that all are equal before God and that oneness and equality belong to the soul. Galatians 3:28 speaks of eschatological equality, i.e., we will be equal in heaven or in the eschaton. Or it is argued: Spiritual interpersonal relationships between Christians have changed, but role and status differences remain. Some scholars even claim that Galatians 3:28 speaks of equal membership but not of equal leadership in the Church.

Widespread in popular and scholarly works is the interpretation which uses the dogmatic categories of "order of creation" and "order of redemption," though neither expression is found in the New Testament.[25] While some traditionalists maintain that women have a different role from men in the order of creation *as well as* in the order of redemption, others argue that before God all are equal. In baptism all have received the gifts of the Spirit and have equal standing before God, but this standing does not extend to their status in society or in the Church.

In his review of the secondary literature on Galatians 3:28, Hans Dieter Betz, who in no way can be suspected of liberation theological bias, has observed that commentaries on Galatians "have consistently denied that Paul's statements have political implications." According to him scholars are prepared to state the opposite of what Paul actually says, in order to preserve a purely "religious" interpretation. In doing so they can strongly emphasize the reality of equality *coram deo* and also "deny that any conclusions can be drawn from this in regard to or about the ecclesiastical office(!) and the political order."[26] While in the last century this "purely religious" argument was often directed against the emancipation of slaves, in this century it is used especially against the ordination of women.

Historical-critical interpretations have come to the form-critical consensus that Galatians 3:26–28 contains pre-Pauline traditional material connected with baptism. The core of this tradition surfaces in Galatians 3:28abc, consisting of three parallel statements: "There is neither Jew nor Greek. There is neither slave nor free. There is no male *and* female." Such a distinction between the pre-Pauline tradition and the Pauline quotation or reformulation of it in Galatians 3:28 and 1 Corinthians 12:13 (and Colossians 3:10–11) allows scholars to explain Paul's theological corrections of the tradition. However, exegetes disagree on whether Paul quotes a "baptismal formula," a "baptismal macarism," a "dominical saying" (verse 28c) or just refers to a traditional baptismal topos. They differ also on the extent of the traditional material and on how to trace its transmission.

The *crux interpretationis* is the statement in verse 28c "neither male and female" since its formulation differs from the first two. These form-critical disagreements lead to competing historical reconstructions and theological interpretations. Every exegete marshals arguments why his/her interpretation is the only valid one and why all the others are faulty. It should be obvious by now that I am not interested here to make the case why my own interpretation is the only accurate historical interpretation since this would deny the multivalency of texts. Rather I want to explore the theological implications of each interpretative strategy for women's liberation struggles. The theologically telling point in every historical-critical interpretation of Galatians 3:28 is how one makes sense of the final statements in verse 28c.

IV

We have seen what words can do. They can heal. They can destroy. They can be spears. They can be prayers. Words can create worlds. Destroy them. Demolish them.... Words can sometimes, by grace, attain the quality of deeds.[27]

Galatians 3:28c, it is generally agreed, does not just abolish social roles but declares that no biological sex differences between male and female exist. It speaks of anthropological unification but not of social equality. This misreading of the text in terms of biological positivism leads to the development of three interpretative strategies:

The *first* strategy acknowledges that the baptismal tradition of Galatians 3:28 speaks about the fervent belief that in baptism the status distinctions between Jews and Greeks, slave and free, and men and women are overcome among Christians. Paul and the household code texts of the post-Pauline literature in turn seek to correct this illusory fantasy of realized eschatology. By dialectically relating Galatians 3:28 with Paul's statements on marriage, women, and slaves in 1 Corinthians and with the *Haustafel* tradition, this interpretation discredits Galatians 3:28 by arguing that its vision had led to social excesses among slaves and women. The spiritual enthusiasts supposedly held that the eschaton had already come and that therefore all sexual and social differences had been abolished. This first interpretative strategy disparages the experience of liberation and equality expressed in Galatians 3:28 as "pre-gnostic," body-denying enthusiasm. It theologically justifies the patriarchal ethos expressed in the *Haustafel* texts.

The *second* approach is "anthropological." It concedes, Galatians 3:28ab could mean that the religious, cultural, and social divisions between Jews and Greeks, slave and free are abolished in the Christian community, since such utopian dreams were alive in antiquity. However, this interpretation continues, such a social interpretation is not possible in view of verse 28c, since the utopian tradition of antiquity could not envision the total abolishment of social sex differences. Therefore, the text is best understood as utopian androgyny rather than as socio-political emancipation. Jewish, Greco-Roman, and especially later Christian gnostic writings testify to the belief that the primordial being was hermaphrodite (male and female) or androgynous (male/female).

If the Christ-Anthropos myth is in the background of verse 28c, then the text states that baptism into Christ has engendered a new androgynous nature of the redeemed. This meant "a metaphysical removal of the *biological* sex distinctions." The "reunification" language of Galatians 3:28abc has its *Sitz im Leben* in the baptismal rite. It is a "performative utterance" and solemn pronouncement. Reinforced by dramatic gesture and ritual it had the power to shape the symbolic universe by which the early Christian group distinguished itself from the surrounding "world." Over against such a "sectarian consciousness" rooted in utopian fantasy and "metaphysical rebellion," Paul insists on the eschatological "not yet" and on the *symbols* of the present differentiated order. Women remain women and men remain men and dress accordingly.[28]

The most recent variation of this "androgynous" interpretation argues that Paul has reworked the tradition of Galatians 3:28 by changing verse 28c from "neither male or female" to "male and female" as well as by adding himself the pairs "neither Jew or Greeks, slave or free." Galatians 3:28c represents a traditional "dominical saying" which occurs only in later gnostic texts but is an oral tradition widespread in certain segments of the early Church. Its meaning lies in Platonic philosophy, perhaps mediated by Philo and Apollos. It assumes that the return to "primordial perfection" entailed the "disembodied sexless state." It was a return to the divine image which was essentially male. Paul in turn rejects the anthropological unification theology of the dominical saying's tradition and insisted on the social unity.

> The initiate must put on Christ. Not put off the flesh. Baptism is not a mystery rite insuring the initiate of oneness with God or with one's heavenly syzygy, but a symbol of social unity in Christ. The church is the new creation in which alienated social groups — Jews/Greeks, slaves/free, men/women — were united.[29]

In short, whatever their historical reconstructions and interpretative strategies, all three "anthropological" interpretations are bent on proving Paul's theology right. They do so by using the dualistic framework either of heresy-orthodoxy, illusion-reality, or realized eschatology-created order. Therefore they read Galatians 3:28c in terms of biological sex rather than social gender distinctions. Moreover, these interpretations take androcentric language at face value. They never question whether not only the third pair of Galatians 3:28 but also the other two pairs Jew/Greek, slave/free speak of men *and* women. Therefore they cannot develop an interpretative model that can make visible the historical "losers," for whom baptism and *ekklêsia* signified a *different* socio-political community, and assembly of equals in the power of the spirit.

The *third* interpretative approach which I have developed in my own work,[30] started with the linguistic difference between the first two "neither-nor" and the last "neither-and" statement of Galatians 3:28. It recognizes that Galatians 3:28c refers to Genesis 1:27 which Jewish exegesis did not understand primarily as connoting primordial androgyny but generally saw it, in the light of Genesis 2 and 3, referring to patriarchal marriage, family and procreation. Verse 28c is therefore best translated by "neither husband and wife." Judaism and Greco-Roman antiquity held that marriage and procreation are civic-religious duties because the family is the foundation and nucleus of the state as well as of religion. Against this social norm which is still alive today, Galatians

3:28c asserts that the institution of marriage is no longer constitutive for the *ekklēsia*, the democratic assembly of free citizens. The Jewish scholar Raphael Loewe perceptively has drawn out the implications of such an interpretation.

> The sociological basis on which Christianity rests is not kinship, as in the case of Judaism, but fellowship [sic] — fellowship in Christ. Such fellowship may acknowledge kinship as a potential ally, it may regard it indifferently . . . or it may repudiate it. . . . Whichever the position it adopts, the ties of kinship are, for Christianity, in the last resort expendable.[31]

This a-familial ethos of Galatians 3:28 does not only assert that religious-cultural status divisions and exploitative dehumanizing relationships between masters and slaves do not define relationships in the Christian community. It also declares that the order of the patriarchal household is not constitutive for it. The text repeats with different social categories that no structures of domination and social-religious elite male privileges exist within the Christian community. By denying the religious and social prerogatives of Jewish males as well as masters and husbands, it accords wives, Jewish women, gentile and slave women and men the new status, equality, and freedom of ecclesial citizenship.

Galatians 3:28 is therefore best understood as a communal-ecclesial self-definition rather than as an anthropological statement about the individual Christian. This third interpretation does not come to the defense of Paul by blaming the historical and theological victims. Nor does it erase from our consciousness that Jews, Greeks, slaves, and freeborn were also women. It can make non-persons visible because it recognizes that gender relations are socially constructed rather than biologically or divinely ordained.

However, one can only comprehend the full significance of such a reading if one does not understand Galatians 3:28 as a climactic statement of Pauline theology, as a prooftext for the "egalitarianism" of early Christianity or as a window to early Christian reality. Only if one contextualizes it within a historical model of socio-political struggle does its historical and theological significance emerge.

A feminist hermeneutics and model of historical reconstruction seeks to reshape our historical and theological self-understanding.[32] It can do so, by displacing for instance androcentric texts and interpretations that marginalize women and other non-persons or silence them altogether. Androcentric language and patriarchal text presuppose women's historical presence and agency but usually do not articulate it. The records of the historical winners marginalize, trivialize, erase and declare as deviant the historical struggles of the subordinated "others" who have refused to become defined by the hegemonic patriarchal politics of inequality and dehumanization.

If androcentric texts and patriarchal records produce the marginality and absence of the "non-persons" in our historical and theological records, then one cannot take these sources as reliable mirror-images of reality. Rather, they must be decoded as complex ideological constructions. The tensions, fissures, contradictions, prescriptions, arguments, and symbolic projections inscribed in androcentric source texts still allow us to read the documents of the historical winners against their linguistic and ideological grain.

V

I am a Black woman writing in a world that defines human as white and male for starters. Everything I do including survival is political.[33]

The contextualization of our interpretations in historical and present experiences of struggle enables us to read their "silences," to fill the "blank spaces" in the text, and to decode the rhetorical strategies of hegemonic texts and interpretations.[34] As rhetorical texts, androcentric biblical texts construct a world in which those whose arguments they oppose either become the "deviant" "others" or are no longer heard at all. Yet freeborn women as well as slave women and men were present in the early Christian movements not only as victims but also as historical agents and theological interlocutors.

My own work has tried to develop such a historical and theological reconstructive model as a political model.[35] I have done so by exploring the contradiction between the experience of patriarchal social-political-religious stratifications on the one side and the experience and vision of democratic structures and well-being for all on the other. Together with other New Testament texts, Galatians 3:28 indicates that such social-political-religious tensions and conflicts existed. They arose between the Christian "house-church" that does not admit of patriarchal household stratifications and its dominant societal patriarchal contexts. This conflict between the early Christian movement and its dominant society soon became also a conflict between the structures and theologies of the *ekklēsia* and those of the household model of Church.[36]

This political contradiction can serve as a heuristic model for reconstructing the rhetorical situation of struggle in the early Christian movements. In such a model diverse texts — such as texts about women's leadership, clues about the life and organization of early Christian communities, Galatians 3:28, Paul's statements in 1 Corinthians and elsewhere, the list of greetings in Romans 16, the household code tradition and its ecclesial adaptation in the Pastorals, Ignatius or 1 Clement — all these texts can be interrelated with each other as an ongoing rhetorical argument.

Such a displacement of texts from their androcentric contexts allows one to re-member them in terms of the conflict that has generated the patriarchal politics of otherness and submission. It allows one to reconstruct memory as a historical-social "subtext" of pre-Pauline, Pauline, and post-Pauline Christianity in its political, societal, cultural, and religious historical contexts. Such a rhetorical-political model of reconstruction also helps one to see the cultural dependencies and effects of this early Christian debate which still surfaces in our New Testament.

The early Christian writings are not the first historical instance where we can locate such a contradiction and debate, nor are they the last ones.[37] The contradiction between the democratic experience and vision of society and religion on the one hand and that of the patriarchal structures of the exploitation and domination on the other, has defined classical Greek philosophies, especially those of Plato and Aristotle,[38] Christian theologies from the New Testament to Augustine, Thomas Aquinas, the Reformers, Kierkegaard, Schleiermacher and up to our own times. It also has generated the Enlightenment articulation of reason and academic disciplines.[39] These hegemonic philosophies and theologies are explicit arguments for the power of the elite men as historical, cultural, and religious subjects. Invoking nature, reason, or divine will, they produce arguments for the exclusion of all his subordinated and subjugated Others as "non-persons" from decision-making citizenship.

To contextualize Galatians 3:28 in a reconstructive model of social-political-religious struggle rather than in that of "orthodoxy-heresy" or "order of creation-redemption" allows us to contextualize our present struggles historically. It enables us to reconstruct early Christian history and theology as memory and vision for the present. It also helps us to understand why the status of all women — not just of elite women — must become the practical criterion for whether a religion can sustain democratic structures and visions.

In short, such a reconstructive model can make the historical "losers" whom the androcentric text excludes, marginalizes, or vilifies centrally present as theological interlocutors and historical subjects. Its *hermeneutic of remembrance* does not work within the constraints of the antiquarian empiricist-factual or the scientific constructivist-value neutral paradigms of historical studies. Rather it explicitly situates itself within the rhetorical emancipatory paradigm of historiography. It does so, because only this paradigm can theoretically acknowledge that historians reconstruct the past in the interest of the present and the future.

Our search for memory and roots is neither antiquarian nor nostalgic, but political, because reconstructions of past reality shape our present historical consciousness. Yet, emancipatory reconstruction of our cultural and religious past is not a fictive creation out of nothing. Rather, it is a disciplined argument for a *different* historical consciousness and imagination. It can engender a theological articulation of Christian identity as a multi-cultural, multi-ecclesial, and multi-religious identity. To be cosmopolitan, democratic, and catholic this identity must remain particular, heterogeneous and provisional, subject to destabilization, renegotiation, and recreation in the diverse liberation struggles.

However, a *hermeneutics of critical theological evaluation* must go hand in hand with such a *hermeneutics of remembrance,* because Christians live texts such as Galatians 3:28 not as *memoria* but proclaim them as authoritative Scripture. Feminists rightly reject the project of reconstruction as one more form of Christian apologetics[40] if it is not accompanied by a critical theological assessment and evaluation of androcentric biblical texts.

Without question, the letter to the Galatians is an androcentric Pauline text that constructs a religious narrative and world in which women are absent. It is formulated to draw the boundary between the Christian group and its Jewish mother community. Its proclamation of equality and oneness in Christ has been understood as cultural and religious sameness. Oneness-theology has engendered the kind of hegemonic unitary Christian identity formulation that does not admit of catholicity as cultural, ecclesial and religious pluriformity and heterogeneity. To become conformed to the image of God or Christ, to achieve Christian identity has meant to "become male" in the horizon of Greek philosophy, Roman imperial theology, and of the Enlightenment, which defines reason and human subjectivity as elite male identity exclusive of *all* women as well as of men of colonialized races and cultures.

Whether such a feminist reading of Galatians 3–5 in terms of the patriarchal "politics of otherness" is justified, must be explored in a critical process of interpretation.[41] This question can only be adjudicated after a careful reading and theological assessment of the androcentric language and theology of Galatians 3–5 in the context of global struggles for freedom and well-being. 1 would suggest, therefore, that this paper is taken as an invitation for the [*Concilium*] discourse to continue such a critical feminist theological process of theological evaluation. To end without a conclusion is to refuse to offer answers to feminist questions that still have to be asked in the centers of patriarchal theology and Church.

NOTES

1. Iris Zavala-Martines, "En la Lucha: The Economic and Socioemotional Struggles of Puerto Rican Women," in Lenora Fulani, ed., *The Psychopathology of Everyday Racism and Sexism*, New York, 1988, pp. 3f.

2. Cf. R. Morgan, *Sisterhood Is Global: The International Women's Movement Anthology*, Garden City, 1984; V. Fabella and M. A. Oduyoye, eds., *With Passion and Compassion: Third World Women Doing Theology*, Maryknoll, N.Y., 1988; D. Eck and Devaki Jain, eds., *Speaking of Faith: Global Perspectives on Women, Religion and Social Change*, Philadelphia, 1987.

3. From "The Song of Questions" of *A Women's Passover Haggadah*, written by E. M. Broner and Naomi Nimrod.

4. See my book *Bread Not Stone: The Challenge of Feminist Biblical Interpretation*, Boston, 1985, and my article "A Feminist Critical Interpretation for Liberation: Martha and Mary: Luke 10:38–42," *Religion and Intellectual Life* 3, no. 2 (1986), pp. 21–36 and the discussions of it in H. Waetjen, ed., *Protocol of the 53rd Colloquy: April 10, 1986*, Berkeley: Center for Hermeneutical Studies, 1987.

5. K. G. Cannon and E. Schüssler Fiorenza. eds., *Interpretation for Liberation*, Atlanta, 1989.

6. I do not understand *patriarchy* either in the sense of sexism and gender dualism or use it as an undefined label. Rather, I construe the term in the "narrow sense" as "father-right and father-might." I understand it as a complex systemic interstructuring of sexism, racism, classism and cultural-religious imperialism that has produced the Western "politics of Otherness." Although patriarchy has adjusted throughout history, its Aristotelian articulation is still powerful today. For a review of the terminology see V. Beechey, "On Patriarchy," *Feminist Review* 3 (1979), pp. 66–82; G. Lerner, *The Creation of Patriarchy*, New York, 1986, pp. 231–41.

7. In distinction to liberation and political theologies, a critical feminist theology insists women cannot be understood just as victims of or collaborators in their oppression. "Solidarity with victims" does not suffice. The self-understanding of women as historical and theological subjects is crucial for a feminist theological reconstruction.

8. For an excellent exploration of this symbol in different theologies see B. Van Iersel and A. Weiler, eds., *Exodus: A Lasting Paradigm, Concilium* 189, Edinburgh, 1987. For a feminist critique of it see C. P. Christ, *Laughter of Aphrodite: Reflections on a Journey to the Goddess*, New York, 1987.

9. Joan Kelly, *Women, History, and Theory*, Chicago, 1984, p. 19.

10. As quoted by Pat Windsor in the *National Catholic Reporter* (30 June 1989), p. 4.

11. Chai Ling organized the hunger strike and took on primary leadership in Tiananmen Square rather than flee the country, although she was convinced that terrible bloodshed would happen. Cf. the *Koppel Report* broadcast by ABC on Tuesday, 19 June 1989.

12. Paula Gunn Allen, "Who Is Your Mother? Red Roots of White Feminism," in *Multicultural Literacy*, St. Paul, 1988, pp. 18f.

13. For the beginning of such an articulation see C. Geffré, G. Gutiérrez, and V. Elizondo, eds., *Different Theologies, Common Responsibility: Babel or Pentecost, Concilium* 171, Edinburgh, 1984.

14. For this expression see G. Gutiérrez, *The Power of the Poor in History,* Maryknoll, N.Y., 1984. It has the advantage that it overcomes the linguistic split between "women" and "the poor, black, Asian, etc.," since this linguistic convention insinuates that women are not black, poor, etc., as well as that black, poor, African or Asian people are not women. See also E. V. Spelman, *Inessential Woman: Problems of Exclusion in Feminist Thought,* Boston, 1988.

15. Cf. Sharon Welch, *Communities of Resistance and Solidarity,* Maryknoll, N.Y., 1985, p. 7: " . . . the referent of the phrase 'liberating God' is not primarily God but liberation. That is, the language here is true not because it corresponds with something in the divine nature but because it leads to actual liberation in history. The truth of God-language and of all theological claims is measured . . . by their fulfilment of its claims in history. . . . "

16. K. B. Jones, "On Authority: Or, Why Women Are Not Entitled to Speak," in I. Diamond and L. Quinby, eds., *Feminism and Foucault: Reflections on Resistance,* Boston, 1988, pp. 119–33.

17. Cf., e.g., A. March, "Female Invisibility in Androcentric Sociological Theory," *Insurgent Sociologist* 11, no. 2 (1982), pp. 99–107; B. Thiele, "Vanishing Acts in Social and Political Thought: Tricks of the Trade," in C. Patemann and E. Gross, *Feminist Challenges: Social and Political Theory,* Boston, 1986, pp. 30–43; and R. Braidotti, "Ethics Revisited: Women and/in Philosophy" ibid., pp. 44–60.

18. Cf. G. Lloyd, *The Man of Reason: "Male" and "Female" in Western Philosophy,* Minneapolis, 1984.

19. For the discussion of "women as subjects," cf. L. Alcoff, "Cultural Feminism Versus Post-Structuralism: The Identity Crisis in Feminist Theory," *Sign* 13 (1988), pp. 405–36; S. Harding, "Rethinking Modernism: Minority vs. Majority Theories," *Cultural Critique* 7 (1987), pp. 187–206.

20. For the expression "womanist" see K. G. Cannon, *Black Womanist Ethics,* Atlanta, 1988, and the forthcoming discussion in *Journal of Feminist Studies.*

21. See, e.g., my Society of Biblical Literature presidential address, "The Ethics of Biblical Interpretation: Decentering Biblical Scholarship," *Journal of Biblical Literature* 107 (1988), pp. 3–17 and my 1988 Harvard Divinity School Convocation address in *Harvard Theological Review.*

22. See my Mowinckel lecture, "Biblical Interpretation and Critical Commitment," *Studia Theologica* 43 (1989), pp. 5–18.

23. Michelle Cliff, "A Journey into Speech," in R. Simonson and S. Walker, eds., *Multicultural Literacy,* p. 59.

24. For extensive bibliographical references, cf. especially the work of H. D. Betz and D. R. MacDonald.

25. For this distinction see my analysis of the household code texts in *Bread Not Stone,* pp. 65–92.

26. H. D. Betz, *Galatians,* Philadelphia, 1979, p. 189 n. 68.

27. Elie Wiesel in dialogue with Robert McAfee Brown in Pacific School of Religion *Bulletin,* Spring 1989.

28. W. A. Meeks, "The Image of the Androgyne," *History of Religions* 13 (1974), p. 108.

29. D. R. MacDonald, *There Is No Male and Female,* Philadelphia, 1987, pp. 125f.

30. For the methodological discussion and execution of such a feminist reconstruction, see my book *In Memory of Her: A Feminist Theological Reconstruction of Christian Origins,* New York, 1983. Basic for such a *hermeneutics of reconstruction* is the distinction between androcentric text and patriarchal system and rhetoric. While all biblical texts are androcentric, i.e., written in grammatically masculine language, they do not all *advocate* patriarchal structures and values.

31. R. Loewe, *The Position of Women in Judaism,* London, 1966, pp. 52f.

32. For a more extensive discussion and bibliography see my article "Text and Reality — Reality as Text: The Problem of a Feminist Historical and Social Reconstruction Based on Texts," *Studia Theologica* 43 (1989), pp. 19–34.

33. Audre Lorde in *The Women's Review of Books* 6, nos. 10–11 (1989), p. 28.

34. Cf. J. Newton, "History as Usual? Feminism and the New Historicism," *Cultural Critique* 9 (1988), pp. 87–121; J. Allen, "Evidence and Silence: Feminism and the Limits of History," in *Feminist Challenges,* ibid., pp. 173–89.

35. See my article "The Politics of Otherness: Biblical Interpretation as a Critical Praxis for Liberation," in Gutiérrez, *Festschrift,* New York, 1989.

36. See my article "Die Anfänge von Kirche und Amt in feministisch-theologischer Sicht," in P. Hoffmann, ed., *Priesterkirche,* Düsseldorf, 1987, pp. 62–95.

37. See S. Moller Okin, *Women in Western Political Thought,* Princeton, 1979.

38. Cf. P. du Bois, *Centaurs and Amazons: Women and the Pre-history of the Great Chain of Being,* Ann Arbor, 1982; idem., *Sowing the Body: Psychoanalysis and Ancient Representation of Women,* Chicago, 1988.

39. Cf. Lowe and Hubbard, eds., *Women's Nature: Rationalizations of Inequality,* New York, 1981; R. May Schott, *Cognition and Eros,* Boston, 1988; S. Benhabib and D. Cornell, eds., *Feminism as Critique,* Minneapolis, 1987; T. de Lauretis, ed., *Feminist Studies/Critical Studies,* Bloomington, 1986. In general, American feminist theory, however, argues that the excluded "others" cannot abandon the Enlightenment's unfinished project of emancipation.

40. See L. Fatum, "Women, Symbolic Universe and Silence," paper read at the Nordisk Forskerkonferanse on "Feminist Reconstruction of Early Christian History: Methodological and Hermeneutical Questions" (9–11 November 1988), to be published.

41. For such a critical assessment see my forthcoming article "You Are 'Sons of God' — Are We? Gal 3:26–4:7 in a Feminist Theological Perspective."

Contributors

Anne Carr was born in Chicago. She studied at Marquette University and at the University of Chicago Divinity School, where she serves as a professor of theology. She has published numerous books, including *A Transforming Grace: Tradition, Symbol, and the Experience of Women*. She has served as a co-director of the Feminist Theology section of *Concilium*.

Chung Hyun Kyung has taught theology at Ewha Women's University in Seoul, Korea. Recently she was appointed to a chair in ecumenism at Union Theological Seminary in New York, where she previously received her doctorate in theology. She is the author of *Struggle to be the Sun Again: Introducing Asian Women's Theology*.

Mary Collins received her doctorate in religious studies at Catholic University in Washington, D.C., where she has also served as a professor of religion and religious education. A Benedictine, she is a founding member of Holy Wisdom Monastery in Wake Forest, N.C. She has served as president of the North American Academy of Liturgy and as a co-director of the Feminist Theology section of *Concilium*.

Mary Condren, a native of Ireland, received her doctorate in theology from Harvard Divinity School. She is the author of *The Serpent and the Goddess: Women, Religion, and Power in Celtic Ireland*.

M. Shawn Copeland is associate professor of theology (systematics) at Marquette University in Milwaukee, Wisconsin. She is a co-editor of the Feminist Theology section of *Concilium* and Associate Convener of the Black Catholic Theological Symposium.

Gabriele Dietrich is professor in the Department of Social Analysis at the Tamilnadu Theological Seminary, Madurai. She is a well-known activist in the women's movement and has also served as vice-president of Pennurimai Iyakkam (Movement for Women's Rights). Originally from Germany, she has lived and worked in India for twenty-four years and has become an Indian citizen.

Julia Esquivel (Velásquez) is a Guatemalan teacher and poet. She studied pastoral theology in the Latin American Biblical Seminary in Costa Rica and in the Bossey Ecumenical Institute in Switzerland. She has published several volumes of poetry.

Ivone Gebara is professor of philosophy and theology at the Theological Institute of Recife and works with base communities and women's groups in Northern Brazil. She has published widely on theology, women's studies, and ecofeminism. She is the co-author of *Mary: Mother of God, Mother of the Poor.*

Elisabeth Gössmann was born in Osnabrück in 1928. She is honorary professor at the Seishin University, Tokyo, and extracurricular professor in the Philosophical Faculty of the University of Munich. She written on the religious history of Japan and women's research in the history of philosophy and theology.

Mary Grey was born in the North of England and studied classics and philosophy at Oxford and theology at Louvain, where she received her doctorate. She is Professor of Feminism and Christianity at the Catholic University of Nijmegen, the Netherlands. She has served as President of the European Society for Women in Theological Research. Her books include *Redeeming the Dream: Feminism, Redemption, and Christianity.*

Catharina Halkes is emeritus professor of feminism and Christianity at the Catholic University of Nijmegen. She is one of the founders of the feminist theological journal *Mara,* and she has published numerous books on Christianity and feminism.

Teresia M. Hinga studied at Nairobi University and received a doctorate in religious studies from the University of Lancaster. Formerly a senior lecturer in the Department of Religious Studies at Kenyatta University, she is currently lecturing in religious studies at De Paul University in Chicago.

Mary Hunt is a feminist theologian from the Roman Catholic tradition. She is the co-founder and co-director of the Women's Alliance for Theology, Ethics, and Ritual, an educational organization in Silver Spring, Maryland. She is the author of *Fierce Tenderness: A Feminist Theology of Friendship.*

Elizabeth A. Johnson is Professor of Theology at Fordham University in New York. She has served as President of the Catholic Theological Society of America. She is the author of several books, including *She Who Is.*

Kwok Pui-lan, the foremost Chinese feminist theologian, received her doctorate at Harvard Divinity School and was formerly on the faculty of the Chinese University of Hong Kong. She is currently on the faculty of the Episcopal Divinity School in Cambridge, Massachusetts. She is the author of *Discovering the Bible in the Non-Biblical World.*

Nantawan Boonprasat Lewis, a native of Thailand, is associate professor of religious studies and ethnic studies at Metropolitan State University, St. Paul/Minneapolis, Minnesota. Actively involved with women's concerns in religion and society, she is co-editor of *Sisters Struggling in the Spirit: A Women of Color Theological Anthology.*

Sallie McFague is Carpenter Professor of Theology at the Vanderbilt School of Divinity. She is the author of numerous books, including *Metaphorical Theology* and *Models of God: Theology in an Ecological, Nuclear Age.*

Mary John Mananzan is National Chairperson of Gabriela, a national federation of women's organizations in the Philippines. A Benedictine, she is also the Dean of St. Scholastica's College in Manila and Director of the Institute of Women's Studies.

E. Ann Matter is Professor of Religious Studies at the University of Pennsylvania in Philadelphia. She is the author of *The Voice of My Beloved: The Song of Songs in Western Medieval Christianity* and the co-editor of *Creative Women in Medieval and Early Modern Italy*

Elisabeth Moltmann-Wendel has a doctorate in theology and writes in the areas of women, theology, and the church. Her publications include *The Women around Jesus, A Land Flowing with Milk and Honey,* and *I Am My Body.*

Diann Neu is a liturgist and psychotherapist, and co-founder and co-director of WATER: Women's Alliance for Theology, Ethics and Ritual. Among her books are *Women-Church Sourcebook* and *Women-Church Celebrations.*

Maria José F. Rosado Nunes is a Brazilian sociologist with a doctorate from the École des Hautes Études en Sciences Sociales in Paris. She is vice president of ISER (Institute for Religious Studies) in Rio de Janeiro and a member of the Brazilian Commission on Citizenship and Reproduction, as well as lecturing on the sociology of religion in São Paulo and holding the chair of feminist studies in São Bernardo do Campo.

Mercy Amba Oduyoye is a native of Ghana who has taught and lectured worldwide. She has served as deputy general secretary of the World Council of Churches in Geneva. Her books include *Hearing and Knowing: Theological Reflections on Christianity in Africa* and *Daughters of Anowa: African Women and Patriarchy.*

Adele Reinhartz is Associate Professor in the area of Judaism and Christianity in the Greco-Roman Era in the Department of Religious Studies, McMaster University in Hamilton, Ontario, Canada. She is the author of *Why Ask My Name? Anonymity and Identity in Biblical Narrative.*

Rosemary Radford Ruether is the Georgia Harkness Professor of Applied Theology at the Garrett-Evangelical Theological Seminary in Evanston, Illinois. Her many books include *Sexism and God-Talk, Women-Church: Theology and Practice of Feminist Liturgical Communities,* and *Disputed Questions.*

Marjorie Procter-Smith received her doctorate in Liturgical Studies from the University of Notre Dame. She has taught liturgy at the Perkins School of Theology in Dallas, Texas. Her books include *Women in Shaker Community and Worship.*

Christine Schaumberger is a German theologian with a particular specialty in feminist liberation theology. She is affiliated with the Gesamthochschule in Kassel, Germany.

Elisabeth Schüssler Fiorenza is Krister Stendahl Professor of New Testament Studies at Harvard Divinity School. A past president of the Society of Biblical Literature, she is the author of many books on New Testament studies and feminist hermeneutics, including *In Memory of Her: A Feminist Theological Reconstruction of Early Christian Origins, Bread Not Stone: The Challenge of Feminist Biblical Interpretation,* and *But She Said.*

Dorothee Sölle was born in Cologne, Germany. She holds graduate degrees from the universities of Göttingen and Cologne, and has taught philosophy, theology, and literature in several German universities and at Union Theological Seminary in New York. Her many books include *Thinking About God, Revolutionary Patience,* and *Of War and Violence.*

Eileen J. Stenzel received her doctorate in theology from the University of Notre Dame. She has taught theology, religious education, and women's studies, and has experience in career counseling with women, rape crisis counseling, and addiction and co-dependency recovery counseling.

Elaine Wainwright, an Australian of Anglo-Irish origin, received her doctorate from the University of Queensland. She is currently lecturer in Biblical Studies and Feminist Studies in Theology in the Brisbane College of Theology.

Janet Walton is a professor of worship at Union Theological Seminary in New York. Her books include *Art and Worship: A Vital Connection* and, as co-editor, *Women at Worship: Interpretations of North American Diversity.*

Delores S. Williams is Paul Tillich Professor of Theology and Culture at Union Theological Seminary in New York City. She is the author of *Sisters in the Wilderness: The Challenge of Womanist God-Talk.*

Sources

1. Elisabeth Schüssler Fiorenza, "For Women in Men's Worlds," from Claude Geffré, Gustavo Gutiérrez, and Virgil Elizondo, eds., *Different Theologies, Common Responsibility*, #171 (1984).

2. Maria José F. Rosado Nunes, "Women's Voices in Latin American Theology," in Elisabeth Schüssler Fiorenza and M. Shawn Copeland, eds., *Feminist Theology in Different Contexts* (1996/1).

3. Elaine Wainwright, "Weaving a Strong Web," in Elisabeth Schüssler Fiorenza and M. Shawn Copeland, eds., *Feminist Theology in Different Contexts* (1996/1).

4. Teresia M. Hinga, "Between Colonialism and Inculturation," in Elisabeth Schüssler Fiorenza and M. Shawn Copeland, eds., *Feminist Theology in Different Contexts* (1996/1).

5. Gabriele Dietrich, "South Asian Feminist Theory," in Elisabeth Schüssler Fiorenza and M. Shawn Copeland, eds., *Feminist Theology in Different Contexts* (1996/1).

6. Christine Schaumberger, "Hunger for Bread and Roses," in Elisabeth Schüssler Fiorenza and Anne Carr, eds., *Women, Work and Poverty*, #194 (1987).

7. M. Shawn Copeland, "Critical Theologies for the Liberation of Women," in Elisabeth Schüssler Fiorenza and M. Shawn Copeland, eds., *Feminist Theology in Different Contexts* (1996/1).

8. Anne Carr, "Women, Work, and Poverty," in Elisabeth Schüssler Fiorenza and Anne Carr, eds., *Women, Work and Poverty* #194 (1987).

9. Nantawan Boonprasat Lewis, "Uneven Development, Capitalism, and Patriarchy," in Elisabeth Schüssler Fiorenza and Anne Carr, eds., *Women, Work and Poverty* #194 (1987).

10. Delores S. Williams, "African-American Women and Domestic Violence," in Elisabeth Schüssler Fiorenza and Mary Shawn Copeland, eds., *Violence Against Women* (1994/1).

11. Julia Esquivel, "Conquered and Violated Women," in Leonardo Boff and Virgil Elizondo, eds., *1492–1992: The Voice of the Victims* (1990/6).

12. Mary Condren, "To Bear Children for the Fatherland," in Anne Carr and Elisabeth Schüssler Fiorenza, eds., *Motherhood: Experience, Institution, Theology*, #206 (1989).

13. Mercy Amba Oduyoye, "Poverty and Motherhood," in Anne Carr and Elisabeth Schüssler Fiorenza, eds., *Motherhood: Experience, Institution, Theology*, #206 (1989).

14. Catharina Halkes, "The Rape of Mother Earth," in Anne Carr and Elisabeth Schüssler Fiorenza, eds., *Motherhood: Experience, Institution, Theology*, #206 (1989).

15. Ivone Gebara, "Option for the Poor as an Option for Poor Women," in Elisabeth Schüssler Fiorenza and Anne Carr, eds., *Women, Work and Poverty* #194 (1987).

16. Dorothee Sölle, "Paternalistic Religion," in John Coleman and Gregory Baum, eds., *Youth Without a Future* #181 (1985).

17. Elisabeth Schüssler Fiorenza, "Breaking the Silence — Becoming Visible," in Elisabeth Schüssler Fiorenza and Mary Collins, eds., *Women: Invisible in Church and Theology*, #182 (1985).

18. Marjorie Proctor-Smith, "Images of Women in the Lectionary," in Elisabeth Schüssler Fiorenza and Mary Collins, eds., *Women: Invisible in Church and Theology*, #182 (1985).

19. Mary John Mananzan, "Education to Femininity or Education to Feminism?" in Anne Carr and Elisabeth Schüssler Fiorenza, eds., *The Special Nature of Women?* (1991/6).

20. "Elisabeth Gössmann, "The Construction of Women's Difference," in Anne Carr and Elisabeth Schüssler Fiorenza, eds., *The Special Nature of Women?* (1991/6).

21. Rosemary Radford Ruether, "Women's Different and Equal Rights in the Church," in Anne Carr and Elisabeth Schüssler Fiorenza, eds., *The Special Nature of Women?* (1991/6).

22. E. Ann Matter, "Ecclesiastical Violence," in Elisabeth Schüssler Fiorenza and Mary Shawn Copeland, eds., *Violence Against Women* (1994/1).

23. Eileen J.Stenzel, "Maria Goretti," in Elisabeth Schüssler Fiorenza and Mary Shawn Copeland, eds., *Violence Against Women* (1994/1).

24. Mary Collins, "Daughters of the Church," in Elisabeth Schüssler Fiorenza and Mary Collins, eds., *Women: Invisible in Church and Theology*, #182 (1985).

25. Mary Grey, "Europe as a Sexist Myth," in Nobert Greinacher and Norbert Mette, eds., *The New Europe: A Challenge for Christians* (1992/2).

26. Kwok Pui-lan, "The Image of the 'White Lady,'" in Anne Carr and Elisabeth Schüssler Fiorenza, eds., *The Special Nature of Women?* (1991/6).

27. Diann Neu, "Our Name Is Church," in Mary Collins and David Power, eds., *Can We Always Celebrate the Eucharist?*, #152 (1982).

28. Chung Hyun Kyung, "Opium or the Seed for Revolution?" in Leonardo Boff and Virgil Elizondo, eds., *Theologies of the Third World*, #199 (1988).

29. Janet Walton, "Ecclesiastical and Feminist Blessing," in Mary Collins and David Power, eds., *Blessing and Power*, #178 (1985).

30. Elisabeth Moltmann-Wendel, "Motherhood or Friendship," in Hans Küng and Jürgen Moltmann, eds., *Mary in the Churches*, #168 (1983).

31. Mary Hunt, "Transforming Moral Theology," in Elisabeth Schüssler Fiorenza and Mary Collins, eds., *Women: Invisible in Church and Theology*, #182 (1985).

32. Elizabeth A. Johnson, "The Maleness of Christ," in Anne Carr and Elisabeth Schüssler Fiorenza, eds., *The Special Nature of Women?* (1991/6).

33. Adele Reinhartz, "Jewish Feminist Theological Discourses," in Elisabeth Schüssler Fiorenza and M. Shawn Copeland, eds., *Feminist Theology in Different Contexts* (1996/1).

34. Sallie McFague, "Mother God," in Anne Carr and Elisabeth Schüssler Fiorenza, eds., *Motherhood: Experience, Institution, Theology*, #206 (1989).

35. Julia Esquivel Velásquez, "Spirituality of the Earth," in Leonardo Boff and Virgil Elizondo, eds., *Ecology and Power* (1995/5).

36. Elisabeth Schüssler Fiorenza, "Justified by All Her Children," *Concilium* Foundation, *On the Threshold of the New Millennium* (1990/1).

Index